INTERNATIONAL COMPARISONS OF PRICES, OUTPUT AND PRODUCTIVITY

CONTRIBUTIONS TO ECONOMIC ANALYSIS

231

ELSEVIER
Amsterdam – Lausanne – New York – Oxford – Shannon – Tokyo

INTERNATIONAL COMPARISONS OF PRICES, OUTPUT AND PRODUCTIVITY

Edited by

D.S. PRASADA RAO
Department of Econometrics
University of New England
Armidale, New South Wales, Australia

and

J. SALAZAR-CARRILLO
Department of Economics
Florida International University
Miami, Florida, USA

1996

ELSEVIER
Amsterdam – Lausanne – New York – Oxford – Shannon – Tokyo

ELSEVIER SCIENCE B.V.
Sara Burgerhartstraat 25
P.O. Box 521, 1000 AM Amsterdam, The Netherlands

ISBN: 0 444 82144 9

This book is printed on acid-free paper.

PRINTED IN THE NETHERLANDS

INTRODUCTION TO THE SERIES

This series consists of a number of hitherto unpublished studies, which are introduced by the editors in the belief that they represent fresh contributions to economic science.

The term "economic analysis" as used in the title of the series has been adopted because it covers both the activities of the theoretical economist and the research worker.

Although the analytical methods used by the various contributors are not the same, they are nevertheless conditioned by the common origin of their studies, namely theoretical problems encountered in practical research. Since for this reason, business cycle research and national accounting, research work on behalf of economic policy, and problems of planning are the main sources of the subjects dealt with, they necessarily determine the manner of approach adopted by the authors. Their methods tend to be "practical" in the sense of not being too far remote from application to actual economic conditions. In additon they are quantitative.

It is the hope of the editors that the publication of these studies will help to stimulate the exchange of scientific information and to reinforce international cooperation in the field of economics.

The Editors

LIST OF CONTRIBUTORS

Sultan Ahmad
The World Bank,
Washington, D.C., U.S.A

Bert Balk
Central Bureau of Statistics,
The Hague, The Netherlands

Jeffrey Bergstrand
University of Notre Dame,
Notre Dame, U.S.A.

Statistics Division
FAO, Rome, Italy

Robert Michael Field
Rockville, Maryland, U.S.A

Zoltan Kenessey
International Statistical Institute,
The Hague, The Netherlands

Salem Khamis
Hemel Hempsted, U.K.

Yoshimasa Kurabayashi
Toyo Eiwa University,
Yokohama, Japan

Elio Lancieri
Banca Nazionale del Lavoro,
Rome, Italy

Lawrence Officer
University of Illinois at Chicago,
Chicago, U.S.A.

Dirk Pilat
OECD, Paris, France

D.S. Prasada Rao
University of New England,
Armidale, Australia

Jorge Salazar-Carrillo
Florida International University,
Miami, U.S.A.

Anthony Selvanathan
Griffith University,
Brisbane, Australia

Michael Ward
The World Bank,
Washington, D.C., U.S.A.

Preface

Crosscountry comparisons of prices, real output and productivity are increasingly being undertaken by international organisations as well as individual researchers and groups around the world. Empirical results emanating from these studies are widely used by economists and applied econometricians. This phenomenal growth in the demand for and supply of results from global, regional and sectoral comparisons has contributed to significant improvements in the aggregation methods used in the compilation of internationally comparable national income aggregates. At the same time, the availability of reliable comparisons has paved the way for novel applications, including several cross-country demand and inequality studies.

The main purpose of the present volume is to bring together a collection of papers representing a cross section of studies describing developments in the field over the last five years. The origins of this volume date back to the conference on "International Comparisons of Price Structures, and their Influence on Productivity and Growth" in 1992 organised with the help of a generous grant from the National Science Foundation. A number of stimulating papers were discussed at that meeting, and this volume presents a selection of papers from that conference and several other papers prepared upon the editors' invitation.

We wish to express our gratitude and appreciation to the authors of the papers included in this volume, and also the participants of the 1992 meeting in Miami for their comments and suggestions which have contributed to significantly improved revisions of the papers. We gratefully acknowledge financial support from the National Science Foundation without which the present volume would not have come into existence. We express our sincere thanks to those who contributed with their technical skills in the preparation of this volume on Latex. In particular, we thank Yoganand Majji, Boon Lee, Arun Guruprasad and Peri Alagappan for their assistance.

D.S. Prasada Rao
J. Salazar-Carrillo

August 1995

OVERVIEW

D.S. Prasada Rao and J. Salazar-Carrillo

Over the last three decades international organizations and individual researchers and research groups around the world have produced an extensive range of international comparisons of prices, real output, real income and productivity and purchasing power parities of currencies. Notable among these have been the International Comparison Program (ICP) of the Statistical Office of the United Nations which is now entering its sixth phase, and from the early 1980s, the International Comparison of Output and Productivity (ICOP) project at the University of Groningen. The increasing availability of internationally comparable real output and productivity estimates has proved a major boon for the community of economists and econometricians interested in the field of international economic comparisons.

It is perhaps surprising that despite the phenomenal growth in the supply of and demand for international comparisons, there has been no consistent growth in the number of readily available publications disseminating the developments in the methodological and applied works involving sectoral, regional and global comparisons. Arguably, the last eminent publication dealing with international comparisons was the 1982 seminal study "World Product and Income" authored by Kravis, Heston and Summers. Consequently, the present volume represents a modest but timely augmentation of the many journal articles yet minimal number of books and monographs on the subject of international comparisons by bringing together contributions from leading scholars from an extensive range of relevant discipline and geographical backgrounds.

The papers in this volume have been classified into two broad groups united by overlapping themes. Part I includes the first group of papers. These are essentially empirical papers intended to provide a clear picture of the various types of international comparisons that have been undertaken by various organizations and individuals. The papers relate to empirical studies of different sectoral and national income aggregates at both regional and global levels. The papers in Part II deal with methodological and analytical issues. As could be expected, discussion of the appropriateness of various aggregation methods for international comparisons accounts for a major component of Part II. Two of the papers in the second section deal with real GDP comparisons, one based on a shortcut/reduced information concept and the other based on the notion of long-run real exchange rates derived using purchasing power parity theory. This section also includes a paper focusing on a theoretical model explaining national price levels which is then used in examining the effects of reduced defence spending.

The first paper by Zoltan Kenessey describes the International Comparison Program (ICP) and traces the historical roots of the project and the contemporary issues affecting ICP. The motivation for the paper stems from the recent publication of the results for Phase V of ICP, the results have an uneven coverage, especially for Latin America, and are based on the regionalised ICP approach. After a brief review of the results from ICP for different regions, the author embarks on a very interesting journey through the history of the project and makes a passionate appeal for the preparation of a detailed bibliography. Given that contributions made in the area of international comparisons are usually published in very disparate sources, and in many cases significant contributions to the debate are included in unpublished expert group meeting reports which are not available in the public domain. Another important factor that is usually not borne in mind by enthusiastic users of ICP results is the quality of the comparisons and the limitations associated with data collection, compilation and many assumptions made in the process of deriving such extensive results at the global level. The Chapter by Kenessey on the ICP in the 1980's and 1990's concludes with an account of many developments related to the ICP, where he describes international comparison work outside the domain of the ICP. This paper provides a useful backdrop to the issues and results described in the other papers of this volume.

The issue of absence of Latin American countries in the latest ICP global comparisons is taken up by Salazar-Carrillo, and he attempts to fill the gap for the region by providing a set of comparisons for the year 1985. The author uses his extensive knowledge of the region and the experience gained through his involvement in this region's comparisons over time to provide a set of results for the countries in Latin America. He uses very detailed category level national price deflators to update the price data to the year 1985 and uses the simple geometric-Walsh method to derive a completely consistent and transitive set of comparisons, and contrasts these results with some of the extrapolations for the Latin American countries from the Penn World Tables and the

World Bank's World Development Report of 1992.

In contrast to the global and regional comparisons described in the previous two chapters, the paper by the Statistics Division of the FAO represents one of the most comprehensive empirical exercises undertaken at the sectoral level. The Food and Agriculture Organization has pioneered work on international comparisons and has been producing statistics in the form of global and regional agricultural output aggregates for over four decades. The present paper describes the latest effort undertaken by the Division to update its international comparisons to the most recent benchmark years of 1985 and 1990. The Division has also taken the opportunity to introduce some modifications to the methodology employed in deriving the purchasing power parities. Methodological improvements reported include a modified Geary-Khamis method which provides purchasing power parities (PPP) for the final output, which is gross output net of feed and seed. The second innovation involves the derivation of internationally comparable agricultural GDP figures. The input expenditures are converted into real terms using input PPPs derived through the use of a multilateral Theil-Tornqvist index formula applied to input price data collected through special surveys. These PPPs are used in deriving real agricultural GDP expressed in a common currency unit. This paper provides summary results, including the PPPs, international prices and real agricultural GDP aggregates for more than a hundred countries, and for the benchmark years 1970, 1975, 1980, 1985 and 1990. The FAO study includes the introduction a neutral currency unit, Agricultural Currency Unit (ACU) for purposes of presenting the results. But the tables in the paper provide all the aggregates in US dollars.

Chapter 4 examines the problem of international comparisons of capital stock. Measurement of capital stock and its comparison over time and across countries is a formidable task, and Ward's paper draws on a recent World Bank study which presents approximate but consistent capital stock estimates for 96 countries. The study applies the standard perpetual inventory model to country specific gross fixed capital formation series in constant 1987 US dollars from the year 1950. The author examines the conceptual issues in the measurement of capital and then discusses the role of capital at length. The results presented show that the rate of capital accumulation in East Asia is much faster than in other regions and most of the growth in assets in that region has been in machinery, transport and other equipment. The author also observes that the relative share of plant, machinery and equipment in the capital stock declined in the 1980's in the case of Europe, Sub-Saharan Africa, Latin America and the Middle East and North Africa. The strengthening of the capital base in East Asia provides a rational explanation as to why economic growth has been most significant in the newly industrialised countries in the region. Appendix Tables for the paper should provide useful information to empirical researchers working on the issues of economic development.

On the subject of economic development and rapid growth, Dirk Pilat's paper focuses on one of the Asian economies, Korea, with the focus on a comparison of prices, output and productivity in Korea and the United States over the period 1963 to 1990. This paper is very impressive in that it attempts to undertake a comparison of the gross domestic product in these countries from the production side of the national accounts. It is a very labour intensive project and the smooth presentation belies the enormous empirical work that lies behind this piece of work. Pilat uses the industry-of-origin approach to the comparisons and compares the real output levels in the agricultural, mining, manufacturing and service sectors of these two economies. The paper outlines the procedures followed in the work, such procedures would be enormously useful for other researchers attempting similar work in this field. Productivity issues are examined using the partial measures of labour and capital productivity as well as the total factor productivity. The productivity gap between these two countries, which is quite wide, is explained in terms of capital intensity, quality of labour inputs, and other factors which include lack of natural resources, land scarcity, poor organisation of production and slow diffusion of knowledge. Time series analysis of productivity suggests that Korea has shown fast growth in productivity, but as the country came from such low levels, its average productivity level is still quite low. Pilat concludes that if Korea succeeds in maintaining the fast productivity growth it has experienced over the last three decades, it may be able to reach productivity levels comparable to those of industrialised countries by the end of the century.

The next paper in this section is a fascinating paper by Robert Michael Field on real gross domestic product of China using a direct comparison of prices in China with those of the United States. The author attempts to answer several questions including: Is China the world's largest economy? Is it the third largest, ranking just ahead of Germany? Is its GDP more than half of the GDP of the United States? In the literature there are several estimates of China's GDP ranging from 300 billion US dollars to more than a 3 trillion dollars, depending on whether the Chinese GDP is converted using the official trade rate of exchange or it is converted using the purchasing power parities. Field's study represents an in depth study of China, and a serious attempt to derive Chinese GDP in US dollars using the industry-of-origin approach. This approach requires a reconciliation of the differences in the accounting approaches followed in the two countries. Michael Field derives a figure of 1137 billion dollars. His figure is towards the bottom range of that in other published papers. A number of useful references and sources of Chinese data are listed in the paper and an appendix containing detailed Chinese and US data for different sectors of these economies is also provided.

The last paper in this section by Lawrence Officer studies the financing of the United Nations (UN) from the perspective of the apportionment of its expenses among member states as determined by the United Nations itself. It examines the tensions; conflicts; and inconsistencies in this process over the entire history of the United Nations. The issue of burden-sharing in international organizations has fallen out of fashion in the academic literature. It is resurrected in Officer's paper for two reasons: first, burden-sharing has continued to be a controversial issue within the UN itself; second, new and improved purchasing-power-parity data has enhanced empirical analysis of the topic. This paper represents a timely analysis and provides an excellent view of the inside workings of the organization on sensitive issues like the assessments. From the view point of the present volume, this paper is a good example of how the results from international comparisons can improve the methodologies underlying the issues such as the UN assessments. The paper provides a succinct account of the methodologies underlying the UN procedures and provides some new and improved methods based on purchasing power parity data.

The Part II of the volume deals with a number of methodological and analytical issues. The first paper in this section by Bert Balk describes the Van IJzeren method for international comparisons. Balk provides a simple description of the Van IJzeren method. The method itself is mathematically complex, and is based on a set of interdependent equations. Properties of this method are described in detail and then contrasted with those of the Geary-Khamis method, the main aggregation procedure used in most international comparisons to date. The paper ends with a simple numerical illustration which provides results from a number of alternative methods. The main purpose of the paper is to popularise this somewhat analytically difficult procedure.

The paper by Khamis examines the principle of consistency in aggregation and argues that the Geary-Khamis method is the natural choice when one is looking for a procedure that satisfies this principle. He argues that the definitions of international prices and purchasing power parities in the Geary-Khamis method provide index numbers satisfying the property of additive consistency. Khamis comments on the use of the EKS method by the OECD and points towards inconsistencies between sub-aggregates and the aggregates at a higher level. His final conclusion is that until a suitable alternative is found the Geary-Khamis method remains as the only method satisfying the principle of aggregation.

The stochastic approach to the construction of index numbers is expounded in the paper by Rao and Selvanathan. The paper describes the stochastic approach which considers the index number problem as one of finding the price change from a set of price relatives. This paper demonstrates the feasibility of deriving standard index number formulae such as the Laspeyres, Paasche and Theil-Tornqvist index numbers, and then proceeds to establish the versatility of stochastic approach in dealing with the problem of multilateral comparisons. The transitive multilateral index numbers due to Caves, Christensen and Diewert and its generalizations are also derived using the stochastic approach. In the last section Rao and Selvanathan derive Geary-Khamis purchasing power parities and international prices using the stochastic approach. One of the advantages of the stochastic approach is that it provides standard errors associated with purchasing power parities unlike the standard index number methods used in international comparisons. This paper advocates the use of regression based methods for international comparisons. The subgroup of papers on aggregation methods for international comparisons conclude with a short paper by Prasada Rao and Salazar- Carrillo on log-change index numbers. In particular, the geometric-Walsh and Rao systems for multilateral comparisons are described and their properties are enunciated. A number of important properties of the Rao system, including its close similarity with the Theil- Tornqvist and Ikle indices, are highlighted.

The last three papers of the volume are different in content to the other papers in this section. Those by Ahmad and Lancieri address the problem of deriving meaningful conversion factors for as many countries as possible and for as many years as possible. Given the background of these authors, they focus mainly on the issue of deriving purchasing power parities or real exchange rates which are stable and simultaneously provide meaningful real per capita income comparisons. Notably these two authors pursue entirely different routes to achieve their goals. Ahmad's paper uses the regression method of shortcut estimation by modelling the deviation of exchange rates from purchasing power parities, for the ICP countries. Estimated models which explain these deviations are then used to obtain extrapolations for countries and time periods outside the period covered by the ICP. The approach used here is similar to that followed in the preparation of the Penn World Tables. The author contrasts his results with those of the World Bank Atlas, Penn World Tables - Mark 5 (PWT5), and attempts to answer the question: Which set of estimates is better? The paper also identifies a number of fruitful areas for further research.

In contrast, Elio Lancieri uses the purchasing power parity (PPP) doctrine to define the long term real exchange rates and provides a new method for estimating real gross domestic product. The paper begins with an excellent summary and critique of the conversion factors available to date, the ICP parities, Penn World Table conversion factors and those from the industry-of-origin approach. Lancieri argues quite convincingly that the situation is far from satisfactory in terms of the reliability of the available conversion factors and their timeliness. He proposes a new method which provides long term exchange rates which perfectly compensate, year-by-year for the inflation differential between countries, in line with the relative PPP doctrine. The resulting exchange rates are termed Adjusted Long Term Exchange Rates (ALTER) and the author provides algebraic proofs of transitivity of the results and demonstrates that these rates can handle situations involving countries experiencing hyper inflation.

The volume concludes with an analytical paper by Jeffrey Bergstrand which tackles the problem of explaining national price levels. Results in this paper form the theoretical basis for empirical regression procedures used in shortcut methods similar to that described in Ahmad's paper. The paper follows on from the author's own work as well as that of Kravis, Lipsey and Clague, which attempts to explain the variability in general price levels across countries using mainly productivity differentials and relative factor endowment differences. The author then turns to the role of fiscal spending on price level differences through a theoretical model. He then examines the effects of reductions in defence spending in industrialized nations on relative national price levels. Bergstrand concludes that, theoretically, the effect of military spending reductions is ambiguous; that the effects depend upon relative factor intensity in production of civilian versus military goods and of civilian tradable versus non-tradable goods, and upon the relative importance in utility of civilian tradable versus nontradable goods. The model developed in the paper is used in an empirical study and the author's conclusion is that reduction in military expenditures are predicted to result in a small real depreciation of a country's currency and thus result in a relatively minor fall in the national price level relative to the world average. Bergstrand's paper demonstrates the need for analytical models which can lay the foundation for shortcut methods which are generally based on intuition and economic reasoning.

In summary, the present volume provides a set of stimulating studies on international comparisons of prices, output and productivity. The papers cover only a small sample of a vast number of developments and innovations in this research field. The papers provide a broad view of the whole exercise of international comparisons. It is the editors' sincere hope that these papers provide a useful reference source for many interested researchers around the world.

Contents

Part II : Methodological Issues

Part I

Global, Regional and Sectoral Comparisons

International Comparisons of Prices, Output and Productivity
Edited by D.S. Prasada Rao and J. Salazar-Carrillo

INTERNATIONAL COMPARISON PROGRAM IN THE 1980's AND 1990's

Zoltan Kenessey[1]
International Statistical Institute
Voorburg, The Netherlands.

1. Introduction

The recent publication of the results for Phase V of the International Comparison Program (ICP) (UN and EUROSTAT, 1994) and of the European comparisons for 1990 [UN, 1994] provides a good opportunity to review the progress of this major international statistical program in the 1980's and 1990's.

The most outstanding current feature is that by the 1990's ICP became world-wide entrenched. The coverage is still uneven, and especially for Latin America, is not as well established as one would like it to be. Problems remain with a number of economies of the former USSR, but progress is being made even in this regard. Moreover comparisons of China and even Vietnam are in the works. Thus, overall, ICP established itself in the 1990's as an important element of world statistical activities.

The organizational arrangements of ICP remain complex. Any world-wide effort, by its nature, engenders complexity. In the case of ICP this is compounded by the funding problems which have been with the program from its inception in the 1960's. In particular, the budgetary limitations at the UN Statistics Division, which is designated for a central role in the program, should be recognized. Fortunately other institutions, especially EUROSTAT, have been able to play major roles in maintaining the ICP momentum in the last two decades.

Also, users do not always understand the nature of the results and the reasons for variability in the comparisons. It is hoped that the publication of the ICP Manual [United Nations, 1992] will reduce con-

[1] Though the author has served as a consultant to the United Nations regarding the compilation of the Phase V ICP report, the views expressed in this paper are entirely personal.

siderably the misunderstandings in this regard. However, a further improvement in the quality of the comparisons, and efforts to strengthen the acceptability of ICP results will probably play a role in solving the remaining problems.

This paper first briefly reviews the evolution of ICP until its recent phase and mentions the plans for the rest of the 1990's. Second, it refers to the main publications with ICP results, as well as to the bibliographical work that would be needed to document the wide ranging international and national work on the comparisons over the last several decades. Third, the overall results of ICP Phase V at the world level are commented on. This is followed, fourthly, by references to the regional comparisons in the same phase. Fifth, data after 1985, especially for 1990 and for the European comparisons, are considered. Finally, in sections six, seven and eight, the quality of the comparisons and some related thoughts are broached.

2. The Evolution of ICP

The United Nations considered working on international comparisons in 1965. At that time the UN Statistical Commission recommended that a study to be made of the available experience in this field, with a view to commencing work later on. The report, which was prepared in 1967 by the present author, was presented to the UN Statistical Commission in early 1968.[2] The Commission approved the proposal and agreed to initiate work on the comparisons. From the beginning the comparisons involved help and participation from several other organizations and from member states of the UN. A significant grant from the Ford Foundation[3] led to the creation of a unit at the University of Pennsylvania in Philadelphia, which worked in close cooperation with staff at the UN Statistical Office (UNSTAT) in New York.

[2]Preparing the report for the UN Statiscal Commission, I first turned to the study by Gilbert and Kravis (1954) for the OECD and to the subsequent comparison by Gilbert and Associates (1958) which were well known at the time. Also, I visited Irving Kravis at the University of Pennsylvania in Philadelphia, where he enthusiastically welcomed the UN's interest in the international comparisons. It was the beginning of a decade-long collaboration with Kravis and of a friendship that lasted until Irving's death. From a scholarly viewpoint, he provided an overview of the subject in Kravis (1984).

[3]At the Ford Foundation Dr. Peter E. De Janosi (today the Director of the well known International Institute in Lexenburg, Austria) was the principal officer involved.

The World Bank and other organizations also helped to finance the new venture. Professor Irving B. Kravis from the University of Pennsylvania was appointed Director of the ICP; he remained in charge of ICP between 1968 and 1984. In the Philadelphia unit key roles were played by Professors Alan Heston and Robert Summers as well. In the New York unit, at the UN Statistical Office the author served as Associate Director of ICP (between 1968 and 1975); with most help from Michael McPeak from the UN staff. For Latin America, the work involved a collaborative effort with ECIEL, and Professor Jorge Salazar-Carillo carried out much of the organization of that work. I wish to mention, that from its inception, the World Bank has been a key contributor and stimulant for ICP; also World Bank staff has been participating in important program, methodological and evaluation work for ICP.

The first volume reporting on Phase I of ICP, together with the description of the methodology was published in 1975 and presented mainly data for 1967 and 1970. The second volume, presenting Phase II results of ICP for 1970 and 1973, appeared in 1978. This was followed in 1982 by the third volume giving Phase III ICP comparisons for 1975. The number of countries involved in Phase I was ten; it increased to sixteen in Phase II; and to thirty four in Phase III. The acronym "ICP" until 1989 referred to "International Comparison Project"; since then it denotes "International Comparison Program" as agreed upon at the session of the UN Statistical Commission in 1989. In Phase IV of ICP sixty countries were involved, and the reference year was 1980; the report on these comparisons appeared in 1986.

Phase V of ICP involved work on sixty four countries with 1985 as its principal reference year. Phase V (as Phase IV) was carried out in a regionalized manner, and the detailed results were compiled into a world matrix of EUROSTAT. The present author served, in the concluding stage of the work, as a consultant to the United Nations, regarding the compilation of the report on Phase V of the ICP (United Nations, 1994a). The next stage of ICP which is now in progress hopefully will cover an even larger number of countries on all continents of the world. Phase VI of ICP will utilize 1993 as its reference year. In the meanwhile, as indicated later, comparisons carried out mainly by the Statistical Office of the European Communities (EUROSTAT) for 1990 provided additional information about developments since 1985 for an important number of countries in Europe and elsewhere.

Between Phase III and Phase IV the ICP work was regionalized. In the first three phases of ICP the principal way of presenting the comparisons was by relying on calculations which reflected the average prices of all participating countries. Since Phase IV, in contrast, the comparisons have been carried out - in the first instance - for regions (or country groups). The world comparisons, in turn, linked these original comparisons to arrive at the comprehensive results. In order to link the comparisons the so-called bridge-country (or link-country) method has been relied on, utilizing data regarding countries which happened to be involved in comparisons for more than one region. A particularly noteworthy example is Austria, which has been involved in comparisons with both Western European and several Eastern European countries. Indeed, the Austrian Central Statistical Office has been a mainstay of the overall international comparison effort and its work is ranked among the leading contributions, along with EUROSTAT and other organizations.

Like some other methodological solutions of ICP, the reliance on link-countries is not without certain drawbacks. Without going into the technicalities, it can be said that world results obtained via the link-country method may give undue weight to the relationships regarding the link-countries. However, the degree and overall significance of this influence is not precisely known. In order to avoid possible distortions emanating from the link-country methodological solution, the application of the core commodity approach will be more widely explored for the 1993 global comparisons. This method involves the identification and pricing of a number of items in all countries compared. Experts disagree on the relative advantages of the link-country and the core commodity approaches; yet there is a growing feeling that only practical quantitative explorations that involve the parallel use of both methods may decide, and probably only after the 1993 round, the superiority of either method.

In the final analysis ICP comparisons are the results of the work of a great many organizations and groups, as well as the participating countries. During the last decade EUROSTAT carried out a particularly outstanding role in the work, but others, including the OECD, and national organizations such as the comparison unit of the Austrian Central Statistical Office (mainly by carrying out work regarding Eastern Europe) contributed very significantly to the world-wide effort. Clearly, without their major inputs the limited resources available at the United Nations (either in New York at UNSTAT or at the regional Economic Commissions of the UN) would not have permitted the performing of the tasks at hand. Also, after Phase III the role of the University of Pennsylvania was changed in the main to advising on methodological matters. At the same time the Statistical Office of the European Communities assumed a largely enhanced role in carrying out international comparisons, in and beyond the sphere of the European countries.

Carrying out world comparisons is more time consuming than comparing countries within regions. While the world comparisons for 1985 were the subject of a report in 1994, the 1985 comparison results for the twelve member countries of the European Community were made first available much earlier, namely in 1987. European comparisons for 1985, covering seventeen OECD countries and three Eastern European countries were published in 1988 by the UN Economic Commission for Europe. Comparisons conducted for 1985 for twenty two African countries carried out by EUROSTAT were issued in 1989. 1985 comparisons for Japan and ten Asian countries were released by the UN Economic Commission for Asia and the Pacific in 1991 in special cooperation with Japan. The 1985 results of Caribbean comparisons produced by EUROSTAT were issued in the same year 1991. Finally, the processing of world comparisons covering 64 countries for the benchmark year 1985 was on the whole completed by EUROSTAT in the summer of 1992 and provided the statistical material for the world report.

The completion of the world-wide comparisons was hampered by various difficulties. A difficulty lain in the small number of interregional, core comparisons which are necessary for linking all the comparisons carried out for various regions and continents. Indeed, the chief problem hampering the finalization of the 1985 world-wide results was the small number of countries available to serve as "bridge-countries" for linking all the regional comparisons with each other. Obviously, the work load on a country that agrees to be compared in more than one regional comparison is an increased one and this circumstance limits the willingness of countries to become "bridge-countries" for ICP.

Phase VI of ICP should yield world results with 1993 as the bench-mark year hopefully only a few years after this reference period. However, fortunately a number of international comparisons are available for later dates than the Phase V ICP results for 1985. First, work undertaken for 1990 under the aegis of EUROSTAT and OECD - covering all twenty four OECD countries and twelve Community countries - is mentioned. In respect to Eastern European countries, the work for 1990 has been complicated by the manifold changes in the transition countries and these comparisons are still in progress. In this work, the many special efforts by the Austrian Central Statistical Office should be again mentioned. The UN Economic Commission for Europe combined results for all 1990 European comparisons and issued their results in 1994 (United Nations, 1994b). However, for the 1990 comparisons participation from countries in Asia (except Japan), Africa and Latin America was lacking.

3. Publications on Comparisons

I am not aware of the existence of a complete or even reasonably adequate and up-to-date bibliography of ICP results or ICP literature. Of course, a complete listing would easily fill a thick volume, perhaps more than one, if extended to all national writings on the subject covering the many languages such literature is known to exist. When input-output work started its world-wide spreading, for a good while international efforts were maintained (by backing from Harvard) to compile the growing bibliography on that subject. Unfortunately, concerning ICP the bibliographical compilations, to my knowledge, have remained much more sporadic. (I am afraid, that work on input-output bibliographies also lost their initial steam).

While a comprehensive bibliography is lacking, here I provide selected references, covering only some sources, which are closely relevant to this article. First, I wish to note that the first three ICP books were published via the World Bank at The Johns Hopkins University Press in Baltimore, Maryland, namely (a) Kravis, Kenessey, Heston and Summers(1975); (b) Kravis, Heston and Summers(1978); and (c) Kravis, Heston and Summers(1982). The results of Phase IV of the ICP were issued jointly by the United Nations and the Commission of the European Communities in UN and EUROSTAT(1986). Publications pertinent to regional results for 1985 which were mentioned earlier include the following: EUROSTAT(1988); OECD(1987); ECE(1988); EUROSTAT(1989); MCA of Japan and ESCAP(1991); and EUROSTAT(1991). Even for national accounting as a whole the literature is very dispersed, yet more accessible (Kenessey, 1993).

4. World Level Results for Phase V

At the world level for 1985, ICP comparisons of GDP per capita (based on international estimates of total GDP divided by the number of population) are available for 56 countries. It seems useful to show the per capita real term GDP results for these countries in 8 major groupings, based on their percentage relationship estimated relative to the US per capita level. It is noted, that comparisons for seven Caribbean countries were also carried out. Unfortunately, it is not entirely clear how - except for consumption - the results for these countries, especially for total GDP, match with the rest. Therefore, in the world tabulation below the Caribbean countries are excluded. The results of the comparison for Nepal (which covered household consumption and government consumption) are also not taken into account in this world table. Judging by the comparisons among the Asian countries, Nepal would fit into the 1-5 per cent grouping.

PER CAPITA GDP LEVEL GROUPINGS
(U.S. level = 100)

Over 60 percent: Australia, Austria, Belgium, Canada, Denmark, Finland, France, Germany, Hong Kong, Italy, Japan, Luxembourg, Netherlands, New Zealand, Norway, Sweden, UK, US.

51-60 percent: No country

41-50 percent: Ireland, Spain.

31-40 percent: Greece, Hungary, Mauritius, Portugal.

21-30 percent: Iran, Korea, Poland, Tunisia, Turkey, Yugoslavia.

11-20 percent: Botswana, Cameroon, Congo, Egypt, Ivory Coast, Morocco, Philippines, Sri Lanka, Swaziland, Thailand.

6-10 percent: Benin, Kenya, Nigeria, Pakistan, Senegal, Zambia, Zimbabwe.

1-5 percent: Bangladesh, Ethiopia, India, Madagascar, Malawi, Mali, Rwanda, Sierra-Leone, Tanzania.

Source: United Nations (1994a), p.5

The eighteen ICP countries which in 1985 attained more than 60 percent of the per capita GDP level in the US were concentrated in three geographic areas, namely Western Europe (12 countries); Asia and the Pacific (4 countries); and North America (2 countries). The 12 European ICP countries in this uppermost grouping were the following: Austria, Belgium, Denmark, Finland, France, Germany, Italy, Luxembourg, The Netherlands, Norway, Sweden, and the UK. The 4 ICP countries belonging to the over 60% grouping in 1985 in Asia and the Pacific were Australia, Hong Kong, Japan, and New Zealand. The 2 countries in North America were Canada and the U.S. In general, 1985 ICP data suggest that economically developed countries had at least two-thirds of the US per capita GDP in real terms in that year.

The middle group of 1985 ICP countries (between 21 and 50 percent of the US per capita GDP level for that year) included 8 European countries, 2 Asian countries, and 2 African countries. The European countries were: Greece, Hungary, Ireland, Poland, Portugal, Spain, Turkey, and Yugoslavia. The 2 Asian countries in this group were Iran and Korea; while the 2 African countries were Mauritius and Tunisia.

The third grouping of 26 countries, defined here as having in 1985 20 percent or less of the per capita US GDP in that year were all from Africa (20 countries) and Asia (6 countries). The African countries were the following: Benin, Botswana, Cameroon, Congo, Egypt, Ethiopia, Ivory Coast, Kenya, Madagascar, Malawi, Mali, Morocco, Nigeria, Rwanda, Senegal, Sierra-Leone, Swaziland, Tanzania, Zambia, and Zimbabwe. The 6 Asian countries in the third group were Bangladesh, India, Pakistan, the Philippines, Sri Lanka, and Thailand. It should be mentioned, that within this third grouping the per capita GDP in 7 of the African and 2 of the Asian countries was less than 5 percent of the US level in 1985. The per capita GDP estimates at international prices in US dollars and the percent of these relative to the US (=100) are reproduced in the Appendix Table at the end of this chapter.

While in 1985 in the uppermost grouping a large number of European countries are listed, and to the third grouping many African countries belonged, the variation within these two geographical areas, and indeed within all regions was quite significant. In respect of this matter the selected results of 1985 comparisons within the regions offer further information, as indicated in the following section. For some analytical issues regarding the world comparisons, several studies are to be found in the volume edited by Salazar-Carillo and Prasada Rao (1988).

5. Regional Results

A summary paper such as this cannot do justice to the detailed work carried on in the individual continents during Phase V of the ICP. Therefore only a few results are highlighted for each region, based on the ICP Data Bases indicated below the tables. For further regional information readers are referred to the sources listed under the References.

5.1 *Europe*

The most advanced ICP work has been concentrated in Europe during the last two decades. Owing to the strength of the work carried out in Europe, in the highlights of regional work seems attractive to place particular emphasis on inter-European results. The European comparison activities have proceeded at particularly high levels of sophistication. In Europe, in addition to EUROSTAT, important work for ICP has been carried out by OECD, by the Austrian Central Statistical Office, and the UN Economic Commission for Europe (ECE).

Phase V of ICP has been implemented in Europe by means of cooperation among several international agencies and the national statistical services of the countries. The three principal components of the European program involved the following:

(a) EUROSTAT undertook the comparison for the following 12 members of the European Union: Belgium, Denmark, France, Germany, Greece, Ireland, Italy, Luxembourg, Netherlands, Portugal, Spain, and the UK.

(b) The Austrian Central Statistical Office played a pivotal role in a set of binary comparisons which were carried out between Austria, on the one hand, and Hungary, Poland, and Yugoslavia, on the other.

(c) Four additional European countries - Finland, Norway, Sweden, and Turkey - forwarded their data to the OECD, which, in cooperation with EUROSTAT, carried out a comparison for 22 of its member countries, which include countries outside Europe: U.S., Canada, Japan, New Zealand and Australia.

Initially, the three component comparisons were conducted separately, but were linked together in the second stage of the work. This was achieved by linking the other two groups of countries to the core EUROSTAT comparison. Among the third group of countries (Finland, Sweden and Norway, as well as Denmark from the first group) a multilateral "Nordic" comparison was carried out, and Denmark served as the bridge country to the core EUROSTAT comparisons.

Table 1
1985 PER CAPITA GDP COMPARISON IN EUROPE,1985 and 1990
(Level of Austria=100)

1980			1990		
Country	Index	Ranking	Country	Index	Ranking
Luxembourg	123.1	1	Switzerland	126.8	1
Norway	123.1	2	Luxembourg	116.5	2
Sweden	112.8	3	Germany FR	110.0	3
Denmark	112.3	4	France	105.0	4
Germany FR	111.7	5	Sweden	103.3	5
France	104.9	6	Denmark	101.4	6
Finland	103.6	7	Austria	100.0	7
Netherlands	103.3	8	Finland	99.7	8
United Kingdom	100.1	9	Iceland	99.7	9
Austria	100.0	10	Belgium	98.8	10
Italy	99.4	11	Norway	98.4	11
Belgium	97.9	12	Italy	96.4	12
Spain	69.7	13	United Kingdom	95.9	13
Ireland	61.9	14	Netherlands	94.9	14
Greece	53.8	15	Spain	70.9	15
Portugal	51.1	16	Ireland	64.1	16
Hungary	47.2	17	Portugal	52.8	17
Yugoslavia	44.2	18	CSFR	50.4	18
Poland	37.1	19	Greece	44.3	19
Turkey	31.2	20	USSR	41.0	20
			Hungary	37.8	21
			Yugoslavia	32.5	22
			Poland	30.4	23
			Turkey	27.7	24
			Romania	20.6	25

Source: United Nations (ICP Data Base, 1992, prel.) United Nations(1994), p.5

As already mentioned, for the second group countries Austria was the bridge country; in this so-called Group II comparison Hungary, Poland and Yugoslavia were compared each with Austria. In the case of Turkey, utilizing the comparison information via the OECD, the data was also linked to the core.

The 1985 European comparison, which covered 20 countries, revealed that 63 percent of the estimated total real GDP of these countries was produced in just four countries: Germany (the data for Germany in the 1985 European ICP report pertain only to the Western part of the Federal Republic of Germany, without Eastern Germany), France, Italy, and the United Kingdom, even though the population share of these countries was only 49 percent of the total, and their area covered only 29 percent of the total territory involved. If data for some other countries, such as the European part of the former Soviet Union, Bulgaria and Romania were added, the total of Germany, France, Italy and the UK would probably show even more strikingly the importance of the development level of these four economies within Europe, relative to their population and geographic area. For the countries included, the per capita GDP indexes were expressed in comparison with the Austrian level (=100).

For the European region by now we also have 1990 comparison results carried out for altogether 25 countries, including the former USSR. The results are also shown in Table 1, taking Austria as 100. There are some differences in the ranking of the countries: for example in 1985 the UK was estimated at the Austrian level while in 1990 about 5 percent below it. Hungary and Yugoslavia in 1990 were dramatically (about 10 percentage points) lower relative to Austria than in 1985. Clearly the great transformations in the region were a factor in this change. It is more difficult to explain the change in Norway's position relative to Austria. Perhaps the relative stability (instability) of the results is also a factor leading to shifts in the percentage rankings, or causing it at least in some part of the shifts.

5.2 *Asia*

In respect of Asia, the ICP work for 1985 was sponsored by the Government of Japan, the Asian Development Bank, and the United Nations Development Program, with assistance from the World Bank. "The organizational and the processing activities of the comparison were shared by the Statistical Office of the United Nations (UNSO) and the Secretariat of the United Nations Economic and Social Commission for Asia and the Pacific (ESCAP). Technical assistance was provided also by experts of the World Bank, of the Statistical Office of the European Communities (EUROSTAT), and of the Statistics Bureau of Japan." (MCA of Japan and ESCAP, 1991 p.77).

The eleven countries participating in the Asian regional comparison were the following: Bangladesh, Hong Kong, India, Iran, Japan, Nepal, Pakistan, the Philippines, Korea, Sri Lanka, and Thailand. In the case of Nepal, the comparison was restricted to consumption only; for the other ten countries it covered the entire GDP. Two of the countries listed - India and Japan - have been ICP participants from Phase I on.

For this comparison, weighted international average prices of the countries involved were developed, into which the original national currency based data was converted. "The converted value data are expressed throughout the study in "Asian dollars". The Asian dollar is a nominal currency which plays the role of a numeraire only. Its purchasing power for the gross domestic product total (taken all participating countries together) equals the purchasing power of the United States dollar in 1985; thus, the total gross domestic product of the whole region, whether expressed in Asian dollars or United States dollars, is the same....The United States dollar was selected as numeraire since it was assumed that this is the currency the purchasing power of which is relatively well known in the entire region." (MCA of Japan and ESCAP, 1991 p.79).

The results of the quantity comparisons were expressed relative to the average ESCAP level, namely the weighted average magnitude of the participating countries. The report of the comparisons underlined that "The per capita quantity indexes...are relatively good approximations of economic development level differences. They cannot be considered, however, as expressions of welfare differences, since gross domestic product, in general, is not supposed to express levels of welfare. Even some economic factor differences, like those of indebtness and its consequences (interest payments), or pollution and other environmental disfunctions are outside the scope of the real product comparison. Nevertheless, since there are no other comparable aggregate national accounting concepts, ICP type real gross domestic products are presumably the best economic development level comparisons one can do in present conditions." (MCA of Japan and ESCAP, 1991 p.80) Beyond the ranking of the countries according to per capita real GDP levels, which in 1985 in Japan and Hong Kong was 4-5 times higher than the Asian average, differences existent in per capita consumption and capital formation levels among the countries are of considerable interest.

Table 2
PER CAPITA GDP COMPARISON IN ASIA,1985
(Average of participating countries=100)

GDP Rank	Country Name	GDP Per Cap.	Household Consumption	Government Consumption	Capital Formation
1	Japan	525.3	486.2	218.4	698.9
2	Hong Kong	454.2	483.1	202.1	451.8
3	Iran	204.1	213.4	212.9	179.5
4	Korea	176.8	164.3	153.2	212.7
5	Thailand	116.2	118.8	272.9	68.7
6	Sri Lanka	81.4	74.8	158.4	76.8
7	Philippines	78.5	93.8	139.4	25.8
8	Pakistan	58.8	63.4	185.4	14.4
9	Bangladesh	36.5	43.7	82.4	7.3
10	India	33.1	36.6	45.7	21.6

Source: United Nations (ICP Data Base, 1992, prel.)

In respect of consumption, for example, the nearly identical levels in Japan and Hong Kong can be noted. Juxtaposed with the per capita total GDP levels, given that the government consumption levels in the two countries were nearly the same, these numbers indicate that the share of capital formation in 1985 was considerably higher in Japan than in Hong Kong. Indeed, this is shown by Japan's per capita capital formation level (7 times above the Asian average) compared to Hong Kong's indicator (4.5 times above the Asian average).

At the other end of the scale, India's consumption level was a bit closer to the Asian average than its per capita GDP level; however, this discrepancy in 1985 was lower than it was the case for Bangladesh. On the other hand, the per capita capital formation level in India was less below the Asian average than for Bangladesh.

International comparisons for China are not yet reflected in the regional (or world) level discussed above in this report. Binary comparison works (such as China-US or China-Japan) have been carried out by various organizations during the recent years. An overview of such efforts, as well as the results of their own estimates, have been provided by Ren Ruoen and Chen Kai(1992, preliminary draft) in Beijing. The results of nine comparisons between China and the US are rather divergent: the per capita GNP of China is ranging from 2 percent to 19 percent of the US level in 1986.

It is encouraging, therefore, that China's State Statistical Bureau has been quite active in promoting participation in ICP. In the 1993 round of ICP comparisons work on Shanghai municipality and Guangdong Province will be included in the ESCAP framework. At the end of 1993 a first meeting on the ICP pilot project was held in Guangzhou, China.

5.3 *Africa*

At the outset of the ICP work in Phase I, one African country - Kenya - was included in the international comparisons. For 1985, the regional comparison involved 22 African countries. Key role in the work was undertaken by EUROSTAT, which earlier - for 1980 coordinated and managed an African regional comparison for 15 countries.

Table 3
PER CAPITA GDP COMPARISON IN AFRICA,1985
(Average of 22 countries=100)

Country	Index	Ranking	Country	Index	Ranking
Mauritius	312	1	Senegal	88	12
Tunisia	248	2	Benin	81	13
Congo	205	3	Kenya	67	14
Botswana	203	4	Zambia	59	15
Egypt	198	5	Madagascar	49	16
Cameroon	176	6	Rwanda	47	17
Swaziland	171	7	Malawi	45	18
Morocco	164	8	Sierra Leone	38	19
Ivory Coast	128	9	Tanzania	32	20
Zimbabwe	123	10	Mali	31	21
Nigeria	90	11	Ethiopia	20	22

Source: United Nations (ICP Data Base, 1992, prel.)

Before showing the summary per capita real term GDP comparisons for the 22 African countries in 1985, it is useful to have a short reference to the Purchasing Parity Standard (PPS) applied in the work, because EUROSTAT used not the currency of one of the countries studied as the numeraire; even though the results were expressed in a single currency, the US dollar. The table above shows the per capita GDP levels in indexed form.

The nearly 16 times difference between the first and the twenty-second ranked countries (Mauritius and Ethiopia, respectively) in

Africa is very large. The same difference, if calculated on the basis of the world summary results is even larger, the first ranked country's per capita GDP being nearly 20 times as large as that of the twenty-second.

5.4 *Caribbean*

While the Caribbean results could not be incorporated in the world matrix of the ICP Phase V report, it seems useful and necessary to include here some references to this work as well.

The Caribbean comparison for 1985 covered the following seven countries: the Bahamas, Barbados, Grenada, Jamaica, St. Lucia, Suriname, Trinidad and Tobago. During Phase V of ICP, beyond the work on the U.S. and Canada, these were the only comparisons carried out in the Americas. Similarly to other Phase IV and V comparisons, which were coordinated by EUROSTAT, the Caribbean work was undertaken by the Statistical Office of the European Communities, in cooperation with the national authorities of the countries involved. At the outset of the project, in the spring of 1987, a workshop for the participating countries was organized and financed by EUROSTAT in Kingston, Jamaica. The meeting was also attended by officials from the Caribbean Community Secretariat, Organisation of Caribbean States, the United Nations Statistical Office, the World Bank, the Inter-American Development Bank, and the ACP Secretariat in Brussels.

At the workshop, the overall methodology, data needs and organization of the project were reviewed. Importantly, a list of products for household consumption and machinery and equipment, as drawn up for the Phase V comparison in Africa, was presented and modified according to the comments from Caribbean countries. On these grounds finally 876 products were priced in the region for consumption, and 164 for equipment goods. These and other needed data were collected by the national statistical offices. The price surveys were carried out between May and October 1989 in the countries concerned, typically during one month of time. In order to estimate the price levels for 1985, which served as the ICP reference year in Phase V, national price index information was used about the price changes between 1989 and 1985. As mentioned, owing to the methodological problems involved it was not feasible to integrate these comparisons with the data obtained for the other comparison in Phase V of ICP. However, the main indexes and rankings within the region are shown in the table below.

Table 4
CARIBBEAN PER CAPITA GDP COMPARISON,1985
(Caribbean average=100)

Country	Index	Ranking
Bahamas	244	1
Trinidad & Tobago	167	2
Barbados	160	3
Suriname	97	4
St. Lucia	63	5
Jamaica	50	6
Grenada	41	7

Source: United Nations (ICP Data Base, 1992, prel.)

6. Data After 1985

By now, world level international comparisons have been available within the ICP for the period 1970 through 1985. Furthermore, comparisons results developed mainly by EUROSTAT, as well as OECD, extend through 1990. Thus, it is possible to have a look at the 1985 ICP estimates in the context of some data for about two decades. Admittedly, the longer-term data are not as comprehensive as the statistics available for 1985. For example, for 1970 the ICP estimates cover only about 1/4 of the number of countries included in 1985. Also, the methodology of estimates developed in Phases IV and V of ICP (owing to the regionalization of the work) is in some respects different from those of the estimates prepared in Phases I through III of ICP.

It also should be borne in mind, that since 1970 the real GDP of the countries has increased. If, for example, the per capita GDP in country A in both 1970 and 1990 were estimated at 40 percent of the US level, this seemingly stagnant percentage masks the fact, that over that 20 year period the US GDP level had increased significantly and so did the GDP level of country A. Indeed, the stability of the relationship suggests, that the economies of both country A and the US have grown at the same rate in respect of the per capita measure. By looking at the real term (inflation adjusted) GDP data in national currency for both country A and the US over time could provide a confirmation of this suggestion, implying that the overall per capita output had the same growth rate in the two countries during the two decades mentioned. Possibly, national real term domestic growth rate data between 1970 and 1990 may not furnish exactly the same results as implied by internationally derived relationships based on ICP estimates. The reasons for potential discrepancies can be manifold; they may relate to differences in weighting (by expenditure categories) and other methodological factors.

Notwithstanding such serious caveats, the data available for countries which were compared in ICP both in 1970 and in 1985 provide some interesting glimpses into the shifts in comparative per capita GDP estimates. The 1970 ICP estimates shown below in the first column of the table are taken from the Phase II ICP results, while in the second column the data for 1985 are from the latest (Phase V) work. The ratios given in the third column are simple divisions of the 1985 percentage (relative to the US) with the same percentage for 1970.

Table 5
PER CAPITA GDP ESTIMATES
(US=100)

Country	1970	1985	1985/1970
Belgium	55.1	64.7	1.17
France	58.2	69.3	1.19
Germany	64.1	73.8	1.15
Hungary	21.6	31.2	1.44
India	2.07	4.5	2.17
Iran	8.37	28.0	3.35
Italy	36.0	65.6	1.82
Japan	39.8	71.5	1.80
Kenya	2.99	6.0	2.01
Korea	5.39	24.1	4.47
Netherlands	50.8	68.2	1.34
Philippines	3.86	10.9	2.82
UK	45.7	66.1	1.45
US	100.0	100.0	1.00

Source: United Nations (ICP Data Base, 1992, prel.)

The table above clearly suggests that in the 1970's and 1980's all countries shown have decreased their distance in respect of their countries' per capita GDP relative to the US. The largest of the percentage gains are shown for countries outside Europe. In Asia, four countries: Korea, Iran, the Philippines and India had shown the largest gains; and there was also a large gain in Kenya in Africa. However, the per capita GDP difference for both India and Kenya remained very large in respect of the US.

OECD calculations for 1990 suggest that several countries shown in the previous table have further reduced their distance relative to the U.S. in respect of GDP per capita. While these data do not cover countries outside the OECD and are not emanating from the set of official ICP estimates, they are of considerable interest in the context of the present paper.

Table 6
OECD PER CAPITA GDP ESTIMATES,1970 and 1990
(US=100)

Country	1990	1990/1970
Germany	85.09	1.33
Japan	82.02	2.06
France	81.08	1.41
Belgium	76.31	1.38
Italy	74.52	2.07
Netherlands	73.33	1.44
UK	73.12	1.60
US	100.00	1.00

Source: The 1990 values are taken from the OECD calculations (OECD, National Accounts Main Aggregates, Vol. 1, 1960-1990, Paris, 1992); the 1970 values are from the ICP.

Among the countries listed, the two fastest "catch-up" trends between 1970 and 1990 were seen for Japan and Italy. In 1970 Japan's per capita GDP was only about 40 percent of the US level and was well below the levels of Belgium, France, Germany, The Netherlands, and the UK (however, it was somewhat higher than the Italian level). By 1990, the Japanese per capita GDP level was higher than in all these countries, with the exception of Germany.

7. Quality of the Comparisons

The first factor influencing the usefulness of international comparisons of GDP and the purchasing power of currencies, such as presented in this report, is the quality of the national statistical data utilized for each country. The quality of national statistical efforts relevant to ICP reflects a great number of circumstances, including budgetary resources in different nations, the availability of skilled statistical staff in countries, the level of record keeping attained in the private and public sectors, etc.

In addition, the statistical methodology applied by countries in the compilation of their basic data and in the aggregation of their series exercises much influence on the quantity as well as on the comparability of the data among countries. Fortunately, over the last few decades countries have increasingly adopted common, internationally recommended statistical guidelines. National data, therefore, became more and more comparable from the viewpoint of methodology, especially in respect of estimates of GDP and its major components. Nevertheless, there remain certain gaps in statistical knowledge practically in all countries of the world, and this circumstance needs to be borne in mind during the utilization of the ICP results for analytical or policy purposes. Usually statistical development levels of countries are correlated with their economic development. There are exceptions to this: there are countries which are considered more advanced in matters of statistics than their per capita GDP may suggest. Moreover, the help of international organizations to countries has been important for filling in gaps in statistical knowledge on various continents. Yet, when everything is said and done, the availability and the quality of statistics needed for successful international comparisons is not always ideal for carrying out the work of the ICP.

The results of international comparisons, at any rate, depend not only on the quality of the underlying national data sets used in the work. The techniques applied in the comparisons also have an impact on the results; therefore the interpretation of the ICP data cannot be isolated from the methodology applied.

Last but not least, the quality of comparisons among countries depends also on the degree of differences existent among them. As a rule, countries close in developmental levels can be compared easier with each other than with countries which are much more or much less developed economically. Similarly, countries of the same region are typically better comparable with each other than they are with countries on different continents. Such difficulties are akin to the problems of comparing economic magnitudes, such as the GDP, in a single country over time. The comparability of the GDP data of a given country is far greater between successive years than over very long time periods.

The problems of comparing a given country's GDP data available for the 19th century and for the 20th century are in many ways similar (and can be of the same magnitude) as comparing distant countries with each other for the same year today.

Other things being equal, the further apart two economic situations are, whether over time within countries or across space among nations, the more difficult it is to compare them. A key factor in this difficulty is the increased share of unique items of production and consumption, which make the comparison of the different situations more problematic. In ICP various techniques have been applied to achieve the desired level of comparability among countries in the West, the East, the North and the South. While this effort is deemed satisfactory for the purposes at hand, particularly given the prevailing resource limitations of the project, the interpretation of the results requires attention, as already mentioned, to the methods of the comparisons which are described later.

Experience has shown, that certain areas of expenditures (for example on services) are less covered in most country statistics than others (for example expenditure on food products). More generally, the quality differences evident across countries cannot always be captured by reliance on detailed specifications for the same. Even if in two countries exactly the same number and quality of commodities can be purchased by the population, it is possible that one of the countries involved has a more extensive and better equipped network of commercial facilities than the other. The specifications, naturally, will not reflect the circumstance that in one country the same goods are readily available within say a 10 kilometre radius for purchasers, while in the other consumers have to travel 100 kilometres to obtain the same. Similarly, the road conditions may make the trips to the commercial facilities a greatly different experience in the two countries. Last but not least, even if the overall quality of the goods and services is similar, their variety (the number of sorts, colors, styles, sizes) may be quite different in various countries.

Nevertheless, since its inception, statisticians working on the ICP amassed a great deal of experience regarding the difficulties and pitfalls of international comparisons. Indeed, considerable experience has been accumulated in respect of spatial comparability even at national levels: within many countries the statistical efforts are faced with the regional variability of economic and social conditions. This is true not only of huge countries such as India or China. Medium and smaller size countries also can be characterized by regional diversity (for example the North and the South of Italy or the Western and Eastern part of Hungary). On the basis of growing national and international experience, the difficulties involved in comparisons across countries can be handled more and more effectively. Indeed, as international comparisons become regular parts (instead of special projects) of the national and international statistical endeavours, the reliability of comparisons will grow further.

8. Related Developments

Among the numerous ICP related developments in recent times I wish to underline the significance of a selected number of items.

8.1 IMF's World Economic Outlook

IMF's "World Economic Outlook" is usually very widely reviewed by the media all over the world. This is related to the quality of the reports as well as to the IMF's operational significance for a large number of countries on all continents. In the context of my review the recent application of revised weights in the Outlook is an important feature. The weights applied by IMF to output growth and other indicators of individual countries in order to aggregate their data into regional, group, or world aggregates. This involves, in effect, determining the shares of each country in world and/or regional/group totals.

In view of the possible distortions and anomalies with the application of exchange-rate based weights, IMF decided instead to adopt purchasing-power-parities based weights for the purposes of aggregating individual country data in the "World Economic Outlook". The change does not necessarily imply the use of the new numbers for country-specific operational purposes by IMF or the World Bank. Indeed, the ICP results are generally not intended for such use within the UN either.

8.2 International Productivity Comparisons

As known, the ICP comparisons are carried out in respect of the "expenditure-side" estimates of GDP. Countries may estimate their GDP also for two other "sides": for the incomes and for the production, and in principle ICP can relate to these "sides" as well. In practice, however, comparisons of the expenditure and the production sides have been accomplished. (Partial "income-side" comparisons, principally for wages, have been explored as well). So far, owing to technical, administrative, and budgeting reasons ICP has not carried out production-side comparisons or income-side studies. However, historically (at least since the Paige-Bombach study and the comparisons of Rostas) there has been interest in the production-side work and research has continued in exploring the matter.

In particular, the International Comparison of Output and Productivity (ICOP), which has been a project of the University of Groningen since 1983, can be mentioned. Following up the earlier work mentioned and the studies of the matter by Angus Maddison, it involves a comparison of real output (value added) in major sectors (agriculture, industry, and services) as well as production sub-sectors within these sectors. It includes labor productivity measures with labor input measured in working hours where possible and also estimating total factor productivity. Maddison and others, including Bart Van Ark, Dirk Pilat, Prasada Rao, Adam Szirmai, have published numerous studies on the subject, especially regarding the international productivity estimates derived from the "production-side" comparisons.

8.3 Gross World Product

Efforts have been also made to utilize the ICP results in the estimation of Gross World Product. In 1993 the Statistical Division of the United Nations issued a special supplement to its National Accounts Statistics Series (United Nations, 1993). The purpose was to assess the changes in the distribution of gross world product (the total of GDP for all individual countries or areas) during the 1970-1989 period. In particular, the study explored the effects of using alternative conversion rates for the original national data in aggregating them into regional and world totals. The conversion rates explored included market exchange and other rates, as well as those based on purchasing power parities (PPP) such as derived in the ICP.

The PPP conversion rates explored in this UN study were based on the Penn World Tables data base, which was developed at the University of Pennsylvania by Robert Summers and Alan Heston. This data base utilizes benchmark ICP estimates and extends their matrix to further years and additional countries.

9. Multiplicity of Results

As all students of international comparisons well know (indeed, as all those familiar with index-number problems understand) comparisons of economic aggregates either over time or across space generally do not provide unique results. Simply put: numerical values calculated with the help of Laspeyres or Paasche (and to continue: Fisher, Divisia, etc) indexes may vary, and their differences can be non-negligible. While this has been a problem for statisticians since the 19th century, for various reasons in international comparisons such problems appear to be magnified. For the future of ICP it is important that the comparison results should be viewed as thoroughly credible.

In order to strengthen ICP and to increase the credibility of its results, at least the following main problems should be addressed: (a) the inherent multiplicity of possible comparison results; (b) the sometimes implausible ICP ranking of countries; and (c) the fear that ICP results may adversely impact international financial actions (such as the membership dues countries pay to the UN or the receipt of grants and aid by countries from international organizations).

I believe that enhancing the credibility of ICP results can be achieved by two principal means:

(a) By establishing world and continental control totals for GDP aggregates; and

(b) by utilizing available but neglected world data (often in physical units of measurement).

It seems both desirable and feasible to establish world and continental (regional) control totals pertaining to Gross Domestic Product. Such controlling totals can be estimated (a) for production by main producing sectors (such as agriculture, mining, manufacturing, construction, trade, services, government), (b) by the use of categories of GDP (such as private consumption, government consumption, capital formation, exports), and (c) by income categories (such as wages and salaries, self-employed income, profits, etc.).

Considerable arrays of national data are available for these categories. As a rule ICP only focuses on category (b) items, depicting the use categories mainly by consumption and capital formation expenditures. Yet data on category (a) and (c) aggregates, even if compiled outside the ICP framework and not subject to detailed ICP work, could help in evaluating the plausibility of ICP results pertaining only to category (b) items.

As a first step, it is desirable establishing approximative world and continental control estimates for (a) GDP by industry, (b) GDP by main categories of use; and (c) GDP by income categories. Just as in national accounts work within a country the data by industrial origin, the data on expenditures, and the data on incomes are juxtaposed to provide opportunities for cross checking and such estimates, the international process would also help in evaluating the plausibility and consistency of the supra-national results. Moreover, the process of developing estimates (for categories a, b, and c both for regions and at the world level), would provide for balancing possibilities and cross-checkings in various ways.

It should be noted that international statistics - from FAO agricultural yearbooks through UN population yearbooks to UN demographic yearbooks - contain much valuable information about countries, which could be utilized for cross-checking the plausibility of ICP results. As a rule these data are not taken into account in developing final ICP world estimates. However, as they are independently collected by various international organizations, they offer opportunities for judging the plausibility of the results. The fact that these data are collected independently, naturally leads to certain problems as well. However, for evaluating the overall ranking of countries and the general plausibility of the ICP estimates, they may offer excellent clues.

The following types of world data could be mapped in the work:
(a) Agricultural production and consumption estimates (FAO)
(b) Caloric intake data (FAO and others)
(c) Energy production and consumption data (UN and others)
(d) Labor data (ILO and others)
(e) Population data (UN and others).

It is well known, that national authorities frequently refer to such types of data (typically outside the national accounts and often in physical unit measures) when they check the plausibility of GDP components and aggregates for their own country. At the international level the plausibility of ICP data could be also enhanced by reference to such magnitudes.

10. Conclusion

The organizational complexity of the ICP work has been a characteristic of it from the beginnings of the program. Nevertheless, there has been a steady progress in respect of the number of countries compared, the quality of the work performed, and the methodological sophistication of the undertaking[4] in general. However, especially if dynamic comparisons are needed, the construction of acceptable longer term time series of real-term comparisons is still one of the tasks ahead.

References

Ark, B. Van and Pilat, D. (1993), 'Cross Country Productivity Levels: Differences and Causes', *Brookings Papers on Economic Activity* (Micro-economics).

ECE (1988), *International Comparisons of Gross Domestic Product in Europe, Statistical Standards and Studies*, No. 41, Geneva.

EUROSTAT (1988), *Purchasing Power Parities and Real Expenditures, Results 1985*, Luxembourg.

EUROSTAT (1989), *Comparisons of Price Levels and Economic Aggregates, 1985, The Results of 22 African Countries*, Luxembourg.

EUROSTAT (1991), *Comparisons of Price Levels and Economic Aggregates, 1985, The Results of 7 Caribbean Countries*, Luxembourg.

Kenessey, Z. (1993), 'Postwar Trends in National Accounts in the Perspective of Earlier Developments' in *The Value Added of National Accounting*, Commemorating 50 years of national accounting in The Netherlands, Netherlands Central Bureau of Statistics, pp. 33-70.

Kenessey, Z., (ed). (1994), *The Accounts of Nations*, Amsterdam, IOS Press.

[4] For a historical overview of the evolution of national accounts since the 1940's see (Kenessey, 1994)

Kravis, I., Kenessey, Z., Heston, A., Summers, R. (1975), *A System of International Comparisons of Gross Product and Purchasing Power*, Johns Hopkins University Press, Baltimore.

Kravis, I., Heston, A., Summers, R. (1978), *International Comparisons of Real Product and Purchasing Power*, Johns Hopkins University Press, Baltimore.

Kravis, I., Heston, A., Summers, R. (1982), *World Product and Income, International Comparisons of Real Gross Product*, Johns Hopkins University press, Baltimore.

Kravis, Irving B. (1984), 'Comparative Studies of National Incomes and Prices', *Journal of Economic Literature*, Vol. XXII, March issue.

Maddison, Angus (1991), *Dynamic Forces in Capitalist Development*, Oxford University Press, London.

MCA of Japan and ESCAP (1991), *Purchasing Power Parity and Quantity Comparisons for the ESCAP Region, 1985*, Tokyo and Bangkok.

OECD (1987), *Purchasing Power Parities and Real Expenditures*, Paris.

OECD (1992), National Accounts Main Aggregates, Vol. 1, 1960-1990, Paris.

Pilat, Dirk (1993), 'The Sectoral Productivity Performance of Japan and the US, 1885-1990', *Review of Income and Wealth*, Series 39, Number 4.

Ren Ruoen and Chen Kai (1992), *'China and the United States: Binary Comparisons of GNP'* (Preliminary draft), Beijing.

Salazar-Carillo, J. (1978), *Prices and Purchasing Power Parities in Latin America: 1960-1972*, OAS Washington, DC.

Salazar-Carillo, J. and D.S. Prasada Rao, (eds.) (1988), *World Comparisons of Incomes, Prices and Product*, North Holland, Amsterdam .

UN and EUROSTAT (1986), *World Comparisons of Purchasing Power and Real Product for 1980*, New York,

ST/ESA/STAT/SER.F/42, (Part I). In 1987 Part II also appeared with detailed results for 60 countries. Part I bears UN publication number E.86.XVI.9, Part II E.86.XVI.10.

United Nations (1992), *Handbook of the International Comparison Programme, Studies in Methods*, New York, Series F, No. 62.

United Nations (1993), *Trends in International Distribution of Gross World Product*, New York, Series X, No. 18.

United Nations and Eurostat (1994a), *World Comparisons of Real Gross Domestic Product and Purchasing Power, 1985.* Phase V of the International Comparison Programme, New York, Series F., No. 64.

United Nations (1994b), *International Comparison of Gross Domestic Product in Europe, 1990.* Results of the European Comparison Programme, New York and Geneva, Conference of European Statisticians, Statistical Standards and Studies, No. 45.

World Bank (1993), *Purchasing Power of Currencies. Comparing National Incomes Using ICP Data. (1975, 1980, 1985, 1990)*, Washington D.C.

Appendix Table
GDP PER CAPITA AT INTERNATIONAL PRICES,1985
(United States = 100)

Country	US$	Index	Country	US$	Index
Africa			Europe		
Benin	1 333	8.1	Austria	10 895	66.1
Botswana	2 671	16.2	Belgium	10 671	64.7
Cameroon	2 724	16.5	Denmark	12 234	74.2
Cote d'Ivoire	1 710	10.4	Finland	11 464	69.5
Congo	2 559	15.5	France	11 434	69.3
Egypt	2 794	16.9	Germany	12 169	73.8
Ethiopia	301	1.8	Greece	5 861	35.5
Kenya	995	6.0	Hungary	5 140	31.2
Madagascar	631	3.8	Ireland	6 740	40.9
Malawi	630	3.8	Italy	10 827	65.6
Mali	365	2.2	Luxembourg	13 416	81.3
Mauritius	5 886	35.7	Netherlands	11 256	68.2
Morocco	2 371	14.4	Norway	13 913	84.4
Nigeria	980	5.9	Poland	4 039	24.5
Rwanda	676	4.1	Portugal	5 568	33.8
Senegal	1 334	8.1	Spain	7 589	46.0
Sierra Leone	630	3.8	Sweden	12 679	76.9
Swaziland	2 344	14.2	Turkey	3 599	21.8
Tunisia	3 446	20.9	U.K.	10 905	66.1
Tanzania	418	2.5	Yugoslavia	4 810	29.2
Zambia	938	5.7			
Zimbabwe	1 684	10.2			
Asia			North America		
Bangladesh	830	5.0	Canada	15 258	92.5
Hong Kong	10 204	61.9	United States	16 494	100.0
India	749	4.5			
Iran	4 619	28.0			
Japan	11 795	71.5	Oceania		
Korea	3 979	24.1	Australia	11 723	71.1
Pakistan	1 342	8.1	New Zealand	10 047	60.9
Philippines	1 791	10.9			
Sri Lanka	1 852	11.2			
Thailand	2 641	16.0			

International Comparisons of Prices, Output and Productivity
Edited by D.S. Prasada Rao and J. Salazar-Carrillo

LATIN AMERICAN COMPARISONS FOR 1985

Jorge Salazar-Carrillo[1]
Florida International University
Miami, U.S.A.

1. Introduction

It is well known that the last benchmark study of the United Nations International Comparison Program (UN-ICP) in which the Latin American countries were appropriately represented was that corresponding to the year 1980.[2] Since these nations represent a significant portion of the world community, both in terms of population and economic activity, it is important attempting to add this grouping to the rest of the existing benchmark estimates. Even though the results of this exercise will not be exactly the same as participation in the ICP comparisons, it will provide an approximation. Such procedures have been undertaken before: Salazar-Carrillo(1977,1983); Salazar-Carrillo and Alonso(1988) and Salazar-Carrillo and Prasada Rao(1988); World Bank(1992) and United Nations(1994). Alternative ways of accomplishing this objective have been followed. The method that has been chosen in this study is to use extrapolations to obtain Latin American estimates for 1985, based on the benchmark comparisons for the region referring to the year 1980. The selection of this methodology is based on the practice of the UN-ICP benchmark comparisons research, to extrapolate, backward and forward, prices and expenditures to a common year, sometimes requiring for countries to be five years apart at the extreme. However, in contrast to other researchers with similar goals, regression methods are not used in estimation in the research

[1]The author would like to thank Dr. Ilona Kovacs of the Institute of Economics of the Hungarian Academy of Sciences in Budapest, and Gustavo Mattos a Ph.D. candidate at the Department of Economics of Florida International University, for their participation in this project. The former worked on the extrapolations of the Latin American data. The latter helped with the calculations of the tables in this chapter. Of course, the ultimate responsibility is entirely mine.

[2]In fact, it would appear that this was the only benchmark year for the UN-ICP project, that started in the late 1960s, in which the representation of these nations was adequate. In the earlier work, as well as in the 1985 comparison, less than half of the Latin American countries were represented.

reported here.

2. Methodology

The 1980 UN-ICP benchmark results will be taken at face value from their publications, which have been amply disseminated and discussed (Kravis et.al, 1982). It should be explained that with respect to the Latin American estimates published in that source, they were mostly the result of incorporating the work done by the ECIEL research network in Latin America[3] to the UN-ICP benchmark of 1980. It may be useful at this juncture to refer to the ECIEL literature prior to 1980, because their comparisons go back as far back as the UN-ICP work. Three articles broke ground in terms of the publications in English, the first being Joseph E Grunwald and Jorge Salazar-Carrillo (1972), immediately followed by Jorge Salazar-Carrillo (1973), and finally Robert Ferber and Jorge Salazar-Carrillo (1975). The 1960s comparisons were reported in Jorge Salazar-Carrillo (1978) with its corresponding Spanish translation. The 1970s comparisons have been reported only in Spanish, see Jorge Salazar-Carrillo (1991). However these results have been published in English in article form in J.Salazar-Carrillo and D.S.Prasada Rao (1988,1990). Although minor discrepancies may have resulted from this blending, the most relevant one is the absence of Mexico from the latter, but not from the ECIEL study. The extrapolation base of 1980 being used here includes Mexico.

In the studies done by Summers and Heston, which mix extrapolations and regressions to present a large set of estimates the world over, the former are constant price value data. An attempt has been made in this paper to extrapolate prices instead. This appears justified because of the criticisms of results that have been obtained substantially by extrapolating the quasi-volumes as done by the above-quoted authors and other researches. It would appear that due to the weak-

[3]ECIEL is the Spanish acronym for Joint Studies for Latin American Economic Integration. This was a program of research organized by the Brookings Institution in 1963, joining as a network the research efforts of the most distinguished centers, institutions, and universities in Latin America. Many studies on the region's economies were put forth by this group, mostly of a comparative nature, and relating to the economic integration of the area. They have been published in English, Spanish and Portuguese, in the form of books, articles and chapters in books. The research program published a periodical called Ensayos ECIEL, and organized about twenty five seminars. They remained active from the early sixties to the late eighties.

nesses in national accounting data and procedures in the developing world, and the greater importance of price statistics in their information systems for adjustment of income levels and policy-making, these should provide a more solid foundation for extrapolating. Also, it seems that for the type of comparative studies that have been undertaken in the last three decades, to place emphasis on the product comparisons belies the fact that most of the independent statistical work involved in the international comparisons work[4] has been in the area of prices. Thus, it makes more sense to concentrate on the extrapolation of the prices of the different types of goods. These are basically consumer prices, investment prices and the overall price level.[5] Finally, it would be very useful to contrast the results of estimation of non-benchmark comparisons using extrapolation methods relying on price information with those utilizing constant value estimates provided by the national accounting authorities.

Bearing on the methods used here, it should be specified that they are the outcome of experiments designed within the previously described ECIEL Program. A summary statement of this research is reported in Aquiles Arellano(1990). The methodology described there has been put to work in this paper. The gist of it is to attempt to extrapolate for each country the prices at the most disaggregated level possible, by using national price indices and indicators that have been experimentally shown to replicate well the benchmark price survey over time. The consumer price indices appear to be the most robust of those extrapolations, in addition constituting the best non-redundant summary measure of the overall price trends in these economies. This procedure is more detailed than what has been attempted and is potentially possible from national accounting data on constant values. It also has the advantage that price data are generally in the public domain, while constant value data seldom are.

[4]This derives from the fact that the main stumbling block in this work is in using exchange rates, in converting values from one currency to another. The alternative is to independently calculate a converter based on the prices of the different countries, which is the concept of the purchasing-power-parity.

[5]Another indication of the weakness in national accounting systems comes from the fact that the implicit deflator of the gross domestic product derived from the estimation of this concept in current and constant prices, is seldom considered reliable enough in national economic analysis and policy to enter prominently in the public discussion. This is in contrast with other price indices that are usually prominently displayed and discussed by the press, like the consumer price indices.

From the previous statements it can be deducted that extrapolation factors are computed resulting from the movement of prices over the time period in question at the sub-category, category or higher grouping level. The application of these extrapolation factors reproduces for 1985 a new sample of national prices for each country in question. This set of prices, combined with geometric average expenditure weights for the 17 Latin American countries included, at the most detailed level permitted by the 1980-85 price extrapolation factors, were utilized to calculate purchasing-power parties (PPPs) for the latter year, through the application of the geometric version of the Walsh Index. This index formula is the one traditionally used since the 1960s in the Latin American comparisons. The formula is given below :

$$I_{j,k} = \Pi_{i=1}^{n}[P_{ik}/P_{ij}]^{w_i}$$

$$\textit{with} \quad w_i = \Pi_{j=1}^{m}(v_{ij})^{1/m}/\Sigma_{i=1}^{n}\Pi_{j=1}^{m}(v_{ij})^{1/m} \quad (1)$$

where subscript i represents commodities; and j and k represent countries, and v stands for value shares. The fact that the sampled items are the same throughout Latin America, together with the characteristics of the Walsh formulation, makes the results transitive and invariant to any base chosen for the presentation of the results. Therefore, the results presented in Table 1 for the international price indices, the result of dividing the PPP, by the exchange rates, would be the same irrespective of the country chosen as a base. Guatemala has been selected because of its price stability and its role as an appropriate bridge country between the Latin American Integration Association (which includes Mexico), and Central America. In addition, the Guatemalan currency (the quetzal) had been used for expressing earlier results, because of its parity with the U.S. dollar at that time. Thus, the selection of Guatemala in this essay will facilitate the contrasting of the present comparisons with the previous ones.[6]

3. Results

As can be seen from Table 1 there were substantial differences in price levels in Latin America in 1985. These are a consequence of a

[6]For future studies probably Panama will be used as the base, since the dollar is its currency. This was not done in the 1980s since this country only recently joined the research program. On the other hand, Nicaragua has not participated in the most recent comparisons because of a political decision by the then ruling socialist Sadinista government.

lack of synchronization between prices in domestic currencies and the levels of exchange rates, which have become much wider over the 1980s probably as a result of the well publicized external debt crisis that affected the area. A follow-up of this phenomenon brought about violent inflationary processes in these nations, coupled with currency devaluations. However, their degree of severity varied widely across the Western Hemisphere, widening price differentials among these countries.

Table 1
Latin American Price Index Numbers at the GDP Level, 1985
(Guatemala = 1.00)

Argentina	0.90
Bolivia	1.81
Brazil	0.61
Colombia	0.57
Costa Rica	0.69
Chile	0.68
Ecuador	0.99
El Salvador	1.46
Guatemala	1.00
Honduras	1.09
Mexico	0.70
Panama	1.02
Paraguay	0.93
Peru	0.51
Republica Dominicana	0.51
Uruguay	0.68
Venezuela	1.22

Source : Own calculations for the purchasing-power parities. The exchange rates are yearly averages taken from the International Monetary Fund, International Financial Statistics, Washington, D.C., several years.

If the purchasing-power parties estimated for 1985 are divided into the gross domestic products of the Latin American nations expressed in local currencies, a real GDP for each country is obtained in a common currency. The next table shows such estimates of real GDPs for each of the 17 Latin American cases covered in the research with their rankings. Since the Guatemalan currency is chosen for the reasons mentioned above as a base country, and the reader is probably unfamiliar with its international value then, it is preferable to convert the figures into an index. This will allow the pinpointing of regional differences, which are further enhanced by the fact that the gross domestic products have been adjusted by population, so as to be expressed in per capita terms. Table 2 shows a smaller regional variation, in the real gross product domestic per head of population when compared with the price indices of the previous table.[7] As in the Table 1, the estimates presented are self-explanatory, and an analysis of the results may certainly generate interesting conclusions.

Table 2
Latin American GDP Per Capita in Index Form,1985
(Guatemala = 1.00)

	Index	Rank
Argentina	228	2
Bolivia	83	15
Brazil	192	4
Colombia	149	8
Costa Rica	154	6.5
Chile	138	10
Ecuador	123	12
El Salvador	24	17
Guatemala	100	14
Honduras	54	16
Mexico	250	1
Panama	154	6.5
Paraguay	121	13
Peru	124	11
Republica Dominicana	146	9
Uruguay	165	5
Venezuela	212	3

Source : Own calculations for the PPP. Gross domestic products in national currencies and population data from World Bank diskettes related with the World Development Report 1992.

[7]The range is wider, though, than in the estimates of price levels because El Salvador represents a lower outlier.

Now that the results have been presented at the maximum level of aggregation, overall national prices and GDPs per capita, it should be noted that these have been calculated as well as the lower levels of aggregation of private consumption expenditures, investment expenditures and government expenditures, following their definition in the then applicable system of national accounts of the United Nations (the 1968 blue book). However, it is not considered that the degree of reliability that can be claimed for these estimates merit their publication, particularly because they constitute extrapolations.[8]

Table 3
Latin American GDP Per Capita in Index Form,1985
(Guatemala = 100)

	Summers-Heston		World Bank	
	Index	Rank	Index	Rank
Argentina	212	3	164	7
Bolivia	68	16	69	15
Brazil	203	6	169	6
Colombia	211	4	172	4.5
Costa Rica	165	9	149	9
Chile	170	8	150	8
Dominican Republic	108	13	99	14
Ecuador	146	10	131	10
El Salvador	74	15	64	16
Guatemala	100	14	100	13
Honduras	54	17	56	17
Mexico	242	1	211	2
Panama	193	7	172	4.5
Paraguay	125	12	103	12
Peru	130	11	115	11
Uruguay	215	2	179	3
Venezuela	208	5	234	1

Source : Own calculations based on estimates presented in Robert Summers and Alan Heston,(1988), and World Bank(1992).

It seems clear that the results obtained in various international comparisons efforts at lower levels of aggregation, are published disregarding the degree of confidence that they deserve.

The overall results, which can be held in trust, should be subjected to further test by comparing them with other available estimates.

[8]However, interested researchers may request these unpublished results if they so desire.

Only two other sources exist for 1985. They are the estimates of Summers and Heston, and the most recent ones and, less well known, of the World Bank. They are shown in Table 3, also expressed in terms of Guatemala as a base, and with the corresponding country rankings. There are significant differences among the results shown in Tables 2 and 3 if the index numbers are considered.[9] However, there is much less variation in the country rankings presented there. Yet, although less demanding, sometimes the ranks can be quite different, as in the case of Venezuela.

Table 4
Absolute Number Differences in the Indices, and their Means

	SH Vs. WB	SH Vs. Own	WB Vs. Own
Argentina	48	16	64
Bolivia	1	15	14
Brazil	34	11	23
Colombia	39	73	34
Costa Rica	16	16	0
Chile	20	16	4
Dominican Republic	9	38	47
Ecuador	15	23	8
El Salvador	10	50	40
Honduras	2	0	2
Mexico	31	8	39
Panama	21	39	18
Paraguay	22	4	18
Peru	15	6	9
Uruguay	36	50	14
Venezuela	26	4	22
Mean	21.6	24.6	23.7
Geometric Mean	15.5	17.1	17.0

Source : Own Calculations, SH=Summers-Heston and WB=World Bank

To examine the index number disagreements in greater detail the absolute and relative differences between the three results are compared in a pairwise manner in Tables 4 and 5. If the results just presented in this Chapter are compared with those of Summers and Heston, the absolute number differentials range from 0 to 73, with a geometric

[9] As well as remarkable similarities in some cases, for example Honduras.

mean of 17.1 and an arithmetic mean of 24.6. When the World Bank numbers are compared with those first published here, they differ less in terms of range (0 to 64), and in both mean differentials. The same is the case for the relative differences, except for the geometric mean of relative number differences. The divergencies between the Summers and Heston (SH) and World Bank (WB) results are narrower, but this is to be expected since their methods are practically the same.[10]

Table 5
Relative Number Differences in the Indices and their Means

	SH Vs. WB	SH Vs. Own	WB Vs. Own
Argentina	25	7	33
Bolivia	2	20	18
Brazil	18	6	13
Colombia	20	42	22
Costa Rica	10	10	0
Chile	12	10	3
Dominican Republic	9	30	38
Ecuador	11	17	6
El Salvador	14	102	91
Honduras	4	0	4
Mexico	14	3	17
Panama	12	22	11
Paraguay	19	3	16
Peru	12	5	16
Uruguay	18	26	8
Venezuela	12	2	10
Mean	12.5	18.0	17.5
Geometric Mean	11.3	11.7	13.2

Source : Own Calculations

The null hypothesis of no association was rejected for a one-tailed test at the 0.05 significance level in the three pairwise comparisons. The accepted alternative hypothesis of positive correlation is predicated on the following high rank correlation values :

$$\text{SH vs. WB} = 0.946$$

[10]In fact, in the course of this research it was surprising to find that there were discrepancies between them in terms of population and GDP in domestic currency. In a few cases the differences were greater than two percent.

SH vs. Own = 0.896

WB vs. Own = 0.867

Thus, it can be deduced that these rankings are highly correlated. However, it should be noted that the index number differences themselves are significantly different from zero.

What remains now to be done is to express the new results here presented in terms that are more easy to refer to, as well as more understandable to the reader. This means expressing them in terms of the United States as a base, as the S.H. and W.B. results have calculated (World Bank,1992).

Table 6
Latin American G.D.P. Per Capita in 1985
(United States = 100)

	SH	WB	Geometric Mean
Argentina	26	25	25
Bolivia	8	10	9
Brazil	25	26	25
Colombia	26	26	26
Costa Rica	20	22	21
Chile	21	23	22
Dominican Republic	13	15	14
Ecuador	18	20	19
El Salvador	9	10	9
Honduras	7	8	8
Mexico	30	32	31
Panama	24	26	25
Paraguay	15	16	16
Peru	16	17	17
Uruguay	26	27	27
Venezuela	25	35	30
United States	100	100	100

Source : Own Calculations, rounded to two digits, and World Bank, World Development Report 1992, op-cit

The third column in Table 6 presents the most valid and reliable comparisons for Latin America in 1985. It is based on our extrapolations bridged alternatively by S.H. and W.B., ultimately combining the two by way of a geometric average. It should be noted that since the reliability of these numbers is limited, we have rounded them to two digits, so as not to give a false impression of exactitude. Anyhow, with a couple of exceptions (like Venezuela) the result of the three columns are very close. Mexico and Venezuela appeared to have the highest income per head in Latin America in 1985, just below one third of the U.S. level. It should be noted that the year 1985 was probably the trough of the decade-long recession suffered by this region in the eighties, as a result of its external debt crisis. A second tier of countries was formed by Uruguay, Chile, Argentina, Brazil and Panama, at about one fourth, or slightly above it, of the U.S. gross domestic product per head of population. On the other hand Honduras, Bolivia and El Salvador had per capita levels of GDP just below 10 per cent of the American levels in 1985. The rest of the Latin American countries ranged from 14 per cent (Guatemala and the Dominican Republic) to 22 per cent (Costa Rica) of the average standard of living in the United States.

4. Conclusions

Based on the survey conducted in 1979-80, a set of benchmark comparisons were undertaken covering the 18 Latin American countries reported here. The survey gathered information on prices, expenditures and quantities (the latter when appropriate and feasible) following the GDP breakdown. The most reliable and complete of these data sets was that referring to prices. Therefore, we chose to extrapolate the benchmark comparisons, which, with the exception of Mexico, were published by the United Nations-International Comparisons Program, on the basis of price series. We also came to the conclusion that the expenditure series by themselves, or in combination with the price series, are not to be trusted given their shallow disaggregation, their weaker statistical base and the relatively lower precision and reporting frequency.

In comparing our results with the alternative estimates for Latin America in 1985, calculated by Summers and Heston and the World Bank, which do not use region-specific methods, and follow a poorer extrapolating methodology, it is found that the overall ranks are close enough as to not reject the hypothesis that they belong to the same universe. In this sense the three studies validate each other. However in absolute and relative terms there are still major discrepancies among the three sets of calculations of GDP's per capita with the United States as a base. Given these circumstances we will clearly recommend the use of our results.

References

Arellano, A(1990), "Extrapolations of Purchasing Power Parities" in Salazar-Carrillo, J. and D.S. Prasada Rao(eds.) *Comparisons of Prices and Real Products in Latin America*, North-Holland, Amsterdam.

Ferber, R. and J. Salazar-Carrillo(1975), "Experience in Generating Micro Data in Latin America" in E.B. Ayal(ed) *Micro Aspects of Development*, Praeger.

Grunwald, J.E and J. Salazar-Carrillo(1972), "Economic Integration, Rates of Exchange and Value Comparisons in Latin America" in Donj-Daly(ed.), *International Comparisons of Prices and Output*, National Bureau of Economic Research.

Kravis, I.B, A. Heston and R. Summers(1982), *World Product and Income*, Johns Hopkins Press, Baltimore

Salazar-Carrillo, J. (1973), "Price, Purchasing Power and Real Product Comparisons in Latin America", *Review of Income and Wealth.*

Salazar-Carrillo, J. (1977), " Latin American Real Product Comparisons of Prices", *The Economic Journal.*

Salazar-Carrillo, J. (1978), *Prices and Purchasing Power Parities in Latin America, 1960-1972*, Organization of American States, Washington, DC.

Salazar-Carrillo, J. (1983), " Real Product and Price Comparisons for Latin America and other World Countries", *Economic Development and Cultural Change*, 31(4).

Salazar-Carrillo, J. (1991) *Poder de Compray Productividad en America Latina*, Centro de Investigation y Docenicia Economica(CIDE), Mexico.

Salazar-Carrillo, J. and I. Alonso(1988), "Real Product and Price Comparisons between Latin America and the Rest of the World", *Review of Income and Wealth.*

Salazar-Carrillo, J. and D.S. Prasada Rao(1988), "Real Product and Price Comparisons among Latin America Countries", in J. Salazar-Carrillo and D.S. Prasada Rao(eds.), *World Comparisons of Incomes, Prices and Product*, North-Holland, Amsterdam.

Salazar-Carrillo, J. and D.S. Prasada Rao(eds.)(1988), *World Comparison of Incomes, Prices and Product*, North-Holland, Amsterdam.

Salazar-Carrillo, J. and D.S. Prasada Rao(eds.)(1990), *Comparisons of Prices and Real Products in Latin America*, North-Holland, Amsterdam.

Summers, R. and A. Heston(1988), " A new set of International Comparisons of Real Product and Price Level Estimates for 130 countries, 1950-1995", *Review of Income and Wealth.*

United Nations(1994), *World Comparisons of Real Gross Domestic Product and Purchasing Power, 1985*, New York.

World Bank(1992), *World Development Report*, Washington, DC.

International Comparisons of Prices, Output and Productivity
Edited by D.S. Prasada Rao and J. Salazar-Carrillo

INTERCOUNTRY COMPARISONS OF AGRICULTURAL OUTPUT AND PRODUCTIVITY, 1970 - 1990

Statistics Division[1]
Food and Agriculture Organization
Rome, Italy

1. Introduction

The work at the Food and Agriculture Organization complements the work of the Statistical Offices of the United Nations, European Union, Organisation for Economic Cooperation and Development, and the World Bank. The so called expenditure approach to international comparisons of GDP has been pursued most extensively within the International Comparisons Project. The ICP has completed five phases so far and has entered Phase VI. The ICP approach results in purchasing power parities of currencies which may be used for comparing the real GDP of different countries. However, in contrast, there has been little work on comparisons based on the industry-of-origin approach. While the ICP results can be applied at the GDP level, it has now been recognized that these results cannot be employed for sectoral comparisons, since the ICP parities are based on prices paid by end users which include trade and marketing margins. The results from the 1985 FAO study as well as the work of Maddison and his associates indicate that the results for different sectors differ significantly from the ICP parities.

The 1985 FAO study represents the biggest effort yet in the area of sectoral comparisons. The coverage of the project is more comprehensive than that of the International Comparisons Project. The data base utilized in the FAO study is broader in scope and the results contrast sharply with those in the ICP. The purchasing power parities of currencies based on agricultural sector prices are, by and large, close to the official exchange rates, whereas the ICP results show considerably lower values for the parities in the case of developing countries. This result suggests that for purposes of agricultural sector comparisons, use of ICP PPPs is quite inappropriate.

[1] Results presented here were the outcome of a study conducted by Professor Prasada Rao who worked as a consultant to the Division

The success of the 1985 project and the popularity of the report indicated a need to update the results to a new benchmark year. The new benchmark years considered here are 1985 and 1990. The aim of the present exercise is wider than a simple update. The present paper endeavours to provide a brief summary of the main results of the new report detailing some of the innovations introduced in the present benchmark comparisons. Details of the new benchmark results are presented in *Intercountry Comparisons of Agricultural Output and Productivity*, Prasada Rao (1993).

The organization of the paper is as follows. Section 2 briefly describes the conceptual framework underlying the comparisons. The data base utilized in the exercise is briefly described in Section 3. Section 4 details the aggregation procedures employed in the study. The main results are presented in Section 5, and the paper is concluded with some remarks in Section 6.

2. Conceptual Framework

The conceptual framework used in the study is based on the Handbook of Economic Accounts for Agriculture (EAA) (FAO, 1974, FAO, 1987 draft). The scope of agriculture considered here is consistent with the ISIC of economic activities of the United Nations. Though ISIC includes Forestry and Fishing and production of agricultural services within Agriculture, the present study encompasses only the production of agricultural commodities which are classified into crops and livestock. Severe data limitations are the main reason for this selection.

Measures of Agricultural Output

Within the framework of economic accounts, four different measures of output may be defined depending upon the level of deduction of inputs used in the production. The inputs used in agricultural production are usually classified by the sector of their origin. The first category of inputs correspond to those agricultural commodities which are used in agricultural production, and these refer to items that are used as seed and feed. The second category of inputs are essentially non-agricultural in nature and produced outside the sphere of agriculture, but used in agricultural production.

The notation used in the paper is as below. For a given set of N output commodities, K non-agricultural inputs and M countries, subscripts i and j refer respectively to commodities and countries. Lower-case letters q, s and f refer, respectively, to quantities of output produced, and quantities of seed and feed inputs used. Letter p refers to price of output, but when used with superscripts s and f refer to seed and feed prices. In practice, seed commodity prices, such as prices of seed potatoes, and eggs for hatching, are generally higher than output prices due to their superior quality. In contrast, feed commodities are usually cheaper. Let X_{kj} and W_{kj} represent the quantity and price of kth non-agricultural input used in country j. The main output concepts used in the study are as below:

Total Output:

$$T_j = \sum_{i=1}^{N} p_{ij} \; q_{ij} \tag{1}$$

which represents the value of total agricultural output in country j.

Gross Output:

$$G_j = \sum_{i=1}^{N} p_{ij} \; q_{ij} \; - \; \sum_{i=1}^{N} p_{ij}^{s} \; s_{ij} \tag{2}$$

is the value of output net of the use of agricultural output used as seed.

Final Output:

$$F_j = \sum_{i} p_{ij} \; q_{ij} \; - \; \sum_{i} p_{ij}^{s} \; s_{ij} \; - \; \sum_{i} p_{ij}^{f} \; f_{ij} \tag{3}$$

is the value of agricultural output net of inputs used as seed and feed. Final output corresponds to the output of the "national farm".

Agricultural GDP:

The agricultural GDP or value added in country j, Y_j, is obtained after deducting the value of non-agricultural inputs used in the production.

$$Y_j = \sum_{i} p_{ij} \; q_{ij} - \sum_{i} p_{ij}^{s} \; s_{ij} - \sum_{i} p_{ij}^{f} \; f_{ij} \; - \; \sum_{k=1}^{k} w_{kj} \; x_{kj} \tag{4}$$

Agricultural Producer Prices

Producer prices at the farm gate are used in the study. The producer prices of output do not include any transport costs or marketing margins. Similarly intermediate consumption should be valued at purchase price paid by producers at the farm gate, which include all the distribution charges.

3. The Data Base

The present study is based exclusively on data from the ICS and the AGROSTAT system of the FAO. The producer prices of output commodities are obtained directly from the ICS. The prices paid for input items, including seed and feed, are compiled from the responses to special FAO questionnaires from the member countries. The output data for different agricultural commodities as well as the seed and feed input quantities are drawn from the ICS.

Data on non-agricultural inputs used are less satisfactory. Main source of information on non-agricultural inputs is the data on Economic Accounts for Agriculture (EAA) collected using special surveys. The EAA data are in the form of expenditures on broad categories of inputs such as the fertilizers, pesticides, fuel and energy and other items. These data are available in a usable form for only 42 countries. Prices paid by farmers for specific non-agricultural inputs are available from special surveys.

Benchmark Years: This study is limited to five benchmark years, viz., 1970, 1975, 1980, 1985 and 1990. But the detailed agricultural GDP comparisons are limited to the year 1985, the year with the most satisfactory data set.

Country Coverage: A total of 103 countries which account for 99 per cent of total world output, and for 98 per cent of the total world population. Due to limited data availability agricultural GDP comparisons are restricted to 42 countries, which are used in obtaining regression-based extrapolations for the remaining countries.

Commodity Coverage: The study is based on a list of 185 agricultural output commodities, 58 commodities used as seed, and 146 commodities used as feed. Quantity data for all these commodities are available from the ICS.

4. The Methodology

The principal aggregation method used in the study is the Geary-Khamis (G-K) method. However the application of this procedure differs from the usual practice, and called a modified G-K method. Since GDP comparisons are the primary concern, it was decided that single deflation procedure would be employed at the highest level feasible.

Output Parities

Given the nature of the data, the following modified Geary-Khamis method is applied at the final output level.

Modified Geary-Khamis Method

If PPP_j and P_i represent, respectively, the purchasing power parity of currency j and the "international average" price of the ith commodity, then the modified system is given by the following equations.

$$P_i = \frac{\sum_j \; [p_{ij} \; q_{ij}]/PPP_j}{\sum_j q_{ij}} \tag{5}$$

$$P_i^s = \frac{\sum_j \; [p_{ij}^s \; s_{ij}]/PPP_j}{\sum_j \; s_{ij}} \tag{6}$$

$$P_i^f = \frac{\sum_j \; [p_{ij}^f \; f_{ij}]/PPP_j}{\sum_j \; f_{ij}} \tag{7}$$

and

$$PPP_j = \frac{\sum_i p_{ij} \; q_{ij} \; - \; \sum_i \; p_{ij}^s \; s_{ij} \; - \; \sum_i \; p_{ij}^f \; f_{ij}}{\sum_i \; p_i \; q_{ij} \; - \; \sum_i \; P_i^s \; s_{ij} \; - \; \sum_i \; p_i^f \; f_{ij}} \tag{8}$$

Input Parities

The input purchasing power parities relating to non-agricultural commodities are obtained using a combination of the Geary-Khamis method and the generalized Theil-Tornqvist index due to Caves, Christensen and Diewert.

The Geary-Khamis method could be employed as price and quantity data were available for three fertilizers: Urea, Triple Superphosphate (TSP) and Muriate of Potash from the FAO Fertilizer Yearbook.

This method resulted in price and expenditure information for the composite item, viz., Fertilizers.

The other non-agricultural inputs considered are pesticides, fuel and energy and others. Expenditure data and, hence, value share information are available for 42 member countries. Expenditure shares for the remaining 61 countries are estimated using the average shares of countries in the regions to which the countries belong. For the commodity groups of pesticides and, fuel and energy a single representative item is priced. In the case of pesticides, 2-4D is selected, and the energy and fuel group is represented by diesel. The ICP parities ares used as a proxy for the "other items" group.

The price and value share information are combined using the Theil-Tornqvist indices for a given pair of countries j and k by

$$TT_{kj} = \Pi_{i=1}^{m} \; [\frac{W_{ij}}{W_{ik}}]^{\frac{v_{ij} + v_{ik}}{2}} \tag{9}$$

The binary indices are used in conjunction with the EKS procedure to yield the Caves, Christensen and Diewert (CCD) indices

$$CCD_{kj} = \Pi_{l=1}^{M} \; [TT_{kl} \; . \; TT_{lj}]^{1/M} \tag{10}$$

This procedure results in the overall non-agricultural input parities for all the countries in the study.

Computation of Real Agricultural GDP: For all the 42 countries with information on actual expenditure information on non-agricultural inputs, the real agricultural GDP can be computed using the double-deflation procedure. Thus

$$Y_j^* = \frac{F_j}{PPP_j^o} - \frac{\sum_{k=1}^{k} W_{kj} \; X_{kj}}{PPP_j^i} \tag{11}$$

where superscripts i and o refer to input and output respectively.

For the remaining countries, the real agricultural GDP is extrapolated using the following regression model postulating the following functional relationship:

$$\frac{X_j^*}{F_j^*} = F(Z_{1j}, \; Z_{2j} \; , ..., \; Z_{pj}, \; U_j) \tag{12}$$

where X_j^* and F_j^* represent the real expenditure on non-agricultural inputs and real final output for country j respectively.

Using a simple log-linear model the extrapolated real agricultural GDP figures for the remaining 61 countries with incomplete data are produced.

5. Results

As it is impossible to present all the results only a selected set from the original report is presented here.

Purchasing Power Parities

Table 1 shows the agricultural parities for the five benchmark years and contrasts them with the official exchange rates. The main feature to note is the general similarity between the parities and the exchange rates. Table 2 compares agricultural parities with the ICP parities at the GDP level. Differences between these two sets of parities are striking.

International Prices

Table 3 presents the international prices of all the commodities covered in the study. These international prices represent average prices expressed in a numeraire currency, namely, the international dollar. This table also provides international prices of all the commodities expressed relative to the price of wheat. International prices of seed and feed commodities are not presented here. These are available in the appendix of the main report, Prasada Rao (1993).

Regional Comparisons

Table 4 provides the total agricultural output by continents at current and constant 1980 prices. The implicit price deflators are presented in Table 4. An interesting picture shows a general decline in agricultural prices during the period 1980 to 1985.

Non-Agricultural Input Parities

The purchasing power parities for non-agricultural inputs calculated using a combination of Theil-Tornqvist and G-K procedures are presented in Table 5. The PPPs for inputs are lower than the corresponding output parities.

Agricultural GDP and Productivity Comparisons

Table 6 presents final output and agricultural GDP figures for all the countries except the eastern European countries and other centrally planned economies. This table also provides per capita and per labour unit agricultural output figures. Similar figures measuring land productivity are also available.

6. Conclusions

Although the present study is an update of the 1985 FAO study, a number of methodological improvements have been introduced during the course of the project. Not all the features of the study are dealt with in this brief summary, a notable omission concerns the proposal to introduce a country-neutral currency - the agricultural currency unit (ACU). The ACU is designed to replace the United States dollar, which is used at present as the numeraire currency, in other words, the international dollar, for purposes of expressing the agricultural output and GDP of different countries in a common currency unit. Chapter 6 of the report by Prasada Rao (1993) deals with the definition of ACU and some of the operational considerations associated with this new concept.

This exercise on intercountry comparisons of agricultural output and productivity also points towards limitations arising out of data deficiency which need to be addressed in the future. In particular, the area of economic accounts, which is central to the concept of agricultural GDP, needs a concerted effort so that more reliable comparisons of agricultural GDP can be obtained for the next benchmark year 1995.

References

Caves, D.W., L.R. Christensen and W.E. Diewert, (1982), "Multilateral Comparison of Output, Input and Productivity Using Superlative Index Numbers", *Economic Journal*, Vol. 92, pp. 73-86.

Caves, D.W., L.R. Christensen and W.E. Diewert, (1982), "The Economic Theory of Index Numbers and the Measurement of Input, Output and Productivity", *Econometrica*, Vol. 50, No. 6, 1982.

Diewert, W.E., (1976) "Exact and Superlative Index Numbers", *Journal of Econometrics*, Vol. 4, pp. 115-145.

Elteto, O. and P. Koves, (1964) "On an Index Number Comparison Problem in International Comparisons" (in Hungarian), *Statistiztikai Szemie*, Vol. 42, pp. 507-518.

FAO, (1974), *Handbook of Economic Accounts for Agriculture*, Rome.

FAO, (1980), "Farm and Input Prices: Collection and Compilation", *FAO Economic and Social Development Paper No. 16*.

FAO, (1986), "Intercountry Comparisons of Agricultural Production Aggregates", *FAO Economic and Social Development Paper No. 61*.

FAO, (1987), "The FAO Agricultural Production Index", *FAO Economic and Social Development Paper No. 63*, Statistics Division, FAO.

FAO, (1987), *Handbook of Economic Accounts for Agriculture*, Rome. (Draft, Mimeographed)

Geary, R.C., (1958), "A Note on Comparisons of Exchange Rates and Purchasing Power Between Countries", *Journal of the Royal Statistical Society*, Vol. 121, 1958.

Khamis, S.H., (1972), "A New System of Index Numbers for National and International Purposes", *Journal of the Royal Statistical Society*, Vol. 135.

Prasada Rao, D.S. (1993), "Intercountry Comparisons of Agricultural Output and Productivity", *FAO Economic and Social Development Paper No. 112*, Rome.

Szulc, B., (1964), "Index Numbers of Multilateral Regional Comparisons" (in Polish), *Prezeglad Statysticzny*, Vol. 3, pp. 239-254.

Theil, H., (1973), "A New Index Number Formula", *Review of Economics and Statistics*, Vol. 53.

Tornqvist, L., (1936), "The Bank of Finland's Consumption Price Index", *Bank of Finland Monthly Bulletin*, No. 10.

United Nations,(1990), *National Accounts Statistics: Main Aggregates and Related Tables, 1987*, New York.

TABLE 1
AGRICULTURAL OUTPUT PPP AND OFFICIAL EXCHANGE RATES - 1970, 1975, 1980, 1985 AND 1990
(UNITS OF NATIONAL CURRENCY PER INTERNATIONAL DOLLAR)

COUNTRIES BY REGION	YEAR 1970		YEAR 1975		YEAR 1980		YEAR 1985		YEAR 1990	
	PPP	EXCHANGE RATE	PPP	EXCHANGE RATE	PPP	EXCHANGE RATE	PPP	EXCHANGE RATE	PPP	EXCHANGE RATE
AFRICA										
ALGERIA	5.203	4.937	5.146	3.944	8.548	3.836	17.426	5.025	20.119	8.840
ANGOLA	19.067	28.750	14.943	25.497	25.595	29.620	54.030	29.620	54.101	29.922
BURUNDI	67.257	87.497	52.628	78.753	79.184	90.001	111.908	120.555	116.735	171.028
CAMEROON	231.039	277.700	221.074	214.133	265.490	210.970	529.628	445.434	570.803	271.518
CHAD	154.653	277.700	165.134	214.133	256.025	210.970	431.078	445.434	358.279	271.518
EGYPT	0.410	0.435	0.363	0.391	0.616	0.700	1.189	0.700	1.278	1.419
ETHIOPIA	2.538	2.500	1.511	2.086	1.917	2.070	2.944	2.070	3.389	2.070
GHANA	1.148	1.020	1.637	1.149	14.103	2.750	86.860	54.113	192.301	326.797
GUINEA	21.139	24.685	36.711	20.650	36.717	18.964	77.189	24.292	469.716	660.066
COTE D'IVOIRE	182.361	277.700	188.846	214.133	270.855	210.970	469.531	445.434	466.634	271.518
KENYA	5.327	7.143	5.944	7.407	7.134	7.463	16.646	16.393	16.063	22.727
MADAGASCAR	160.447	277.700	174.626	214.133	217.908	210.970	647.422	661.375	830.320	1492.537
MALAWI	0.590	0.833	0.496	0.865	0.528	0.812	0.977	1.706	1.105	2.725
MALI	140.971	277.700	132.465	214.133	199.497	210.970	346.309	445.434	345.486	271.518
MOROCCO	5.176	5.060	6.037	4.049	7.876	3.930	12.139	10.054	12.059	8.233
MOZAMBIQUE	24.616	28.750	23.152	25.497	26.175	49.985	76.540	43.159	892.108	925.926
NIGER	179.598	277.700	207.696	214.133	320.914	210.970	558.298	445.434	540.266	271.518
NIGERIA	1.004	0.714	1.292	0.615	1.943	0.546	4.127	0.894	12.768	8.038
RWANDA	81.764	100.000	70.062	92.851	69.399	92.842	128.015	101.092	91.868	82.600
SENEGAL	174.148	277.700	164.158	214.133	184.204	210.970	426.089	445.434	365.833	271.518
SOMALIA	6.702	7.143	6.986	6.950	11.016	6.295	80.988	39.364	88.689	N.A.
SOUTH AFRICA	0.605	0.714	0.701	0.732	0.855	0.778	1.632	2.193	1.916	2.584
SUDAN	0.286	0.348	0.367	0.348	0.709	0.500	2.735	2.288	15.791	4.505
TANZANIA	4.933	7.143	5.854	7.407	9.663	8.197	40.537	17.443	85.152	195.056
TUNISIA	0.543	0.525	0.428	0.402	0.505	0.405	0.979	0.832	1.086	0.877
UGANDA	0.058	0.071	0.094	0.741	0.516	0.742	9.846	6.369	717.654	428.850
BURKINA FASO	184.912	277.700	152.512	214.133	293.919	210.970	487.125	445.434	368.256	271.518
ZAIRE	0.387	0.500	1.033	0.500	11.867	2.758	41.940	49.554	49.058	718.580
ZIMBABWE	0.546	0.714	0.517	0.568	0.602	0.643	1.507	1.613	1.985	2.451
NORTH AND CENTRAL AMERICA										
CANADA	0.853	1.047	0.995	1.017	1.257	1.170	1.446	1.366	1.325	1.167
COSTA RICA	7.204	6.625	8.178	8.570	11.218	8.570	62.065	50.536	65.663	91.274
CUBA	0.571	1.000	0.494	0.802	0.511	0.716	0.668	0.921	0.977	N.A.
DOMINICAN RP	0.928	1.000	1.077	1.000	0.981	1.000	4.953	3.115	10.732	8.290
EL SALVADOR	2.678	2.500	1.611	2.500	3.602	2.500	3.992	2.500	5.993	8.030
GUATEMALA	1.074	1.000	0.885	1.000	1.064	1.000	1.514	1.000	2.470	5.015
HAITI	4.574	5.000	4.448	5.000	5.090	5.000	9.762	5.000	8.694	5.000
HONDURAS	1.724	2.000	1.284	2.000	1.381	2.000	2.019	2.000	2.465	2.000
MEXICO	12.472	12.500	14.834	12.497	27.589	22.950	315.578	246.002	4170.871	2808.989
NICARAGUA	8.625	7.000	7.412	7.026	10.084	10.050	44.387	24.372	725.906	705.000
UNITED STATES OF AMERICA	1.000	1.000	1.000	1.000	1.000	1.000	1.000	1.000	1.000	1.000
SOUTH AMERICA										
ARGENTINA	2.283	3.759	14.801	36.580	96.189	183.717	0.294	0.602	2345.648	4876.000
BOLIVIA	9.365	11.876	16.270	20.000	3.918	2.451	0.449	0.440	2.355	3.173
BRAZIL	2.392	4.494	7.612	8.204	4.818	5.271	4.837	6.200	44.592	68.300
CHILE	1.103	1.202	378.554	491.110	50.036	39.000	127.804	161.081	210.957	305.062
COLOMBIA	16.392	18.334	25.022	31.151	48.891	47.225	131.728	140.095	215.964	499.251
ECUADOR	14.665	20.377	18.400	25.000	23.033	25.000	107.400	68.889	369.114	761.615
PARAGUAY	60.964	125.992	83.591	125.945	121.191	125.992	269.921	306.670	821.099	1229.810
PERU	34.042	38.700	42.126	40.601	277.920	286.287	5.958	10.101	1865.303	1878.860
URUGUAY	0.100	0.250	1.098	2.273	6.794	9.075	81.587	101.430	1033.693	1171.050
VENEZUELA	4.652	4.499	4.460	4.285	5.736	4.293	11.274	7.500	26.732	46.751

TABLE 1 CONTINUED

COUNTRIES BY REGION	YEAR 1970		YEAR 1975		YEAR 1980		YEAR 1985		YEAR 1990	
	PPP	EXCHANGE RATE	PPP	EXCHANGE RATE	PPP	EXCHANGE RATE	PPP	EXCHANGE RATE	PPP	EXCHANGE RATE
ASIA										
AFGHANISTAN	77.204	45.000	48.831	45.000	56.182	44.267	134.056	50.600	390.344	50.600
BANGLADESH	4.884	4.762	16.774	11.236	12.850	15.385	27.443	28.571	27.031	34.483
MYANMAR	3.142	4.762	4.406	6.452	4.021	6.623	6.440	8.403	11.948	6.329
SRI LANKA	6.560	5.952	8.692	6.993	11.669	16.393	22.309	27.027	26.347	40.000
CHINA	2.247	2.463	1.434	1.866	1.586	1.497	2.447	2.933	2.801	4.785
INDIA	7.313	7.519	7.798	8.333	7.167	7.874	12.664	12.346	16.561	17.544
INDONESIA	270.171	363.504	406.287	414.938	758.137	626.959	1571.058	1109.878	1979.978	1845.018
IRAN, ISLAMIC REP. OF	86.623	75.752	85.118	67.622	156.056	70.607	362.429	90.884	419.875	67.995
IRAQ	0.531	0.357	0.424	0.296	0.475	0.295	1.176	0.311	1.623	0.311
ISRAEL	0.456	0.350	0.929	0.637	5.037	4.902	1.370	1.076	2.674	2.016
JAPAN	771.852	359.971	796.090	296.736	619.828	225.836	869.554	236.742	688.621	144.092
CAMBODIA	39.713	55.540	193.506	N.A.	336.184	N.A.	560.896	N.A.	509.583	N.A.
KOREA, D P RP	383.271	N.A.	492.658	N.A.	939.296	N.A.	1414.652	N.A.	1193.666	N.A.
KOREA, REPUBLIC OF	504.821	310.559	780.687	483.092	1331.919	606.061	2270.272	869.565	1930.052	707.714
LAOS	537.750	N.A.	1802.928	N.A.	2439.540	N.A.	5115.742	N.A.	5767.855	N.A.
MALAYSIA	3.613	3.061	3.483	2.386	3.085	2.176	4.271	2.482	4.221	2.705
MONGOLIA	2.647	N.A.	2.290	N.A.	2.000	N.A.	3.264	N.A.	3.567	N.A.
NEPAL	12.784	10.125	10.675	10.986	10.632	12.000	18.293	18.137	21.545	29.356
PAKISTAN	5.668	4.762	8.839	9.901	9.442	9.901	12.828	15.873	12.882	21.739
PHILIPPINES	4.644	5.952	6.242	7.246	6.484	7.519	18.295	18.519	25.366	24.390
SAUDI ARABIA, KINGDOM OF	7.030	4.500	5.724	3.517	5.785	3.327	9.580	3.622	11.743	3.745
SYRIA	3.495	3.820	3.459	3.700	4.931	3.925	10.644	3.925	14.534	11.225
THAILAND	10.992	20.800	13.400	20.379	14.780	20.476	18.035	27.149	20.407	25.562
TURKEY	13.559	10.800	21.780	14.428	106.946	73.584	579.451	519.480	2113.014	2631.579
VIET NAM	5.251	N.A.	12.380	N.A.	20.427	N.A.	33.780	N.A.	40.159	N.A.
EUROPE										
ALBANIA	7.024	N.A.	5.567	N.A.	7.432	N.A.	13.198	N.A.	15.234	N.A.
AUSTRIA	26.581	26.000	20.647	17.379	18.053	12.917	22.948	20.517	19.449	11.340
BELGIUM-LUXEMBOURG	52.407	50.000	46.635	36.670	39.517	29.199	59.672	58.928	51.674	33.322
BULGARIA	2.238	1.170	1.560	0.969	1.598	0.858	2.047	1.030	1.939	N.A.
CZECHOSLOVAK, FED. REP.	24.551	27.000	15.648	20.930	14.329	14.270	18.051	17.140	16.812	17.950
DENMARK	6.625	7.500	6.949	5.733	7.429	5.628	11.381	10.519	10.168	6.173
FINLAND	5.634	4.200	6.158	3.679	6.945	3.727	13.332	6.162	13.129	3.816
FRANCE	7.059	5.554	7.878	4.280	8.114	4.220	12.598	8.911	11.599	5.431
GERMAN, NEW LANDER	6.155	4.200	4.180	3.480	3.896	3.300	7.289	3.640	5.848	N.A.
GERMANY, FEDERAL REP.	4.118	3.660	3.530	2.454	3.177	1.815	3.438	2.920	2.688	1.612
GREECE	36.924	30.000	38.917	32.123	70.526	42.495	187.550	137.684	246.181	158.378
HUNGARY	41.656	30.000	28.564	20.449	27.799	32.387	40.980	50.075	47.585	63.171
IRELAND	0.339	0.417	0.493	0.450	0.578	0.486	0.842	0.938	0.905	0.603
ITALY	777.395	625.000	860.088	653.595	1270.269	854.701	2499.273	1901.141	2332.853	1196.172
NETHERLANDS	3.671	3.620	3.332	2.523	2.544	1.985	3.363	3.293	4.043	1.816
NORWAY	10.905	7.143	9.850	5.212	10.122	4.936	14.499	8.552	14.937	6.247
POLAND	32.223	40.000	26.950	3.320	36.197	44.220	137.981	147.189	555.341	9523.809
PORTUGAL	31.354	28.750	34.845	25.497	88.824	50.028	227.406	170.126	230.230	142.207
ROMANIA	13.468	20.000	9.455	20.000	7.743	18.000	9.574	17.094	30.128	22.432
SPAIN	75.123	69.999	73.228	57.471	92.734	71.521	185.075	169.635	164.844	101.626
SWEDEN	6.603	5.173	5.981	4.141	6.448	4.227	10.407	8.565	11.245	5.910
SWITZERLAND	6.102	4.313	4.792	2.579	3.719	1.673	4.826	2.432	4.180	1.382
UNITED KINGDOM	0.405	0.417	0.533	0.450	0.567	0.430	0.779	0.772	0.771	0.560
YUGOSLAVIA	12.783	12.500	19.316	17.361	33.912	24.640	255.230	270.160	83580	113180
OCEANIA										
AUSTRALIA	0.672	0.893	0.602	0.763	0.779	0.878	1.111	1.427	1.185	1.280
NEW ZEALAND	0.606	0.893	0.523	0.823	0.703	1.028	1.156	2.008	1.114	1.704
PAPUA NEW GUINEA	0.808	0.893	1.312	0.763	1.245	0.670	1.937	1.000	2.534	0.955
FORMER USSR	2.236	0.900	1.556	0.722	1.263	0.646	2.087	0.838	2.052	0.584

TABLE 2
AGRICULTURAL OUTPUT PPP, PPP FOR TOTAL GDP AND OFFICIAL EXCHANGE RATES - 1980 AND 1985
(UNITS OF NATIONAL CURRENCY PER INTERNATIONAL DOLLAR)

COUNTRIES BY REGION	1980 PPP FOR AGRICULTURE	1980 PPP FOR TOTAL GDP	1980 OFFICIAL EXCHANGE RATE	1980 RATIO: PPP TO EXCHANGE RATE	1980 PPP RATIO: AGRICULTURE TO TOTAL GDP	1985 PPP FOR AGRICULTURE	1985 PPP FOR TOTAL GDP	1985 OFFICIAL EXCHANGE RATE	1985 RATIO: PPP TO EXCHANGE RATE	1985 PPP RATIO: AGRICULTURE TO TOTAL GDP
AFRICA										
ALGERIA	8.548	N.A.	3.836	2.228	N.A.	17.426	N.A.	5.025	3.468	N.A.
ANGOLA	25.595	N.A.	29.620	0.864	N.A.	54.030	N.A.	29.620	1.824	N.A.
BURUNDI	79.184	N.A.	90.001	0.880	N.A.	111.908	N.A.	120.555	0.928	N.A.
CAMEROON	265.490	193.300	210.970	1.258	1.373	529.628	160.450	445.434	1.189	3.301
CHAD	256.025	N.A.	210.970	1.214	N.A.	431.078	N.A.	445.434	0.968	N.A.
EGYPT	0.616	N.A.	0.700	0.880	N.A.	1.189	0.169	0.700	1.699	7.036
ETHIOPIA	1.917	1.002	2.070	0.926	1.913	2.944	0.847	2.070	1.422	3.476
GHANA	14.103	N.A.	2.750	5.128	N.A.	86.860	N.A.	54.113	1.605	N.A.
GUINEA	36.717	N.A.	18.964	1.936	N.A.	77.189	N.A.	24.292	3.178	N.A.
COTE D'IVOIRE	270.855	197.200	210.970	1.284	1.374	469.531	165.169	445.434	1.054	2.843
KENYA	7.134	4.918	7.463	0.956	1.451	16.646	5.536	16.393	1.015	3.007
MADAGASCAR	217.908	136.900	210.970	1.033	1.592	647.422	242.674	661.375	0.979	2.668
MALAWI	0.528	N.A.	0.812	0.650	N.A.	0.977	0.503	1.706	0.573	1.942
MALI	199.497	251.500	210.970	0.946	0.793	346.309	167.135	445.434	0.777	2.072
MOROCCO	7.876	2.866	3.930	2.004	2.748	12.139	2.560	10.054	1.207	4.742
MOZAMBIQUE	26.175	N.A.	49.985	0.524	N.A.	76.540	N.A.	43.159	1.773	N.A.
NIGER	320.914	N.A.	210.970	1.521	N.A.	558.298	N.A.	445.434	1.253	N.A.
NIGERIA	1.943	0.605	0.546	3.559	3.212	4.127	0.701	0.894	4.616	5.887
RWANDA	69.399	N.A.	92.842	0.747	N.A.	128.015	44.412	101.092	1.266	2.882
SENEGAL	184.204	157.000	210.970	0.873	1.173	426.089	141.349	445.434	0.957	3.014
SOMALIA	11.016	N.A.	6.295	1.750	N.A.	80.988	N.A.	39.364	2.057	N.A.
SOUTH AFRICA	0.855	N.A.	0.778	1.099	N.A.	1.632	N.A.	2.193	0.744	N.A.
SUDAN	0.709	N.A.	0.500	1.418	N.A.	2.735	N.A.	2.288	1.195	N.A.
TANZANIA	9.663	5.778	8.197	1.179	1.672	40.537	12.000	17.443	2.324	3.378
TUNISIA	0.505	0.278	0.405	1.247	1.817	0.979	0.299	0.832	1.177	3.274
UGANDA	0.516	N.A.	0.742	0.695	N.A.	9.846	N.A.	6.369	1.546	N.A.
BURKINA FASO	293.919	N.A.	210.970	1.393	N.A.	487.125	N.A.	445.434	1.094	N.A.
ZAIRE	11.867	N.A.	2.758	4.303	N.A.	41.940	N.A.	49.554	0.846	N.A.
ZIMBABWE	0.602	0.525	0.643	0.936	1.147	1.507	0.621	1.613	0.934	2.427
NORTH AND CENTRAL AMERICA										
CANADA	1.257	1.080	1.170	1.074	1.164	1.446	1.220	1.366	1.059	1.185
COSTA RICA	11.218	5.790	8.570	1.309	1.937	62.065	N.A.	50.536	1.228	N.A.
CUBA	0.511	N.A.	0.716	0.714	N.A.	0.668	N.A.	0.921	0.725	N.A.
DOMINICAN RP	0.981	0.594	1.000	0.981	1.652	4.953	N.A.	3.115	1.590	N.A.
EL SALVADOR	3.602	1.310	2.500	1.441	2.750	3.992	N.A.	2.500	1.597	N.A.
GUATEMALA	1.064	0.467	1.000	1.064	2.278	1.514	N.A.	1.000	1.514	N.A.
HAITI	5.090	N.A.	5.000	1.018	N.A.	9.762	N.A.	5.000	1.952	N.A.
HONDURAS	1.381	1.120	2.000	0.690	1.233	2.019	N.A.	2.000	1.009	N.A.
MEXICO	27.589	N.A.	22.950	1.202	N.A.	315.578	N.A.	246.002	1.233	N.A.
NICARAGUA	10.084	N.A.	10.050	1.003	N.A.	44.387	N.A.	24.372	1.821	N.A.
UNITED STATES OF AMERICA	1.000	1.000	1.000	1.000	1.000	1.000	1.000	1.000	1.000	1.000

TABLE 2 - CONTINUED

COUNTRIES BY REGION	1980 PPP FOR AGRICULTURE	1980 PPP FOR TOTAL GDP	1980 OFFICIAL EXCHANGE RATE	1980 RATIO: PPP TO EXCHANGE RATE	1980 PPP RATIO: AGRICULTURE TO TOTAL GDP	1985 PPP FOR AGRICULTURE	1985 PPP FOR TOTAL GDP	1985 OFFICIAL EXCHANGE RATE	1985 RATIO: PPP TO EXCHANGE RATE	1985 PPP RATIO: AGRICULTURE TO TOTAL GDP
SOUTH AMERICA										
ARGENTINA	96.189	260.400	183.717	0.524	0.369	0.294	N.A.	0.602	0.488	N.A.
BOLIVIA	3.918	14.510	2.451	1.599	0.270	0.449	N.A.	0.440	1.020	N.A.
BRAZIL	4.818	3.252	5.271	0.914	1.482	4.837	N.A.	6.200	0.780	N.A.
CHILE	50.036	26.670	39.000	1.283	1.876	127.804	N.A.	161.081	0.793	N.A.
COLOMBIA	48.891	21.990	47.225	1.035	2.223	131.728	N.A.	140.095	0.940	N.A.
ECUADOR	23.033	14.160	25.000	0.921	1.627	107.400	N.A.	68.889	1.559	N.A.
PARAGUAY	121.191	83.870	125.992	0.962	1.445	269.921	N.A.	306.670	0.880	N.A.
PERU	277.920	130.000	286.287	0.971	2.138	5.958	N.A.	10.101	0.590	N.A.
URUGUAY	6.794	7.580	9.075	0.749	0.896	81.587	N.A.	101.430	0.804	N.A.
VENEZUELA	5.736	3.140	4.293	1.336	1.827	11.274	N.A.	7.500	1.503	N.A.
ASIA										
AFGHANISTAN	56.182	N.A.	44.267	1.269	N.A.	134.056	N.A.	50.600	2.649	N.A.
BANGLADESH	12.850	N.A.	15.385	0.835	N.A.	27.443	4.999	28.571	0.961	5.490
MYANMAR	4.021	N.A.	6.623	0.607	N.A.	6.440	N.A.	8.403	0.766	N.A.
SRI LANKA	11.669	3.770	16.393	0.712	3.095	22.309	5.486	27.027	0.825	4.067
CHINA	1.586	N.A.	1.497	1.059	N.A.	2.447	N.A.	2.933	0.834	N.A.
INDIA	7.167	3.370	7.874	0.910	2.127	12.664	4.745	12.346	1.026	2.669
INDONESIA	758.137	280.000	626.959	1.209	2.708	1571.058	N.A.	1109.878	1.416	N.A.
IRAN, ISLAMIC REP. OF	156.056	N.A.	70.607	2.210	N.A.	362.429	N.A.	90.884	3.988	N.A.
IRAQ	0.475	N.A.	0.295	1.610	N.A.	1.176	N.A.	0.311	3.781	N.A.
ISRAEL	5.037	4.140	4.902	1.028	1.217	1.370	N.A.	1.076	1.273	N.A.
JAPAN	619.828	240.000	225.836	2.745	2.583	869.554	222.000	236.742	3.673	3.917
CAMBODIA	336.184	N.A.	N.A.	N.A.	N.A.	560.896	N.A.	N.A.	N.A.	N.A.
KOREA, D P RP	939.296	N.A.	N.A.	N.A.	N.A.	1414.652	N.A.	N.A.	N.A.	N.A.
KOREA, REPUBLIC OF	1331.919	384.000	606.061	2.198	3.469	2270.272	464.148	869.565	2.611	4.891
LAOS	2439.540	N.A.	N.A.	N.A.	N.A.	5115.742	N.A.	N.A.	N.A.	N.A.
MALAYSIA	3.085	N.A.	2.176	1.418	N.A.	4.271	N.A.	2.482	1.721	N.A.
MONGOLIA	2.000	N.A.	N.A.	N.A.	N.A.	3.264	N.A.	N.A.	N.A.	N.A.
NEPAL	10.632	N.A.	12.000	0.886	N.A.	18.293	N.A.	18.137	1.009	N.A.
PAKISTAN	9.442	3.130	9.901	0.954	3.017	12.828	3.980	15.873	0.808	3.223
PHILIPPINES	6.484	3.180	7.519	0.862	2.039	18.295	5.845	18.519	0.988	3.130
SAUDI ARABIA, KINGDOM OF	5.785	N.A.	3.327	1.739	N.A.	9.580	N.A.	3.622	2.645	N.A.
SYRIA	4.931	N.A.	3.925	1.256	N.A.	10.644	N.A.	3.925	2.712	N.A.
THAILAND	14.780	N.A.	20.476	0.722	N.A.	18.035	8.184	27.149	0.664	2.204
TURKEY	106.946	N.A.	73.584	1.453	N.A.	579.451	153.300	519.480	1.115	3.780
VIET NAM	20.427	N.A.	N.A.	N.A.	N.A.	33.780	N.A.	N.A.	N.A.	N.A.

TABLE 2 - CONTINUED

COUNTRIES BY REGION	1980 PPP FOR AGRICULTURE	1980 PPP FOR TOTAL GDP	1980 OFFICIAL EXCHANGE RATE	1980 RATIO: PPP TO EXCHANGE RATE	1980 PPP RATIO: AGRICULTURE TO TOTAL GDP	1985 PPP FOR AGRICULTURE	1985 PPP FOR TOTAL GDP	1985 OFFICIAL EXCHANGE RATE	1985 RATIO: PPP TO EXCHANGE RATE	1985 PPP RATIO: AGRICULTURE TO TOTAL GDP
EUROPE										
ALBANIA	7.432	N.A.	N.A.	N.A.	N.A.	13.198	N.A.	N.A.	N.A.	N.A.
AUSTRIA	18.053	15.390	12.917	1.398	1.173	22.948	16.600	20.517	1.118	1.382
BELGIUM-LUXEMBOURG	39.517	36.610	29.199	1.353	1.079	59.672	44.600	58.928	1.013	1.338
BULGARIA	1.598	N.A.	0.858	1.862	N.A.	2.047	N.A.	1.030	1.987	N.A.
CZECHOSLOVAK. FED. REP.	14.329	N.A.	14.270	1.004	N.A.	18.051	N.A.	17.140	1.053	N.A.
DENMARK	7.429	7.430	5.628	1.320	1.000	11.381	9.800	10.519	1.082	1.161
FINLAND	6.945	4.520	3.727	1.863	1.537	13.332	5.970	6.162	2.164	2.233
FRANCE	8.114	5.240	4.220	1.923	1.548	12.598	7.270	8.911	1.414	1.733
GERMAN. NEW LANDER	3.896	N.A.	3.300	1.181	N.A.	7.289	N.A.	3.640	2.002	N.A.
GERMANY, FEDERAL REP.	3.177	2.370	1.815	1.750	1.341	3.438	2.480	2.920	1.177	1.386
GREECE	70.526	35.420	42.495	1.660	1.991	187.550	77.300	137.684	1.362	2.426
HUNGARY	27.799	13.550	32.387	0.858	2.052	40.980	18.550	50.075	0.818	2.209
IRELAND	0.578	0.461	0.486	1.189	1.254	0.842	0.723	0.938	0.898	1.165
ITALY	1270.269	759.000	854.701	1.486	1.674	2499.273	1302.000	1901.141	1.315	1.920
NETHERLANDS	2.544	2.530	1.985	1.282	1.006	3.363	2.550	3.293	1.021	1.319
NORWAY	10.122	6.160	4.936	2.051	1.643	14.499	8.630	8.552	1.695	1.680
POLAND	36.197	16.140	44.220	0.819	2.243	137.981	75.786	147.189	0.937	1.821
PORTUGAL	88.824	31.660	50.028	1.775	2.806	227.406	66.200	170.126	1.337	3.435
ROMANIA	7.743	N.A.	18.000	0.430	N.A.	9.574	N.A.	17.094	0.560	N.A.
SPAIN	92.734	63.650	71.521	1.297	1.457	185.075	95.300	169.635	1.091	1.942
SWEDEN	6.448	N.A.	4.227	1.525	N.A.	10.407	8.510	8.565	1.215	1.223
SWITZERLAND	3.719	N.A.	1.673	2.223	N.A.	4.826	N.A.	2.432	1.984	N.A.
UNITED KINGDOM	0.567	0.487	0.430	1.319	1.164	0.779	0.568	0.772	1.009	1.371
YUGOSLAVIA	33.912	19.420	24.640	1.376	1.746	255.230	113.465	270.160	0.945	2.249
OCEANIA										
AUSTRALIA	0.779	N.A.	0.878	0.887	N.A.	1.111	1.240	1.427	0.779	0.896
NEW ZEALAND	0.703	N.A.	1.028	0.684	N.A.	1.156	1.350	2.008	0.576	0.856
PAPUA NEW GUINEA	1.245	N.A.	0.670	1.858	N.A.	1.937	N.A.	1.000	1.937	N.A.
FORMER USSR	1.263	N.A.	0.646	1.955	N.A.	2.087	N.A.	0.838	2.490	N.A.

TABLE 3

INTERNATIONAL PRICES OF AGRICULTURAL COMMODITIES - 1970, 1975, 1980, 1985 AND 1990

COMMODITIES BY GROUP	YEAR 1970		YEAR 1975		YEAR 1980		YEAR 1985		YEAR 1990	
	INTER-NATIONAL PRICE	RELATIVE PRICE	INTER-NATIONAL PRICE	RELATIVE PRICE	INTER-NATIONAL PRICE	RELATIVE PRICE	INTER-NATIONAL PRICE	RELATIVE PRICE	INTER-NATIONAL PRICE	RELATIVE PRICE
CEREALS										
WHEAT	69.89	100	125.85	100	146.78	100	121.27	100	142.91	100
RICE, PADDY	100.52	143.81	179.34	142.5	220.12	149.96	164.55	135.7	197.44	138.15
BARLEY	57.9	82.84	104.69	83.19	122.04	83.15	98.07	80.88	114.31	79.99
MAIZE	61.23	87.6	109.06	86.66	140.74	95.88	116.26	95.87	128.03	89.58
POP CORN	69.35	99.22	203.9	162.02	231.49	157.71	264	217.7	230	160.94
RYE	73.89	105.71	110.87	88.1	129.17	88	105.48	86.98	105.63	73.91
OATS	52.74	75.45	94.32	74.95	111.34	75.85	87.14	71.86	113.79	79.62
MILLET	73.77	105.55	114.05	90.63	129.06	87.93	130.97	108	167.46	117.17
SORGHUM	65.29	93.41	112.8	89.63	138.91	94.64	112.3	92.61	133.23	93.23
BUCKWHEAT	79.84	114.22	165.23	131.29	245.9	167.53	198.25	163.48	263.07	184.07
QUINOA	156.83	224.37	309.7	246.09	340.29	231.84	337.97	278.7	376.86	263.7
FONIO	68.77	98.39	100.72	80.04	122.78	83.65	185.94	153.33	136.01	95.17
TRITICALE	95.68	136.89	174.33	138.53	212.24	144.6	144.63	119.26	142.77	99.9
CANARY SEED	129.52	185.31	366.48	291.21	300.54	204.76	279.25	230.28	388.1	271.56
MIXED GRAIN	64.75	92.64	99.88	79.37	114.41	77.95	116.94	96.43	176.8	123.71
CEREALS NES	105.18	150.49	167.09	132.77	209.77	142.91	183.7	151.48	250.6	175.35
STARCH ROOTS AND TUBERS										
POTATOES	47.13	67.43	88.41	70.25	126.64	86.28	84.16	69.4	111.56	78.06
SWEET POTATOES	35.24	50.42	64.28	51.08	84.43	57.52	66.63	54.95	81.73	57.19
CASSAVA	32.17	46.02	55.08	43.76	90.3	61.52	77.03	63.52	74.62	52.21
YAUTIA (COCOYAM)	88.86	127.13	181.29	144.06	252.48	172.01	163.53	134.86	143.44	100.37
TARO (COCO YAM)	76.1	108.88	147.22	116.98	183.5	125.02	109.86	90.6	101.34	70.91
YAMS	65.48	93.68	107.35	85.3	201.84	137.51	180.94	149.21	212.8	148.9
ROOTS AND TUBERS NES	47.1	67.38	87.43	69.48	137.65	93.78	98.17	80.96	114.86	80.37
SUGAR CROPS										
SUGAR CANE	9.84	14.08	17.97	14.28	26.43	18.01	24.58	20.27	21.01	14.7
SUGAR BEETS	15.05	21.53	25.33	20.13	33.96	23.14	28.59	23.58	33.33	23.32
PULSES, NUTS AND SEED										
BEANS, DRY	180.58	258.35	330.87	262.92	496.8	338.47	346.76	285.95	573.04	400.97
BROAD BEANS, DRY	104.85	150.02	188.47	149.76	233.79	159.28	179.54	148.06	213.21	149.19
PEAS, DRY	72.23	103.34	154.77	122.98	216.92	147.78	160.48	132.34	219.79	153.79
CHICK-PEAS	125.83	180.03	265.33	210.83	424.06	288.91	585.21	482.59	755.35	528.53
COW PEAS, DRY	117.86	168.63	209.47	166.45	198.27	135.08	196.4	161.96	151.66	106.12
PIGEON PEAS	139.24	199.21	225.51	179.2	365.64	249.11	522.69	431.03	744.01	520.6
LENTILS	136.88	195.84	272.18	216.28	434.68	296.14	468.72	386.52	565.46	395.67
LUPINS	85.65	122.53	156.04	123.99	355.75	242.37	204.74	168.83	180.5	126.3
PULSES NES	149.20	213.46	269.16	213.88	385.35	262.54	315.37	260.07	347.58	243.21
BRAZIL NUTS	215.86	308.84	242.06	192.35	450.82	307.14	19.85	16.37	517.52	362.12
CASHEW NUTS	163.41	233.79	258.77	205.62	479.61	326.75	287.23	236.86	678.32	474.64
CHESTNUTS	141.51	202.46	254.65	202.35	458.31	312.24	458.82	378.36	785.03	549.3
ALMONDS	429.17	614.02	562.11	446.66	1548.6	1055.05	1040.74	858.23	1645.63	1151.49
WALNUTS	371.99	532.21	532.9	423.45	861.51	586.94	779.9	643.13	1125.03	787.2
PISTACHIOS	984.09	1407.95	1611.02	1280.13	2711.03	1847.01	2153.99	1776.26	3826.03	2677.16
HAZELNUTS (FILBERTS)	483.45	691.67	561.26	445.99	893.03	608.41	791.18	652.44	1316.8	921.4
NUTS NES	505.05	722.59	735.99	584.83	1141.42	777.64	1094.79	902.81	1162.44	813.39
SOYBEANS	114.28	163.5	187.77	149.21	282.49	192.46	255.26	210.5	275.8	192.98
GROUNDNUTS IN SHELL	169.47	242.46	352.74	280.29	523.24	356.48	398.96	329	466.92	326.71
COCONUTS	51.83	74.15	66.47	52.82	137.32	93.55	117.5	96.89	129.54	90.64

TABLE 3 - CONTINUED

COMMODITIES BY GROUP	YEAR 1970		YEAR 1975		YEAR 1980		YEAR 1985		YEAR 1990	
	INTER-NATIONAL PRICE	RELATIVE PRICE	INTER-NATIONAL PRICE	RELATIVE PRICE	INTER-NATIONAL PRICE	RELATIVE PRICE	INTER-NATIONAL PRICE	RELATIVE PRICE	INTER-NATIONAL PRICE	RELATIVE PRICE
COPRA	600.44	859.06	693.77	551.28	1292.19	880.36	1027.62	847.41	1619.34	1133.09
PALM KERNELS	124.32	177.86	176.08	139.91	204.5	139.32	180.83	149.12	180.91	126.59
PALM OIL	171.60	245.51	289.95	230.39	450.22	306.73	330.03	272.15	352.51	246.66
OLIVES	168	240.36	314.81	250.16	433.32	295.22	453.51	373.98	391.88	274.21
KARITE NUTS (SHEANUTS)	55.61	79.57	89.96	71.48	141.06	96.1	188.14	155.15	128.32	89.78
CASTOR BEANS	151.53	216.8	264.33	210.04	400.93	273.15	569.18	469.36	463.32	324.19
SUNFLOWER SEED	111.36	159.32	184.38	146.51	247.93	168.91	247.94	204.46	276.6	193.54
RAPESEED	173.65	248.44	284.99	226.45	345.43	235.34	295.25	243.47	348.39	243.78
TUNG NUTS	131.95	188.78	236.63	188.03	273.13	186.08	209.69	172.91	212.41	148.63
SAFFLOWER SEED	136.41	195.17	233.77	185.75	325.43	221.71	374.58	308.9	385.16	269.51
SESAME SEED	240.24	343.72	450.87	358.27	658.57	448.68	565.16	466.05	646.92	452.67
MUSTARD SEED	118.46	169.48	270.51	214.95	317.41	216.25	247.66	204.23	272.31	190.54
POPPY SEED	413.06	590.97	687.78	546.52	603.77	411.34	538.11	443.74	750.82	525.37
MELONSEED	93.68	134.03	131.28	104.31	164.6	112.14	175.88	145.03	152.65	106.81
VEGETABLE TALLOW	69.34	99.21	158.09	125.62	195.45	133.16	143.03	117.94	160.61	112.38
STILLINGIA OIL	84.26	120.55	171.88	136.58	195.45	133.16	143.03	117.94	149.9	104.89
KAPOKSEED IN SHELL	343.09	490.86	273.47	217.31	201.27	137.12	123.71	102.01	124.77	87.3
COTTONSEED	72.26	103.38	118.19	93.91	166.02	113.11	159.16	131.25	180.92	126.6
LINSEED	120.27	172.07	267.34	212.43	349.63	238.2	245.26	202.25	264.08	184.78
HEMPSEED	213.29	305.16	331.39	263.32	777.25	529.54	559.35	461.26	617.51	432.09
OILSEEDS NES	175.69	251.36	259.88	206.5	335.88	228.83	275.86	227.48	317.57	222.21
VEGETABLES EXCLUDING MELONS										
CABBAGES	49.62	71	78.08	62.04	100.29	68.32	83.98	69.25	115.37	80.73
ARTICHOKES	197.3	282.29	277.69	220.65	385.58	262.69	452.85	373.44	598	418.44
ASPARAGUS	443.6	634.66	708.83	563.24	1169.45	796.74	1120.57	924.06	1487.04	1040.52
LETTUCE	115.22	164.85	183.29	145.64	230.99	157.37	229.31	189.09	315.21	220.56
SPINACH	92.05	131.7	167.02	132.71	252.51	172.03	221.81	182.91	321.09	224.68
TOMATOES	74.26	106.24	133.64	106.19	184.66	125.81	145.26	119.78	195.61	136.88
CAULIFLOWER	84.58	121.01	133.32	105.94	193.91	132.11	187.86	154.92	215.27	150.63
PUMPKINS, SQUASH, GOURDS	78.53	112.35	156.65	124.48	213.45	145.42	167.03	137.74	222.7	155.83
CUCUMBERS AND GHERKINS	99.94	142.99	157.71	125.32	231.29	157.58	196.24	161.82	249.58	174.64
EGGPLANTS	84.49	120.87	157.6	125.23	187.04	127.43	159.03	131.14	211.13	147.73
CHILLIES+PEPPERS, GREEN	112.8	161.38	190.42	151.31	265.58	180.94	261.09	215.31	346.7	242.59
ONIONS+SHALLOTS, GREEN	88.6	126.76	136.12	108.16	185.67	126.5	152.56	125.81	169.64	118.7
ONIONS, DRY	91.42	130.79	154.28	122.59	230.36	156.94	173.29	142.9	215.57	150.84
GARLIC	279.42	399.77	475.98	378.22	603.97	411.48	558.04	460.18	686.13	480.1
BEANS, GREEN	162.15	232	253.6	201.51	362.46	246.94	339.51	279.97	464.02	324.68
PEAS, GREEN	92.22	131.94	144.48	114.8	201.99	137.61	180.91	149.19	230.44	161.25
BROAD BEANS, GREEN	99.31	142.08	141.19	112.19	217.21	147.99	222.98	183.88	203.52	142.41
STRING BEANS	170.22	243.53	237.54	188.75	251.71	171.49	295.14	243.39	520.31	364.07
CARROTS	58.72	84	110.1	87.48	136.25	92.82	118.08	97.38	144.17	100.88
GREEN CORN (MAIZE)	77.52	110.9	121.86	96.83	139.99	95.37	132.26	109.07	152.36	106.61
MUSHROOMS	489.44	700.25	857.01	680.99	1343.64	915.41	1246.7	1028.07	1582.82	1107.54
CHICORY ROOTS	158.02	226.09	191.3	152.01	286.62	195.27	287.98	237.48	298.22	208.67
CAROBS	52.65	75.33	76.04	60.42	118.29	80.59	224.2	184.88	197.61	138.27
VEGETABLES FRESH NES	52.63	75.3	98.48	78.25	141.3	96.27	132.89	109.58	154.7	108.25

TABLE 3 - CONTINUED

COMMODITIES BY GROUP	YEAR 1970 INTER-NATIONAL PRICE	YEAR 1970 RELATIVE PRICE	YEAR 1975 INTER-NATIONAL PRICE	YEAR 1975 RELATIVE PRICE	YEAR 1980 INTER-NATIONAL PRICE	YEAR 1980 RELATIVE PRICE	YEAR 1985 INTER-NATIONAL PRICE	YEAR 1985 RELATIVE PRICE	YEAR 1990 INTER-NATIONAL PRICE	YEAR 1990 RELATIVE PRICE
FRUITS INCLUDING MELONS										
BANANAS	67.84	97.06	108.17	85.96	148.21	100.98	149.88	123.6	163.84	114.64
PLANTAINS	40.79	58.36	65.11	51.74	129.45	88.19	122.08	100.67	150.12	105.04
ORANGES	70.9	101.43	104.35	82.92	162.05	110.4	209.14	172.47	213.86	149.64
TANG.MAND.CLEMENT.SATSMA	105.36	150.75	121.21	96.32	214.8	146.34	236.79	195.27	257.03	179.85
LEMONS AND LIMES	108.64	155.43	141.89	112.74	252.27	171.87	227.47	187.58	274.9	192.35
GRAPEFRUIT AND POMELO	72.92	104.33	86.06	68.38	156.05	106.31	179.91	148.36	225.63	157.88
CITRUS FRUIT NES	106.26	152.03	154.87	123.06	213.8	145.66	242.51	199.98	210	146.95
APPLES	90.74	129.82	163.7	130.08	214.09	145.86	207.35	170.99	311.17	217.73
PEARS	89.34	127.82	164.32	130.57	216.63	147.59	222.46	183.44	377.74	264.31
QUINCES	89.13	127.51	144.59	114.89	219.88	149.8	192.46	158.71	241.03	168.65
APRICOTS	137.64	196.93	240.89	191.42	346.47	236.05	297.05	244.96	396.43	277.39
SOUR CHERRIES	189.98	271.81	293.01	232.83	429.46	292.58	292.44	241.16	475.44	332.67
CHERRIES	213.85	305.96	376.48	299.16	574.69	391.53	462.92	381.74	636.98	445.71
PEACHES AND NECTARINES	133.17	190.52	252.04	200.28	320.26	218.19	285.29	235.26	349.29	244.4
PLUMS	98.8	141.35	194.97	154.93	272.96	185.97	243.3	200.63	289.2	202.36
STONE FRUIT NES, FRESH	96.95	138.7	164.94	131.06	228.83	155.9	209.23	172.54	191.65	134.1
STRAWBERRIES	385.7	551.82	637.74	506.75	838.08	570.97	825.97	681.12	1021.14	714.52
RASPBERRIES	328.64	470.18	526.47	418.34	793.13	540.35	718.27	592.32	906.87	634.55
GOOSEBERRIES	221.18	316.45	405.98	322.6	478.74	326.17	486.7	401.35	675.58	472.72
CURRANTS	288.11	412.21	507.55	403.3	490.04	333.86	391.67	322.98	572.89	400.86
BLUEBERRIES	578.32	827.41	678.09	538.82	1026.74	699.51	1120.19	923.75	1461.31	1022.51
CRANBERRIES	267.54	382.77	288.24	229.04	726.99	495.29	1200.43	989.92	1408.19	985.34
BERRIES NES	106.29	152.07	160.61	127.63	268.92	183.21	268.26	221.22	360.31	252.12
GRAPES	103.69	148.36	219.8	174.66	281.56	191.83	225.55	186	317.44	222.12
WATERMELONS	43.57	62.34	77.5	61.58	116.86	79.62	92	75.87	120.82	84.54
CANTALOUPES+OTH MELONS	82.64	118.24	141.52	112.45	203.09	138.36	143.55	118.37	205.3	143.65
FIGS	113.32	162.13	218.39	173.54	334.77	228.08	275.64	227.3	456.22	319.23
MANGOES	84.03	120.22	134.08	106.54	212.02	144.45	192.71	158.92	220.74	154.46
AVOCADOS	129.27	184.95	265.69	211.12	354.05	241.21	295.97	244.07	343.78	240.55
PINEAPPLES	73.32	104.9	112.04	89.03	152.78	104.09	169.61	139.86	179.89	125.87
DATES	112.38	160.78	160.91	127.86	303.72	206.92	280.19	231.05	356.78	249.65
PERSIMMONS	155.99	223.17	288.79	229.47	447.54	304.91	229.54	189.29	357.23	249.96
PAPAYAS	89.18	127.59	123.06	97.79	166.81	113.65	167.26	137.93	143.19	100.19
FRUIT TROPICAL FRESH NES	163.01	233.22	164.56	130.76	185.37	126.29	189.07	155.92	216.99	151.83
FRUIT FRESH NES	93.34	133.55	158.29	125.78	213.04	145.14	178.38	147.1	200.56	140.34
STIMULANTS										
COFFEE, GREEN	664.37	950.53	1555.08	1235.69	1562.55	1064.56	821.82	677.7	1209.59	846.38
COCOA BEANS	420.74	601.95	688.66	547.22	1024.81	698.19	712.57	587.61	1197.53	837.94
TEA	626.88	896.9	918.59	729.93	1461.7	995.84	1067.78	880.53	1028.55	719.7
MATE	364.22	521.09	1143.35	908.52	407.45	277.59	220.22	181.6	364.58	255.11
HOPS	1601.98	2291.98	2157.71	1714.55	3562.77	2427.29	3456.76	2850.58	4024.53	2816.05
SPICES										
PEPPER,WHITE/LONG/BLACK	723.75	1035.47	1117.67	888.12	1512.04	1030.14	1231.63	1015.64	2141	1498.1
PIMENTO, ALLSPICE	571.45	817.59	874.22	694.67	1059.25	721.66	1142.97	942.54	1348.92	943.87
VANILLA	1282.68	1835.15	1622.59	1289.33	2939.91	2002.94	1835.69	1513.78	1695.27	1186.22
CINNAMON (CANELLA)	656.18	938.81	729.95	580.03	1252.98	853.64	1164.66	960.43	1270.52	889.01
CLOVES, WHOLE+STEMS	2640.03	3777.13	2574.65	2045.85	4423.3	3013.57	4749.49	3916.61	7060	4940.04
NUTMEG, MACE, CARDAMONS	621.02	888.5	825.01	655.57	1739.49	1185.1	1526.78	1259.04	2024.49	1416.58
ANISE, BADIAN, FENNEL	387.34	554.17	669.49	531.99	754.61	514.11	549.94	453.5	651.57	455.92
SPICES NES	343.22	491.04	476.96	379	507.45	345.72	389.56	321.24	413.88	289.6
OIL OF CITRONELLA	40779.37	58343.75	22141.97	17594.3	13930.28	9490.59	1554.57	1281.96	915.85	640.84
PEPPERMINT	702.35	1004.86	1767.91	1404.81	1911.8	1302.5	854	704.24	1126.43	788.19
ESSENTIAL OILS NES	7940.89	11361.16	15700.16	12475.55	15522.96	10575.68	12943.76	10673.91	13329.29	9326.79
PYRETHRUM, DRIED FLOWERS	704.91	1008.53	1067.29	848.09	2425.88	1652.74	667.95	550.82	759.7	531.58

TABLE 3 - CONTINUED

COMMODITIES BY GROUP	YEAR 1970		YEAR 1975		YEAR 1980		YEAR 1985		YEAR 1990	
	INTER-NATIONAL PRICE	RELATIVE PRICE	INTER-NATIONAL PRICE	RELATIVE PRICE	INTER-NATIONAL PRICE	RELATIVE PRICE	INTER-NATIONAL PRICE	RELATIVE PRICE	INTER-NATIONAL PRICE	RELATIVE PRICE
FIBRE CROPS										
COTTON LINT	691.54	989.4	1137.37	903.77	1472.38	1003.12	1017.95	839.44	1281.75	896.87
FLAX FIBRE AND TOW	492.62	704.79	925.23	735.2	1249.57	851.33	958.37	790.31	996.68	697.4
HEMP FIBRE AND TOW	420.78	602.02	737.73	586.21	765.5	521.53	577.95	476.6	662.13	463.31
KAPOK FIBRE	789.88	1130.1	722.62	574.2	684.34	466.23	467.08	385.17	485.83	339.95
JUTE	193.64	277.05	231.71	184.12	340.88	232.24	347.02	286.16	202.26	141.53
JUTE-LIKE FIBRES	153.63	219.8	236.93	188.26	295.41	201.26	213.06	175.7	238.52	166.9
RAMIE	488.41	698.77	786.6	625.04	1084.93	739.15	2832.33	2335.65	4196.29	2936.23
SISAL	160.3	229.34	439.53	349.25	391.54	266.75	395.95	326.52	284.15	198.83
AGAVE FIBRES NES	229.47	328.31	502.06	398.94	500.63	341.07	452.74	373.35	529.75	370.68
ABACA (MANILA HEMP)	141.28	202.13	410.9	326.51	428	291.59	378.79	312.36	473.91	331.6
FIBRE CROPS NES	166.61	238.37	506.27	402.29	541.89	369.18	332.56	274.24	558.72	390.95
TOBACCO LEAVES	882.43	1262.51	1368.29	1087.26	1748.21	1191.04	1345.41	1109.48	1502.43	1051.28
NATURAL RUBBER	387.94	555.03	391.65	311.21	753.17	513.13	506.63	417.79	653.2	457.06
NATURAL GUMS	856.15	1224.91	1068.37	848.94	998.03	679.95	68.91	56.82	270.89	189.55
LIVESTOCK PRODUCTS										
COW MILK, WHOLE, FRESH	100.38	143.62	164.56	130.76	229.61	156.43	224.12	184.82	286.48	200.45
INDIGENOUS CATTLE MEAT	960.71	1374.5	1392.43	1106.44	2181.43	1486.2	1918.89	1582.39	2450.3	1714.53
BUFFALO MILK	140.82	201.47	239.68	190.45	311.04	211.91	286.94	236.62	319.39	223.48
INDIGENOUS BUFFALO MEAT	477.51	683.19	796.03	632.53	1161.91	791.6	961.96	793.27	1055.28	738.4
SHEEP MILK	157.18	224.88	251.62	199.94	313.2	213.38	291.95	240.75	359.72	251.7
WOOL, GREASY	1180.98	1689.64	2033.48	1615.83	3023.85	2060.13	2583.83	2130.73	3281.47	2296.11
INDIGENOUS SHEEP MEAT	812.67	1162.71	1360.93	1081.41	2071.75	1411.47	1820.85	1501.55	2281.51	1596.42
GOAT MILK	126.93	181.61	208.56	165.72	263.19	179.31	248.68	205.07	285.5	199.77
INDIGENOUS GOAT MEAT	773.7	1106.95	1325.54	1053.29	1926.36	1312.41	1644.39	1356.02	1822.23	1275.05
INDIGENOUS PIGMEAT	749.81	1072.77	1231.24	978.36	1378.97	939.48	1189.84	981.19	1348.78	943.77
HEN EGGS	624.82	893.94	903.06	717.58	1116.11	760.4	888.24	732.48	1129.52	790.35
INDIGENOUS DUCK MEAT	753.41	1077.92	1144.04	909.07	1202.97	819.57	1299.08	1071.27	1587.37	1110.72
INDIGENOUS GEESE MEAT	938.16	1342.25	1292.66	1027.16	1621.74	1104.88	1514.11	1248.59	1655.28	1158.23
INDIGENOUS OTHER POULTRY	2555.09	3655.61	1859.4	1477.5	1588.89	1082.5	1673.78	1380.26	1851.34	1295.42
INDIGENOUS TURKEY MEAT	705.27	1009.04	1054.01	837.53	1234.35	840.95	1306.16	1077.11	1328.82	929.8
EGGS EXCL HEN	854.81	1222.99	1143.75	908.84	1468.66	1000.58	1039.6	857.29	1101.57	770.79
INDIGENOUS CHICKEN MEAT	674.5	965.02	1072.36	852.11	1302.76	887.56	1098.55	905.9	1338.65	936.69
INDIGENOUS HORSE MEAT	626.96	897	1176.13	934.57	1727.14	1176.69	1309.71	1080.03	1604.21	1122.5
INDIGENOUS ASS MEAT	848.34	1213.73	1578.2	1254.06	1615.97	1100.95	1208.09	996.24	1269.12	888.03
INDIGENOUS MULE MEAT	657.9	941.26	1551.78	1233.07	1690.97	1152.04	1256.82	1036.42	1252.73	876.56
CAMEL MILK	143.76	205.68	250.17	198.79	301.39	205.34	265.95	219.31	293.77	205.56
INDIGENOUS CAMEL MEAT	623.31	891.79	991.2	787.62	1309.68	892.27	1186.81	978.69	1298.04	908.27
RABBIT MEAT INDIGENOUS	1125.06	1609.65	1516.42	1204.97	1988.15	1354.51	1626.21	1341.03	1790.39	1252.78
INDIGENOUS RODENTS	960.97	1374.88	1536.51	1220.93	3271.63	2228.94	1903.42	1569.63	887.59	621.07
INDIGENOUS OTHER CAMEL	960.97	1374.88	1536.51	1220.93	3297.25	2246.39	1909.49	1574.64	882.58	617.56
GAME MEAT	708.66	1013.89	1016.14	807.44	1315.93	896.53	1185.23	977.38	1374.02	961.43
MEAT NES	585.13	837.16	984.12	782	1275.49	868.98	918.81	757.68	1014.23	709.68
HONEY	539.61	772.03	1068.57	849.1	1304.15	888.51	1343.01	1107.49	1765.71	1235.5
COCOONS, REELABLE	1302.43	1863.42	1970.03	1565.41	2711.63	1847.42	2415.14	1991.62	3746.24	2621.33

TABLE 4
TOTAL AGRICULTURAL OUTPUT BY CONTINENT
(IN THOUSANDS OF INTERNATIONAL DOLLARS)

	AT CURRENT PRICES				
CONTINENT	1970	1975	1980	1985	1990
AFRICA	21542048	39817024	58188192	55584848	75814576
NORTH AND CENTRAL AMERICA	62998992	117531312	174599680	170076000	207811616
SOUTH AMERICA	24018048	46507312	74173296	74686288	96355888
ASIA	106041712	208851968	318671360	326218752	457489408
EUROPE	77777056	143429296	207816064	191789248	236623520
OCEANIA	7568091	13394627	19661888	19558608	25777600
FORMER USSR	44599008	75741072	107403248	97726896	134615440

	AT 1980 PRICES				
CONTINENT	1970	1975	1980	1985	1990
AFRICA	51490256	55738496	58188192	65503232	74802336
NORTH AND CENTRAL AMERICA	139013600	157863360	174599680	197450864	201812464
SOUTH AMERICA	55775776	63857392	74173296	86746384	94665408
ASIA	238316288	275354880	318671360	393993216	463260416
EUROPE	173262512	189367792	207816064	221274208	221620192
OCEANIA	17775008	18977568	19661888	22506928	23977920
FORMER USSR	99625424	100803568	107403248	114897728	127181568

IMPLICIT PRICE DEFLATORS BY CONTINENT

CONTINENT	1970	1975	1980	1985	1990
AFRICA	41.83	71.43	100	84.85	101.35
NORTH AND CENTRAL AMERICA	45.31	74.45	100	86.13	102.97
SOUTH AMERICA	43.06	72.83	100	86.09	101.78
ASIA	44.49	75.84	100	82.79	98.75
EUROPE	44.89	75.74	100	86.67	106.77
OCEANIA	42.57	70.58	100	86.9	107.5
FORMER USSR	44.76	75.13	100	85.05	105.84

TABLE 5
PPP FOR AGRICULTURAL OUTPUT AND NON-AGRICULTURAL INPUTS AND EXCHANGE RATE - 1985
(UNITS OF NATIONAL CURRENCY PER INTERNATIONAL DOLLAR)

COUNTRIES BY REGION		PPP FOR AGRICULTURAL OUTPUT	PPP FOR NON-AGRICULTURAL INPUT	EXCHANGE RATE
AFRICA				
	ALGERIA	17.426	4.389	5.025
	ANGOLA	54.030	50.726	29.620
	BURUNDI	111.908	118.286	120.555
	CAMEROON	529.628	405.676	445.434
	CHAD	431.078	365.302	445.434
	EGYPT	1.189	0.719	0.700
	ETHIOPIA	2.944	1.349	2.070
	GHANA	86.860	54.216	54.113
	GUINEA	77.189	35.462	24.292
	COTE D'IVOIRE	469.531	488.089	445.434
	KENYA	16.646	12.587	16.393
	MADAGASCAR	647.422	572.802	661.375
	MALAWI	0.977	1.176	1.706
	MALI	346.309	437.634	445.434
	MOROCCO	12.139	7.723	10.054
	MOZAMBIQUE	76.540	57.073	43.159
	NIGER	558.298	319.031	445.434
	NIGERIA	4.127	0.891	0.894
	RWANDA	128.015	113.256	101.092
	SENEGAL	426.089	236.073	445.434
	SOMALIA	80.988	37.612	39.364
	SOUTH AFRICA	1.632	1.369	2.193
	SUDAN	2.735	2.359	2.288
	TANZANIA	40.537	17.395	17.443
	TUNISIA	0.979	0.445	0.832
	UGANDA	9.846	2.657	6.369
	BURKINA FASO	487.125	290.823	445.434
	ZAIRE	41.940	50.834	49.554
	ZIMBABWE	1.507	1.440	1.613
NORTH AND CENTRAL AMERICA				
	CANADA	1.446	1.325	1.366
	COSTA RICA	62.065	49.431	50.536
	CUBA	0.668	0.829	0.921
	DOMINICAN RP	4.953	1.899	3.115
	EL SALVADOR	3.992	3.361	2.500
	GUATEMALA	1.514	0.836	1.000
	HAITI	9.762	3.074	5.000
	HONDURAS	2.019	2.019	2.000
	MEXICO	315.578	146.060	246.002
	NICARAGUA	44.387	39.461	24.372
	UNITED STATES OF AMERICA	1.000	1.000	1.000

TABLE 5 - CONTINUED

COUNTRIES BY REGION	PPP FOR AGRICULTURAL OUTPUT	PPP FOR NON-AGRICULTURAL INPUT	EXCHANGE RATE
SOUTH AMERICA			
ARGENTINA	0.294	0.448	0.602
BOLIVIA	0.449	0.268	0.440
BRAZIL	4.837	5.456	6.200
CHILE	127.804	161.048	161.081
COLOMBIA	131.728	117.469	140.095
ECUADOR	107.400	62.852	68.889
PARAGUAY	269.921	335.965	306.670
PERU	5.958	8.970	10.101
URUGUAY	81.587	80.945	101.430
VENEZUELA	11.274	3.777	7.500
ASIA			
AFGHANISTAN	134.056	43.343	50.600
BANGLADESH	27.443	13.079	28.571
MYANMAR	6.440	3.506	8.403
SRI LANKA	22.309	12.813	27.027
CHINA	2.447	2.798	2.933
INDIA	12.664	6.988	12.346
INDONESIA	1571.058	553.848	1109.878
IRAN, ISLAMIC REP. OF	362.429	57.324	90.884
IRAQ	1.176	0.405	0.311
ISRAEL	1.370	1.106	1.076
JAPAN	869.554	365.506	236.742
CAMBODIA	560.896	N.A.	N.A.
KOREA, D P RP	1414.652	1.336	N.A.
KOREA, REPUBLIC OF	2270.272	801.195	869.565
LAOS	5115.742	60.505	N.A.
MALAYSIA	4.271	2.034	2.482
MONGOLIA	3.264	3.226	N.A.
NEPAL	18.293	10.651	18.137
PAKISTAN	12.828	8.158	15.873
PHILIPPINES	18.295	16.982	18.519
SAUDI ARABIA, KINGDOM OF	9.580	2.543	3.622
SYRIA	10.644	3.170	3.925
THAILAND	18.035	18.448	27.149
TURKEY	579.451	297.824	519.480
VIET NAM	33.780	1.155	N.A.

TABLE 5 - CONTINUED

COUNTRIES BY REGION		PPP FOR AGRICULTURAL OUTPUT	PPP FOR NON-AGRICULTURAL INPUT	EXCHANGE RATE
EUROPE				
	ALBANIA	13.198	2.994	N.A.
	AUSTRIA	22.948	22.793	20.517
	BELGIUM-LUXEMBOURG	59.672	48.456	58.928
	BULGARIA	2.047	2.089	1.030
	CZECHOSLOVAK, FED. REP.	18.051	13.466	17.140
	DENMARK	11.381	9.164	10.519
	FINLAND	13.332	7.049	6.162
	FRANCE	12.598	8.570	8.911
	GERMAN, NEW LANDER	7.289	2.948	3.640
	GERMANY, FEDERAL REP.	3.438	2.852	2.920
	GREECE	187.550	86.736	137.684
	HUNGARY	40.980	27.069	50.075
	IRELAND	0.842	1.086	0.938
	ITALY	2499.273	1576.828	1901.141
	NETHERLANDS	3.363	2.951	3.293
	NORWAY	14.499	9.266	8.552
	POLAND	137.981	88.163	147.189
	PORTUGAL	227.406	102.393	170.126
	ROMANIA	9.574	27.142	17.094
	SPAIN	185.075	136.735	169.635
	SWEDEN	10.407	10.068	8.565
	SWITZERLAND	4.826	3.056	2.432
	UNITED KINGDOM	0.779	0.739	0.772
	YUGOSLAVIA	255.230	232.472	270.160
OCEANIA				
	AUSTRALIA	1.111	1.639	1.427
	NEW ZEALAND	1.156	1.865	2.008
	PAPUA NEW GUINEA	1.937	0.816	1.000
	FORMER USSR	2.087	0.902	0.838

TABLE 6
FINAL OUTPUT, AGRICULTURAL GDP, AGRICULTURAL GDP PER CAPITA AND AGRICULTURAL GDP PER LABOUR UNIT - 1985
(IN INTERNATIONAL DOLLARS AND AS INDEX)

COUNTRIES BY REGION	FINAL OUTPUT (1000 INT.$)	AGRICULTURAL GDP (1000 INT.$)	AGRICULTURAL GDP PER CAPITA (INT.$)	INDEX OF AGRICULTURAL GDP PER CAPITA (AV.=100)	AGRICULTURAL GDP PER LABOUR UNIT (INT.$)	INDEX OF AGRICULTURAL GDP PER LABOUR UNIT (AV.=100)
AFRICA						
ALGERIA	1492251	1152763	52.9	42.7	891.3	120.3
ANGOLA	530398	449087	51.3	41.4	168.1	22.7
BURUNDI	565007	493364	104.3	84.2	210.6	28.4
CAMEROON	1214446	952611	94.8	76.5	373	50.3
CHAD	442970	395129	78.7	63.5	278.4	37.6
EGYPT	5303674	4096558	88.1	71.1	744.1	100.4
ETHIOPIA	2703233	2428043	56.4	45.5	166.7	22.5
GHANA	1253973	1094216	85.2	68.8	427.7	57.7
GUINEA	483803	417570	83.7	67.6	241.6	32.6
COTE D'IVOIRE	1974117	1581267	159.2	128.5	654.8	88.4
KENYA	1977518	1681879	83.7	67.5	252.8	34.1
MADAGASCAR	1473458	1174051	114.7	92.6	324.3	43.8
MALAWI	634193	546801	74.5	60.1	219.1	29.6
MALI	729244	645162	81.5	65.8	301.4	40.7
MOROCCO	2325588	1691865	76.8	62	623.1	84.1
MOZAMBIQUE	793599	679717	49.6	40	109.6	14.8
NIGER	436733	382490	57.9	46.7	124.1	16.7
NIGERIA	6249990	5161242	56.1	45.3	214.6	29
RWANDA	734482	632168	103.6	83.6	225.8	30.5
SENEGAL	565273	470702	73.8	59.6	210.3	28.4
SOMALIA	1011165	896600	140.8	113.6	456.4	61.6
SOUTH AFRICA	5277780	3786279	119.9	96.8	2131.5	287.7
SUDAN	2766744	2382166	109.2	88.1	510.7	68.9
TANZANIA	2481783	2171808	95.5	77	235.2	31.7
TUNISIA	1152135	864907	119.1	96.1	1285.4	173.5
UGANDA	1994313	1728670	110.5	89.2	293.6	39.6
BURKINA FASO	537097	468402	59.5	48	127.9	17.3
ZAIRE	2514866	2262876	74.4	60.1	282.6	38.1
ZIMBABWE	1059151	843931	101.8	82.1	361.3	48.8
NORTH AND CENTRAL AMERICA						
CANADA	11189197	6164128	244.6	197.4	11618.4	1568.1
COSTA RICA	734455	482096	182.5	147.2	1937.1	261.4
DOMINICAN RP	1029856	810084	126.3	101.9	1009.9	136.3
EL SALVADOR	569394	492355	103.3	83.3	830.3	112.1
GUATEMALA	1041743	827664	103.9	83.9	677.6	91.5
HAITI	619796	525153	89.2	72	296.7	40
HONDURAS	615608	512432	116.9	94.4	671.5	90.6
MEXICO	12816850	9871538	124.4	100.4	1113.3	150.3
NICARAGUA	468326	362343	110.7	89.4	859.6	116
UNITED STATES OF AMERICA	106438448	64544272	269.7	217.7	19327.7	2608.5

TABLE 6 - CONTINUED

COUNTRIES BY REGION	FINAL OUTPUT (1000 INT.$)	AGRICULTURAL GDP (1000 INT.$)	AGRICULTURAL GDP PER CAPITA (INT.$)	INDEX OF AGRICULTURAL GDP PER CAPITA (AV.=100)	AGRICULTURAL GDP PER LABOUR UNIT (INT.$)	INDEX OF AGRICULTURAL GDP PER LABOUR UNIT (AV.=100)
SOUTH AMERICA						
ARGENTINA	15940693	11434259	377	304.2	9024.3	1218
BOLIVIA	863248	708036	111.1	89.7	811.1	109.5
BRAZIL	34286016	25100784	185.2	149.4	1832.1	247.3
CHILE	1874108	1354792	111.8	90.2	2255.9	304.5
COLOMBIA	4980331	3696899	123.7	99.8	1305.8	176.2
ECUADOR	1625514	1261398	135.4	109.3	1294.2	174.7
PARAGUAY	1401176	1086331	294.1	237.4	1817.2	245.3
PERU	1956684	1519560	78.3	63.2	659.1	89
URUGUAY	1409259	1048065	348.4	281.2	6195.2	836.1
VENEZUELA	2263020	1656304	95.6	77.2	2121.6	286.3
ASIA						
BANGLADESH	5976823	5051611	49.9	40.3	244	32.9
SRI LANKA	1779963	1414002	87.8	70.8	455.1	61.4
INDIA	67680720	56256208	73.1	59	281.6	38
INDONESIA	16449938	13457693	80.4	64.9	399	53.9
IRAN, ISLAMIC REP. OF	6087870	4324822	90.8	73.3	1042.8	140.7
IRAQ	1479900	1116140	70.2	56.7	1070.1	144.4
ISRAEL	1110718	567798	134.2	108.3	6963.1	939.8
JAPAN	11461827	5897110	48.8	39.4	1159.8	156.5
KOREA, REPUBLIC OF	3988895	2945001	72.2	58.2	578.9	78.1
MALAYSIA	3606501	2632385	167.9	135.5	1169.7	157.9
NEPAL	1244453	1069482	63.2	51	162.9	22
PAKISTAN	10426668	8238110	79.8	64.4	520.4	70.2
PHILIPPINES	7533072	6510081	118.1	95.3	665.7	89.8
SAUDI ARABIA, KINGDOM OF	424217	291606	25.1	20.3	195.5	26.4
SYRIA	1984270	1173894	112.2	90.6	1647.9	222.4
THAILAND	9471548	7351815	142.5	115	407.8	55
TURKEY	11370495	8397111	166.8	134.6	722.1	97.5
EUROPE						
AUSTRIA	2376785	1565826	207.2	167.2	6155.4	830.8
BELGIUM-LUXEMBOURG	2704164	1353434	132.4	106.8	13976.1	1886.3
DENMARK	3298053	1857133	363.2	293.1	11419.3	1541.2
FINLAND	1435938	902774	184.2	148.6	3682.6	497
FRANCE	24734144	15251074	276.4	223.1	9213.5	1243.5
GERMANY, FEDERAL REP.	15419053	8061081	132.1	106.6	6021.9	812.7
GREECE	4471171	2986742	300.6	242.6	2852.3	385
HUNGARY	4477098	3164412	297.2	239.8	4179.9	564.1
IRELAND	2719490	2039345	576.1	464.9	9655	1303.1
ITALY	16813040	13542904	237	191.3	6472.6	873.6
NETHERLANDS	6396469	4206317	290.4	234.3	15973.1	2155.8
NORWAY	856981	470825	113.4	91.5	3476.2	469.2
PORTUGAL	1514147	1058540	104.2	84.1	1174.1	158.5
SPAIN	12483638	8241698	213.5	172.3	4378.5	590.9
SWEDEN	2159611	1213269	145.3	117.3	6135.8	828.1
SWITZERLAND	1676377	1064331	164.5	132.7	6514.8	879.3
UNITED KINGDOM	11191308	6464099	113.8	91.8	10190.3	1375.3
YUGOSLAVIA	5170091	3926684	169.8	137	1414.6	190.9
OCEANIA						
AUSTRALIA	12401929	8758242	554.9	447.8	20240.3	2731.7
NEW ZEALAND	5406857	3824269	1177.7	950.4	26752.1	3610.6
PAPUA NEW GUINEA	883550	708695	204.8	165.3	592.5	80
TOTAL	553470478	392347393	123.9		740.9	

ORDER NO: 1AJU5616
ORDER DATE: 05/22/97

INTERNATIONAL COMPARISONS OF PRICES, OUTPUT N
AND PRODUCTIVITY / EDITED BY D.S. PRASADA RAO T
AND J. A
CONTRIBUTIONS TO ECO S

ELSEVIER SCIENCE PUBLI 1996 1 VOLS
98.50 CLOTH

0-444-82144-9 96-352
N8-933017

QTY ORDERED: 001
QTY SHIPPED: 001
670901/0014

BLACKWELL NORTH AMERICA

International Comparisons of Prices, Output and Productivity
Edited by D.S. Prasada Rao and J. Salazar-Carrillo

A PERSPECTIVE ON INTERNATIONAL COMPARISONS OF CAPITAL [1]

Michael Ward
Country Operations Division
The World Bank Group
Washington D.C., U.S.A.

1. Introduction

The role of capital in explaining growth and the value of benefits accruing to the community resulting from the use of capital cannot be properly determined without appropriate data. When making comparisons across countries, determining consistent and standardized measures for a concept like capital poses a number of methodological questions. Their satisfactory resolution can assist analysts in making economic policy formulation more meaningful and operationally relevant. [2]

The assumptions underlying new ideas about economic growth, and the theories based upon which they rest, are hard to test and the relevant data to support them difficult to find. Despite recent developments in theory, and the crucial significance economists traditionally attach to the role played by capital in explaining growth, little progress has been made in measuring what economists perceive (not always unambiguously) as capital. Like money, capital is what capital does, and the importance of capital may lie more in the economic services it delivers rather than what it costs. This capacity to deliver something worthwhile determines the real value of fixed capital assets to economic activity. A user-oriented, demand perspective, matched

[1] This paper is a part of a wider research enquiry at The World Bank on "Levels of Service" measurement being carried out by Peter Cook and Jonathan Stevens. It draws heavily on the findings of an unofficial internal World Bank study by Michael Hee and Raquel Fok that was able to generate capital stock estimates for 96 countries (see below).

[2] The World Bank, for example, globally finances from a capital fund investment projects designed to support sustainable socio-economic development in its member countries. While such investments are intended to help borrowers achieve development, allocations are made on a country by country basis and the use of capital is not optimized in a truly global economic sense.

to the more customary supply side approach, can potentially enhance policy makers' understanding of the capital.

2. Background

A fundamental, almost unquestioned, assumption of development agencies and donors is that capital investment will promote growth and development. Yet, across countries, there is no common measure of capital (even assuming the concept and definition are the same) providing a consistent assessment of the economic value of productive assests in different geographic situations.

Conventionally, comparisons of relative growth and productivity performance between countries have been carried out mostly using "within country" variables to explain differences. The approach has been to link output in a given country to domestic capital and internal labor factors to describe variations in that country's economic activity. Since the end results of such exercises are apparently "unit free" (growth, percentage changes in net output per capita, etc.) they are deemed to be directly comparable across countries. Few seek to question the intrinsic validity of inter-country comparisons and whether the explanatory "input" variables – if measured on a cross-sectional basis – are truly comparable. From an analytic perspective, these studies do not allow policymakers to conclude very much about the actual size and importance of the contribution of capital to the process of development in different countries. The results fail to help those disbursing funds to identify where investment is most effective in raising output and income levels when a broader international perspective is needed.

This lack of uniformity means that disbursements of the world's limited resources of capital, internationally, have to be conducted not on the basis of the real overall returns to the assets concerned, but on individual country assessments using indicators other than the economic value of capital in use. Improved methods must be sought to determine appropriate allocations of aid and investment.

3. Capital Stock Estimates

3.1 The World Bank Study

Comparable capital stock estimates for developing countries are few and far between. They are generally limited to only a small handful of regionally specific countries.[3]. An exception is a recent (1993) internal World Bank Study[4] which presents approximate but consistent capital stock estimates for 96 economies. This study applies the standard perpetual inventory model (PIM) to country specific gross fixed capital formation series (GFCF) in constant 1987 US dollars over the period 1950 to 1990. Unfortunately, this study, although the first comprehensive one of its kind, is subject to important limitations. It adopts some highly restricting statistical assumptions that include uniform service lives for the different classes of physical assets in all the countries studied. In all cases, lifetimes of 35 years for buildings and construction and 15 years for machinery, transport and other equipment are assumed. The model also applies a simple standard rectangular or single exit distribution for capital retirements for both assets. The service lives are based on the respective unweighted average of a set lifetimes in a sample of countries. They are deemed to remain constant over the whole 40 year period of the calculations. In addition, the constituent country specific investment series are initially converted into constant 1987 US dollars at the prevailing nominal exchange rate (IMF "rf" series) to put them all on a standard (but not equivalent, nor uniform) valuation basis.

3.2 A Review of the Results

Perhaps surprisingly in the circumstances, these broad approximations for capital give rise to results that are analytically interesting and far from counter intuitive. They show that the rate of capital accumulation in East Asia is much faster than in other regions and that the most impressive growth in assets in that region has been in machinery, transport and other equipment. This strongly supports the belief that embodied technical progress incorporated within new equipment, in particular through imported machinery, has been absorbed fastest in East Asia and has contributed significantly to income growth in the region. The results also reveal that, by comparison, the relative share of plant, machinery and equipment in the capital stock declines over the decade of the 1980s in the case of Europe, Sub-Saharan Africa, Latin America and the Middle East and North Africa. Only in the OECD countries has the share of machinery also been rising. Furthermore, the absolute share of machinery in the capital stock is the highest for

[3]See for example, Andre Hofman (1992).

[4]Michael Hee and Raquel Fok (1993), Socio-Economic Data Division, IEC, The World Bank, Washington, D.C.

East Asia and lowest for the Middle East and North Africa. Calculated on a per capita basis, the differences appear even more marked. This strengthening of the capital base is impressive and provides a rational explanation as to why economic growth has been most significant in the new industrial countries of East Asia (Hong Kong, Singapore, Indonesia, Korea, Malaysia and Thailand) and China.

Annex Table A.1 provides details of the estimates of the Total Gross Capital Stock (in millions of constant 1987 US dollars) in the 96 countries covered by this study. [5] For the reasons explained above, the results should be treated with considerable caution.

3.3 Methodological Improvements

What is necessary, then, to move these most recent analytically useful capital measures on to a more sound conceptual basis? In terms of the basic methodological framework, estimation approach and aggregation procedures, there is little alternative to using the PIM with all its well recognized limitations (See Annex 1 for a summary). In getting closer to the "real" situation, however, significant progress can be made by shifting to a purchasing power parity basis when compiling the fundamental country based GFCF series employed in generating the essential capital stock estimates. The main purpose of converting the basic GFCF expenditure series reported in national currencies into international dollars using relevant sector level (not overall GDP) purchasing power parities (PPPs) instead of exchange rates is to secure estimates of investment on the basis of a common currency denominator that eliminates the differences between countries in relative price levels. In this way, the value of investment and the associated return of capital can be compared in a uniform and equivalent manner across countries. Depending on the specific aims of the study, and whether comparable estimates of real change over time are required, a decision whether to use a single year's PPP (such as the latest "replacement cost" year) or a sequence of annual PPPs will have to be made. Given that PPPs are more stable than exchange rates over time and are linked more closely to relative trends in domestic inflation (although perhaps less so in the case of imported machinery and equipment), it is not so

[5] The study provides component estimates for the two main sub-aggregates: (a) Building and Construction; and (b) Transport Machinery and Other Equipment. Additionally, calculations of the Gross Capital:Output (GCP) ratios, 1980-1990, are made for all 96 countries.

materially important to select a single base reference year to effect this transformation process.

In addition, it would be desirable to dispense with the present "consistency" assumptions about uniform lengths of life and standard single exit retirement function across all countries. If good information exists about the actual lifetimes of different classes of assets, these would have more meaning. Though country specific lifetime estimates represent historical experience with already retired capital, they tend more closely to reflect the reality of existing practices. Modifying the length of life assumptions over time to take account of faster rates of technical progress and more rapid scrapping patterns might also yield some improvement. In a related context, if the analytical interest is mainly in the relationship between production capacity and development potential, it may not be necessary to introduce additional capital utilization coefficients to adjust the derived capital stock estimates to reflect the real productive contribution of such assets in practice. Such a sophistication, however, would help better explain actual growth performance.

More important, real technical progress may be hidden in the price of an asset. The investment deflators used in each country should take account, therefore of the quality improvements incorporated over time in the new productive assets added to the existing capital stocks. [6] For much the same reason, a separate account must be made of second hand purchases of used assets and for major repairs and refurbishings which will add to productive potential. Not only this but, in analyzing price trends in this area, special care must be taken to eliminate the effects of individual accounting revaluations undertaken by business enterprises since these can introduce distortions into the basic asset series. In principle, however, in moving from an historical cost basis of valuation (at which the original GFCF acquisitions are made and investment is valued in the national accounts) to a replacement cost basis of assessment, such assets revaluations should be already taken care of methodologically.

Evidence suggests that, with the exception of a handful of OECD

[6] For many developing countries relying on imported machinery and equipment mainly from the advanced industrial countries, it seems likely that the technical developments in capital goods producing industries will have a very similar impact in each of the receiving countries.

countries and primarily in the area of computers, no adjustments are made for quality and "efficiency enhancing" factors in the corresponding investment price series used as deflators. Clearly, for analytical purposes, it is important to retain consistency between the national accounts GNP and growth measures and the component investment and implicit capital stock figures. Essentially, therefore, if the deflators only measure observed price changes, then the residual unexplained variable in any regression analysis will, to a significant extent, reflect inherent technical progress. This would apply particularly where growth is related to investment in machinery and equipment.

4. Measuring the Role of Capital

How can economists better assess the relative importance of capital in different countries? If by "important" economists mean "how large is the capital stock?" (compared with other factors used in the production process), described above, using the value of the existing stock of capital assets at replacement cost as the appropriate yardstick. But, it is not certain that this is a very useful concept for policy purposes. Some would argue the resulting aggregate does not properly reflect the value of that capital, i.e. its real contribution to output and usefulness to society, and that the valuation basis is not the same across assets and compared with labor, particularly between countries.

4.1 The Conventional Method

Customarily defined, the stock of capital in any country is the accumulation of successive investments, adjusted appropriately for retirements, valued on a chosen consistent basis (not historical cost). What economists term "investment" in this context is measured statistically as gross fixed capital formation. The United Nations System of National Accounts (SNA, 1968 and 1993) defines gross fixed capital formation as the outlays (including own account production) on additions of new durable goods to the existing stock of fixed assets. A capital good is a commodity that is durable, generally possessing a lifetime of at least a year. (Military equipment, buildings and structures – with the exception of hospitals serving the general public – are conventionally excluded.) A productive asset contributes directly and indirectly, in combination with other types of assets, to future income generation via the continuous flow of production services it provides. For some purposes, it is useful to think of a capital good as anything that is too costly to buy out of a single year profit and loss account or too large to constitute a regular itemized cost charged to the government's current budget. Most capital goods, therefore, must be purchased from internally accumulated savings within an enterprise, including official budget surpluses, out of own funds obtained from other sources, and from borrowing (savings generated elsewhere in the system). In developing countries, a large share of capital assets are obtained from external sources. The process of physical capital formation cannot be divorced from the basic means of capital financing, and the question of true capital cost – and hence real capital prices – cannot always be easily determined. Furthermore, differences over time and across countries between national prices and international prices arise because of exchange rate movements, and variations in tariffs and quotas.

The economic value of an asset is normally assumed to be the present (i.e. discounted) value of the stream of future net income that is expected to yield over its lifetime. Many assets, however, do not earn any clearly identifiable financial return, nor one that can be attributed specifically to their use in productive activity. In the public sector, in particular, it is difficult to assess even the contribution of roads and bridges to output, let alone the value of state owned capital like prisons or even the Central Statistical Office. Similar problems are faced when valuing other public assets used in a collective context and in combination with other factors. Yet public assets and institutions like parks and prisons provide (most would agree) important services. The intrinsic value of capital, or rather its net worth, lies not so much in its monetary acquisition cost but in the inherent value of the services it provides to society. Some services can be marketed directly. Other goods and services (to the production of which such capital has contributed) provided collectively to the community may be valued differently. Ultimately, all public assets – although they often have no directly measurable output value – allow people to produce new commodities in a better way, in the broadest sense.

The traditional means of evaluating fixed assets may thus prove less than satisfactory in certain contexts. In many advanced industrial countries where the more conventional yardsticks have fallen short in providing relevant signals for policy action, simply on practical costing grounds, the combination of narrow short term financial perspectives and limited traditional accounting practices have contributed to arbitrary measures of the real value of the capital. Such accounting practices could lead to inappropriate assessments of the rate of depreciation and to inadequate measures of the loss of value of physical capital during use, even in financial terms. At the extreme, in many developing countries, it is evident that key public investments have been allowed to deteriorate. This is partly because the public infrastructure cannot be readily connected to a market and to pecuniary returns of output. Present procedures of valuing capital, therefore, would show a capital "value" where it does not exist. The method used provides no scope for placing a satisfactory value on the importance of the service an asset provides and the resulting need, therefore, to maintain it. [7]

4.2 An Alternative Perspective on Capital

The quantity, quality and reliability of the flow of services, and the actual carrying capacity of installed assets, really matter when it comes to measuring the real contribution of capital to an economy. To carry out these assessments properly, however, it is necessary first to identify relevant output and impact indicators and then resolve some critical questions of aggregation, scale ordering and weights.

Investment in capital assets and their maintenance of can be viewed as decisions which are based on the value that decision-makers place on existing assets. Investment decisions are mostly "partial" and hence, estimates of rates of return should be evaluated in the context of how the additional assets harmonize with the existing stock of capital, and how they balance with other factors already in place. As investment accumulates and the stock of capital expands, the introduction of assets will tend to represent a progressively smaller component of the total capital stock. The ability of this new investment to provide future services will depend on how well it can be integrated harmoniously into the existing stock of capital and how satisfactorily it will blend in with the pattern of service this capital already delivers, since the latter will comprise the dominant characteristic of the level of service provided.

4.3 The Measurement of Capital Services

In theory, if product and factor markets are functioning effectively, the price of an asset, or its present value, represents the discounted cost, in current prices, of the future income streams that are expected to result from the contribution capital makes to productive

[7]A parallel can be found in the degradation of natural environmental assets, where present generations use up scarce, non-renewable resources because they are not required to pay the costs of resource depletion, and their replacement. They are concerned to benefit only from their extraction.

activity. But, reflecting the conflicting arguments that have raged over the meaning of capital, policymakers are now confronted by a choice between monetary or physical indicators to measure output streams. Since capital forms an important component of the production function, as a concept, it appears to sit firmly on the supply side of the equation. But, as has been evident over successive business cycles, the capacity to produce is not the same as the actual contribution to production. The length of life of a piece of capital, for example, is linked to the enterprise as a going economic concern. Both physical and financial factors may cut that life short – or, indeed, prolong it. In the case of both installed productive capital and social overhead capital, the availability of supply factors available to generate output does not determine their use, nor their usefulness, or their utilization. Thus, the traditional practice of using the cost of the capital to best represent the value of capital in productive activity may be misleading.

A more meaningful approach may be to consider the importance of capital from the standpoint of the demand for its real services. This is particularly relevant in the case of infrastructural facilities and social overhead capital where the direct link to production performance is unclear and non-market situations often apply. An approach that focusses on the value of services received by users and, therefore, on measures of demand, output, the actual level of services delivered, is often measurable and comparable using physical indicators. Early social cost benefit analysis strove to quantify this when appraising large projects. The distinction between the two approaches, however, rests more with the financial marketability of output and the perception that certain forms of capital constitute direct rather than indirect components of final output value. Roads, vehicles, railways, ships, aircraft, telephones, water supply and even street lighting, for example, all have an identifiable (if not always easily measurable) end-uses and their output can be quantified. Such capital serves both intermediate and final demand. Plant and machinery and factory buildings, on the other hand, only provide an indirect contribution to output. As factor inputs, used in combination with other factors, their individual contribution to final output are often less evidently quantifiable, but their specific machine output can usually be physically determined.

The usefulness of physical indicators, and, specifically, the highly detailed technical measures of capital goods developed for the International Comparison Program (ICP) in facilitating this evaluation process have been little examined. The technical characteristics of capital e.g.

power/output specifications, can be defined, and hedonic regression procedures used to weight and aggregate different characteristics and convert them into consistent and equivalent value terms. Alternatives to conventional measures of capital based on the Perpetual Inventory Model (PIM) may be not only feasible, but also more meaningful, at least in some policy and operational contexts.

5. Concluding Observations

In many countries, despite the extensive array of technical and financial data now available pertaining to investment goods, economists still know remarkable little about either the actual real amount of capital in a country at a particular moment of time, or how this capital can be compared, in equivalent terms, with similar capital available in other countries. This makes it difficult for analysts – who need to differentiate between the quality, reliability and utilization of various pieces of capital – to assess issues like relative productivity and overall efficiency. They need more robust measures to try to explain variations in economic growth and the contribution that different factors – and various components of capital – make to that growth. [8] Their aim should be to help policymakers use scarce resources more sparingly and assist users to derive a higher economic rate of return from the more efficient allocation of capital to different activities across the world.

Capital is a means to production; the better the capital, the higher the potential final output. Measures attaching significance to the physical and technical characteristics of assets (rather than these assets being represented by money values) may have much to recommend them. Because factors like labor and land contribute in varying degrees to the production process, it can be potentially confusing to measure the contribution of capital to output in any terms other than in respect of the service it renders. For example, some capital may be in place but, for legal reasons, e.g. filings for bankruptcy, (as with the airline industry), patent infringement, etc. it may not be possible to utilize the assets concerned, even though they are still potentially productive. Service output measures can improve understanding the role of capital in economic growth. Many measures of capital, on the other hand, tend to get unduly influenced by market imperfections, changing economic

[8] Capital helps to explain increases in productive capacity rather than production itself. As a stock of assets, it merely indicates what potentially determines the rate and, perhaps more interestingly, the pattern of economic growth.

circumstances, and distorted exchange rates. Generally, these value measures relate only to "stock" or capacity concepts. Significantly, however, it is only in combination with other production factors – land, labor and entrepreneurship – that capital possesses any importance.

APPENDIX I
THE PIM AND ASSET LIFETIME ASSUMPTIONS

a. General

The Perpetual Inventory Model (PIM) is the most commonly used method of measuring capital. In theory, the PIM arrives at an identical value to that obtained in a full census of capital. This is only true, however, if all the inherent length of life and survival assumptions basic to the methodology correspond exactly with those actually used by Government and private enterprises and faithfully reflect reality in the use of capital. Even though the PIM may achieve this matching, the method will still fail to represent the true value of capital. To what precise extent, researchers may never know, not least because the census method itself is severely flawed and subject to human inaccuracy when applied in practice. Such differences arise mainly on account of individual idiosyncrasies and the virtual impossibility of implementing robust standardized procedures to evaluate personally, on a unit by unit basis, the value of assets at their current replacement cost. But some industrial countries are moving towards a more direct measurement approach in certain areas.

In the case of developing countries, the basic compilation problems are significantly compounded by pricing issues. Capital is in large part imported (even in the case of building and construction work) and equivalent local "values" reflect, *inter alia*, overseas supplier costs, prevailing exchange rates, as well as the usual delivery, installation and set up charges for putting equipment in place.

b. Lifetimes

Fundamental to the PIM is the length of life assumptions. These are far more important than the associated survival functions.

In developing countries, the average length of life of capital, in practice, probably has less to do with basic technical issues than with the ability of the country to adequately maintain its stock of roads, plant, and equipment etc.. It also depends on the country's ability to borrow capital from banks and donors. Simple observation clearly reveals that actual lifetimes have little to do with the assumed lifetimes determined by formal depreciation procedures (in any financial accounting sense) and economic obsolescence. Depreciation, or capital assumption, requires asset users to keep capital not just in working order but also at a level close to that perceived in the original design specifications, i.e. to maintain intact the projected carrying capacity of the asset in question over its intended lifetime. In turn, the initially assumed lifetimes should reflect the expected use of the respective physical assets concerned. The actual lengths of life, however, will depend on a variety of factors, few of which are inherently related to the initial value of a piece of capital. Several of the more important factors affecting a machine's service life and actual asset utilization in general, particularly in developing countries, are listed below :

(a) Unavailability of foreign exchange to invest in new replacement capital;

(b) No access to funds to acquire the necessary spare parts to keep existing capital in operation ;

(c) Lack of raw material inputs, fuel and other energy supplies to keep machinery working ;

(d) Dependence on foreign suppliers; limited (and sometimes unpredictable) assurance about the quantity (or quality) of foreign supplies ;

(e) Lower quality capital, imperfect models, secondhand and rehabilitated machines, repaired plant, etc ;

(f) Absence of local operational knowledge, technical know-how and repair skills ;

(g) Poor management, irregular supervision, combined with unsatisfactory regular maintenance ;

(h) Adverse locational factors and poor adaptation to local physical conditions ;

(i) Inadequate interface with inter-related natural resource endowments and other natural phenomena (heat, humidity, uneven terrain, etc.) ; and

(j) Higher risk of accidents.

All these features significantly affect the use of capital, its lifetime and its degree of utilization.

Better quality repairs and replacements by improved spare parts may help improve the real performance of capital installed, and lower basic cost per unit of output. Over the passage of time, there may also be accelerated technical progress, improved learning processes and new materials that enhance asset values. Some of these developments will be incorporated later into the design and construction of new equipment and structures.

Abnormal asset lives, whether excessively long or unexpectedly short, are not uncommon. These lifetimes will vary over time as other economic conditions change. There is rarely a smooth spectrum of technical change.

APPENDIX II
CAPITAL SERVICE MEASUREMENTS: AN EXAMPLE

Public service decision analysis for infrastructure can be illustrated by the case of a service allocation for a water supply system serving two areas in a community possessing, respectively, two types of service: one using household connections to middle income consumers and one by standpipe to low income consumers. Each type of service contributes to public welfare and has its service characteristics (and costs) valued in different ways by the users. To assess the effects on public welfare of improved service to each of the communities, the following steps should be carried out :

(a) First, the characteristics of the water actually received by each user group need to be measured (e.g. percent impurities, color, percent of time available, etc.,).

(b) Second, technical knowledge must be employed to determine the effects of operations and maintenance decisions and condition of equipment on the operations of the water supply system which are reflected in service characteristics.

(c) Third, some common unit of service value must be employed so that the benefit to each use of changing service characteristics can be estimated.

(d) Fourth, the link between service improvement and the cost of service improvements must be estimated.

Once these measures are available, the allocation rule can be implemented. For each area, the aggregate benefit associated with each unit of service improvement is assessed by adding together the separate benefits for each user group. This is then divided by the estimated cost of a unit of service improvement, yielding the marginal benefit-cost ratio (MBCR) for service improvements in each area. The provision of resources can then be adjusted until the MBCR's for the two areas are approximately equalized.

References

Ahmad, Y.J., S. EL Serafy, and E. Lutz (1989), *Environmental Accounting for Sustainable Development*, The World Bank, Washington, DC.

Aukrust, Odd, and Juule Bjerke (1959), "Real Capital and Economic Growth in Norway 1900-56", *The Review of Income and Wealth*, Series VIII.

Barna, Tibor (1959), "Alternative Methods of Measuring Capital", *The Review of Income and Wealth*, Series VIII.

Biorn, Erik, Erling Holmoy, and Oystein Olsen (1985), *Gross and Net Capital, and The Form of The Survival Function - Some Norwegian Evidence*, Discussion Paper No.11, Central Bureau of Statistics, Norway.

Delong, Bradford J., and Lawrence Summers (1991), "Equipment Investment and Economic Growth",*Quarterly Journal of Economics.*

El Serafy, S. (1989), "The Proper Calculation of Income from Depletable Natural Resources", Ahmad, Y.J., S. El Serafy, and E. Lutz, *Environmental Accounting for Sustainable Development*, The World Bank, Washington, DC.

Harrison, Anne (1992), *Natural Assets and National Income*, Environment Department Working Paper No. 1992-43, World Bank, Washington, DC.

Michael Hee and Raquel Fok(1993), "Physical Capital Stock: Estimates for Developing Economies", *Socio-Economic Data Division*, IEC, The World Bank, Washington, DC.

Hicks, J.R. (1946), *Value and Capital*, Oxford University Press,London.

Hofman, Andre A. (1992), "Capital Accumulation in Latin America: A Six Country Comparison for 1959-80", *The Review of Income and Wealth*, Series 38, No. 4, pp. 365-401.

Goldsmith, R.W. (1951), "A Perpetual Inventory of National Wealth", *Studies in Income and Wealth*, Vol. 14.

Keuning, Steven J. (1989), *An Estimate of The Fixed Capital Stock by Industry and Type of Capital Good in Indonesia*, Institute of Social and Advisory Service, The Hague.

Kumar, Jagdish, R.P. Katyal, and S.P. Sharma (1986), "Estimates of Capital Stocks in India", *The Review of Income and Wealth*, Vol.9, No.1

Lutz, Ernst, and Mohan Munasinghe (1991), "Accounting for the Environment", Finance and Development, Vol. 28, No.1, International Monetary Fund and The World Bank, Washington, DC.

Maddison, Angus (1993), *Standardized Estimates of Fixed Investment and Capital Stock at Constant Prices: A Long Run Survey for 6 Countries*, University of Groningen, mimeo.

Miller, Edward D. (1990), "Can a Perpetual Inventory Capital Stock be Used for Production Function Parameter Estimation?", *The Review of Income and Wealth*, Series 36, Vol.1

OECD (1988), *Capital Stock Statistics: Recent Development*, Note by the Secretariat at the Meeting of National Accounts Experts, OECD, Paris.

OECD (1993),*Methods Used by OECD Countries to Measure Stocks of Fixed Capital*, OECD, Paris.

Tengblad, Ake, and Nanan Westerlund (1976), "Capital Stock and Capital Consumption Estimates by Industries in the Swedish National Accounts", *The Review of Income and Wealth*, Series 22, No.4.

U.S. Department of Commerce (1987), *Fixed Reproducible Tangible Wealth in the United States*, 1925-85, Washington, DC.

Ward, Michael (1976), *The Measurement of Capital: The Methodology of Capital Stock Estimates in OECD Countries*, OECD, Paris.

World Bank (1993), *The East Asian Miracle: Economic Growth and Public Policy* ,Oxford University Press, Washington, DC.

Annex Table A.1: Estimates of Total Gross Capital Stock
(in million constant 1987 US$)

	1980	1981	1982	1983	1984	1985	1986	1987	1988	1989	1990
AFRICA	643,268	683,310	721,109	753,927	783,017	804,143	821,907	836,094	850,834	864,920	880,856
1 Benin	4,172	4,654	5,166	5,394	5,569	5,700	5,816	5,928	6,025	6,181	6,339
2 Botswana	2,312	2,625	2,920	3,162	3,370	3,693	3,892	4,120	4,403	4,846	--
3 Cameroon	12,727	14,621	16,715	19,007	21,177	23,425	27,076	29,663	31,116	32,065	--
4 Congo	9,184	10,112	11,432	12,583	13,571	14,445	15,013	15,402	15,677	15,924	16,384
5 Cote d'Ivoire	25,417	27,434	29,103	30,466	31,077	31,771	32,435	33,066	33,404	33,515	33,564
6 Ethiopia	10,753	11,079	11,526	12,037	12,581	12,841	13,164	13,557	13,968	14,337	14,507
7 Gabon	19,732	21,219	22,644	24,134	25,548	27,050	28,276	28,822	29,428	29,505	29,605
8 Ghana	9,061	9,202	9,459	9,653	9,838	9,986	10,147	10,507	10,072	11,512	--
9 Kenya	24,718	26,208	27,136	27,552	27,971	29,927	27,915	28,293	28,855	29,642	30,356
10 Lesotho	939	1,100	1,290	1,400	1,533	1,711	1,841	1,980	2,161	2,346	2,520
11 Madagascar	5,591	5,705	5,900	5,997	6,097	6,105	6,111	6,167	6,299	6,446	6,673
12 Malawi	4,362	4,534	4,709	4,853	4,975	5,037	5,065	5,080	5,204	5,319	5,523
13 Mali	3,072	3,254	3,453	3,626	3,812	4,051	4,362	4,654	4,951	5,300	5,583
14 Mauritius	4,207	4,371	4,499	4,638	4,789	4,931	5,106	5,350	5,686	6,025	6,342
15 Nigeria	102,775	11,610	118,052	122,900	125,199	126,289	126,939	127,097	127,264	127,468	--
16 Rwanda	1,603	1,745	1,944	2,172	2,452	2,714	3,103	3,407	3,689	3,913	3,983
17 Senegal	11,154	11,425	11,718	12,012	12,299	12,420	12,609	12,831	13,085	13,317	13,515
18 Sierra Leone	979	1,023	1,054	1,080	1,106	1,102	1,125	1,145	1,190	1,229	--
19 South Africa	262,468	280,909	298,972	315,827	332,022	345,181	354,176	362,430	371,279	380,565	387,916
20 Sudan	22,436	23,232	25,436	27,443	29,357	30,331	31,631	32,540	33,430	33,805	--
21 Swaziland	2,079	2,174	2,260	2,406	2,518	2,620	2,693	2,704	2,717	2,717	--
22 Tanzania	10,474	10,957	11,504	11,736	12,107	12,384	12,630	13,069	13,582	14,270	--
23 Togi	3,759	4,048	4,301	4,488	4,713	4,957	5,198	5,368	5,553	5,761	5,892
24 Uganda	23,291	23,192	23,013	22,849	22,759	22,458	22,253	21,690	21,258	20,904	20,430
25 Zaire	9,074	9,921	10,753	11,701	12,615	13,414	14,182	14,920	15,751	16,471	17,003
26 Zambia	37,265	36,138	34,353	32,114	30,492	27,712	24,868	21,775	19,052	16,467	--
27 Zimbabwe	19,665	20,740	21,790	22,699	23,467	23,888	24,282	24,530	24,828	25,085	25,238

Annex Table A.1: Estimates of Total Gross Capital Stock
(in million constant 1987 US$)

	1980	1981	1982	1983	1984	1985	1986	1987	1988	1989	1990
ASIA	1,807,992	1,958,409	2,125,195	2,303,215	2,493,067	2,682,511	2,881,748	3,110,059	3,363,533	3,621,071	3,905,753
28 Bangladesh	28,621	30,460	32,182	33,244	34,454	35,628	36,780	38,413	39,853	41,127	42,482
29 China	350,567	374,385	408,979	450,204	501,086	562,430	631,547	713,262	804,026	877,289	951,016
30 Hong Kong	78,698	87,793	96,869	105,124	113,471	121,507	130,047	140,075	150,679	161,600	173,341
31 India	628,322	664,169	701,220	738,149	776,251	810,775	845,216	884,129	926,051	969,691	1,013,160
32 Indonesia	96,545	110,580	125,703	141,166	155,656	170,333	186,213	202,814	221,420	242,478	267,894
33 Korea, Rep.	165,017	182,736	202,063	224,495	249,018	275,520	305,137	339,925	379,364	425,502	483,363
34 Malaysia	57,440	65,270	73,784	83,014	92,534	100,708	106,979	112,728	119,351	128,288	139,525
35 Pakistan	49,093	51,379	54,093	57,274	60,780	64,505	68,456	72,704	76,779	81,468	86,155
36 Philippines	81,948	89,866	97,952	106,674	112,874	116,011	118,788	122,028	125,821	130,753	135,873
37 Singapore	44,641	50,505	57,529	65,097	73,201	79,957	85,569	91,247	97,278	104,429	113,208
38 Sri Lanka	12,271	13,719	15,270	16,888	18,372	19,574	20,874	22,211	23,774	25,155	26,508
39 Thailand	93,525	101,590	109,176	117,740	127,196	135,016	142,387	151,131	161,902	175,582	193,430
LATIN AMERICA	2,044,658	2,188,417	2,313,069	2,404,994	2,494,505	2,569,615	2,651,054	2,730,153	2,800,546	2,861,712	2,913,434
40 Argentina	317,701	329,692	338,871	346,725	352,313	351,994	351,764	353,150	353,551	351,198	348,018
41 Bolivia	22,082	22,845	23,503	23,570	23,594	23,359	22,964	22,566	22,418	22,214	21,689
42 Brazil	763,306	818,658	869,968	910,208	949,160	987,371	1,035,577	1,080,099	1,117,370	1,151,946	1,178,585
43 Chile	52,721	55,522	57,166	58,403	59,819	60,693	61,702	63,238	64,978	67,395	69,953
44 Colombia	71,579	76,396	81,493	86,468	91,592	95,369	99,491	103,601	108,265	112,213	115,908
45 Costa Rica	10,282	10,846	11,202	11,601	12,127	12,599	13,109	13,670	14,160	14,742	15,419
46 Dominican Rep.	10,939	11,814	12,470	13,219	14,022	14,700	15,330	16,259	17,287	18,429	19,187
47 Ecuador	37,026	39,768	42,461	44,273	45,940	47,356	48,745	50,323	51,584	52,502	53,046
48 El Salvador	10,540	10,790	10,987	11,226	11,492	11,715	11,961	12,143	12,363	12,584	12,601
49 Gautemala	15,831	16,677	17,317	17,545	17,730	17,803	17,836	18,055	18,320	18,636	18,874
50 Hondurus	9,226	9,711	10,135	10,619	11,199	11,636	11,967	12,230	12,486	12,792	12,976
51 Jamaica	20,229	20,498	20,705	20,768	20,748	20,514	20,362	20,415	20,282	20,364	20,254
52 Mexio	381,509	421,493	452,040	471,205	491,743	510,460	525,100	538,300	552,141	566,684	584,467
53 Panama	13,895	14,890	15,931	16,664	17,295	17,824	18,456	18,966	18,984	18,923	19,097
54 Paraguay	7,135	8,393	9,373	10,065	10,761	11,445	12,144	12,879	13,576	14,357	15,207
55 Peru	73,454	77,968	82,367	85,233	87,936	89,846	92,440	95,652	97,456	98,102	98,722
56 Trinidad & Tobago	14,300	15,600	17,019	18,264	19,492	20,707	21,605	22,281	22,875	23,368	23,841
57 Uruguay	22,957	24,648	25,934	26,595	26,948	26,567	26,171	26,253	26,561	26,590	26,497
58 Venezuela	189,947	202,210	214,127	222,345	230,599	237,660	244,331	250,077	255,893	258,677	259,097

Annex Table A.1: Estimates of Total Gross Capital Stock
(in million constant 1987 US$)

	1980	1981	1982	1983	1984	1985	1986	1987	1988	1989	1990
MIDDLE EAST/ N.AFRICA	1,476,900	1,575,242	1,666,516	1,754,630	1,839,629	1,910,445	1,971,518	2,023,241	2,068,707	2,112,616	--
59 Algeria	194,642	213,263	232,028	251,561	271,486	289,303	306,466	321,541	334,643	346,337	357,247
60 Cyprus	9,077	9,714	10,369	11,002	11,776	12,405	12,985	13,592	14,259	15,076	15,860
61 Egypt , Arab Rep.	42,580	47,258	53,191	59,737	66,538	73,493	79,492	84,866	90,334	95,577	100,091
62 Iran, Islamic Rep.	541,807	565,184	588,225	617,514	645,722	669,761	688,507	704,326	718,901	734,892	749,351
63 Israel	96,094	101,429	106,926	112,719	117,240	120,302	122,799	125,699	128,195	130,407	133,617
64 Jordan	7,888	9,500	11,153	12,490	13,675	14,699	15,069	16,997	17,974	18,756	19,470
65 Libya	275,234	284,646	201,127	269,576	258,963	250,983	243,471	234,028	224,149	210,494	--
66 Morocco	46,496	49,912	53,770	57,011	60,143	62,770	65,372	67,007	70,540	73,612	76,798
67 Saudi Arabia	211,163	237,864	276,879	295,795	321,304	338,788	354,245	369,197	381,727	397,024	--
68 Syrian Arab Rep.	25,953	28,845	31,865	34,990	38,187	41,235	43,996	45,512	46,958	48,165	--
69 Tunisia	25,466	27,629	29,903	32,227	34,594	36,706	38,316	39,676	41,029	42,276	43,687
EUROPE	829,630	870,784	910,325	947,684	978,732	1,004,102	1,028,769	1,053,296	1,074,658	1,096,740	1,119,660
70 Greece	154,322	161,779	160,957	175,908	181,034	186,968	191,502	195,401	199,282	204,341	210,084
71 Hungary	82,803	87,889	92,624	97,139	101,326	104,757	108,137	112,040	115,354	118,852	121,590
72 Malta	3,752	3,990	4,261	4,566	4,812	5,047	5,279	5,630	6,003	6,388	--
73 Portugal	127,836	133,992	140,248	145,959	149,496	151,762	154,276	157,530	162,115	168,504	176,428
74 Turkey	172,132	180,899	190,323	199,557	208,545	217,793	228,133	238,497	246,938	253,417	260,112
75 Yugoslavia	288,785	302,236	313,912	324,554	332,718	337,775	341,442	344,198	344,966	345,239	344,971

Annex Table A.1: Estimates of Total Gross Capital Stock
(in million constant 1987 US$)

	1980	1981	1982	1983	1984	1985	1986	1987	1988	1989	1990
OECD	36,696,431	30,394,336	39,998,255	41,634,286	43,370,712	44,000,081	46,301,491	47,888,784	49,572,009	51,399,703	53,346,465
76 Australia	715,827	752,175	783,319	814,955	849,985	879,060	906,367	935,361	970,938	1,006,316	1,034,750
77 Austria	417,130	437,335	455,511	473,610	491,770	507,242	522,192	537,084	554,605	572,636	591,679
78 Belgium	447,750	463,851	479,500	494,249	508,896	518,332	528,497	539,193	552,297	567,423	585,065
79 Canada	1,017,869	1,086,514	1,146,755	1,206,986	1,268,029	1,322,427	1,300,693	1,445,530	1,516,206	1,591,235	1,661,135
80 Denmark	350,616	359,575	369,227	378,879	390,127	399,393	411,747	423,273	432,503	441,117	450,633
81 Finland	327,461	341,816	357,500	374,151	389,581	401,090	412.012	423,490	436,592	452,271	466,125
82 France	2,77,160	2,912,437	3,047,734	3,175,886	3,290,806	3,382,824	3,475,089	3,572,835	3,679,182	3,799,633	3,929,572
83 Germany	3,979,515	4,134,936	4,383,694	4,435,673	4,577,587	4,674,212	4,774,471	4,877,879	4,982,146	5,104,297	5,239,743
84 Iceland	14,074	14,892	15,702	16,436	17,273	17,972	18,562	19,333	20,012	20,570	21,191
85 Ireland	75,794	81,171	86.318	90,842	95,209	98,431	101,308	103,965	106,375	109,696	113,545
86 Italy	2,476,461	2,592,696	2,691,093	2,801,209	2,907,513	2,996,390	3,082,925	3,171,381	3,260,298	3,350,992	3,448,496
87 Japan	6,953,869	7,426,069	7,888,558	8,342,288	8,815,371	9,284,718	9,710,617	10,322,344	10,925,051	11,610,058	12,384,781
88 Luxembourg	22,967	23,738	24,585	25,372	26,130	26,531	27,258	28,078	29,067	29,998	31,180
89 Netherlands	773,033	799,294	823,851	847,892	873,791	891,743	912,721	935,614	957,519	981,630	1,007,156
90 New Zealand	129,042	133,549	138,769	144,739	150,816	155,430	159,693	164,185	168,236	172,279	176,627
91 Norway	306,729	332,393	335,079	349,110	366,786	376,734	389,771	403,440	416,052	427,955	432,366
92 Spain	925,130	965,769	1,006,829	1,046,496	1,081,657	1,112,048	1,146,065	1,187,101	1,232,696	1,284,144	1,340,927
93 Sweden	521,107	538,844	556,286	574,344	593,375	608,012	623,230	639,754	656,267	674,759	692,749
94 Switzerland	615,892	641,997	667,159	693,437	720,787	746,657	769,310	796,605	826,047	857,246	890,497
95 United Kingdom	1,043,805	1,896,572	1,952,937	2,012,537	2,080,974	2,136,220	2,194,764	2,262,302	2,337,466	2,419,434	2,499,944
96 United States	12,005,132	12,468,715	12,880,774	13,336,064	13,874,235	14,266,595	14,683,392	15,100,047	15,512,454	15,925,957	16,348,290

International Comparisons of Prices, Output and Productivity
Edited by D.S. Prasada Rao and J. Salazar-Carrillo

COMPARATIVE PRICE AND PRODUCTIVITY LEVELS: KOREA AND THE UNITED STATES, 1963-1990

Dirk Pilat
Groningen Growth and Development Centre
University of Groningen

1. Introduction

International comparisons of economic performance have become an important topic in economic research. Increasingly, countries look beyond their own borders to find better solutions to their economic problems and to help improve their own performance. Partly, this is the result of the emergence of the GATT- system and the move to free trade, which has caused economies to become much more open to international competition. This has resulted in much more pressure on countries to keep up with best performance. Before these developments only some sectors, mainly those producing tradable goods, were subject to international competition and had to improve their performance continually to keep up with international developments. Nowadays, services are also increasingly becoming part of international trade. Therefore, knowledge of international best practice, expressed in productivity levels, or international cost levels, expressed in relative price levels, has become more important.

Unfortunately, productivity comparisons between countries are not so simple as they may seem. Each country's output is expressed in national currency units and therefore not directly comparable. Converting to a similar currency with the exchange rate does not solve the problem. Exchange rates are heavily influenced by capital flows, speculation and government intervention, and at best only reflect price differences for tradable goods. For these reasons, reliable price indicators are needed to convert each country's output to a similar currency.

There are two main approaches to this problem. The best known is the expenditure approach. It is based on detailed price comparisons of consumer and investment goods. Large price surveys are held in each country, carefully matching products. The individual price ratios are aggregated to more meaningful expenditure categories, such as food products, clothing, transport, and so on. The approach was developed in the early 1950s (Gilbert and Kravis, 1954) and came to its peak in the 1970s and early 1980s during the work in the International Comparisons Project (ICP, see Kravis, Heston and Summers, 1982). Nowadays, international organisations such as Eurostat and OECD regularly publish comparative GDP estimates based on the approach, and short-cut estimates are available for 130 countries (Summers and Heston, 1991). This approach is highly useful for comparative analysis of expenditure and living standards, but gives only limited information on sectoral productivity and price levels.

The second approach is based on a sectoral perspective. Producer price levels are compared for main sectors such as agriculture, manufacturing and services. In addition, input price levels have to be derived, because both production and intermediate input have to be deflated to end up with total GDP. This approach dates back to the work of Rostas (1948) and Paige and Bombach (1959). In recent years, it has received more attention from economists. Work at the University of Groningen in the ICOP (International Comparisons of Output and Productivity)-project since 1983 has tried to revive the approach. Following studies for agriculture and mining, most work has been on manufacturing (Van Ark and Pilat, 1993; Van Ark, 1995). Recently the focus of research has moved to output measurement in services (Pilat, 1994a). Other organisations and researchers have also picked up the industry-of-origin approach. FAO (1986) now publishes comparisons of agricultural output and prices for most countries in the world. The National Institute of Economic and Social Research (NIESR) also has made several studies with this approach (Smith, Hitchens and Davies, 1982; Smith and Hitchens, 1985; O'Mahony, 1992).

In essence, the approach is quite simple. If prices and quantities of comparable products are available, individual price ratios can be aggregated as follows:

$$PPP_j^{XU(X)} = \frac{\sum_{i=1}^{n} P_{ij}^X * Q_{ij}^X}{\sum_{i=1}^{n} P_{ij}^U * Q_{ij}^X} \tag{1}$$

at quantity weights of country X (or alternatively at quantity weights of country U), where P is price and Q quantity, and where i=1..n is the number of comparable products in industry j. The PPP shown in the formula is comparable to a Paasche price index in intertemporal comparisons, and its alternative at quantity weights of country U is comparable to a Laspeyres price index. Usually the geometric (or Fisher) average of Paasche and Laspeyres PPPs is preferred as the final PPP.

Direct comparisons can be made mainly for sectors producing clear and definable goods, for which statistical offices produce price and quantity information. Apart from agriculture, mining and manufacturing, this is also the case for some services, such as transport and electricity, gas and water. If extensive price comparisons can not be made, the comparison may have to be based on a limited number of price indicators, sometimes derived from the ICP- investigation, or on relevant volume indicators.

In theory, PPPs have to be derived for both output and intermediate input and a PPP for GDP has to be derived by double deflation, similar to standard national accounts practice. Unfortunately, very little information is available on prices and quantities of intermediate inputs. With limited information, double deflation is very susceptible to measurement error, especially if the ratio of value added to output is very small (Kravis, 1976). This paper uses the adjusted single indicator method (Paige and Bombach, 1959), which applies output PPPs also to the deflation of intermediate inputs, but weights the resulting PPPs at the value added level to derive a final PPP at the total GDP level.

The paper estimates and discusses comparative price and productivity levels between Korea and the United States for the period 1963 to 1990. A benchmark comparison for Korea and the United States is made for 1985. In addition, the benchmark is updated to 1990 for most indicators, and backdated to 1963, to derive a more intertemporal perspective of price and productivity levels.

2. Productivity and Price Levels in 1985

2.1 *Data Requirements for International Comparisons*

Comparisons of output and productivity across countries depend on consistent, reliable and comprehensive national accounts and census sources. These should preferably include both output (GDP) and employment data. For the United States, BEA's national accounts provides such a framework. For Korea, data sources are less comprehensive and the national accounts provide no data on labour input.

Table 1
Reconciliation of Basic Sources and National Accounts
South Korea, 1985

	Agricul ture (a)	Mining	Manufac turing (b)	Construc tion	Wholesale & Retail Trade
Gross Value of Output (bn. Won)					
- Census	10,547.8	1,042.8	78,628.3	16,875.7	11,794.6
- National Accounts	12,367.7	1,272.2	95,597.6	14,626.4	14,340.2
Census Value Added (bn. Won)	-	758.9	27,502.4	6,761.6	5,258.2
Gross Value Added (bn. Won)					
- Census (c)	7,322.3	653.3	16,582.9	6,174.9	7,965.2
- National Accounts	8,585.6	797.1	20,161.8	5,351.9	9,684.4
Employment (1000s)					
- Census	4,230	91	2,663	860	2,304
- National Accounts	3,722	154	3,500	908	3,370
GVA per Person (1000 Won)					
- Census	1,731	7,217	6,227	7,184	3,458
- National Accounts	2,307	5,176	5,761	5,894	2,874

Notes: (a) Excluding forestry and fisheries, breakdown national accounts based on Bank of Korea, 1985 Input-Output Tables, Seoul, 1988.
(b) Manufacturing census figures are adjusted for small establishments.
(c) Estimate based on ratio gross value added/gross value of output from the national accounts.

Sources: Gross value of output and gross value added national accounts from Bank of Korea, National Accounts 1990, Seoul, 1990, employment from Bank of Korea, 1985 Input-Output Tables, Seoul, 1988; census information for agriculture from NSO, Korea Statistical Yearbook 1992, Seoul, 1992; mining and manufacturing from EPB, Report on Mining and Manufacturing Survey 1985, Seoul, 1987, with adjustment for small establishments from EPB, Report on Mining and Manufacturing Census, 1983 and 1988 issues; construction from EPB, 1985 Census of Construction, Seoul, 1987; census employment in distribution based on EPB, 1986 Wholesale and Retail Trade Census, Seoul, 1988, adjusted to 1985.

Korean data for GDP at factor cost are available in quite some detail and can be derived from the Bank of Korea's national accounts (Bank of Korea, 1990). The weakest aspect of the Korean data are its figures on labour input (Lindauer, 1984). There are a number of establishment surveys by the Ministry of Labor, but these cover only the formal economy and primarily its larger establishments. The only annually available, comprehensive source on Korean employment is the Economically Active Population Survey of the Economic Planning Board, which is primarily a household survey. The survey distinguishes only the major sectors of the economy.

For the benchmark year 1985, detailed employment figures are provided by the Bank of Korea in their 1985 Input-Output Tables. This source offers the most consistent framework of output and employment information for Korea. Unfortunately, these data are only available for a few benchmark years, which implies that data from the Economically Active Population Survey must be used for time series analysis. Figures for hours worked per person in Korea by sector also have a much weaker basis than in the United States. Since 1970 the Ministry of Labor's Report on the Monthly Labor Survey provides estimates of hours worked for the nonagricultural business sector of the economy, but these are based on a relatively small survey.

The output and productivity comparisons in this paper are primarily based on national accounts data. However, there are a number of comprehensive census sources which can also be used for productivity analysis. Table 1 shows output, employment and productivity estimates for the five sectors for which census information is available. The census data on agriculture and mining cover more than 80 percent of total output. In manufacturing, the coverage is somewhat lower, since the national accounts make some imputations for informal activity and include some information for manufacturing establishments not covered by the Korean manufacturing census. For construction and wholesale and retail trade, there is a much larger gap between the census source and the national accounts. The construction census covers only a limited number of large licensed companies and excluded unlicensed companies, own-account construction and construction by the government. Wholesale and retail trade is a sector with a lot of informal activity. It is therefore to be expected that the census does not cover all persons engaged in this sector.

To achieve a comprehensive overview of comparative output and productivity in the Korean economy it is necessary to use the national accounts. However, for more detailed industry or sectoral analysis, the censuses provide very useful information. In particular for manufacturing (Pilat, 1994b), the census provides a much more useful source for detailed analysis than the national accounts.

2.2 *Measuring Sectoral Output*

Agriculture

Comparisons of output in agriculture are fairly simple to make. The number of products involved is limited and quality differences between countries are less of a problem than they are in, for instance, manufacturing. A recent FAO study (Prasada Rao, 1993) covered almost 100 countries, which together produced more than 99 percent of world agricultural output. The comparison between Korea and the United States for 1985 is based on this study. In addition, I made a separate comparison for fisheries, which is excluded in most agricultural comparisons, but is fairly important in the Korean case. Relative output in this sector is based on the total quantity of fish caught. The PPPs for agriculture and fisheries are weighted by their respective GDP figures to derive a PPP for agriculture and fisheries combined. This PPP is also applied to forestry, for which no separate output indicators were derived.

Mining

For mining, the approach is also quite simple. Output in mining depends on the natural resource base, and can therefore differ substantially between countries. Korea's mining sector is fairly small. Its production consists mainly of coal and some metal ores. The United States produces a much wider range of minerals and is a leading producer in several products. The 1985 price comparisons covered more than 80 percent of total mining output in both countries (Pilat, 1994a).

Manufacturing

The manufacturing sector is the most extensively studied sector in international comparisons. Van Ark and Pilat (1993) and Van Ark (1994) give a detailed account of the methods and procedures of comparisons for this sector. Unlike agriculture and mining, manufacturing comparisons are based on a limited sample of products. Many manufacturing products are unique to one country and cannot be compared with another (for instance: Boeing 747s in the United States, supertankers in Korea). In addition, manufacturing products are much less homogeneous than agricultural and mining products. Furthermore, detailed information on manufacturing production is often not disclosed, especially if the number of firms producing a product in a country is small.

The detailed manufacturing comparison between Korea and the United States is extensively discussed elsewhere (Pilat, 1994b). It is based on the manufacturing census in both countries, which supplies detail by product and by industry. The 1987 comparison made price comparisons for products which covered almost 37 percent of total manufacturing output in Korea and 21 percent in the United States. For the comparison for the economy as a whole the 1987 PPP was backdated to 1985, using GDP deflators in Korea and the United States.

Electricity, Gas and Water

This is one of the least complicated service sectors. Output consists mainly of supply of electricity, gas and water, for which suitable volume indicators are available and price indicators can be derived.

Construction

Construction output is of a heterogeneous nature, and varies between countries. Although most statistical offices provide some information on the total size or surface of buildings constructed, this is not sufficient for a detailed comparison. Since a direct industry of origin comparison did not seem feasible, I used a proxy PPP for construction expenditure from the ICP project. The ICP PPPs have the advantage that they relate to specified buildings, and are therefore more comparable between countries. In addition, expenditure on construction and output of the construction sector are not that different. In general, there are no trade and transport margins involved in construction. There is also still very little international trade in construction. Furthermore, almost all output of the construction sector is part of final demand, as it has almost no intermediate component. The price data collected by the ICP project therefore cover the same construction projects as would be covered by an industry of origin approach. The three major objections to the use of an ICP PPP as a proxy for an output PPP are therefore of limited relevance to the construction sector. The only factor which may still distort ICP proxies for sectoral purposes are taxes and subsidies. On the whole, however, the two approaches should lead to comparable results.

Transport and Communication

The approach in this sector was similar to that in electricity, gas and water. For most components of output, good quantity indicators are available. The best indicators for transport are based on passenger and ton kilometres. For communication, it is possible to look at the number of phone calls, mail delivered, and so on. There are considerable structural differences in this sector between the two countries. In Korea, passenger transport is predominantly by rail, which is only a small component in the USA. In the United States, car passenger transport is more important, but since this is largely private, it is not part of the transport sector. Other structural differences are the much larger weight of rail freight transport in the United States, and the minor position of air passenger transport in Korea.

A special problem in transport is the so-called terminal element (Smith, Hitchens and Davies, 1982). The output of the transport industry consists not only of the physical movement of persons or goods, but includes loading and unloading services. The relative importance of the terminal service depends on the distance travelled. For short distances its share in total output may be fairly large. A large weight of terminal services can reduce the productivity of the transport system. Since terminal services in Korea are much more important than in the United States, where distances are much larger, this effect tends to reduce Korean productivity. I have not made a correction for this factor, communication.

Wholesale and Retail Trade

The 'product' of this sector consists of the intermediation between producers and consumers. Distribution does not produce any physical products directly, apart from some production by butchers and bakers. It is therefore not possible to base a comparison on a direct product match. Also, there are no ICP proxy PPPs for this sector, since it is an intermediate sector which does not figure in the ICP investigation. I used the approach applied by Smith and Hitchens (1985), who converted total sales for different wholesale and retail categories by the corresponding ICP PPP for the corresponding expenditure category. After summing the matched sales by wholesale and retail trade an average reweighed PPP for both segments can be derived (Pilat, 1994a).

Mulder and Maddison (1993) have recently attempted to use a different procedure for this sector in a comparison between Mexico and the United States for 1975. They converted sales values by detailed category with ICP PPPs for that category, and the intermediate inputs in the same category with product PPPs derived from sectoral ICOP comparisons between Mexico and the United States. This approach gives a double deflated PPP for value added. However, for detailed segments of distribution this approach may lead to negative value added or other unsatisfactory results. Mulder and Maddison therefore also presented single deflated results.

Finance, Insurance and Real Estate

Information on finance is often restricted to monetary indicators. Total output in finance can be related to the total volume of transactions (the transactions approach), or to the net interest received on the deposits held by banks (the liquidity approach) (see Mark, 1982). Recent studies (Smith, 1989) seem to favour the transaction approach for output measurement. I have also adopted this latter approach, and have defined the total volume of transactions as M2, which is the sum of cash currency, demand deposits and time and savings deposits. This was suggested by Goldsmith (1983) as a good indicator for the degree of financial intermediation of an economy. Relative financial output is therefore based on M2, which was converted by the PPP for the whole economy from the ICP work. Since the degree of financial intermediation in South Korea (the ratio of M2 to GDP) is substantially lower than in the United States, output in the financial sector is relatively low in Korea.

A separate comparison for insurance was based on the total number of life insurance policies. This is the largest component of the insurance industry. Unfortunately, no comparative information was available on other insurance policies.

Real estate involves the renting and operation of nonresidential and residential dwellings, and some related activities. It includes the operation of owner-occupied dwellings. The estimate of relative output in real estate is based on the total value of the residential capital stock in Korea and the United States. The capital stock figures are based on national sources (Pyo, 1992; BEA, 1993), using non-standardised assumptions for the lifetime of structures and equipment. Residential capital stocks were converted to a common currency by ICP PPPs for residential investment supplied by Alan Heston. The resulting quantity relation is subsequently applied to GDP in real estate to derive a PPP.

Services and Government

Output measurement in education is quite difficult. Volume series in national accounts are quite often based on input indicators, such as the number of teachers. The measurement here is based on the total number of students, adjusted for students' relative achievement. Achievement levels are derived from the tests of the International Association for the Evaluation of Educational Achievement (IAEEA, 1991), which show Korea ahead of the United States in primary and secondary education. The association tested students aged 10 and 11, aged 14 and 15, and students in the final year of secondary education. The results for these age groups were taken to be representative for achievement levels of primary, secondary and tertiary education, respectively. The total number of students in each type of school was weighted by its relative achievement level. The three levels of schooling were given the same weight.

Other services combines the activities of, amongst others, health services, business services, personal services, recreation services, legal services and social services. For some of these output or price measures may be found, for others very little information is available. The PPP for this sector is based on the ICP proxies for health services, recreation services, personal care and miscellaneous services, weighted with per capita expenditure.

Output in government is still very difficult to measure. In most countries, volume movements are still based on the numbers of persons employed, sometimes adjusted for estimated productivity improvements. For this sector I also resorted to the use of an ICP proxy, which in the ICP comparisons was based partly on input measures and partly on prices of some specified government services.

2.3 *Output, Productivity and Price Levels, 1985*

The PPP for total gross domestic product is the weighted average of all sectoral PPPs, weighted by their corresponding GDP. In addition to the sectors discussed above, an adjustment was made for imputed bank services and for the statistical discrepancy. The PPP for imputed bank services is the same as for financial services, whereas the one for the statistical discrepancy is the same as that for GDP as a whole.

The price and productivity levels by sector for 1985 are presented in table 2. Similar to the Japanese case (Pilat, 1993), there are extreme variations between sectors. In agriculture, the Korean productivity level is even below that of Japan (see Pilat, 1994a), at only 5 percent of the US level. The high PPP for this sector, as well as the low labour productivity level, make Korea's performance remarkable similar to that of Japan. The small scale of farming, and primarily the protectionist agricultural policies followed in Korea have given very few incentives to farmers to rationalise production and improve their efficiency.

Mining production in Korea is dominated by coal. There is no production of gas and oil in Korea, which are both capital intensive and highly productive parts of the mining industry. Productivity in this sector is therefore also far behind the United States.

Manufacturing is the most interesting sector in terms of Korea's productive performance. It is the sector upon which much of Korea's success has been built and where Korean firms have been extremely successful. There are substantial differences within the manufacturing sector (Pilat, 1994b), but overall Korean productivity in 1985 was less than 20 percent of the US level. This figure appears remarkably low for such a successful exporter of manufacturing products. However, the average level masks considerable variation within manufacturing, and successful exporting industries generally have higher productivity levels than domestically oriented industries. In addition, the low productivity levels are generally not at odds with the low labour costs in Korean manufacturing.

Another relatively successful sector in Korea is construction. Korean firms have been heavily involved in construction in the Middle East and even today construction is one of the fast growing activities in the

Korean economy. However, although price levels are substantially below those in the United States, productivity is still below 40 percent of the US level.

The productivity levels in the rest of the economy show extreme variations. The highest productivity is found in education. Output in this sector is based on the number of students adjusted for relative achievement. However, there are a number of problems involved here. First, as Hill (1977) has noted, part of the output in this sector depends not on the performance of the sector itself, but on the students using the service. Since students in Korea, as in Japan, study much longer hours than their counterparts in the United States, their achievement is very high. The question is whether this should be considered part of the output of the educational sector, as the result of an educational system which succeeds in making students work hard, or if it should be considered as a separate component.

Another problem concerns the achievement levels themselves. These are available only on a comparable basis for a limited number of subjects, primarily science and mathematics. These are traditionally subjects which are stressed much more in the Japanese and Korean schooling system than in the United States. They may therefore give an overstatement of achievement for all subjects. A related problem concerns the growing criticism of schooling in Japan and Korea where creativity is concerned. Although schools in Japan and Korea are good in replication, they are much less able in teaching students to think creatively and develop their own ideas. This is traditionally an area where the Western education system has performed better, and where standard achievement tests have little to offer on a comparative basis. Low price levels for education were also found in the ICP investigation for several other developing countries. Although the ICP measures were based primarily on indicators for inputs, they do indicate that services, and especially non-market services are much cheaper in developing countries than in industrialised countries (Bhagwati, 1984).

The high productivity level of non-market services in Korea is also visible in the data for government. The health sector is probably also highly productive compared to the United States, but it is disguised in other services, and is therefore mixed with several market services with much lower relative productivity levels.

Table 2
Comparative Output, Productivity and Price Levels
Korea/United States, 1985

	Purchasing Power Parity (Won/$US)	Real GDP Korea	GDP per Person Engaged Korea (USA=100)	GDP per Hour Worked Korea	Relative Price Level Korea (a) (USA=100)
Agriculture, Forestry & Fisheries	1809.5	6.0	5.9	5.0	208
Mining	991.0	0.8	5.5	5.3	114
Manufacturing	708.4	3.8	25.0	17.3	81
Electricity, Gas & Water	1274.9	1.6	32.8	24.2	147
Construction	519.7	6.6	50.7	38.7	60
Transport & Communication					
- Transport & Storage	617.8	5.1	31.6	21.2	71
- Communication	301.8	5.0	94.8	70.8	35
Wholesale & Retail Trade	731.3	2.4	24.4	14.7	84
Finance, Insurance & Real Estate					
- Finance	990.7	2.1	35.1	26.8	114
- Insurance	347.6	3.1	62.3	48.1	40
- Real Estate	496.5	2.2	20.9	14.0	57
Services & Government					
- Education	148.8	13.3	277.0	174.6	17
- Other Services	345.4	2.7	60.6	38.5	40
- Government	326.0	3.3	92.7	58.4	38
Total Economy	572.1	3.5	31.0	20.6	66

Note: (a) The 1985 exchange rate was 870 Won to the US dollar.
Source: Pilat (1994a).

3. Productivity Growth in the Postwar Period

The benchmark estimates show that Korea has only reached high productivity levels only in some services. This may seem at odds with the fast productivity growth which Korea experienced in the last three decades. However, Korea came from very low productivity levels and has simply not had enough time to catch up with a high-income country such as the United States.

Table 3
Growth of GDP per Hour Worked by Sector
Korea and Korea/United States, 1963-90
(annual average compound growth rates)

KOREA	1963-73	1973-79	1979-90	1963-90
Agriculture, Forestry & Fisheries	2.87	4.50	4.67	3.96
Mining	9.08	-7.47	1.40	2.08
Manufacturing	7.63	5.61	6.41	6.68
Electricity, Gas & Water	11.62	12.98	10.65	11.52
Construction	9.39	0.81	5.66	5.92
Transport & Communication	11.98	6.38	4.95	7.82
Wholesale & Retail Trade	5.48	1.37	3.53	3.76
Finance, Insurance & Real Estate	1.96	-0.98	-0.29	0.38
Services & Government	1.97	1.18	1.14	1.45
Total Economy	4.14	4.71	5.62	4.87
KOREA/UNITED STATES	1963-73	1973-79	1979-90	1963-90
Agriculture, Forestry & Fisheries	-0.85	3.24	-0.09	0.36
Mining	6.37	0.32	-0.46	2.20
Manufacturing	4.48	4.33	3.59	4.08
Electricity, Gas & Water	6.91	14.12	9.00	9.33
Construction	12.87	2.85	6.94	8.16
Transport & Communication	8.33	3.42	2.88	4.99
Wholesale & Retail Trade	2.85	0.03	1.89	1.83
Finance, Insurance & Real Estate	0.91	-1.03	-0.24	0.01
Services & Government	1.02	0.84	1.14	1.03
Total Economy	2.18	4.10	4.67	3.62

Source: Pilat (1994a).

Korea's comparative productivity growth is presented in table 3. In the period 1963-90 GDP per hour worked rose 4.9 percent annually. GDP itself grew much faster, but employment more than doubled between from 1963 to 1990 and hours worked increased as well. The best performance in productivity terms was in utilities, followed by manufacturing, construction and transport and communication. Some productivity improvement was made in agriculture and wholesale and retail trade, whereas mining, finance, insurance and real estate and services and government made hardly any progress.

The bottom part of table 3 shows relative productivity growth between Korea and the United States. In comparative terms, most progress was made in electricity, gas and water and in construction. US productivity in manufacturing rose fairly rapidly during the whole period, so comparative performance in manufacturing was somewhat disappointing. In agriculture, finance, insurance and real estate, and in services and government, Korea did not catch up much with the United States. In finance, insurance and real estate it even fell behind during the 1970s.

Table 4
GDP per Hour Worked, by Sector
Korea/United States, 1963-90
(USA=100)

	1963	1970	1975	1980	1985	1990
Agriculture, Forestry & Fisheries	4.3	4.3	4.0	4.2	5.0	4.8
Mining	4.2	2.6	9.3	7.1	5.3	7.5
Manufacturing						
Census	5.2	8.4	11.7	13.7	16.5	28.1
National Accounts	7.1	10.0	11.8	14.6	17.3	20.9
Electricity, Gas & Water	2.2	4.7	5.4	10.9	24.2	24.7
Construction	6.6	21.7	19.4	26.3	38.7	54.7
Transport & Communication	7.8	13.0	20.4	21.1	25.8	29.0
Wholesale & Retail Trade	13.2	15.8	18.5	14.7	14.7	21.6
Finance, Insurance & Real Estate	26.5	24.7	27.9	23.8	23.1	26.5
Services & Government	48.9	45.2	56.0	57.5	58.6	64.5
Total Economy	10.6	13.2	13.9	16.3	20.6	27.6

Source: Based on tables 2 and 3; manufacturing census estimate from Pilat (1994a).

The international comparisons from table 2, for the benchmark 1985, and the time series underlying table 3 are combined in table 4. Agricultural productivity remained at a very low productivity level of less than 5 percent of the United States. Again, this pattern is remarkably similar to that of Japan, where agriculture also stagnated during the postwar period.

The table shows two estimates for manufacturing. One is based on the national accounts series, the other uses the basic census sources. The estimates are remarkably similar, except for the last two years, where the census shows a rapid productivity increase and the national accounts a slow one. Productivity in mining remained at a very low level.

The bottom part of the table shows the service sectors of the economy. By 1963, services and government, but also finance, insurance and real estate already had relatively high productivity levels. In finance, insurance and real estate, as well as in wholesale and retail trade, productivity catch up was limited. In services and government, international productivity differences seem generally much smaller than in goods- producing sectors, such as agriculture and manufacturing, which is confirmed by the Korean productivity levels. Overall, GDP per hour worked rose from only 10.6 percent of the United States in 1963 to 27.6 percent in 1990. GDP per person engaged rose from 11.2 percent in 1963 to 36.6 percent in 1990.

4 Explaining Productivity Levels

What explains the still rather low labour productivity levels in the Korean economy? This section looks primarily at capital intensity and quality of labour as explanatory factors, but also discusses some complementary factors.

4.1 *Capital Intensity*

Estimates of Korean capital stock have been made by Pyo (1988, 1992). The lack of data before 1953, two major wars and the division of the country make it difficult to derive estimates of Korean capital stocks based on the perpetual inventory method, in particular for subsectors. Pyo's estimates are based on benchmark surveys of capital stocks and updated with investment series through the polynomial benchmark method (Pyo, 1988). These figures are available in considerable detail and correspond to the ISIC sectoral breakdown. For the United States, I have used estimates published by BEA (BEA, 1993).

Graph 1 shows the available stock of capital per person engaged, in Korea as a percentage of the United States. There is little difference between capital intensity developments including and excluding structures. Most attention has recently been focussed on capital equipment as the main driver of productivity change and economic growth (De Long and Summers, 1992). In 1963, Korean workers had on average only 6 to 7 percent of the equipment of their US counterparts at their disposal. In manufacturing, this ratio was substantially higher, but fell during part of the 1960s, as investment in capital equipment did not keep up with employment growth in manufacturing (Pilat, 1994a). Since the 1960s, the stock of equipment per person has expanded rapidly, but in 1989, Korean workers still had only 35 percent of the capital equipment of their US counterparts.

Within the economy there are several areas where Korean capital intensity is still very low. This is primarily the case in agriculture and mining. Low capital intensity is partly a reflection of the relative factor endowments of Korea and the United States. Greater availability of labour at low cost and relative scarcity of capital makes it imperative for Korea to use labour-intensive production processes. Recently, Korean wages have rapidly increased and capital intensity will have to rise substantially as well.

Graph 1
Capital Stock and Capital Equipment per Person, Korea/United States, 1963-89

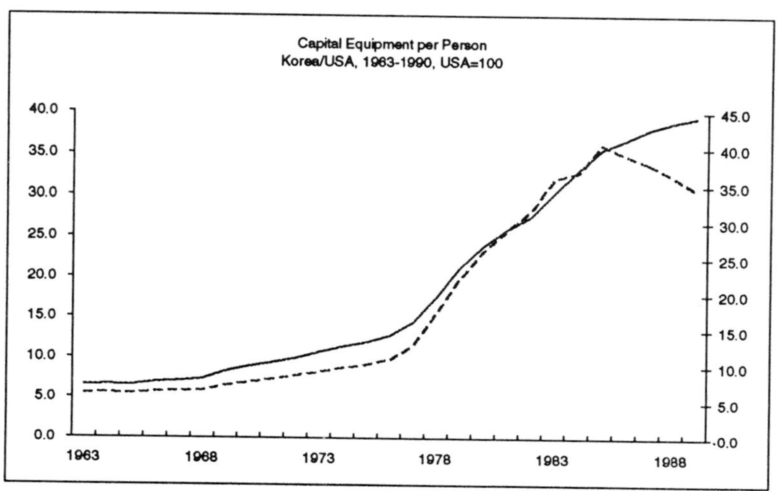

Sources: Capital stock Korea from Pyo (1988, 1992), for United States from BEA (1993); persons engaged from Pilat (1994a).

Differences in capital intensity explain only a limited part of the productivity gap between the two countries, even though the gap in capital intensity is quite substantial. This is partly the result of the low share of capital in total income, only 30 to 35 percent on average. Recent growth theorists have argued that the coefficient of capital may be substantially higher if account is taken of externalities. Table 5 shows the explanatory value of capital for three alternative capital shares, namely the actual average share based on factor incomes (approximately 0.35), 0.5 and 0.7.

Table 5
Labour Productivity, Capital Intensity
and Joint Factor Productivity
Korea/United States, 1963-89, USA=100

	1963	1970	1975	1980	1985	1989
Whole Economy						
GDP per Hour Worked	8.7	10.9	11.4	13.5	17.0	21.1
Capital Stock per Person	6.6	8.9	11.9	23.8	35.5	39.4
Equipment per Person	6.2	7.8	10.3	26.1	40.5	34.5
Joint Factor Productivity						
Average capital share	29.9	29.1	29.8	25.7	29.3	34.0
Capital share = 0.5	37.6	41.5	40.1	34.0	35.6	41.8
Capital share = 0.7	67.4	70.9	66.2	49.2	47.8	54.9
Capital Productivity	169.2	165.2	146.7	89.7	77.9	86.6

Sources: Whole economy GDP per hour based on table 4, capital stock from BEA (1993) and Pyo (1992) converted to 1985 US dollar with 1985 PPPs supplied by Alan Heston.

With capital's share at 0.5, capital intensity 'explains' 29 percent of the overall productivity gap in 1963 and 21 percent in 1989. Joint factor productivity is a combination of two partial productivity measures, labour productivity and capital productivity. The relatively large explanatory effect of capital intensity is related to relatively high capital productivity.

4.2 *The Quality of Labour Input*

Education has been an important component of Korean economic growth. A substantial part of growth between 1963 and 1990 can be directly related to education (Pilat, 1994a). To what extent does a low level of education still play a role in explaining productivity differences between Korea and the United States? Table 6 shows the distribution of the Korean workforce over four educational levels.

Table 6
Distribution of Employment According to Highest Level of General Education, Korea/United States, 1987

	Elementary or Junior High School	Senior High School	Junior College	Senior College & University	Total
Korea					
Manufacturing	47.4	43.7	3.1	5.8	100.0
Whole Economy	40.9	44.0	4.2	10.8	100.0
United States					
Manufacturing	20.8	45.0	16.5	17.7	100.0
Whole Economy	16.6	40.0	20.5	22.9	100.0

Sources: Korea from Ministry of Labor, Yearbook of Labor Statistics 1988, Seoul, 1988; United States from BLS, Current Population Survey 1987, Washington DC, 1991.

The Korean workforce has on average a lower level of education than that of the United States. More than 40 percent of the workforce had less than senior high school in 1987 and only 11 percent had a college or university degree. Weighting the employment distribution with relative earnings weights shows that the Korean workforce has reached a 'quality' level of almost 90 percent of the United States. The explanatory effect of education is therefore, at least directly, quite small.

In manufacturing, the average level of schooling is lower in both countries. Less than 10 percent of the Korean workforce had more than a high school degree in 1987, compared with almost 35 percent in the United States.

Formal education is only one component of the contribution of labour quality to productivity differences across countries. In-company training can also play a major role and for Japan research suggests that this is an important factor contributing to productivity performance. This is less evident for Korea, but in general it appears that the quality of the workforce is not an immediate constraint on Korean productivity performance.

4.3 *Other Explanations*

Low capital intensity still explains a substantial part of the productivity gap between the two countries. Differences in education and training, however, appear limited and play only a small role. Other explanations have to be found therefore. One possible explanation are structural differences. If the Korean economy is relatively more engaged in activities with low absolute productivity than the US economy, its overall productivity level will be lower. Adjusting for this structural effect (Pilat, 1994a) suggests a rather limited contribution, however. Some specific factors, such as lack of natural resources and land scarcity may help explain low productivity in agriculture and mining.

The remaining productivity gap may to a considerable degree have to be explained from efficiency differences, such as poorer organisation of production, overstaffing, lack of specialisation or slow diffusion of knowledge (Pack and Westphal, 1986). Such evidence is ill suited to quantification at the macro-level and must be gathered from industry-specific studies. Further research in this area may have to rely more on such micro- economic evidence.

5 Relative Price Levels

International comparisons of sectoral output and productivity also provide information on relative price levels of countries. The relative price level is defined as the purchasing power parity divided by the exchange rate (Heston and Summers, 1993). Price levels are regarded as one of the important byproducts of international comparisons and have been extensively discussed in the literature (Kravis and Lipsey, 1983; Falvey and Gemmel, 1991).

Table 7
Alternative Conversion Factors for GDP
Korea/United States, 1975-85 (Won/$US)

	Purchasing Power Parities			Relative Price Levels		
	1975	1980	1985	1975	1980	1985
ICP Benchmarks (Fisher PPP)	219.6	467.7	540.1	45.4	77.0	62.1
Penn World Table Mark V	215.7	416.9	510.4	44.6	68.6	58.7
ICOP Benchmarks (Fisher PPP)	317.4	546.5a	579.0	65.6	90.0a	66.6
Exchange Rate	484.0	607.4	870.0	100.0	100.0	100.0

Note: (a) Updated result, using GDP deflators from Pilat (1994a).

Sources: ICP benchmarks from Kravis, et al. (1982) and from ICP files supplied by Alan Heston; Penn World Table V from Summers and Heston (1991); ICOP PPPs from table 2 and Pilat (1994a); exchange rate from IMF, International Financial Statistics, Washington DC, various issues.

Until recently the ICP investigation was the only source of information on relative price levels of countries. However, the industry of origin approach offers an alternative source for such information. Table 7 compares the Korea/USA ICP benchmark results for 1970 through 1990 with the ICOP benchmarks and its updates. The table also supplies the estimates from the Penn World Table (version V, see Summers and Heston, 1991) and the exchange rate for the same years.

In particular for 1975 there appears to be a significant difference between the ICP estimates (both the benchmark and the Penn World Table estimate), and the industry of origin estimate. For 1985 the difference is much smaller. Pilat (1994a) shows that for total GDP the two ICOP estimates for 1975 and 1985 were reasonably consistent. Consistency of the two ICOP PPPs implies that the ICP estimates shown for these years are apparently much less consistent. The difference in results between the two approaches has not yet been scrutinised carefully. However, even without the international comparative aspect, national accounts for several countries show large discrepancies between the expenditure approach and the industry of origin approach. Paige and

Bombach (1959) also found a big gap between their industry of origin estimates and the expenditure estimates of Gilbert and Kravis (1954). This is an area where more research needs to be done.

Graph 2
Purchasing Power Parities and the Exchange Rate
Korea/United States, 1953-90 (Won/$US)

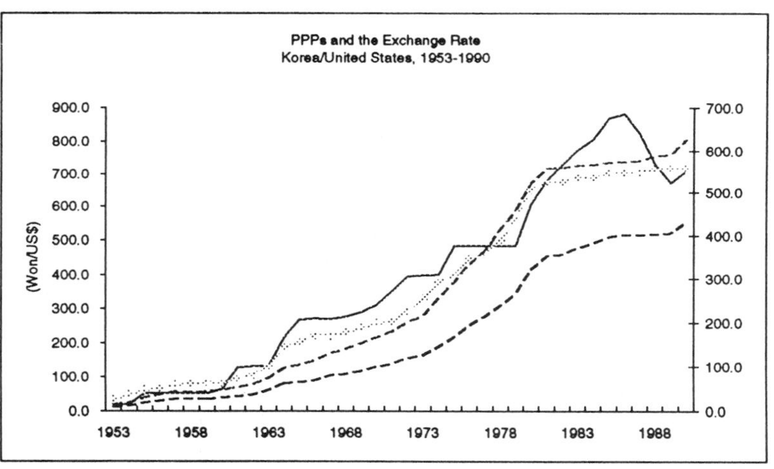

Source: Based on 1985 benchmark, time series from Pilat (1994a).

Graph 2 shows the updated PPPs for total GDP, from both the ICOP and ICP approaches, and the updated PPP for manufacturing. Because of relatively high rates of inflation during its process of economic development and to remain competitive with its exports, the Korean Won has depreciated almost continuously since 1953. Since 1986 this pattern has changed as the Won appreciated. The two PPPs for GDP are a reflection of the relative price changes between Korea and the United States. Both show a rapid growth of the PPP up to 1981, after which inflation in Korea levelled off. The movements of the PPPs are quite similar, and the level for both is also substantially below the exchange rate, which reflects the low price levels generally found for developing countries such as Korea (Bhagwati, 1984).

The PPP for manufacturing is significantly higher than the PPPs for GDP. Before 1961, the manufacturing PPP was almost double the exchange rate. After 1961, continuous devaluations of the Won have kept the manufacturing PPP and the exchange rate close together, except for a short period in the late 1970s, as the Korean Won became somewhat overvalued. Since the appreciation of the Won in 1986, manufacturing PPPs have risen significantly above the exchange rate. In this respect, Korea still conforms to the Balassa model (Balassa, 1964), i.e. its manufacturing price level is considerably above its GDP price level, which is caused by low prices of services.

Table 8
Sectoral Relative Price Levels
Korea/United States, 1953-90
(USA=100)

	1953	1960	1965	1973	1980	1985	1990
Agriculture, Forestry & Fisheries	191	186	103	99	215	213	285
Mining	80	134	59	64	56	56	96
Manufacturing	166	127	74	81	106	81	111
Electricity, Gas & Water	462	441	269	253	280	161	155
Construction	124	144	49	37	65	47	90
Transport & Communication	152	188	66	83	113	93	124
Wholesale & Retail Trade	117	84	60	72	106	87	108
Finance, Insurance & Real Estate	125	74	28	38	83	58	79
Services & Government	19	27	10	16	35	29	44
Total Economy	87	80	42	58	93	71	96

Sources: Based on table 2; updated with GDP deflators from Pilat (1994).

There are also quite large differences between PPPs and relative price levels for different sectors of the economy. Table 8 illustrates these differences. In 1953, the Korean Won was set at a very high level, resulting in high price levels in almost every sector of the economy. The US government put intense pressure on the Rhee government to devalue the Won, but this devaluation came about only after the fall of Rhee's government in 1960 (Haggard, Kim and Moon, 1990). Up to 1965 the relative price level fell gradually as the Won depreciated much faster than suggested by relative inflation figures.

Similar to the Japanese situation, the agricultural price level in Korea moved to great heights. In 1990 it was almost three times the US price level, suggesting high rates of protection in this sector. The PPP for manufacturing has stayed close to the exchange rate, leading to Korean price levels comparable to those in the United States. However, within manufacturing there are considerable differences between sectors, and several branches have price levels below those in the United States, giving a strong competitive position to these branches. The largest gap between US and Korean price levels is in services and government, where Korea was at price levels less than 45 percent of those in the United States.

6 Concluding Remarks

This paper has provided an overview of Korean comparative price and productivity performance since 1963, based on an industry-of-origin approach. During this period, Korea has shown fast growth in productivity, but as the country came from such low levels, its average productivity level is still quite low. However, if Korea succeeds in maintaining the fast productivity growth it has experienced over the last three decades it may be able to reach productivity levels comparable to those of industrialised countries by the end of the century.

Analysis of productivity levels based on macro-economic assessments of capital intensity, labour quality and structural effects provide only limited insights in the main factors driving productivity performance. Much of the remaining differences in productivity across countries, and even among industrialised countries, appear associated with pure efficiency differences (Van Ark and Pilat, 1993; McKinsey, 1993). More work combining micro-economic and macro-economic analysis is required to gain deeper insights in the important phenomena at hand.

References

Ark, B. van (1995) , *The Economics of Convergence - A Comparative Analysis of Industrial Productivity since 1950*, Edward Elgar, Aldershot, forthcoming.

Ark, B. van and D. Pilat (1993) , 'Productivity Levels in Germany, Japan and the United States: Differences and Causes', *Brookings*

Papers on Economic Activity (Microeconomics), No. 2, pp. 1-69.

Balassa, B. (1964) , 'The Purchasing Power Parity Doctrine: A Reappraisal', *Journal of Political Economy*, Vol. 72, February, pp. 584-96.

Bhagwati, J.N. (1984) , 'Why are Services Cheaper in the Poor Countries', *Economic Journal*, Vol. 94, pp. 279-86.

Falvey, R.E. and N. Gemmell (1991) , 'Explaining Service-Price Differences in International Comparisons', *American Economic Review*, Vol. 81, December, pp. 1295-309.

FAO (1986) , *Intercountry Comparisons of Agricultural Production Aggregates*, FAO Economic and Social Development Paper, No. 61, Rome.

Gilbert, M. and I.B. Kravis (1954) , *An International Comparison of National Products and the Purchasing Power of Currencies*, OECC, Paris.

Goldsmith, R.W. (1983) , *The Financial Development of India, Japan and the United States D A Trilateral Institutional, Statistical, and Analytical Comparison*, Yale University Press, London.

Haggard, S., B.K. Kim and C.I. Moon (1990) , *The Transition to Export-Led Growth in South Korea, 1954-1966*, World Bank Working Papers WPS 546, Washington DC, November.

Heston, A. and R. Summers (1993) , 'Temporal Consistency of Benchmark Estimates and Catch-Up', in: A. Szirmai, B. van Ark and D. Pilat (eds), *Explaining Economic Growth - Essays in Honour of Angus Maddison*, North Holland, Amsterdam, pp. 353-73.

Hill, T.P. (1977) , 'On Goods and Services', *Review of Income and Wealth*, Series 23, no. 4, December, pp. 315-38.

IAEEA (1991) , *Science Achievement in 24 Countries*, International Association for the Evaluation of Educational Achievement, Pergamon Press.

Kravis, I.B. (1976) , 'A Survey of International Comparisons of Productivity', *The Economic Journal*, Vol. 86, March, pp. 1-44.

Kravis, I.B., A. Heston and R. Summers (1982) , *World Product and Income*, Johns Hopkins University Press, Baltimore.

Kravis, I.B. and R.E. Lipsey (1983) , *Toward an Explanation of National Price Levels*, Princeton Studies in International Finance, No. 52, November.

Lindauer, D.L. (1984) , *Labor Market Behavior in the Republic of Korea*, World Bank Staff Working Paper No. 641, World Bank, Washington DC.

Mark, J.A. (1982) , 'Measuring Productivity in Service Industries', *Monthly Labor Review*, Vol. 105, June, pp. 3-8.

McKinsey (1993) , *Manufacturing Productivity*, McKinsey Global Institute, Washington DC.

Mulder, N. and A. Maddison (1993) , *The International Comparison of Performance in Distribution: Value Added, Labour Productivity, and Purchasing Power Parities in Mexican and US Wholesale and Retail Trade 1975/7*, Groningen Growth and Development Centre, Research Memorandum GDD2.

O'Mahony, M. (1992) , 'Productivity Levels in British and German Manufacturing Industry', *National Institute Economic Review*, February, pp. 46-63.

Paige, D. and G. Bombach (1959) , *A Comparison of National Output and Productivity*, OECC, Paris.

Pack, H. (1987) , *Productivity, Technology and Industrial Development - A Case Study in Textiles*, Oxford University Press, New York.

Pack, H., and L.E. Westphal (1986) , 'Industrial Strategy and Technological Change - Theory versus Reality', *Journal of Development Economics*, Vol. 22, pp. 87-128.

Pilat, D. (1993) , 'The Sectoral Productivity Performance of Japan and the United States, 1885-1990', *Review of Income and Wealth*, Vol. 39, No. 4, December, pp. 357-75.

Pilat, D. (1994a) , *The Economics of Rapid Growth: The Experience of Japan and Korea*, Edward Elgar Publishers, Aldershot.

Pilat, D.(1994b) , 'Comparative Productivity in Korean Manufacturing, 1967-1987', *Journal of Development Economics*, forthcoming.

Prasada Rao, D.S. (1993) , *International Comparisons of Agricultural Output and Productivity*, FAO Economic and Social Development Paper No. 112, FAO, Rome.

Pyo, H.K. (1988) , *Estimates of Capital Stock and Capital/Output Coefficients by Industries for the Republic of Korea (1953-1986)*, KDI Working Paper No. 8810, Korea Development Institute, Seoul.

Pyo, H.K. (1992) , *A Synthetic Estimate of the National Wealth of Korea, 1953-1990*, KDI Working Paper No. 9212, Korea Development Institute, Seoul, May.

Rostas, L. (1948) , *Comparative Productivity in British and American Industry*, Cambridge University Press, Cambridge.

Smith, A.D. (1989) , 'New Measures of British Service Outputs', *National Institute Economic Review*, May, pp. 75D88.

Smith, A.D. and D.M.W.N. Hitchens (1985) , *Productivity in the Distributive Trades D A Comparison of Britain, America and Germany* Cambridge University Press, Cambridge.

Smith, A.D., D.M.W.N. Hitchens and S. Davies (1982) , *International Industrial Productivity*, Cambridge University Press, Cambridge.

Souza, A.J. de, and C. Michalka (1988) , 'A Methodology for Collecting Construction Prices', in: J. Salazar-Carillo and D.S. Prasada Rao (eds), *Comparisons of Prices and Real Products in Latin America*, North Holland, Amsterdam.

Summers, R. and A. Heston (1991) , 'The Penn World Table (Mark 5); An Expanded Set of International Comparisons, 1950-1988', *Quarterly Journal of Economics*, Vol. CVI, No. 2, May, pp. 327-68.

Statistical Sources:

Bank of Korea (1990) , *National Accounts 1990*, Seoul, 1990.

Bank of Korea, *Input-Output Tables*, Seoul, various issues.

Bureau of Economic Analysis (BEA) (1993) , *Fixed Reproducible Tangible Wealth in the United States, 1925-1989*, Washington DC.

Bureau of Labor Statistics (1991) , *Current Population Survey 1987*, Washington DC.

Economic Planning Board (EPB) , *Economically Active Population Survey*, Seoul, various issues.

Economic Planning Board (EPB) , *Report on Mining and Manufacturing Survey*, Seoul, various issues.

Economic Planning Board (EPB) , *Report on Mining and Manufacturing Census*, Seoul, various issues.

Economic Planning Board (EPB) , *Wholesale and Retail Census*, Seoul, various issues.

Economic Planning Board (EPB) , *Census of Construction*, Seoul, various issues.

International Monetary Fund (IMF) , *International Financial Statistics*, Washington DC, various issues.

Ministry of Labor , *Report on the Monthly Labor Survey*, Seoul, various issues.

Ministry of Labor (1988) , *Yearbook of Labor Statistics 1988*, Seoul.

National Statistical Office (1992) , *Korea Statistical Yearbook 1992*, Seoul.

International Comparisons of Prices, Output and Productivity
Edited by D.S. Prasada Rao and J. Salazar-Carrillo

CHINA: THE DOLLAR VALUE OF GROSS DOMESTIC PRODUCT

Robert Michael Field
11020 Wickshire Way Rockville, MD
U.S.A.

I. Introduction

Is China the world's second largest economy?[1] Is it the third largest, ranking just ahead of Germany? [2] Or is it ninth, sandwiched between Brazil and Australia?[3] Is its GDP more than half of the GDP of the United States? Or a quarter? Or less than a tenth?

In the past three years, at least half a dozen estimates of China's GDP have been published that range from some 300 billion US dollars to more than 3 trillion dollars. The lower figures were converted from *yuan* at the official trade rate of exchange; the higher were obtained by the calculation of purchasing power parities (PPPs). [4] But even

---

[1]Summers, Robert, and Heston, Alan, "The PENN World Table (Mark 5) : An Expanded Set of International Comparisons, 1950-1988," *The Quarterly Journal of Economics*, May 1991, p. 239 ff. The latest revision of the data (PWT, Mark 5.5), which has data through 1990, is available on diskette from the National Bureau of Economic Research in Cambridge, Massachusetts.

[2]International Monetary Fund, *World Economic Outlook, May 1993*, pp. 116-117. China's ranking is based on the shares of GDP in the world total given in Table 33, except for China's, which is taken from Chart 32.

[3]World Bank, *World Development Report 1993*, pp. 242-243.

[4]Early in its world, the United Nations International Comparison Programme found that "the purchasing power of the currency of low-income countries relative to that of very high-income countries is often two or three times as great as the exchange rate would indicate" and that the use of the exchange rate to convert national-accounts aggregates would "lead to a correspondingly large understatement of the low-income countries's relative real income". See Irving B. Kravis, Alan Heston and Robert Summers, *World Product and Income: International comparisons of real gross product*, 1982, p. 3.

The IMF concluded recently that "[market exchange rate] weights may not be accurate measures of the relative economic size of countries" (see Annex IV, "Revised Weights for the *World Economic Outlook*" in IMF, *op. cit.*) and has switched to the use of PPP weights to measure of the share of a country's GDP in world or regional totals.

among the PPP estimates, the highest is 2.7 times the lowest. This chapter presents a new PPP estimate of 1.5 trillion *dollars* in 1992, which puts China's per capita GDP at about the same level as India's.

Section 2 discusses the idiosyncrasies of the system of national accounts now used in China and its relationship to the material product system of accounts inherited from the former Soviet Union. Section 3.1 presents an estimate of China's GDP in current and constant *yuan* and dollars. Section 3.2 compares it with recent estimates of the World Bank, the International Monetary Fund, and PENN World Tables. Section 4 examines the outlook for future work on China's GDP. The derivation of the estimate presented in this chapter is shown in detail in the statistical appendix.

2. A Note on China's National Accounts[5]

When China joined the World Bank in 1980, its statisticians began to study standard national accounts (SNA) and the national accounts of other countries, and to produce explanatory material and estimates, particularly for the tertiary sector.[6] Officially published gross national product data first appeared in the 1986 statistical communique on social and economic development and the 1987 statistical yearbook. In the last six years, the Chinese have published an increasing amount of detail:[7]

The 1988 yearbook - series in current prices and indexes for the primary, secondary, and tertiary sectors ;

The 1990 yearbook - a series and an index for construction ;

The 1991 yearbook - series and indexes for industry, freight transport, and commerce ;

[5]This presentation of China's national accounts in an input-output format is taken from Robert Michael Field, "Macroeconomy : Fluctuation and Change", *China's Economic Reform*, Walter Galenson, *ed.*, San Francisco: The 1990 Institute, 1992, pp. 232-236.

[6]For a detailed account of the process by which these GNP data were developed, see Jeffrey R. Taylor, "Gross National Product Statistics for China", *China Statistics Monthly*, No. 5-6-7, August-September-October 1988, pp. 1-6.

[7]See State Statistical Bureau, *Zhongguo tongji nianjian, 1988,* Beijing : Tongji chubanshe, 1988 and the volumes for succeeding years.

The 1992 yearbook - a series and an index for gross domestic product.

And finally, in August 1991, I obtained from officials at the State Statistical Bureau (SSB) a series and an index for nonmaterial services.[8] Except for the figures in the 1987 input-output table[9], the SSB has never published statistics on GDP by final expenditure – that is, on private consumption, gross fixed investment, changes in inventory, government spending, or net exports.[10]

Since the 1950s, the Chinese have used–and still continue to use–the material product system (MPS) of national accounts. This system, which is loosely based on the Marxist labor theory of value, was developed in the Soviet Union and was used only in socialist (or formerly socialist) countries. Under MPS, only economic activities that produce, transport or otherwise facilitate the production of physical objects are included. For example, transport is limited to the movement of freight, and services such as health, education, finance, insurance, and public administration are ignored.[11]

The two major concepts used in MPS accounting are:

- National income (*guomin shouru*), which is equal to the sum of the net values of the five material production sectors. The differences between national income and GDP are that national income (1) excludes depreciation, and (2) includes only those nonmaterial services that are used as inputs by the material production sectors.

---

[8] Because the data have been revised since then, the data on nonmaterial services can no longer be used, but they do indicate that the data could have been added to the statistical yearbook.

[9] State Planning Commission, Centre of Economic Forecasting and State Statistical Bureau, Department of Statistics on Balances of National Economy, *Input-Output Tables of China, 1981*, Honolulu: University of Hawaii Press, 1987.

[10] Cheng Xiaonong–who was working as a research fellow at the Chinese Institute for Economic Reform in 1987–made a set of unofficial estimates for 1978-1986 that was published in "The Macroeconomy in the Reform: Distribution and Utilization of National Income", *Jingji yanjiu* [Economic Research], No. 8, 1987, pp. 16-28.

[11] For an excellent treatment of China's national income accounts and the methods by which the data are compiled, see Shigeru Ishikawa, *National Income Formation and Capital Formation in Mainland China*, Tokyo: The Institute of Asian Economic Affairs, 1965.

- National income utilized (*guomin shouru shiyong*), which is equal to the sum of household consumption, institutional consumption, and accumulation. National income utilized corresponds most closely to the SNA concept of gross domestic purchases. The differences are that (1) household and institutional consumption under MPS include some nonmaterial services; (2) household consumption is narrower and institutional consumption broader than the corresponding SNA concepts of consumption and government; and (3) the MPS concept of accumulation excludes investment whereas the SNA concept of investment includes them.

These categories are related in the same way as GDP calculated by industry and GDP calculated by final expenditure. The MPS identity is: $NI = C + A + X - M + L + S$ where NI equals national income, and C, A, X, M, L, and S equal consumption, accumulation, exports, imports, material losses, and statistical discrepancy, respectively.

The clearest way to show the difference between national income and GDP is to examine the small MPS and SNA input-output tables for 1987 shown in Figures 1 and 2.[12] The five material production sectors shown in Figure 1 are agriculture, industry, construction, freight transport, and commerce. Depreciation is not included in intermediate input, but neither is it included in net value. The Chinese calculate the net value of agriculture by the "production method" (gross value less the value of material input); the net value of construction, freight transport and commerce by the "distribution method" (the sum of wages, profit, taxes, and interest); and the net value of industry by both methods.[13]

---

[12]Because the SSB used preliminary figures to balance the 1987 input-output tables, national income, consumption, and accumulation in the MPS table and GDP in the SNA table differ only slightly from the values published in the statistical yearbook. See, for example, State Statistical Bureau, *Zhongguo tongji niannjian*, I99I, pp. 31, 32, and 40.

[13]The net value of output at large and medium industrial enterprises in 1987 calculated by the two methods (in billion current *yuan*) is, as follows:

Production method 189.4
Distribution method 189.8

See State Statistical Bureau, *Zhongguo dazhongxing gongye chiye* [China's Large and Medium Scale Enterprises], Beijing: China Urban Economics Society Press, 1989, p 310.

Figure 1. China: MPS Input-Output Table for 1987 in Billion *Yuan*

	Agriculture	Industry	Construction	Freight transport	Commerce	Major repair	Household consumption	Institutional consumption	Accumulation	Net exports	Statistical discrepancy	Gross value
Agriculture	68.8	136.5	1.2	0.0	9.1	0.0	218.0	2.6	21.6	7.8	2.0	467.6
Industry	61.4	652.0	155.6	18.9	31.5	56.9	282.9	53.5	102.3	-31.2	-2.5	1381.3
Construction	0.0	0.0	0.0	0.0	0.0	63.6	0.0	0.0	179.5	0.0	0.0	243.1
Freight transport	4.6	25.4	5.9	0.6	1.2	1.0	13.2	5.1	2.8	8.5	-0.1	68.2
Commerce	4.3	61.3	9.2	1.4	4.2	2.1	35.5	15.5	7.4	-9.5	0.1	131.5
Depreciation	10.1	63.2	5.1	10.5	5.9							
Netvalue	318.3	443.0	66.1	36.8	79.6							
Gross value	467.6	1381.3	243.1	68.2	131.5							

Source: State Statistical Bureau, *Zhongguo touru chanchu biao, 1987 niandu* [Input-Output Table of China, 1987], Beijing: Zhongguo tongji chubanshe, 1991, pp. 322-325.

Figure 2. China: SNA Input-Output Table for 1987 in Billion *Yuan*

	Agriculture	Industry	Construction	Freight transport	Commerce	Non-material services	Household consumption	Institutional consumption	Investment	Net exports	Statistical discrepancy	Gross value
Agriculture	68.8	136.5	1.2	0.0	9.1	2.3	217.6	0.7	21.6	7.8	2.0	467.6
Industry	61.4	652.0	155.6	18.9	31.5	65.2	260.2	11.5	159.2	-31.9	-2.4	1381.3
Construction	0.0	0.0	0.0	0.0	0.0	0.0	0.0	0.0	243.1	0.0	0.0	243.1
Freight transport	4.6	25.4	5.9	0.6	1.2	6.0	12.2	0.1	3.9	8.5	-0.1	68.2
Commerce	4.3	61.3	9.2	1.4	4.2	5.7	33.5	11.8	9.5	-9.5	0.1	131.5
Non-material services	8.2	33.6	1166	4.3	22.4	21.5	70.9	108.9	0.0	3.4	-0.1	274.7
Value added	320.2	472.6	69.5	43.0	63.2	173.9						
Gross value	467.6	1381.3	243.1	68.2	131.5	274.7						

Source: State Statistical Bureau, *Zhongguo touru chanchu biao, 1987 niandu* [Input-Output Table of China, 1987], Beijing: Zhongguo tongji chubanshe, 1991, pp. 24-27.

Final demand consists of major repair and renewal of fixed assets, household consumption, institutional consumption, accumulation, net exports, and a statistical discrepancy. Just as depreciation is not part of national income, so major repair and renewal of fixed assets is not part of national income utilized.[14] The SNA input-output table shown in Figure 2 uses the same five material production sectors as the MPS table but adds a row and column for nonmaterial services. Points to observe about the tables are that:

- The intermediate inputs of the material production sectors are the same in both tables.

- The relationship between value added (SNA) and net value (MPS) for the material production sectors is

$$\text{VA} = \text{NY} + \text{D} - \text{NMS}$$

- where VA equals value added and NV, D, and NMS equal net value, depreciation and the nonmaterial services buried in net value. This is true because the gross values and material inputs are the same.

- Investment (SNA) equals accumulation (MPS) plus major repair and renewal of fixed assets (MPS).

- The sum of the differences between household consumption, institutional consumption, and net exports in the two systems of accounts equals nonmaterial services (SNA) for the material production sectors.

- And finally, estimates of the intermediate consumption of services by the service sector and the final demand for nonmaterial services (which are not included in MPS) must be added.

[14] In the early input-output tables, major repair and renewal of fixed assets was forced to equal depreciation because of the identity that equates national income with the sum of consumption, accumulation, and net exports. See State Planning Commission, Centre of Economic Forecasting and State Statistical Bureau, Department of Statistics on Balances of National Economy, *Input-Output Tables of China, 1981*, Honolulu: University of Hawaii Press, 1987, p. 18.

The continued use of the category institutional consumption as part of final demand in the SNA table is the clearest indication we have that the Chinese have not gone over completely to SNA but have adjusted data collected under the MPS to approximate the categories required by SNA. In fact, they have been working on a new system of national accounts designed to take advantage of those features of each system they consider to be important and to show what they consider to be "Chinese characteristics". However, they have expressed their intention to adopt the revised SNA (1993) standard and to publish more detailed data.

3. The Dollar Value of Gross Domestic Product

3.1 The Field/Taylor Estimate

The Field/Taylor estimate of China's GDP on a PPP basis–in current and constant *yuan* and dollars – is shown in Table 1.[15] In the last 15 years, GDP rose from 359 billion *yuan* to 2,402 billion *yuan*; the aggregate yuan/dollar price ratio rose from 1.237 to 1.618; and the dollar value of GDP rose from $290 billion to $1,485 billion. The indexes of real growth (with 1978 as 100) were 322 in 1990 *yuan* and 331 in 1990 dollars. The Field/Taylor estimate is based on 1981 purchasing power parities by industry of origin for 1981. The PPPs for the six major industries (agriculture, industry, [16] construction, transport, commerce, and nonmaterial services) are derived from the *yuan*/dollar price ratios prepared by Taylor in 1987. [17] The PPPs for agriculture and industry are calculated in two stages, with the unweighted average of the price ratios within branches and the value-added weighted average of the price ratios between branches. The PPP for each industry was moved to other years by adjusting it by the ratio of the Chinese to the US implicit price deflator for the respective industries in the

[15]I am responsible for the calculation of the estimate presented in this chapter but have referred to it as the Field/Taylor estimate to give Jeffrey R. Taylor full credit for the purchasing power parities on which it is based and without which it would not have been possible. Taylor was at the US Bureau of the Census at the time and is currently at the IMF. The IMF estimate was prepared before Taylor joined the Fund.

[16]Industry is defined as mining, manufacturing, and the generation of electric power.

[17]Jeffrey R. Taylor, *Dollar GNP Estimates for China*, Center for International Research, U.S. Bureau of the Census, CIR Staff Paper, No. 59, March 1991.

given year[18]. The Chinese deflators were calculated from value added in current *yuan* and indexes for 1978-1992. [19] The US deflators were calculated by concording value added in current and 1987 dollars for 1978-1990 [20] to Chinese sectors of production and calculating implicit dollar price deflators by industry. [21] Finally, the *yuan*/dollar price ratios are calculated, [22] and the dollar value of GDP by industry is derived from the original data in *yuan* and the PPPs. [23] The differences between the estimate presented here and the original Taylor estimate are that this estimate: (1) uses revised and updated Chinese data; (2) is deflated by indexes for six industries rather than Taylor's three – which were all that were available at the time; and (3) is in both current and 1990 dollars whereas the Taylor estimate is in 1981 dollars for all years.

3.2. A Comparison with Other Recent Estimates

The Field/Taylor estimate of China's GDP is compared with three recent estimates of the dollar value of China's GDP for selected years since 1985 in Table 2. The Field/ Taylor and the IMF estimates (which are between 1.2 and 1.5 trillion dollars in 1991) are at the low end of the range, whereas the PENN World Table estimate (3.4 trillion dollars) is at the high end. The World Bank estimate (1.9 trillion dollars) lies in between. All four estimates are derived by the purchasing power parity method, the two lowest using PPPs by industry of origin and the two highest using PPPs by final expenditure. They are given as reported or as derived from data in their respective sources–except for that of the International Monetary Fund (which I had to reconstruct on the basis of several conversations with specialists at the Fund).

[18]That is, by the change in Chinese prices relative to those in the US within the respective industries.

[19]See Appendix Table A1.

[20]See Appendix Table A3. In 1991, the Bureau of Economic Analysis of the US Department of Commerce revised its method of estimating GDP, controlled the totals to figures from the 1987 input-output table and switched to 1987 constant prices rather than those for 1982.

[21]See Appendix Table A4.

[22]See Appendix Table A5

[23]See Appendix Table A6.

Table 1. China: Gross Domestic Product

	Current prices			Constant prices	
	Billion *yuan*	Yuan/ dollar ratios	Billion dollars	Billion 1990 *yuan*	Billion 1990 dollars
1978	358.81	1.237	290.1	671.0	419.8
1979	399.81	1.163	343.8	719.0	449.6
1980	447.00	1.222	365.7	765.0	481.0
1981	477.51	1.145	417.2	802.4	503.6
1982	518.23	1.128	459.4	873.4	550.6
1983	578.70	1.176	492.2	962.2	607.8
1984	692.82	1.102	628.5	1101.5	697.1
1985	852.74	1.247	683.6	1233.8	782.5
1986	968.76	1.350	717.7	130g.6	827.1
1987	1130.71	1.360	831.7	1477.7	942.g
1988	1407.42	1.463	962.3	1633.7	1044.2
1989	1599.76	1.502	1065.3	1700.7	1092.7
1990	1768.13	1.555	1137.4	1768.1	1137.4
1991	2018.83	1.580	1277.7	1909.9	1224.5
1992	2402.02	1.618	1484.6	2163.2	1388.4

Sources:
Current prices: Billion yuan: Appendix Table A1; *Yuan/dollar ratios*: Derived from the figures in current *yuan* and current dollars; *Billion dollars*: Appendix Table A6.
Constant prices: Billion 1990 yuan: Derived from the figures for 1990 in current *yuan*; and the indexes in Appendix Table Al; *Billion 1990 dollars*: Appendix Table A6.

Estimates Based on Final Expenditure

The World Bank estimate is based on 1986 PPPs that were compiled in China by Ren Ruoen and Chen Kai during 1989-90.[24] They moved the estimate forward to 1991 by the real rate of growth in China and deflated it to 1991 dollars by the implicit US GDP price deflater.

Table 2
China: Alternative Estimates of Gross Domestic Product in Billion Current Dollars

	By industry of origin		By final expenditure	
	Field Taylor	International Monetary Fund	World Bank	PENN World Tables
1985	684			1903
1986	718		1114	2074
1990	1137	1295		3061
1991	1278	1455	1931	3439

Sources: See the text.

[24] Ren Ruoen and Chen Kai, "An Expenditure-Based Bilateral Comparison of Gross Domestic Product Between China and the United States", May 1993. Ren is at the School of Business Management of the Beijing University of Aeronautics and Astronautics. He was a Visiting Scholar at MIT in 1991/92 and a consultant to the World Bank in 1992/93. Chen is at the Economic Development Center of the Ministry of Posts and Telecommunications in Beijing.

The price ratios are based on 210 bilateral comparisons for consumption, 103 for investment, and one for government. The Chinese prices are national averages, where available; otherwise, Ren and Chen used the average of prices in ten geographically dispersed cities [25] .The US prices are drawn from standard government sources,[26] advertisements in papers such as The New York Times, survey reports by consulting firms, and interviews with Chinese scholars living in different US cities. Ren and Chen present price ratios with Chinese and US weights, and their geometric mean; they use the geometric mean to convert China's GDP to dollars.

The PENN world tables estimate is based on 1985 PPPs for consumption, investment,and government. Generally speaking, countries report prices for 400 or so commodities to the UN International Comparison Programme (ICP). These prices are used to derive ratios of the prices in the local currency to the prices in dollars; then the price ratios are grouped and averaged in two stages to obtain 150 detailed price parities and finally PPPs for consumption, investment, and government. [27]

The source of the PPPs used in the PENN World Tables, however, is not known. The authors have never published the details of their estimate for China, and at that time the Chinese had not participated in the ICP. In the past, however, they made extensive use of the PPPs that Professor Irving Kravis estimated following his trip to China in 1975. In his article [28] characterized his estimates as frail "and said they should be regarded as subject to a much wider margin of error"

[25]The national average prices are drawn from SSB, Zhongguo tongji niannjian, 1987 [China Statistical Yearbook, 1987]; State Price Bureau, Zhonggong jiaorong wujia shouce [Price Handbook for Heavy Industry and Transportation], Beijing: Zhongguo Jingji chubanshe, 1986; newspapers; magazines; and other sources. The other prices were collected in sample surveys conducted by research teams that were sent to Beijing, Chengdu, Guangzhou, Kunming, Nanjing, Shanghai, Shenyang, Taiyuan, Wuhan, and Xian.

[26]Sources such as Bureau of the Census, Statistical Abstract of the United States; Bureau of Labor Statistics (BLS), CPI Detailed Report; BLS, Producer Prices and Price Indexes Data; and BL S, Producer Price Indexes Data.

[27]Summers, Robert, and Heston, Alan, "the PENN World Table (Mark 5): An Expanded Set of International Comparisons, 1950-1988", the Quarterly Journal of Economics, May 1991, p. 239 ff.

[28]Kravis , Irving B., "An Approximation of the Relative Real Per Capita GDP of the People's Republic of China", Journal of Comparative Economics, No. 1, 1981, pp. 60-78.

than those for the four lowest-income countries in phase 2 of the ICP (which were regarded as having a 5-percent precision interval).

I moved the PENN World Tables estimate for 1990 in 1990 dollars forward to l991 by the real rate of growth in China and deflated it to 1991 dollars by the implicit US GDP price deflater in order to compare it with the other three estimates.

Despite the fact that the World Bank and the PENN World Tables both start with a figure of 970 billion yuan for China's GDP in 1986, the dollar value of their estimates are very different. To show the nature of the difference, the PPPs for consumption, investment, and government in 1986 are shown in Table 3. The World Bank PPPs for consumption, and government in 1986 are shown in Table 3. The World Bank PPPs for consumption, and investment are half again and nearly double those of the PENN World Tables. Only the PPPs for government are close. In the absence of detail for either estimate, it is not possible to say why they are so different.

Estimates Based on Industry of Origin

Although a figure of 2 trillion dollars is frequently attributed to the IMF[29], the Fund has never released its estimate. To reconstruct the IMF estimate, I followed the procedure it used: (1) I moved Taylor's estimate for 1989 in 1981 dollars to 1990 (the base year the IMF used) by the real rate of growth in China, and (2) deflated it to 1990 dollars by the implicit US GDP price deflater. I then moved it to 1991 in the same way in order to compare the estimate with the other three estimates. By implicit US GDP price deflater, I then moved it to 1991 in the same way in order to compare the estimate with the other three estimates. By basing its estimate on Taylor's figure for 1989 in 1981 dollars, however, the IMF overlooked revised data for the earlier years, and did not take advantage of the data on the six major industries that have become available since Taylor made his estimate to double deflate his 1981 PPPs to 1990.

The Field/Taylor estimate, which makes allowances for these circumstances, is discussed, above.

[29]See, for example, *The Wall Street Journal*, May 28, 1993

4. The Outlook for Work on the Dollar Value of China's GDP

The range between the dollar GDP estimates adopted by international organizations (the IMF and the World Bank) and well-respected organizations (the PENN World Tables) is disturbing. I do not believe

Table 3
China: World Bank and PENN World Tables PPPs for 1986

	World Bank			PENN
	Chinese weights	US weights	Geometric mean	PENN World Tables
Total	0.4880	1.5541	0.8709	0.4679
Consumption	0.4704	0.1867	0.7814	0.5397
Investment	0.9635	2.8417	1.6547	0.861
Government	0.1215	0.1215	0.1215	0.1281

Sources: Ren Ruoen and Chen Kai, "An Expenditure-Based Bilateral Comparison of Gross Domestic Product Between China and the United States", May 1993 (Draft). Summers, Robert, and Heston, Alan, "The PENN World Table (Mark 5): An Expanded Set of International Comparisons, 1950-1988", The *Quarterly* Journal of Economics, May 1991, p. 239 ff. The latest revision of the data (PWT, Mark 5.5), which has data through 1990, is available on diskette from the National Bureau of Economic Research in Cambridge, Massachusetts.

that China has the second or third largest economy in the world, and I draw some comfort from the fact - shown in the tabulation below - that the Field/Taylor estimate of China's GDP per capita (which falls at the lower end of the range) was about the same as India's in 1990 and

1991. However, the range is so wide, the size of the Chinese economy so large, and its ostensible rate of growth so rapid that all of them (including the Field/Taylor estimate) remain open to question.

	GDP (billion dollars)	GDP per capita (dollars)
China		
1990	1,137	1,003
1991	1,278	1,112
India		
1990 (PWT55)	907	1,068
1991 (WB)	996	1,150

Future research will be able to take advantage of more and better data on the Chinese economy. It seems likely that the SSB will:

Release more detailed data on value added by economic sector:

Publish the 1992 input-output table (which will provide data on final expenditure for a second year);

Switch to the full SNA system; and

Compile and release SNA data on final expenditure.

Furthermore, the hoped-for release of the 1990 ICP data for China should help narrow the range of uncertainty about the PPPs, but will not resolve it as the ICP data will only contain information on Shanghai and Guangdong - which are not provinces that can be considered typical of China as a whole. The research problem will then be how to adjust the PPPs for Shanghai and Guangdong to make them representative of the country as a whole.

In short, differences of opinion about the dollar value of china's GDP will remain for some time, but the estimates are likely to converge as more information becomes available and as more work is done.

Meanwhile, the subject continues to be of interest to academics and of great practical importance to China, as their access to credit at concessionary terms from the World Bank depends in part on estimates of dollars GDP.

Appendix Table A1. China: Gross Domestic Product in Current Yuan, Indexes, and Implicit Price Deflators, by Industry

	Total	Agriculture	Industry	Construction	Transport	Commerce	Services
BILLION CURRENT YUAN							
1978	358.81	101.84	160.70	13.82	17.28	26.55	38.62
1979	399.81	125.89	176.97	14.38	18.42	22.02	42.13
1980	447.00	135.94	199.65	19.55	20.50	21.36	50.00
1981	477.51	154.56	204.84	20.71	21.11	22.79	53.50
1982	518.23	176.16	216.23	22.07	23.67	15.96	64.14
1983	578.70	196.08	237.56	27.06	26.49	17.10	74.41
1984	692.82	229.55	278.90	31.67	32.71	28.51	91.48
1985	852.74	254.16	344.87	41.79	40.69	57.70	113.53
1986	968.76	276.39	396.70	52.57	47.56	59.66	135.88
1987	1130.71	320.43	458.58	66.58	54.49	71.42	159.21
1988	1407.42	383.10	577.72	81.00	66.10	98.00	201.50
1989	1599.76	422.80	648.40	79.40	78.60	101.20	269.36
1990	1768.13	501.70	685.80	85.94	111.76	83.70	299.23
1991	2018.83	528.86	808.71	101.51	127.70	124.55	327.50
1992	2402.02	574.40	1012.84	144.68	140.21	141.16	388.73
INDEX (1978=100)							
1978	100.0	100.0	100.0	100.0	100.0	100.0	100.0
1979	107.6	106.1	108.7	102.0	107.7	108.8	107.1
1980	116.0	104.6	122.4	129.2	113.8	107.4	119.7
1981	121.2	111.9	124.5	133.3	116.0	127.6	124.3
1982	131.2	124.8	131.7	137.9	129.5	120.0	147.1
1983	144.9	135.1	144.5	161.4	142.5	134.8	167.4
1984	166.0	152.6	166.0	179.0	163.8	153.6	199.3
1985	187.4	155.4	196.2	218.7	185.9	188.5	230.1
1986	203.3	160.5	215.2	253.4	209.7	201.1	223.6
1987	225.9	168.1	243.6	298.7	230.7	222.5	296.3
1988	251.3	172.3	280.8	322.5	261.5	250.3	337.9
1989	262.2	177.6	295.0	295.3	273.8	227.4	382.0
1990	272.4	190.7	304.9	298.8	279.2	213.1	399.6
1991	294.2	195.2	346.9	327.4	322.5	220.5	409.0
1992	333.0	203.1	418.1	405.3	351.8	237.1	451.3
IMPLICIT PRICE DEFLATORS (PERCENTAGE CHANGE FROM PREVIOUS YEAR)							
1979	3.6	16.5	1.3	2.0	-1.0	-23.8	1.9
1980	3.7	9.5	0.2	7.3	5.3	-1.7	6.2
1981	2.2	6.3	0.9	2.7	1.0	-10.2	3.0
1982	0.3	2.2	-0.2	3.0	0.4	-25.5	1.3
1983	1.1	2.8	0.1	4.8	1.7	-4.6	2.0
1984	4.5	3.6	2.2	5.5	7.4	46.3	3.3
1985	9.0	8.7	4.6	8.0	9.6	64.9	7.5
1986	4.7	5.3	4.9	8.6	3.6	-3.1	23.1
1987	5.0	10.7	2.1	7.4	4.1	8.2	-11.6
1988	11.9	16.6	9.3	12.7	7.0	22.0	11.0
1989	8.9	7.1	6.8	7.1	13.6	13.7	18.3
1990	6.4	10.5	2.3	7.0	39.4	-11.7	6.2
1991	5.7	3.0	3.6	7.8	-1.1	43.8	6.9
1992	5.1	4.4	3.9	15.1	0.7	5.4	7.6

Sources:

Billion Current yuan:

Services: Derived as tertiary industry less transport and commerce. For the value of tertiary industry, see State Statistical Bureau, Zhongguo tongji nianjian, 1993 [China Statistical Yearbook], Beijing: Tongji chubanshe, 1993, p. 31-32.

Other industries: Ibid.

Indexes:

Services:

1978-1990: State Statistical Bureau, Department of Statistics on Balances of National Economy, June 1991.

1981-1992: Appendix Table A2.

Other industries: Ibid.

Implicit price deflators: Derived from the data in current yuan and the indexes.

Appendix Table A2. China: Derivation of an Index of Value Added in Services

	Tertiary	Transport	Commerce	Services
REPORTED INDEX (1978=100)				
1980	114.3	113.8	107.4	119.7
1981	122.2	116.0	127.6	
1982	135.2	129.5	120.0	
1983	152.3	142.5	134.8	
1984	178.3	163.8	153.6	
1985	207.9	185.9	188.5	
1986	213.0	209.7	201.1	
1987	260.8	230.7	222.5	
1988	296.2	261.5	250.3	
1989	316.2	273.8	227.4	
1990	323.0	279.2	213.1	
1991	340.8	322.5	220.5	
1992	373.4	351.8	237.1	
BILLION 1980 YUAN				
1980	91.86	20.50	21.36	50.00
1981	98.21	20.90	25.38	51.94
1982	108.66	23.33	23.87	61.46
1983	122.40	25.67	26.81	69.92
1984	143.30	29.51	30.55	83.24
1985	167.08	33.49	37.49	96.11
1986	171.18	37.78	40.00	93.41
1987	209.60	41.56	44.25	123.79
1988	238.05	47.11	49.78	141.16
1989	254.12	49.32	45.23	159.57
1990	259.59	50.30	42.38	166.91
BILLION 1990 YUAN				
1990	494.69	111.76	83.70	299.23
1991	521.95	129.09	86.61	306.25
1992	571.88	140.82	93.13	337.93
ESTIMATED INDEX (1978=100)				
1980				119.7
1981				124.3
1982				147.1
1983				167.4
1984				199.3
1985				230.1
1986				223.6
1987				296.3
1988				337.9
1989				382.0
1990				399.6
1991				409.0
1992				451.3

Sources:
Reported index:
Tertiary, transport and commerce: State Stastistical Bureau, Zhongguo tongji nianjian, 1993 [China Statistical Yearbook], Beijing: Tongji chubanshe, 1993, pp. 31-32.
Services: State Statistical Bureau, Department Statistics on Balances of National Economy, June 1991.
Billion 1980 yuan:
Tertiary, transport and commerce:
1980: Ibid.
1981-1990: Derived from the value added in 1980 and reported indexes.
Services: Derived as the residual.
Estimated index: Derived from the index number for 1980 provided by the State Statistical Bureau and the estimated value added in 1980 and 1990 yuan.

Appendix Table A3. United States: Gross Domestic Product in Current and 1987 Dollars, by Industry

	1972 Standard Industrial Classification									
	1978	1979	1980	1981	1982	1983	1984	1985	1986	1987
BILLION CURRENT DOLLARS										
Gross domestic product	2232.7	2488.6	2708.0	3030.6	3149.6	3405.0	3777.2	4038.7	4268.6	4539.9
Private industries	1954.6	2180.9	2370.2	2661.7	2769.0	2979.9	3340.4	3570.8	3755.3	4019.4
Agriculture	63.3	74.6	66.7	81.1	77.0	62.7	83.7	84.3	81.7	88.5
Mining	61.4	71.2	112.6	148.1	146.1	127.9	137.1	130.6	82.7	83.0
Construction	110.7	124.8	128.7	129.4	129.4	137.9	161.2	179.2	201.9	213.0
Manufacturing	521.9	575.7	588.3	653.0	747.5	693.3	773.9	798.5	829.3	878.4
Transportation	202.2	219.1	242.2	273.3	292.1	326.7	358.8	378.0	393.8	419.9
Electricity	58.6	60.9	70.4	83.5	94.7	109.8	122.2	129.4	130.2	139.5
Wholesale trade	157.1	178.6	191.6	212.7	216.5	223.6	258.4	276.6	290.9	302.6
Retail trade	214.9	233.2	244.7	269.3	286.6	321.1	361.3	390.9	418.7	440.1
Finance	328.6	370.8	418.4	469.6	503.9	565.3	619.0	681.8	743.5	809.9
Services	294.6	333.0	377.0	425.1	469.8	521.3	586.9	650.9	712.8	784.0
Government	270.5	293.9	324.2	358.1	388.0	415.0	445.9	481.8	512.1	545.3
Statistical discrepancy	7.6	13.8	13.6	10.9	-7.4	10.2	-9.0	-13.9	1.2	-24.8
BILLION 1987 DOLLARS										
Gross domestic product	3703.5	3796.8	3776.3	3843.1	3760.3	3906.6	4148.5	4279.8	4404.5	4539.9
Private industries	3169.7	3238.1	3202.7	3272.6	3246.3	3361.8	3620.4	3759.2	3871.2	4019.4
Agriculture	59.2	62.4	63.2	72.7	73.3	68.4	71.5	81.9	84.5	88.5
Mining	85.0	71.9	79.9	74.2	73.1	71.3	82.0	83.3	83.0	83.0
Construction	198.8	200.3	185.4	174.7	164.9	170.0	190.9	209.0	209.1	213.0
Manufacturing	773.1	337.1	725.4	746.7	711.1	733.8	791.4	810.5	819.1	878.4
Transportation	325.1	335.5	336.3	337.1	331.3	351.7	377.6	381.8	386.9	419.9
Electricity	123.2	123.1	121.6	121.9	114.9	116.8	124.7	128.6	126.5	139.5
Wholesale trade	185.8	195.8	190.5	207.5	218.2	224.2	259.5	273.0	307.1	302.6
Retail trade	338.1	334.8	320.1	330.6	336.8	365.1	397.7	421.4	453.2	440.1
Finance	631.0	667.4	692.8	704.7	708.4	727.9	762.1	776.4	776.6	809.9
Services	573.5	592.8	609.0	64.4	629.2	649.5	687.8	722.0	751.7	784.0
Government	488.3	498.6	508.9	511.6	507.1	512.5	516.9	527.5	536.4	545.3
Statistical discrepancy	12.2	20.6	19.0	13.6	-8.7	11.5	-9.8	-14.7	1.3	-24.8
Residual	33.4	39.6	45.7	45.3	15.6	20.8	21.0	7.7	-4.4	0.0

Appendix Table A3. United States: Gross Domestic Product in Current and 1987 Dollars, by Industry

	1987 Standard Industrial Classification					
	1987	1988	1989	1990	1991	1992
BILLION CURRENT DOLLARS						
Gross domestic product	4539.9	4900.4	5250.8	5522.2	5677.5	5950.7
Private industries	4019.4	4344.0	4622.2	4842.7		
Agriculture	88.5	90.8	104.8	111.3		
Mining	83.0	87.9	84.2	98.5		
Construction	213.0	227.6	235.9	241.3		
Manufacturing	877.8	961.0	1004.6	1018.3		
Transportation	419.8	442.1	463.3	481.9		
Electricity	139.5	143.4	154.5	160.4		
Wholesale trade	303.1	331.0	351.6	359.7		
Retail trade	441.8	471.7	502.5	515.8		
Finance	809.7	866.3	926.5	974.7		
Services	782.5	865.5	948.8	1041.0		
Government	545.3	584.8	627.6	674.1		
Statistical discrepancy	-24.8	-28.4	1.1	5.4		
BILLION 1987 DOLLARS						
Gross domestic product	4539.9	4718.6	4838.0	4877.5	4821.0	4922.6
Private industries	4019.4	4188.0	4288.8	4311.4		
Agriculture	88.5	85.1	88.0	94.2		
Mining	83.0	94.4	83.7	87.7		
Construction	213.0	211.2	212.8	208.5		
Manufacturing	877.8	924.6	932.4	922.8		
Transportation	419.8	431.5	443.0	456.0		
Electricity	139.5	146.3	152.6	154.8		
Wholesale trade	303.1	313.4	329.4	323.1		
Retail trade	441.8	467.0	483.7	478.0		
Finance	809.7	847.4	869.0	868.3		
Services	782.5	813.5	846.8	872.9		
Government	545.3	555.9	567.0	581.7		
Statistical discrepancy	-24.8	-27.4	0.9	4.9		
Residual	0.0	2.1	-18.6	-20.5		

Source: Survey of Current Business, May, 1993, pp.51 ans 54, and July 1993, p. 7.

Appendix Table A4. United States: Gross Domestic Product in Current and 1987 Dollars, and Implicit Price Deflators, by Industry

	1972 Standard Industrial Classification									
	1978	1979	1980	1981	1982	1983	1984	1985	1986	1987
BILLION CURRENT DOLLARS										
Gross domestic product	2232.7	2488.6	2708.0	3030.6	3149.6	3405.0	3777.2	4038.7	4268.6	4539.9
Agriculture	63.3	74.6	66.7	81.1	77.0	62.7	83.7	84.3	81.7	88.5
Industry	641.9	705.5	761.8	871.5	877.1	915.9	1020.8	1051.3	1041.4	1091.6
Construction	110.7	124.8	128.7	129.4	129.4	137.9	161.2	179.2	201.9	213.0
Transportation	143.6	160.5	181.3	202.9	208.6	232.0	249.0	255.8	264.4	289.7
Commerce	372.0	411.8	436.3	482.0	503.1	544.7	619.7	667.5	709.6	742.7
Services	893.7	997.7	1119.6	1252.8	1361.7	1501.6	1651.8	1814.5	1968.4	2139.2
BILLION 1987 DOLLARS										
Gross domestic product	3703.5	3796.8	3776.3	3843.1	3760.3	3906.6	4148.5	4279.8	4404.5	4539.9
Agriculture	59.2	62.4	63.2	72.7	73.3	68.4	71.5	81.9	84.5	88.5
Industry	981.3	972.1	926.9	942.8	899.1	921.9	998.1	1022.4	1028.6	1100.9
Construction	198.8	200.3	185.4	174.7	164.9	170.0	190.9	209.0	209.1	213.0
Transportation	201.9	212.4	214.7	215.2	216.4	234.9	252.9	253.2	260.4	280.4
Commerce	523.9	530.6	510.6	538.1	555.0	589.3	657.2	694.4	760.3	742.7
Services	1692.8	1758.8	1810.7	1840.7	1844.7	1889.9	1966.8	2025.9	2064.7	2139.2
IMPLICIT PRICE DEFLATORS (PERCENTAGE CHANGE FROM PREVIOUS YEAR)										
Gross domestic product		8.7	9.4	10.0	6.2	4.1	4.5	3.6	2.7	3.2
Agriculture		11.8	-11.7	5.7	-5.8	-12.7	27.7	-12.1	-6.1	3.4
Industry		10.9	13.2	12.5	5.5	1.8	2.9	0.5	-1.5	-2.1
Construction		11.9	11.4	6.7	5.9	3.4	4.1	1.5	12.6	3.6
Transportation		6.2	11.7	11.7	2.2	2.5	-0.3	2.6	0.5	1.8
Commerce		9.3	10.1	4.8	1.2	2.0	2.0	1.9	-2.9	7.1
Services		7.4	9.0	10.1	8.5	7.6	5.7	6.6	6.4	4.9

Appendix Table A4. United States: Gross Domestic Product in Current and 1987 Dollars, and Implicit Price Deflators, by Industry

	1987 Standard Industrial Classification					
	1987	1988	1989	1990	1991	1992
BILLION CURRENT DOLLARS						
Gross domestic product	4539.9	4900.4	5250.8	5522.2	5677.5	5950.7
Agriculture	88.5	90.8	104.8	111.3		
Industry	1100.3	1192.3	1243.3	1277.2		
Construction	213.0	227.6	235.9	241.3		
Transportation	280.3	298.7	308.8	321.5		
Commerce	744.9	802.7	854.1	875.5		
Services	2137.5	2316.6	2502.9	2689.8		
BILLION 1987 DOLLARS						
Gross domestic product	4539.9	4718.6	4838.0	4877.5	4821.0	4922.6
Agriculture	88.5	85.1	88.0	94.2		
Industry	1100.3	1165.3	1168.7	1165.3		
Construction	213.0	211.2	212.8	208.5		
Transportation	280.3	285.2	290.4	301.2		
Commerce	744.9	780.4	813.1	801.1		
Services	2137.5	2216.8	2282.8	2322.9		
IMPLICIT PRICE DEFLATORS (PERCENTAGE CHANGE FROM PREVIOUS YEAR)						
Gross domestic product		3.9	4.5	4.3	4.0	2.6
Agriculture		6.7	11.6	-0.8		
Industry		2.3	4.0	3.0		
Construction		7.8	2.9	4.4		
Transportation		4.7	1.5	0.4		
Commerce		2.9	2.1	4.0		
Services		4.5	4.9	5.6		

Notes:

1. The industries in this table are derived from Appendix Table A3, as follows:
   Total = Domestic industries
   Agriculture = Agriculture
   Industry = Mining + Manufacturing + Electricity
   Construction = Construction
   Transport = Transport - Electricity
   Commerce = Wholesale trade + Retail trade
   Services = Finance +services + Government
2. The implicit price deflators are derived from the data in current and 1987 prices.

Source: **Appendix table A3.**

Appendix Table A5. Yuan/Dollar Price Ratios

	Total	Agriculture	Industry	Construction	Transport	Commerce	Services
1978		0.715	1.919	1.349	1.435	2.318	1.319
1979		0.745	1.752	1.230	1.337	1.491	1.250
1980		0.925	1.550	1.185	1.260	1.331	1.218
1981		0.930	1.390	1.140	1.140	1.140	1.140
1982		1.009	1.314	1.108	1.120	0.839	1.065
1983		1.189	1.292	1.123	1.112	0.785	1.009
1984		0.965	1.283	1.139	1.198	1.125	0.986
1985		1.193	1.335	1.211	1.280	1.821	0.993
1986		1.338	1.422	1.168	1.319	1.817	1.149
1987		1.432	1.483	1.211	1.350	1.835	0.969
1988		1.565	1.584	1.267	1.380	2.176	1.029
1989		1.501	1.627	1.318	1.543	2.422	1.160
1990	1.555	1.672	1.616	1.351	2.144	2.055	1.166
1991	1.580						
1992	1.618						

Sources:

Individual industries: Derived from the 1981 yuan/dollar price ratios in Jeffrey R. Taylor, Dollar GNP Estimates for China, U.S. Bureau of the Census, Center for International Research, CIR Staff Paper No. 59, March 1991, and the implicit price deflators in Appendix Tables A1 and A4.

Total:

1990: Derived from the total in current yuan and current dollars. See Appendix Tables A1 and A6.

1991-1992: Derived from the 1990 yuan/dollar price ratio and the implicit yuan and dollar price deflators. See Appendix Tables A1 and A4.

Appendix Table A6. China: Gross Domestic Product in U.S. Dollars, by Industry

	Total	Agriculture	Industry	Construction	Transport	Commerce	Services
BILLION CURRENT U.S. DOLLARS							
1978	290.1	142.4	83.8	10.2	12.0	12.4	29.3
1979	343.8	168.9	101.0	11.7	13.8	14.8	33.7
1980	365.7	147.0	128.8	16.5	16.3	16.1	41.0
1981	417.2	166.2	147.4	18.2	18.5	20.0	46.9
1982	459.4	174.5	164.5	19.9	21.1	19.0	60.2
1983	492.2	164.9	183.8	24.1	23.8	21.8	73.8
1984	628.5	237.8	217.4	27.8	27.3	25.3	92.8
1985	683.6	213.0	258.3	34.5	31.8	31.7	114.3
1986	717.7	206.6	279.0	45.0	36.0	32.8	118.2
1987	831.7	223.8	309.3	55.0	40.4	38.9	164.3
1988	962.3	244.8	364.8	63.9	47.9	45.0	195.9
1989	1065.3	281.6	398.5	60.2	50.9	41.8	232.3
1990	1137.4	300.0	424.3	63.6	52.1	40.7	256.6
1991	1277.7						
1992	1484.6						
BILLION 1990 U.S. DOLLARS							
1978	419.8	157.3	139.2	21.3	18.7	19.1	64.2
1979	449.6	166.9	151.3	21.7	20.1	20.8	68.8
1980	481.0	164.5	170.3	27.5	21.2	20.5	76.9
1981	503.6	176.0	173.3	28.4	21.7	24.4	79.8
1982	550.6	196.3	183.3	29.4	24.2	22.9	94.5
1983	607.8	212.5	201.1	34.4	26.6	25.8	107.5
1984	697.1	240.0	231.0	38.1	30.6	29.4	128.0
1985	782.5	244.5	273.0	46.6	34.7	36.0	147.8
1986	827.1	252.5	299.5	54.0	39.2	38.4	143.6
1987	942.9	264.4	339.0	63.6	43.1	42.5	190.3
1988	1044.2	271.0	390.8	68.7	48.8	47.8	217.0
1989	1092.7	279.4	410.5	62.9	51.1	43.5	245.3
1990	1137.4	300.0	424.3	63.6	52.1	40.7	256.6
1991	1224.5	307.1	482.8	69.7	60.2	42.1	262.6
1992	1388.4	319.5	581.8	86.3	65.7	45.3	289.8

Sources:
Current U.S. dollars:
1978-1990:
Total: Derived as the sum of individual industries.
Individual industries: Derived from the data in current yuan in Appendix table A1 and the yuan/dollar price ratios in Appendix table A5.
1991-1992: Derived from the data in current yuan in Appendix Table A1 and the yuan/dollar price ratios in Appendix Table A5.
1990 U.S. dollars:
Total : Derived as the sum of individual industries.
Individual industries: Derived from the data for 1990 in current yuan and the indexes for 1978-1992 in Appendix Table A1 and the yuan/dollar price ratios for 1990 in Appendix Table A5.

International Comparisons of Prices, Output and Productivity
Edited by D.S. Prasada Rao and J. Salazar-Carrillo

AN ASSESSMENT OF THE UNITED NATIONS SCALE OF ASSESSMENTS, 1946-1994

Lawrence H. Officer
University of Illinois at Chicago
Chicago, USA

Never have so many argued so much about so little money as in the United Nations. – Stoessinger (1964, p. 3)

1. Concept And Application of Scale of Assessments

The focus of this study is the UN scale of assessments, the percentage allocation of UN expenses to its members.[1] Each member state is assigned an assessment rate or assessment, computed to two decimal places, and the sum of the assessments over all countries is typically 100.00 percentage points or, in UN terminology, 10,000 points (a point being one-hundredth of a percentage point).

Two implications follow. First, determination of the scale is a zero-sum game, a clear invitation to country conflict. Second, the amount (generally required to be in dollars) contributed by a country is the product of three factors: (1) the UN budget, (2) one-hundredth the country's assessment rate, and (3) the proportion of the amount due to the United Nations [the product of (1) and (2)] that the country elects to contribute. A country dissatisfied with its assessment rate (or with the UN budget or the activities financed by the budget) can elect a low third factor (below unity) and become in arrears in its UN

[1]For a related study, but focused on the developing countries and the time period 1986-94, see Officer (1994). Sources of institutional information about the scale of assessments are United Nations, General Assembly, Report of the Committee on Contributions (cited as CC Report) and Scale of Assessments for the Apportionment of the Expenses of the United Nations: Report of the Fifth Committee (cited as FC Report), 1st - 46th sessions, 1946-1991, and Note by the Secretariat, Evolution of the Methodology for the Scale of Assessments and its Current Application (cited as Evolution), 24 April 1989; United Nations, Yearbook of the United Nations, 1946-47 to 1986; U.S. Department of State, United States Participation in the United Nations, various issues 1946-47 to 1989.

contribution.[2]

2. Selection of Scales for Study

The objective of this study is to present a history of the UN scale of assessments from three standpoints: first, accepting both the scale and the procedure used by the UN in setting the scale, and analyzing the steps in this procedure (sections 3, 4 and 5); second, accepting the scale itself but simplifying and reinterpreting the procedure via an econometric model (sections 6 and 7); third, rejecting both the UN procedure and the resultant scale, developing an "ideal" scale in its place (sections 8 and 9). The techniques of the second and third standpoints involve moving cross-section analysis over time. Therefore a time series of scales must be identified and selected.

According to the UN Charter, the General Assembly (GA) is responsible for apportioning the expenses of the UN among its members. The GA appoints a Committee on Contributions (CC) to make recommendations concerning that task. Primary elements of the CC's recommendations are the assessment scale itself and the scale period (the year or years for which the scale is applicable), with a three-year scale period envisaged in the GA's rules of procedure. Underlying the

---

[2]The regular budget of the United Nations is distinguished from financing of peacekeeping operations. The scale of assessments has always had direct and precise application to the regular budget. Over the UN history, some peacekeeping activities have been paid from the regular budget, but these operations have uniformly been minor in expense and only two (Jerusalem and India-Pakistan) remain. In two other cases (West New Guinea and Yemen), in the early 1960s, parties to the dispute divided the total costs of the UN presence among themselves. One peacekeeping force (Cyprus) has always been financed by voluntary contributions. The original UN Emergency Force (1956-67), stationed in Egypt, and the UN Congo Force (1960-64) were the first truly expensive peacekeeping undertakings. They were financed on the basis of the scale of assessments for the regular budget but as modified by voluntary contributions and rebates to developing countries.

Since 1973, a special assessment scale has been applied to all new peacekeeping operations. Member countries are divided into four mutually exclusive groups: developed countries, paying their respective regular-budget assessment rates; developing countries, paying 20 percent of their regular rates; least developed countries, paying 10 percent; and permanent members of the Security Council, paying their regular rates plus the shortfall from the developing-country groups in proportion to their regular rates. For histories of the financing of UN peacekeeping operations, see Stoessinger (1964) and James (1989).

CC's recommendations is the "statistical base period", the period for the statistical data used by the CC to determine the scale. In spite of a typical condition of contentious GA debate on any recommended scale, only rarely does that body alter the recommendations of the CC, due largely to the fact that guidelines for the CC's work are set by the GA itself.

Consider the concept of the decision period, the year in which the CC recommends a scale and the GA decides to establish a scale. A decision period yields the pertinent scale of assessments, the scale period, and the underlying statistical base period. The methodology for selecting the time series of scales for this study is as follows:

1. *Consider only decision periods at which all member countries are considered jointly.* The principal reason is that scales are then determined in a pure general-equilibrium setting, with uniform treatment of countries. New members, added between selected decision periods, are excluded until the next decision period. A subsidiary reason for this rule is that the sum of assessments generally totals the original 100.00 percentage points, instead of a higher number derived from adding the assessments of new members to the original number.
2. *Where more than one scale utilizes a given statistical base period, select the scale with the larger number of countries (always the later scale).* This maximizes the size of the country sample.
3. *Exclude scale periods where changes in the scale are trivial* (1948 and 1949).

The resulting time series of quintuples–decision period, scale period, statistical base period, and (representing the scale) UN membership and sum of assessments–are listed in Table 1.[3] The scales themselves are found in the source to the table.

3. Properties of Components of The Scale

The elements of the scale are the steps in the procedure of determining the scale. They may be characterized in three different ways.

[3] All the tables are presented at the end of the paper.

First, a scale element may be objective or subjective in nature. The objective elements are based on statistical data, involve a rigid procedure and order of application, and are completely performed prior to application of the subjective elements. The subjective elements are based on the judgment of the CC and the order of their application is irrelevant (except that, beginning with the 1992-94 scale, the subjective elements became dependent entirely on the voluntary acceptance of additional points by donor countries).[4]

Second, a scale element corresponds to one or more assessment principles embedded in GA resolutions, even though the GA does not always make this correspondence explicit. Ability to pay is and always has been the fundamental principle for the scale. In a resolution of February 13, 1946, the GA stated: "The expenses of the United Nations should be apportioned broadly according to capacity to pay." A GA resolution of December 21, 1991 (among others over the years) reaffirms that "the capacity of Member States to pay is the fundamental criterion for determining the scale of assessments."

Three other principles of assessment have been noted by the GA. Collective financial responsibility is propounded in a GA resolution of December 14, 1976. Level of development is a principle present in many GA resolutions, perhaps best stated as the requirement of drawing up scales "on the basis of...the continuing disparity between the economies of developed and developing countries" (GA resolution of December 14, 1976). Limited assessment change is a principle described as "the need to prevent extreme and excessive variations of individual rates of assessments between two successive scales" in a GA resolution of December 18, 1981 (and similarly elsewhere).

Third, a scale element may have the effect of making the scale progressive, proportional, or regressive–but in two distinct senses. Let A_i denote the assessment of country i, where typically $\Sigma A_i = 100.00$, YS_i the income of country i as a percentage of total income over all countries (so that $\Sigma YS_i = \Sigma A_i$), and YP_i the per capita income of country i (leaving aside the issues of income definition and comparison across countries). Then according as the effect of the element is $\partial A_i / \partial YS_i$ greater than, equal to, or less than unity, the scale is progressive, proportional, or regressive with respect to total income and

[4]It may be noted that the UN reserves the term "element" only for what are called here the "objective elements."

that element. Also, according as the effect of the element is $\partial A_i/\partial YP_i$ greater than, equal to, or less than zero, the scale is progressive, proportional, or regressive with respect to per capita income and that element. The two senses of progressivity are not distinguished in the existing literature.

4. History of The Scale Elements

Consider first the objective scale elements, arranged according to assessment principle, beginning with ability to pay. For the early scales the income concept was net national product (**NNP**) at factor cost; from the 1965 scale onward it was **NNP** at market prices. **NNP** as an income concept makes the scale proportional with respect to total income; for if the procedure were to stop right here, the scale would be identical to the percentage distribution of **NNP** (what the UN calls the national-income scale, but is better described as the **NNP** scale). From the 1986-88 scale onward, **NNP** was replaced by debt-adjusted income, obtained by subtracting repayment of foreign-debt principal (with interest payments already excluded from **NNP**), this element probably making the scale progressive with respect to per capita income.

In every scale, the income of poor countries has been reduced via a low-per-capita-income allowance, making the scale progressive with respect to per capita income. The percentage reduction of income is given by the formula $G[(L-YP_i)/L]$, where G is the gradient (the maximum percentage reduction) and L the per-capita-income limit (income is reduced only if $YP_i < L$). Over the years, G and L have been increased from the original 40 percent and \$1000 to 85 percent and \$2600 in the 1992-94 scale.

For each country, income in current (not constant) prices is averaged over the statistical base period; but, first, annual income must be expressed in a common currency, the U.S. dollar. The principal conversion factor is the current exchange rate (**ER**), in annual-average form. A subsidiary conversion factor is relative purchasing power parity: a base year is selected, and the current-year conversion factor is the product of the base-year exchange rate and the domestic/U.S. current-to-base-year price-index ratio. Eventually called **PARE** (price-adjusted rate of exchange) by the CC and viewed by that body as the ideal conversion factor, its use to date is rare: an unknown, but clearly small, number of cases in early scales and seven countries in the 1992-94 scale.[5]

The CC has considered absolute purchasing power parity (**PPP**) as a conversion factor, but rejected it, primarily for perceived lack of data. Surprisingly, it has evinced no awareness of the exchange-rate conversion bias (**ERCB**), well-known in the economic literature: the positive correlation of **PPP/ER** (both numerator and denominator expressed as number of units of domestic currency per dollar) with per capita income, that implies income is biased downward for lower-income relative to higher-income countries when estimated by nominal (**ER**-converted) income rather than expressed directly in real (**PPP**-converted) terms. The **UN NNP** scale is best termed the nominal **NNP** scale, the percentage distribution of the average of annual nominal **NNP** over the statistical base period. The **ERCB** transforms the proportionality of the nominal **NNP** scale with respect to total income into progressivity of the corresponding real NNP scale with respect to per capita income.[6]

Turning to *collective financial responsibility*, this principle justifies a ceiling (maximum assessment), per-capita ceiling (maximum per-capita assessment, that of the country with the highest assessment), and floor (minimum assessment). The ceiling, with values for all scales shown in the second column of Table 5, has been applicable only to the United States. The floor, originally set at 0.04 percent, changed to 0.02 with the 1974-76 scale and to 0.01 with the 1978-79 scale, has also been in existence for all scales. As the "UN Membership" columns of Table 1 show, in the order of half the members have been assessed at the floor since the 1968-70 scale. The per-capita ceiling, in existence for the 1951-1976 scales, was enjoyed by only a few countries. All three elements are regressive–the ceiling and floor with respect to both total and per capita income, the per-capita ceiling with respect to per capita income.

Level of development provides a second justification of the low

---

[5]Also, in the 1986-88 scale, World Bank data (that employ a kind of relative-**PPP** concept) were used for three countries. For some scales in the 1970s, the problem of conversion was obviated for a few countries, by direct estimation of **NNP** in U.S. dollars.

[6]The implicit real progressivity of a nominally proportional tax was recognized by writers in the traditional burden-sharing literature, though they did not distinguish the two senses of progressivity. See Neale (1961, pp. 36-37), Uri (1963, pp. 46-47), and Pincus (1965, pp. 66-67).

per-capita income allowance and also underlies "no increase in the assessments of the least developed countries" (the latter in effect since the 1983-85 scale). *Limited assessment change* relates to many elements over the years: minimal change in the scale (1948-50 and 1966-67 scales; see Table 1 for details), maximum of ten-percent change in a given assessment (1951 scale), partial removal of discrepancies from income adjusted for low per-capita-income allowance or from ceiling (1952-55 scales), a longer statistical base period (1978-), and a "scheme of limits" (1986-) involving eight assessment brackets each with a maximum percentage change and a maximum percentage-point change.

The hypothetical assessment scale based only on the objective elements is called the *machine scale* and results from the *scale methodology*, that is, application of the elements in a specific order with predetermined methods to reallocate the points shifted by each element.[7]

Considering now the subjective elements of the scale, the process of applying them is called *mitigation of the scale or ad hoc adjustment.* Under ability to pay, mitigation typically corrects for data problems, such as the prewar statistical base period (1946-47 scales) and varying data quality among countries (1951-61 scales). Mitigation has also allowed for casualty losses (due to wars or natural disasters) and such elements as **PARE**, economic events beyond the base period, external debt, and ability to secure foreign exchange–without incorporation in the scale methodology.

Under *level of development*, increases of assessments for developing countries have been mitigated or downward adjustments in assessments made. Similarly, for *limited assessment change*, changes (especially increases) in assessments were mitigated prior to establishment of the scheme of limits. The actual scale of assessments, called the *official scale*, is obtained by mitigating the machine scale, that is, redistributing points in that scale by applying ad hoc adjustment.

5. Importance of The Scale Elements

The quantitative importance of an individual element in the scale is the number of percentage points redistributed among member states by the step (in the UN scale procedure) corresponding to that element

[7]For a complete description of the scale methodology for the 1986-94 scales, see CC Report, 44th sess., 1989, pp. 5, 8, and 46th sess., 1991, pp. 7-9.

relative to the hypothetical scale determined at the *end of the preceding step.* While other definitions are possible, this one respects both the UN scale procedure (the scale methodology plus ad hoc adjustment) and the UN scale itself, which is the viewpoint of sections 3 to 5.

Rows (1) to (6) of Table 2 (inclusive of notes) present all that is known, or can be computed, regarding the importance of individual elements in the scales from 1946 to 1992-94. Until the 1989-91 scale, information is scattered, because the CC was traditionally secretive regarding quantitative aspects of its work.[8] Taking the nominal-NNP scale as the basis, rows (1) to (6), in order, completely specify the remainder of the UN scale methodology plus ad hoc adjustment, except for the exclusion of "no increase in the assessments of the least developed countries."[9]

Because the information for a given element in the scale is so scattered, it is hard to discern behavior over time; but something can be said for each element. Debt adjustment entered the machine scale in 1986-88. It is highly probable that, in spite of a different schemata, that element redistributed less than one percentage point in that period, as it did in the two subsequent periods. The low-per-capita-income allowance is clearly of substantial importance since 1978-79. For earlier scales, it is reasonable to surmise that its impact was somewhat less, because of the lower gradient in the formula.

An upper limit to the number of points redistributed by the floor is the product of the floor assessment and the number of floor countries (countries assessed at the floor, some of which would be there even without application of the floor constraint). For the four available scale

[8]Only in the year 1959 did the CC agree to permit a member state to see its own specific data (income, conversion factor, population, low per-capita-income allowance)–and that in response to a GA resolution (December 10, 1958). It refused to release data for other countries to an individual member, even though, obviously, "it was difficult to ascertain whether increases in assessments were justified without access to the national income data for all Member States" (FC Report, 25th sess., 1970, p. 2). Member countries were treated no differently from scholars; they had to wait patiently for the CC to publish in its future Reports such parts of the data documentation underlying its work as it decided. In fact, the CC released neither the machine scale nor country-comparative income data until the 1983-85 scale.

[9]This element of the scale methodology redistributed 0.02 percentage points in 1983-85 (CC Report, 37th sess., 1982, p. 9) and zero points in the later scales.

periods in Table 2, the ratio of the floor's actual point redistribution to the upper limit is in the .50 - .61 range. If a ratio of .6 is used, the maximum effect of the floor occurred in 1971-73, with importance of 63 x .04 x .6 = 1.51 percentage points.

Of all the elements, the ceiling's importance in the missing periods is the most uncertain. The lower ceiling over time (to 1974-76) increases the effect, but the reduction in U.S. relative nominal income acts to reduce it. The available figures suggest that, on balance, the trend in the ceiling's importance is downward. Information about the scheme of limits is complete for its existence; its importance has been increasing over time. However, there is reason to believe the GA will decide to terminate the scheme of limits.

Except for the 1983-85 aberration, the importance of mitigation has had an upward trend from the early scales (see also *Evolution*, p. 15). Cumulative criticism in the GA against mitigation, combined with making the acceptance of points purely voluntary, decreased the importance of mitigation in 1992-94.

Absent the elements that follow nominal **NNP**, the official scale would be the nominal-**NNP** scale. Information on the latter scale exists only for the scale periods exhibited in Table 2. For the 1986-94 scales, the nominal-**NNP** scale itself is known; for the 1983-85 scale, what is available is only dollar-denominated **NNP**–denoted as NNP_i for country i–and only for countries with assessment above 0.03 percent.[10]

The net joint effect of all scale elements that follow nominal NNP, these elements represented by rows (1) to (6), is $(\Sigma \mid A_i - NNPS_i \mid /2$, where A_i is country i's official-scale assessment and $NNPS_i$ its **NNP**-scale assessment. This computation is made directly for the 1986-94 scales; but for 1983-85 one must resort to a three-step process. First, for the sample, s1, of countries with $A_i > 0.03$, the hypothetical $NNPS_i$ for a UN membership of s1 is $NNP_i(\Sigma^* A_i / \Sigma^* NNP_i)$, where Σ^* denotes restricted summation, in this case over the set s1 of i. Second, the net joint effect of the scale elements following nominal **NNP** is $Es1 \equiv (\Sigma^* \mid A_i - NNPS_i \mid)/2$. Third, for the full **UN** membership the effect is estimated as $Es1(\Sigma A_i / \Sigma^* A_i)$, where, as usual, Σ denotes unrestricted summation, that is, over the set of countries constituting the entire

[10] Data sources are CC Report, 38th sess., 1983, pp. 24-25; 45th sess., 1990, pp. 45-56; 46th sess., 1991, pp. 29-36.

UN membership. The underlying assumption is that the proportion of points redistributed (from the nominal-**NNP** scale) outside the sample (that is, for the $i \notin s1$) is that same as within it (that is, for the $i \in s1$).[11]

The resulting net joint effect of the scale elements following nominal **NNP**, these elements represented by rows (1) to (6), is shown in row (7). The effect, number of points redistributed from the nominal-NNP scale, has range approximately 10-13 percentage points for the 1983-94 scales, meaning that nominal **NNP** accounts for 87 - 90 percent of the scale.

6. Country Conflicts And Groupings

Throughout UN history, the work of the CC and debate in the GA has been replete with country-group conflicts regarding the scale of assessment. Four issues can be discerned. First, the United States has always argued, from the principle of sovereign equality of UN members (in Article 2 of the UN Charter), for the existence of the ceiling element in the scale methodology and for reductions in the ceiling level. Opposition to the U.S. position, from the Soviet bloc and from developing countries, centered on incompatibility of the ceiling with the ability-to-pay principle and the unique benefits the United States derived from UN membership (for example, UN headquarters in New York, payment of assessments in U.S. dollars).

Second, in the 1950s and 1960s countries of the Soviet bloc complained vigorously about increases in their assessments, claiming that their heavy war damage was being ignored and that a systematic effort to reduce assessments of Western countries at Eastern European and USSR expense was occurring. The United States and others countered that these assessment shifts reflected changes in relative capacities to pay and application of the ceiling, the latter legitimate via the principle of sovereign equality. The Soviet bloc also asserted that improper data were used for their economies and, in particular, complained that their turnover taxes were included in CC estimates of their **NNP**, while indirect taxes of other countries were excluded. The shift to **NNP** at market prices from factor cost was made to solve this problem of data

[11]It may be noted that $\Sigma A_i = 100.00$ while $\Sigma^* A_i = 98.78$, the latter the percentage sample coverage. For the other scale periods, the sample coverage is 100 percent, except that two new members (Marshall Islands and Micronesia, with assessment 0.01 each) are excluded from the 1992-94 computation.

comparability.

Third, as early as 1951 but especially from the late 1960s, there was controversy in the General Assembly whenever assessments of some developed countries were reduced while those of some developing countries were increased. At the extreme, the proposal was sometimes advanced that as long as the disparity between developed and developing countries persisted, the total assessment of developed countries should not decrease at the expense of that of developing countries. Counter-arguments (made by developed countries) were that this suggestion was incompatible with the principles of ability to pay and collective financial responsibility, and that assessment was legitimately on an individual-country rather than group basis.

Fourth, the "middle-income" countries, essentially developed countries other than the United States, view themselves as an unprotected group, enjoying neither the ceiling (or, while in effect, the per-capita ceiling, except for a few countries) nor low-per-capita-income allowance and other concessions to the developing countries, and thus most subject to passive increases in assessment.

These tensions suggest that the scale be examined from the standpoint of four country groups: the United States (considered a one-country group), other developed countries, Eastern Europe inclusive of the USSR, and developing countries. Basically, countries are assigned to the groups according to the classification of the United Nations Statistical Office (UNSO) in its various publications.[12]

The inclusion of many scale elements and/or changes in the values of the parameters of the elements were a result of country-group

[12] "Other developed countries" consists of the members of the Organization of Economic Co-operation and Development, but excluding the United States and Turkey, plus Liechtenstein, South Africa, Malta, and Israel, the last two countries beginning with the 1974-76 scale (consistent with the 1973 decision period and the UNSO reclassification of these countries from developing to developed status in 1972-73). "Eastern Europe" comprises the countries of the traditional Soviet bloc: Albania, Bulgaria, Czechoslovakia, German Democratic Republic, Hungary, Poland, Romania, the USSR or the countries of the ex-USSR (1992-94 scale), and Yugoslavia (1946-50 scales). The UNSO reclassification of Turkey and Yugoslavia from developed to developing (in 1972 and 1985, respectively) is an illogical direction of change; these countries are considered always developing (except Yugoslavia when in the Soviet bloc).

pressure, conflict, and compromise. The first change in the income concept, from factor cost to market prices, can be viewed as a response to Soviet-bloc complaint. The second change, incorporation of debt adjustment, emanated from developing-country pressure. The very existence of the ceiling in the scale and every reduction in its value were results of U.S. initiative and power, albeit the ceiling level was subject to compromise. The developing-country group has fought for reductions in the floor level; naturally, it has been opposed by the developed countries. The per-capita ceiling (now defunct) can be interpreted as an effort by some higher-income countries (especially Canada and Sweden) in the "middle-income" group to achieve protection from being passive recipients of points resulting from other-groups' influence on the scale. The developing-country and Soviet-bloc groups traditionally were vociferous in their opposition to both ceilings.

While the existence of the low-per-capita-income allowance in the scale was not a result of developing-country pressure, the increase in the values of its parameters over time certainly was. The developing group pushed successfully for other concessions, including "no increase in the assessments of the least developed countries," a longer statistical base period, and the scheme of limits (the last two elements considered a means of protecting growing countries of the group from increases in assessment). Much mitigation activity by the CC has been a response to developing-group insistence that increases in its assessments be moderated, that decreases be initiated, and that its problems of external debt, foreign exchange, and natural disasters be recognized. With so many inter-group tensions and conflicts at work, the very principle of limited assessment change can be considered a technique of reducing the impact of these confrontations.

7. Positive Analysis of UN Scale

To this point both the official scale and the UN procedure of obtaining the scale have been accepted. Now the scale is retained but the UN procedure is replaced by an alternative approach. The early writers on international burden-sharing described a progressive assessment as "each country contributing a percentage of its national income but with this percentage dependent on relative income per capita (Schelling, 1955, p. 12).[13] Though these authors did not suggest it, a

[13] Similar or related statements are made by Robbins (1950, p. 16), Hoag (1957, p. 530), Neale (1961, p. 36), and Uri (1963, p. 46).

direct expression of the relationship in real-income terms follows naturally. The relationship involves progressivity with respect to only per capita income. Suppose that it is complemented by progressivity with respect to total income, with the amount of each type of progressivity left open, and that country-group effects are included. Then one may test the extent to which the UN scale methodology plus ad hoc adjustment–constituting a complex, multi-step procedure, in large part a resultant of country-group conflict and compromise, and based on nominal income—can be replaced by a simple model, paying explicit attention to country groups, and grounded on real income. The relationship, however, cannot be directly applicable to countries assessed at the ceiling or floor, because the country assessment may be set by the constraint rather than by the scale methodology (plus ad hoc adjustment) in the UN or by the model here.

The relationship may be stated as an econometric equation as follows, for a given scale (pertaining, of course, to a given scale period):

$$R_i = K \cdot F^{DC_i} \cdot G^{EE_i} \cdot YK_i^H \cdot u_i \tag{1}$$

R_i is country i's assessment-income ratio normalized by the mean ratio over the countries in the sample. Specifically, $R_i \equiv (A_i/Y_i)/(mean\ (A_i/Y_i)$, where A_i is country i's official assessment rate and Y_i its real income. The mean R_i over countries in the sample is unity.

DC_i and EE_i are dichotomous variables with value unity if country i is in the developed-country (DC_i) or Eastern European (EE_i) group, respectively, zero otherwise. $YK_i \equiv YP_i/YP_{US'}$, the ratio of country i to U.S. per capita real income. Parameters of the equation are K, F, G, H; and u_i is country i's error term, assumed to be identically and independently distributed for all i, with an expected value of unity.[14]

[14]Homoscedasticity (the key to an identical distribution across i) is a reasonable assumption, because the dependent variable ($R_i \equiv normalized\ A_i/Y_i$) is in ratio form. (It would be decidedly unreasonable were A_i the dependent variable and Y_i an explanatory variable.) Because the data are cross-sectional, independence of u_i from u_j, $i \neq j$, can be accepted. Independence of u_i, all i, from DC_i and EE_i is assured by the variables' nonstochastic status. While YK_i is stochastic, it may reasonably be assumed to be distributed independently of u_i, all i. The reason is that a country's UN dollar assessment–one-hundredth the UN budget multiplied by A_i or, equivalently, by $R_i \cdot Y_i \cdot mean(A_i/Y_i)$–is extremely small relative to the country's income. For example, excluding floor countries, the ratio of "dollar

Country-group effects are as follows. The percentage effect on the assessment-income ratio of being developed is $100 \cdot (F - 1)$ and that of being Eastern European is $100 \cdot (G - 1)$. Favoritism to developing countries is implied by F, $G > 1$. Progressivity of the scale is measured as follows. According as the elasticity (H) of the assessment-income ratio (R_i) with respect to per capita income (YK_i) is greater than, equal to, or less than zero, the scale may be deemed progressive, proportional, or regressive with respect to per capita income. Recalling that R_i is A_i/Y_i normalized to a mean of unity; according as K (for developing countries), $K \cdot F$ (for developed countries), or $K \cdot G$ (for Eastern Europe) is greater than, equal to, or less than unity, the scale (subset of A_i) for that group is progressive, proportional, or regressive with respect to total income (Y_i).

The analysis in this section is positive (because the UN scale, the set A_i, underlies the dependent variable) and disaggregative (in the sense that all countries in the sample are given equal weight in estimating equation (1)). While its official scale is accepted, the UN measure of assessable income, meaning income inclusive of the low-per-capita-income allowance, is not.[15] The variable Y_i differs from UN assessable income in five respects: the income concept is gross national product (**GNP**) rather than **NNP**, in constant rather than current prices, and exclusive of debt adjustment for all scales; the conversion factor is **PPP** rather than **ER**; and progressivity is determined by the data and specified equation rather than predetermined. However, the unweighted average of annual income is taken over the statistical base period, and the mid-period population figure is used to compute per-capita income, both in accordance with UN procedure.[16]

---

assessment for 1989" to "nominal **NNP** averaged annually over the statistical base period, 1977-86," ranges from 0.002 to 0.012 of one percent (CC Report, 44th sess., 1989, pp. 42-46). These numbers are too low for a discernible effect of a country's assessment rate (A_i) on its income (Y_i) and thence on per capita income (YP_i).

[15]Under the allowance, the relief (income subtracted from low-income countries) is redistributed to high-income countries (those with per-capita income above the limit) in proportion to their incomes. Prior to the 1980-82 scale, the relief was distributed to all countries, both low-income and high-income, which reduced the progressive effect of the allowance.

[16]Mid-period population means the middle year of a base period with an odd-year length, the average of the two middle years for a base period with an even-year length. Justification of the income concept and conversion factor is provided in section 8. Data sources and construction of variables are in appendix B and the first paragraph of appendix A.

Equation (1) is estimated separately for all scale periods delimited in section 2 and listed in Table 1. This moving cross-section analysis provides answers to four questions. First, how close does the equation approximate the UN scale for the various scale periods? Second, is the UN scale progressive in terms of real income and how has its progressivity changed over UN history? Third, are there country-group effects (for example, favoritism to developing countries) distinguishable from the influence of per-capita income in determination of the scale, and how have these effects changed over time? Fourth, how have the highest-assessed countries fared relative to the equation's predictions?

To estimate equation (1), ordinary least-squares is applied to the equation transformed into logarithmic form.[17] Among the constant term and the variables DC_i, EE_i, and YK_i, the subset that maximizes $\bar{R}^2$ is included in the regression. Because the initial statistical base period was prewar, the CC included effects of "war dislocation" and "war improvement" in the preparation of its original recommended scale. Therefore a dichotomous variable, DI_i (1 if dislocated by World War II, 0 otherwise), is included in the equation for the 1947 and 1950 scale periods.[18] The samples exclude the United States (always the sole ceiling country), all countries assessed at the floor, and China until 1980-82.[19]

---

[17]The fitted regression is $\hat{lnR_i} = \hat{k} + \hat{f} \cdot DC_i + \hat{g} \cdot EE_i + \hat{h} \cdot lnYK_i$, where $\hat{k}$, $\hat{f}$, $\hat{g}$, $\hat{h}$ are least-squares estimates of its parameters and $\hat{lnR_i}$ is the fitted value of lnR_i. Estimates of the parameters of equation (1) are $\hat{K} = e^{\hat{k}}$, $\hat{F} = e^{\hat{f}}$, $\hat{G} = e^{\hat{g}}$, $\hat{H} = \hat{h}$; the fitted value of R_i is $\hat{R}_i = e^{\hat{lnR_i}}$; and the fitted value of A_i is $\hat{A}_i = \hat{R}_i \cdot Y_i \cdot mean(A_i/Y_i)$.

[18]It is not clear whether the CC procedure took the form of updating income figures or of ad hoc adjustment, but no matter. While the GA altered the CC initial scale, it did so principally by imposing a ceiling and floor, and the countries subject to these constraints are excluded from the sample. Countries with unity value of DI_i are those that had been occupied (totally or partially) by Germany or Japan, plus the United Kingdom. DI_i is applied to the 1950 scale period because of minimal changes in the scale through that period.

[19]Inclusion of the United States and the floor countries could seriously bias the regression, as extreme observations (the one having an assessment-income ratio below, the others above that predicted by its per-capita income and country group). China's assessment was far above that justified by its income when the country was represented by the Republic of China, because of the legal fiction that the Republic represented all of China and the initial establishment of China's assessment at the level of France, for lack of Chinese data. The gross overassessment continued after representation was switched to the People's Republic, until China submitted income and population data (1980-82 scale). The inclusion of China in earlier samples would

Estimates of equation (1) are presented in Table 3, with t-values in parentheses below coefficients. There are two measures of sample size: N, the number of countries, and ΣA, the total assessment of the countries in the sample. The latter statistic understates the sample coverage because the United States, the floor countries, and China until 1980-82 are excluded by default. The percentage coverage, meaning ΣA as a percent of the total assessment of the potential sample, is 78 percent in 1947, 88 percent in 1950, 93 percent in 1951, and over 99 percent in the subsequent scale periods.

Approximation to UN scale: Two measures of goodness of fit are used. The first is r^2, the squared correlation between R_i and $\hat{R}_i$, which measures the direct predictive ability of equation (1) over the sample period. However, the ultimate interest is A_i, for which the predictive power of equation (1) may be gauged by Theil's inequality coefficient, U, where $U^2 = \Sigma(\hat{A}_i - A_i)^2/\Sigma A_i^2$. A perfect fit implies U = 0, while the naive model $\tilde{A}_i = 0$, all i, yields U = 1. (See note 16 for the computation of $\hat{R}_i$ and $\hat{A}_i$.) Considering the cross-sectional nature of the equation, the goodness-of-fit is impressive for most scale periods. The r^2 is above .50 from 1959-61 onward and U is below .25 for the majority of the scale periods. From 1958 onward, all explanatory variables are present and their coefficients are frequently highly significant. In all cases coefficients have the theoretically correct sign. Also, the magnitudes of the country-group coefficients are as expected: those of DC and EE both above unity in all scales from 1952 (favoritism toward developing countries), that of DI below unity in 1947 (recognition of war damage). It can be concluded that equation (1) constitutes a surprisingly good model of UN scale determination.

Progressivity and country-group effects: Per-capita income elasticity ($\hat{H}$) is always positive, implying scale progressivity with respect to per capita income. Though the coefficient is uniformly inelastic, there is an upward trend in its value. The developing countries face a progressive scale with respect to total income for those scales for which the constant term exceeds unity (1947 and 1983-94). In contrast, except for 1947 and 1947-51, respectively, all developed and Eastern European countries encounter a progressive scale (the product of the constant and the respective coefficient above unity). From the late 1960s to the early 1980s the country-group percentage effects against these groups and in

---

severely bias the regression in the same direction as the floor countries.

favor of developing countries actually exceeds 100 percent.

Highest-assessed countries: In every scale period, the countries with the four highest assessments account for more than half, and sometimes almost two-thirds, of total assessments.[20] So it is of interest to explore the extent to which these countries are overassessed or underassessed in light of equation (1). Table 4 lists, for each scale period, the four highest-assessed countries together with their pertinent statistics. Consider first the normalized assessment-income ratio (R_i), shown in the first part of the table. For most scale periods, all four countries have values above, sometimes substantially above, the sample mean (unity)–meaning that they were "overassessed" by this simple measure.

For the 1954 to 1971-73 periods, the USSR assessment-income ratio is the highest among all the sample countries; whereas from 1952 onward the U.S. ratio is the lowest of the four highest-assessed countries. Yet in all scale periods USSR per capita income is lowest and U.S. highest among the highest-assessed countries. So the ceiling was effective in limiting the U.S. assessment-income ratio relative to that of the other high-assessed countries. Also, the USSR had justification from 1952 (when its assessment increased by 41 percent over 1951, followed by further annual increases of 25 and 15 percent) in complaining of its assessment relative to that of the high-income Western countries.

Consider now the statistic ($A_i - \hat{A}_i$), the actual minus fitted assessment for country i, shown in the second part of Table 4.[21] This statistic measures, in percentage points, the overassessment (if positive) or underassessment (if negative) of country i relative to the estimated equation (1). The United States always benefits from the ceiling, and its underassessment is at a maximum in the 1980-94 scales.[22] In contrast, the other high-assessed countries are, with two minor exceptions, uniformly overassessed for all scale periods.

The overassessment of the USSR (or ex-USSR, for 1992-94) is shown even more clearly, exceeding that of the remaining high-assessment countries in 1947 and then uniformly from the 1953 scale.

---

[20]China, tied with France for the fourth highest assessment in 1947-52, is excluded from the analysis.

[21]Although the United States is not in the sample, its $\hat{A}_i$ may be computed as for other countries.

[22]The effects of the ceiling in Table 4 differ from those in Table 2 because the point of reference is the estimated equation (1) as distinct from the UN scale methodology.

Incredibly, the USSR overassessment dwarfs that of Japan, especially in the most recent scales. Looked at another way, Japan's assessment is close to being "on the regression line," while the USSR assessment is "above the line."

8. Properties of A Normative Scale

The third viewpoint of the study involves rejection of not only the UN procedure of obtaining its scale but also the official scale itself. An ideal scale is derived and used to evaluate the official scale. Because it is used in a normative analysis, the ideal scale is called the "normative scale." In this section properties of the normative scale are established.

Number of assessment principles: The multiplicity of assessment principles in the UN "scale methodology plus ad hoc adjustment" fosters dissension and bargaining as distinct from adherence to principle. The political difficulty of constructing a scale is magnified, because the relative weights of the various principles require determination and this is both the evident initial step in constructing the scale and the obvious initial subject of conflict. Multiple criteria also make the scale procedure complex, and it can be surmised that a complex procedure enhances the scope for country-group conflict. So a single assessment principle has the dual advantage of defusing political tensions and of simplicity, with the added benefit of a favorable interaction of the two benefits.

Selection of assessment principle: Given that a single assessment criterion is to be selected, ability to pay is the obvious choice. It is the most notable principle of national tax systems and is consistent with economists' concepts of horizontal and vertical equity. It also happens to be the most important principle underlying the UN scale procedure both legally and empirically (as shown in sections 3 and 5, respectively).

Income concept: To measure ability to pay, a strong case can be made for a multidimensional approach, inclusive of wealth and of social and economic indicators of development, as has often been discussed in the UN itself. However, data limitations and the objective of simplicity dictate resort to income, here as in the UN. National rather than domestic product and market prices rather than factor cost (the first always UN practice, the second since the 1965 scale) are the better indicators of ability to pay (for all scale periods). However, contrary to UN procedure, gross rather than net product (**GNP** rather than **NNP**) is taken. The use of GNP enhances international comparability, because accounting depreciation varies with tax law and rulings and with data quality. Also, with **GNP** measuring total output, it is a matter of choice how much of it is devoted to depreciation–and it is arguable that ability to pay be independent of that choice.

The UN shift to debt-adjusted income is not followed. This inclusion of a capital-account transaction in current income violates a national-accounting precept. Also, asymmetrically, while subtracting repayment of debt principal from income, the UN concept adds neither the original borrowing to debtor's income nor the repaid principal to lender's income.

Denomination of income: **GNP** in constant rather than current prices is adopted (contrary to UN practice), because mere price change does not alter a country's ability to pay. To convert constant-price **GNP** to a common currency, **PPP** is utilized, in opposition to the CC selection of **ER** supplemented by **PARE**. The advantages of **PPP** over **ER** are threefold. First, **ER** is based on a weighting pattern of "output" that is nebulous and related directly only to tradables; whereas **PPP** (**GNP** concept) has a precise weighting pattern based on shares of tradables and nontradables (and their components) in national production. Second, in contrast to **ER**, **PPP** is not subject to the **ERCB**. Third, **ER**, unlike **PPP**, is influenced by factors irrelevant to international income comparison, for example, speculation and exchange-market intervention. The disadvantages of **PARE** relative to **PPP** are that (i) the former corrects only for differential changes in price levels relative to exchange rates rather than providing appropriate conversion factors for price levels themselves, and (ii) the amount of **PARE** correction varies with the base year chosen and in fact can be negative.[23]

Progressivity: The amount of progressivity that the scale should contain is inherently arbitrary. Therefore the UN explicit progressivity is accepted, which enhances comparability with the official scale. Specifically, the UN low-per-capita-allowance formula is taken, but with the per-capita-income limit re-expressed in real-income terms. Note

---

[23]An important reason given by the CC for its rejections of constant-price data and of **PPP** is lack of data; but it can be argued with some justification that this excuse no longer has validity (see appendix B).

that the elements in the UN scale under the ability-to-pay criterion that affect progressivity implicitly (**ER** conversion factor, debt adjustment) are excluded, as are, of course, all elements under the other assessment principles and the entirety of ad hoc adjustment.

Base period: A three-year "normative base period" is selected, because it is a good compromise between the principal advantage of a shorter base period (reflecting current economic conditions) and that of a longer one (reducing the effect of fluctuations in income). The early statistical base periods of less than three years are retained as evolutionary to the three-year period; but the CC abandonment of the three year-period in 1977 is rejected because it was founded on the limited assessment change principle rather than ability to pay.[24]

Attention to country groups: Because the UN scale is so reflective of country-group tensions, the "normative scale" should be oriented to an evaluation of the assessments of country groups. In contrast, the UN procedure for setting the scale is on an individual-country basis.

9. Normative Analysis of UN Scale

Application of the methodology of section 8 yields (for each scale period) a normative assessment, N^j, for each group j, where j = United States (US), other developed countries (DC), Eastern Europe (EE), and developing countries (DL).[25] The normative assessment can be compared with the actual assessment, A^j, for each country group.[26] The actual assessment (A^j) and actual-normative assessment differential ($A^j - N^j$) for each country group are shown in Table 5 for each scale period. Looking at actual assessment (A^j), other developed countries increase their assessment almost throughout UN history (except for the early 1950s), so that by 1992-94 they account for over half the total assessment. In contrast, the United States to 1974-76, Eastern Europe from 1968-70, and developing countries from 1952 enjoy almost continuous reductions in their assessment.

[24] The base period was extended "in order to alleviate the sharp variations in the rates of assessment of countries whose national incomes had risen rapidly in the early 1970s" (CC Report, 42nd sess., 1987, p. 9). The normative base periods are presented in Table 1.

[25] Derivation of the normative scale is provided in appendix A.

[26] Note that $A^j = \Sigma A_i, i \in j$, and that $\Sigma A^j = \Sigma N^j$ = total assessments, given in the last column of Table 1.

Group overassessment ($A^j - N^j > 0$) or underassessment ($A^j - N^j < 0$) follows patterns. The effect of the ceiling on the U.S. assessment is strongest in 1950-64, with the constraint becoming inconsequential and eventually non-binding in 1980-94.[27] Other developed countries are overassessed in the early scales, underassessed in 1958-73, and then increasingly overassessed. After 1947, Eastern Europe is always overassessed; but there is a downward trend from 1962-64. Developing countries are overassessed in 1950-64; but from 1953 there is a steady decrease in their overassessment, and there is a switch in 1966-67 to steadily increasing underassessment. While *collective financial responsibility* (represented by the ceiling) has had reduced impact over time, *level of development* has become increasingly powerful.

The total intergroup transfer of points, $(\Sigma \mid A^j - N^j \mid)/2$, measures how close the official scale is to its normative equivalent. Of the 21 scale periods, nine involve a "fit" of over 90 percent (corresponding to an intergroup transfer of under ten percentage points) and twelve a "fit" of 80 - 90 percent.

10. Summary And Conclusions

Three approaches are used to examine the UN scale of assessments, meaning the apportionment of UN expenses among its member countries, over the entire UN history. First, *both the scale and the UN procedure of determining it are accepted.* It is shown that the elements in determination of the scale emanate from various assessment principles, that the UN use of the exchange rate to express income in a common currency involves a hidden progressivity in the scale, and that the relative importance of the various elements in the scale is measurable (though information is complete only for recent scales).

Second, *the UN scale is accepted but the procedure is simplified and rationalized.* Progressivity is found to increase over time and there are strong country-group effects in favor of developing countries. Regarding the highest-assessed countries, the United States is underassessed, the USSR overassessed, and Japan assessed close to what the model predicts.

Third, *the UN scale is rejected in favor of a normative alter-*

---

[27] These results are strikingly divergent from those of section 7 and Table 4; but the "norm" there (a fitted regression equation) is substantially different.

native. From this standpoint, the U.S. underassessment is small by the 1980s, while developing countries enjoy increasing underassessment from the mid-1960s. Overassessment of Eastern Europe tends to decrease from the mid-1950s, but that of developed countries other than the United States increases from the mid-1970s. Due largely to the overassessment of other developed countries, by 1992-94 developed countries (including the United States) accounted for over three-quarters of the UN scale. In contrast, and in spite of strong and persistent complaints about their apportionment of UN expenses, the developing countries by 1992-94 paid almost twenty percentage points less than their normative share.

Appendix A: Computation of Normative Scale

Step 1: Compute **PPP**-converted **GNP** in constant prices ("real **GNP**," Y_i) and per-capita real **GNP** (YP_i) for each country i for which data are available, for the given normative base period (with the set of resulting i denoted as s2). In accordance with UN practice, (i) the *unweighted average* of annual **GNP** and (ii) the *mid-period* population, are taken from the $GNPM_i$ and P_i series, respectively, in step 7 of appendix B.

Step 2: Convert the per-capita-income limit of the UN low-per-capita-allowance formula to its real-**GNP** equivalent. This is done by multiplying the UN limit for the base period by the ratio of "U.S. real **GNP** (Y_{US})" to "U.S. nominal **NNP** (national income, for 1947 to 1957-59) averaged over the base period."[28]

Step 3: For each country calculate *real assessable income* (YB_i), that is, real **GNP** adjusted for the low-per-capita-income allowance. The converted income limit of step 2 is applied with the UN gradient.

Step 4: Sum the YB_i into country groups: $YB^j = \Sigma YB_i$, $i \in j$, where j = US, DC, EE, DL.

Step 5: Adjust the YB^j for differential sample coverage: $YC^j = (A^j/A^j_s) \cdot YB^j$; where $A^j_s = \Sigma A_i$, $i \in j$ and $i \in s2$, is the sample coverage for group j (see footnote 25).

[28]The source of U.S. nominal data is U.S. Department of Commerce (1986) and Survey of Current Business, various issues.

Step 6: Adjust the YC^j so they sum to total assessments (given by the last column of Table 1 for the specific scale period). The result is the normative scale: $N^j = (\Sigma A^j / \Sigma YC^j) \cdot YC^j$.

Step 7: Compute the sample coverage, ΣA^j_s. For 1947, 1950, and 1951, coverage is 82, 87, and 90 percentage points. For the remaining scale periods, it exceeds 99 percent.

Appendix B: Income And Population Data

The objective is to have, for each country i, an annual time series of (1) **PPP**-converted, U.S.-dollar-denominated **GNP** in constant prices and (2) population, enveloping the statistical (and hence, by default, normative) base periods corresponding to the scale periods for which country i was a UN member. Further, these time series should be consistent both over time and across countries. The series are obtained from the following steps.

Step 1: From Summers and Heston (1991), obtain the annual series on real **GDP** per capita (international dollars, 1985 prices, Laspeyres index), denoted as $GDPL_i$, and on population (thousands of persons), denoted as P_i, for each UN member i for as much of the requisite time period as their series encompass.[29] Their maximum coverage for a given country is 1950-88.[30] These Summers-Heston **GDP** data, except for their divergence from **GNP**, fulfill the conceptual requirements to serve as the required input for step 1 of appendix A: the year 1985 emanates from a **PPP** computation; figures for other years are extrapolated using national-accounts series at constant prices (Summers and Heston, 1991, p. 343).

Step 2: Compute real **GDP** in millions of international dollars: $GDPM_i = (P_i \cdot GDPL_i)/1000$.

Step 3: Multiply $GDPM_i$ by the ratio of **GNP** in current prices to **GDP** in current prices (for the years for which data on this ratio exist–otherwise assume a unity ratio).[31] The result is $GNPM_i$, real **GNP** in millions of international dollars.

[29] The population figures for Nigeria in 1957-59 are corrected by adding 10 million.

[30] For countries in their Table B3, **GDPL** for 1985 is computed as the product of .01, relative per capita **GDP**, and U.S. 1985 **GDPL**.

[31] Data sources for the ratio are World Bank, World Tables, and UN, Yearbook of National Accounts Statistics, various issues.

Step 4: For cross-country consistency, the Summers and Heston (1991) data fix the country coverage. However, it is possible, and indeed desirable, to extend their temporal coverage for the given countries. Let $GNPM_i^l$ denote $GNPM_i$ for the latest available year, ℓ (usually, though not always, 1988), and $GNPM_i^e$ for the earliest available year, e (1950 at the earliest). Using all available published data sources, two series of output at constant domestic prices, denoted as $GNPC_i$, are developed, data permitting.[32] One series begins in year ℓ and ends in 1989; another begins in 1938-40 (the average of whatever of these years are available) and ends in year e.[33] The first series extends $GNPM_i$ forward to 1989 (or as close to that year as data availability permits) by means of the multiplicative factor $GNPM_i^l/GNPC_i^l$; the second series extends $GNPM_i$ backward to 1938-40 (or 1950, or as far back as data permit) by means of the multiplicative factor $GNPM_i^e/GNPC_i^e$, where $GNPC_i^l$ ($GNPC_i^e$) is $GNPC_i$ in year ℓ (e).[34]

Step 5: Using the same technique as for $GNPM_i$, extend P_i forward to 1991 and backward to 1938-40 (or rather as much in either direction as correspondence with the extended $GNPM_i$ series warrants).[35]

Step 6: Adjust the $GNPM_i$ and P_i series for merger or separation of countries. For Germany for 1980-89, add the $GNPM_i$ (and P_i) series for the Federal Republic of Germany and the German Democratic Republic. For the United Arab Republic for 1955-57, add the series

[32] The data sources fall into six categories: (1) earlier versions of the Penn World Table [of which Summers and Heston (1991) constitute the fifth version]: Summers, Kravis, and Heston (1980), Summers and Heston (1988); (2) World Bank, World Tables, various issues; (3) historical-statistics volumes: Mitchell (1975, 1982, 1983), U.S. Bureau of the Census (1975); (4) United Nations, Statistics of National Income and Expenditure and Yearbook of National Accounts Statistics, various issues; (5) publications of the Research Project on National Income in East Central Europe: Alton (1980), Alton and others (1990), Lazarcik (1969); (6) Central Intelligence Agency, Handbook of Economic Statistics, various issues.

[33] Different series of $GNPC_i$ or the same series with different base years are linked on the basis of one-year overlaps. Should a consistent series have gaps, it is interpolated linearly to obtain the missing annual observations.

[34] This aggregative extrapolation technique is consistent with the Summers-Heston Laspeyres income concept while enabling expansion of the observations beyond that limited by their approach of extrapolating on a disaggregative basis (consumption, investment, government spending, exports, and imports separately).

[35] Data sources are UN, Demographic Yearbook, and World Bank, World Tables, various issues.

for Egypt and Syria. For Pakistan (East plus West) for 1959-68, add the $GNPM_i$ series for Bangladesh and Pakistan. Extend the series backward to 1949 via $GNPC_i$ for Pakistan (East plus West). Similarly, for the 1950-68 P_i, add the series for Bangladesh and Pakistan, and extend it to 1949 via a population series for Pakistan (East plus West).

Step 7: The resulting annual $GNPM_i$ and P_i series are the inputs into (i) step 1 of appendix A, followed by the remainder of appendix A, for section 9 and (ii) step 1 of appendix A revised so that "statistical base period" replaces "normative base period," for section 7.

References

Alton, Thad P.(1980), *Economic Growth in Eastern Europe 1965-1979.* Occasional Paper No. 59, Research Project on National Income in East Central Europe. New York: L.W. International Financial Research.

Alton, Thad P., and others(1990), *Economic Growth in Eastern Europe 1975-1989.* Occasional Paper No. 110, Research Project on National Income in East Central Europe. New York: L.W. International Financial Research.

Hoag, Malcolm W. (1957), "Economic Problems of Alliance," *Journal of Political Economy*, 65, pp. 522-34.

James, Alan. (1989), "The Security Council: Paying for Peacekeeping," in David P. Forsythe, *The United Nations in the World Political Economy*, pp. 13-35. New York: St. Martin's Press.

Lazarcik, Gregor. (1969), *Czechoslovak Gross National Product by Sector of Origin and by Final Use, 1937 and 1948-1965*, Occasional Paper No. 26, Research Project on National Income in East Central Europe. New York: Columbia University.

Mitchell, B. R. (1975), *European Historical Statistics, 1750-1970.* New York: Columbia University Press.

Mitchell, B. R. (1982), *International Historical Statistics: Africa and Asia.* New York: New York University Press.

Mitchell, B. R. (1983), *International Historical Statistics: The Americas and Australasia.* Detroit: Gale Research Company.

Neale, Alan D. (1961), *The Flow of Resources from Rich to Poor.* Occasional Papers in International Affairs, No. 2. Harvard University, Center for International Affairs.

Officer, Lawrence H. (1994), "An Assessment of the United Nations Scale of Assessments from a Developing-Country Standpoint," *Journal of International Money and Finance*,13, pp. 415-28.

Pincus, John. (1965), *Economic Aid and International Cost Sharing.* Baltimore: Johns Hopkins Press.

Robbins, Lionel. (1950), "Towards the Atlantic Community," *Lloyds Bank Review* pp. 1-24.

Schelling, Thomas C. (1955), *International Cost-Sharing Arrangements.* Essays in International Finance, No. 24. International Finance Section, Princeton University.

Stoessinger, John G. (1964), *Financing the United Nations System.* Washington, DC: The Brookings Institution.

Summers, Robert, and Alan Heston. (1988), "A New Set of International Comparisons of Real Product and Price Levels Estimates for 130 Countries, 1950-1985," *Review of Income and Wealth*, 34, pp. 1-25.

Summers, Robert, and Alan Heston. (1991), "The Penn World Table (Mark 5): An Expanded Set of International Comparisons, 1950-1988," *Quarterly Journal of Economics*,106, pp. 327-68.

Summers, Robert, Irving B. Kravis, and Alan Heston. (1980), "International Comparisons of Real Product and its Composition, 1950-77," *Review of Income and Wealth*, 26, pp. 19-66.

Uri, Pierre. (1963), *Partnership for Progress.* New York: Harper & Row.

U.S. Bureau of the Census.(1975), *Historical Statistics of the United States, Colonial Times to 1970.* Washington, DC: U.S. Government Printing Office.

U.S. Department of Commerce. (1986), *The National Income and Product Accounts of the United States, 1929-82: Statistical Tables.* Washington, DC: U.S. Government Printing Office.

Table 1
Delineation of Scale Periods, 1946-1994

Decision Period (Year)	Scale Period	Stat. Base Period[a]	Norm. Base Period[b]	UN Membership[c]		Sum of Assessments
				Total[d]	Floor[e]	
1946	1947[f]	1938-40	1938-40	52	7	100.00
1949	1950[g]	1948[h]	1948	57	8	100.00
1950	1951	1949[h]	1949	57	8	100.00
1951	1952	1950[h]	1950	58	8	100.00
1952	1953	1950-51	1950-51	58	9	100.00
1953	1954	1950-52	1950-52	58	9	100.00
1954	1955	1951-53	1951-53	58	9	100.00
1957	1958[i]	1952-54	1952-54	80	14	100.00
1958	1959-61	1955-57	1955-57	79[j]	16	100.00
1961	1962-64	1957-59	1957-59	98[k]	32	100.00[l]
1965	1966-67[m]	1960-62	1960-62	115[n]	51	99.82
1967	1968-70	1963-65	1963-65	120	57	100.00
1970	1971-73	1966-68	1966-68	124	63	100.00
1973	1974-76	1969-71	1969-71	133	70	100.00
1976	1977	1972-74	1972-74	142	81	100.00
1977	1978-79	1969-75	1973-75	145	66	100.00
1979	1980-82	1971-77	1975-77	149	70	100.00
1982	1983-85	1971-80	1978-80	155	78	100.00
1985	1986-88	1974-83	1981-83	157	78	100.00
1988	1989-91	1977-86	1984-86	157	79	100.00
1991	1992-94	1980-89	1987-89	161	84	100.02

Source: CC Report and FC Report, 1st - 46th sessions, 1946-1991.

[a]Statistical base period, used by UN and in sections II - VII of text. [b]Normative base period, used in sections VIII - IX of text. [c]Number of countries assessed at time scale was decided. Excludes new members assessed after decision period. [d]Components of USSR (scale periods 1946-1991) or ex-USSR (scale period 1992-94) counted as one country. [e]Number of countries assessed at floor rate. [f]Scale for 1946 decided at same time with same statistical base period but three fewer countries. [g]Scale for 1948 differs from 1947 by inclusion of two new members with the sum of their assessments (0.31) balanced by reduction in the assessment for Sweden. Scale for 1949 differs from 1948 by inclusion

of one new member with its assessment of 0.15 balanced by reduction in assessment for Sweden of 0.04 and for United Kingdom of 0.11. Scale for 1950 differs from 1949 by division of assessment for "India and Pakistan" (formerly assessment for India, unchanged since scale for 1947) into assessments for India and Pakistan separately, and by inclusion of one new member with its assessment of 0.12 balanced by reduction in assessment for Sweden of 0.02 and for United States of 0.10.

[h]Actually, the latest year for which income data are available for a country, of which probably the modal year.

[i]Scale for 1956-57 (decided in 1956) has same statistical base period but six fewer countries.

[j]United Arab Republic, joining Egypt and Syria, reduced UN membership by one.

[k]Syria and United Arab Republic (Egypt) counted as two members again. Necessity for allocation of assessment of former joint United Arab Republic to these two members noted in 1961 decision period, though not established until 1962.

[l]Excludes retroactive downward revisions in assessments for Czechoslovakia and Hungary, decided in 1963.

[m]Scale for 1965 decided at same time with same statistical base period but three fewer countries. Differs from 1966-67 scale by a higher assessment for Malaysia and exclusion of the three new members (one of which, Singapore, was then part of Malaysia).

[n]Excludes Indonesia, which temporarily withdrew from the United Nations in January 1965 (before the 1965 decision period).

Table 2
Importance of Elements in Scale[a]
(No. of percentage points redistributed)[b]

Element	Scale Period			
	1983-85	1986-88	1989-91	1992-94
(1) Debt adjustment			.87	.71
(2) Low-per-capita-income allowance[c]	9.50		8.35	8.27
(3) Floor[d]			.47	.51
(4) Ceiling[e]			5.68	5.51
(5) Scheme of Limits		1.79	3.54	3.82
(6) Mitigation[f]	1.52	.69	.77	.50
(7) Net effect of (1)-(6)[g]	9.88	11.67	12.90	11.73

Source: Rows (1) - (6); 1989-91, 1992-94–CC Report, 44th sess., 1989, p. 34; 46th sess., 1991, p. 44. Row (2), 1978-79–CC Report, 32nd sess., 1977, pp. 19, 22; 1980-82–CC Report, 34th sess., 1979, p. 13; 1983-85–CC Report, 37th sess., 1982, p. 7. Row (4), 1962-64–FC Report, 17th sess., 1962, p. 2; 1968-70–CC Report, 24th sess., 1969, p. 19; 1971-73–FC Report, 27th sess., 1972, p. 3. Row (5), 1986-88–CC Report, 45th sess., 1990, p. 6. Row (6), 1971-73–Evolution, p. 15; 1986-88–CC Report, 45th sess., 1990, p. 56. Row (7)–see section V of text.

Rows (3) and (4), 1946 and 1947: The CC did not apply the principle of collective financial responsibility to its initial, 1946-48, recommended scale, resulting in a U.S. assessment of 49.89 percent. The GA rejected the CC scale and imposed a ceiling of 39.89 percent, a floor of 0.04 percent, and one-year scale periods. The importance of the ceiling is clearly ten percentage points; that of the floor is computed as $\Sigma \mid A_i - B_i \mid$, where A_i is country i's assessment for 1947, B_i its assessment recommended by the CC, and i runs over all countries for which $B_i < 0.04$.

Row (6), 1983-85: The CC incorrectly calculates the importance of mitigation in 1983-85 as 0.63 percentage points (CC Report, 45th sess., 1990, p. 50). The true figure, 1.52 percentage points, is computed as $(\Sigma \mid A_i - M_i \mid)/2$, where A_i is country i's official assessment and M_i its machine-scale assessment (source for the latter, CC Report, 37th sess., 1982, pp. 52-22). The explanation for the CC's error is that in constructing the 1983-85 scale, two mitigation processes occurred; first, the usual one, to obtain the CC recommended scale from the machine scale; second, an additional 0.63 percentage points redistributed because the GA would not accept the recommended scale. The CC computation, incorrectly, used the original recommended scale instead of the machine scale.

[a]A blank space indicates the figure is not available. A dash indicates the element is not applicable. [b]Basis is nominal NNP at factor cost (1946-64), nominal NNP at market prices (1965-94). [c]Other scale periods: 1978-79, 5.81; 1980-82, 8.85. [d]Other scale periods: 1946 and 1947, 0.14. [e]Other scale periods: 1946 and 1947, 10.00; 1962-64, 6.48; 1968-70, 7.91; 1971-73, 6.88. [f]Other scale period: 1971-73, 0.20 - 0.25. [g]And of "No increase in the assessments of the least developed countries."

Table 3
Regressions for Assessment-Income Ratio

Scale Period	Constant[a]	Coefficient of DC	Coefficient of EE	Income Elasticity[c]	Goodness of Fit r^2	Goodness of Fit U	Sample Size N	Sample Size ΣA
1947	1.62 (2.18)	0.70[d] (1.94)		0.41 (2.52)	.31	.15	19	42.11
1950	0.78 (2.67)	1.57 (2.92)	—	—	.29	.17	26	47.49
1951	0.79 (2.69)	1.51 (2.94)	—	—	.27	.18	28	51.09
1952	0.77 (3.49)	1.59 (3.50)	1.52 (1.76)	—	.18	.14	45	56.55
1953	0.76 (3.92)	1.64 (3.90)	1.81 (2.57)	—	.28	.17	44	58.43
1954	0.75 (4.14)	1.67 (4.10)	1.95 (2.94)	—	.34	.20	44	60.22
1955	0.73 (4.41)	1.74 (4.41)	2.01 (3.06)	—	.38	.24	44	60.69
1958	—	1.29 (2.93)	1.53 (2.66)	0.13 (4.56)	.27	.37	60	61.48
1959-61	—	1.47 (4.79)	1.69 (3.58)	0.18 (6.65)	.53	.36	58	61.49
1962-64	—	1.48 (4.54)	1.94 (4.21)	0.20 (6.88)	.56	.34	60	61.76
1966-67	0.76 (1.78)	1.89 (4.57)	2.25 (4.50)	0.12 (1.54)	.55	.36	60	61.37
1968-70	0.74 (1.86)	2.01 (4.77)	2.31 (4.50)	0.13 (1.63)	.59	.35	59	61.91
1971-73	0.65 (2.94)	2.33 (6.25)	2.45 (5.11)	0.10 (1.33)	.64	.33	57	61.75
1974-76	0.62 (3.50)	2.78 (7.96)	3.00 (7.07)	0.21 (3.00)	.79	.28	59	67.96
1977	—	2.00 (9.45)	2.58 (7.17)	0.56 (16.4)	.80	.21	57	67.72
1978-79	—	2.29 (10.73)	2.75 (7.18)	0.51 (17.70)	.85	.22	73	68.61
1980-82	—	2.26 (10.10)	2.40 (5.92)	0.52 (17.13)	.83	.21	74	74.10
1983-85	1.21 (1.62)	2.07 (6.05)	2.04 (4.48)	0.69 (10.50)	.82	.23	72	74.06
1986-88	1.39 (2.81)	1.87 (5.22)	1.86 (3.85)	0.79 (11.47)	.78	.23	75	74.05
1989-91	1.49 (2.95)	1.73 (4.10)	1.70 (2.99)	0.82 (10.28)	.74	.23	73	73.91
1992-94	1.68 (3.56)	1.61 (3.46)	1.38 (1.73)	0.87 (10.44)	.79	.26	68	73.52

Source: see section VII of text.

[a]A dash indicates that the constant is taken as unity, because its inclusion in the regression reduces $\overline{R^2}$.

[b]A dash indicates that the coefficient is taken as unity, because inclusion of the variable in the regression reduces $\overline{R^2}$.

[c]A dash indicates that elasticity is taken as zero, because inclusion of the income variable reduces $\overline{R^2}$.

[d]Variable is DI.

Variables
Assessment-Income Ratio: normalized to unit mean
DC = 1 if developed country, 0 otherwise
EE = 1 if Eastern European country, 0 otherwise
DI = 1 if dislocated by World War II, 0 otherwise
Income: ratio of per-capita income to U.S. per-capita income

Goodness of Fit
r^2 = squared correlation between actual and fitted assessment-income ratio
U = Theil's U statistic for actual and fitted assessment

Sample Size N = number of countries
ΣA = total assessment of countries in sample

Table 4
Statistics for Countries With Four Highest Assessments

Scale Period	Normalized Assessment-Income Ratio[a]				Actual minus Fitted Assessment[b]			
	U.S.	USSR	U.K. Japan[c]	Franc GER[d]	U.S.	USSR	U.K. Japan[c]	France GER[d]
1947	1.20	0.72	1.13	1.01	-14.13	1.22	0.84	0.69
1950	1.04	0.89	1.43	1.39	-6.57	0.98	1.70	0.77
1951	1.06	0.92	1.45	1.28	-4.89	1.20	1.99	0.42
1952	1.03	1.33	1.44	1.28	-7.31	1.32	1.58	0.22
1953	0.96	1.70	1.43	1.29	-10.08	2.79	1.37	0.20
1954	0.89	1.91	1.36	1.25	-13.36	3.93	0.79	0.02
1955	0.89	2.06	1.27	1.30	-14.32	5.02	-0.06	0.13
1958	1.05	2.16	1.31	1.46	-7.74	6.77	0.59	1.11
1959-61	1.19	2.16	1.53	1.82	-7.53	6.43	0.99	1.88
1962-64	1.28	2.34	1.63	1.76	-4.92	6.50	1.32	1.54
1966-67	1.37	2.38	1.68	1.83	-1.41	6.72	1.37	1.61
1968-70	1.38	2.36	1.62	1.76	-2.62	6.67	0.88	1.26
1971-73	1.41	2.26	1.59	1.80	-2.34	6.28	0.55	1.19
1974-76	1.29	2.22	1.39	1.85	-8.01	5.41	-0.49	1.06
1977	1.26	1.83	1.51	1.97	-14.52	3.59	0.31	1.44
1978-79	1.45	2.16	1.78	2.25	-14.37	4.02	0.42	1.29
1980-82	1.34	1.85	1.75	2.25	-17.21	3.73	0.35	1.45
1983-85	1.30	1.71	1.80	2.26	-23.13	4.24	0.50	1.21
1986-88	1.33	1.65	1.84	2.27	-24.14	4.18	0.47	1.04
1989-91	1.24	1.54	1.77	2.15	-26.79	4.15	0.09	0.87
1992-94	1.25	1.50	1.90	2.14	-29.20	4.80	0.22	1.26

Source–Normalized assessment-income ratio and fitted assessment: see section VII of text. Actual assessment: CC Report and FC Report, various sessions, 1946-1991.

[a]Dependent variable in Table 3 regressions.

[b]Measured in percentage points. Fitted assessment from Table 3 regressions.

[c]U.K. for scale periods 1947 to 1971-73, Japan for scale periods 1974-76 to 1992-94.

[d]France for scale periods 1947 to 1971-73, Federal Republic of Germany for scale periods 1974-76 to 1989-91, Germany for scale period 1992-94.

Table 5
Actual and Normative Assessments, by Country Group
(percentage points)

Scale Period	United States		Other Developed Countries		Eastern Europe		Developing Countries	
	Actual	Actual minus Normative	Actual	Actual minus Normative	Actual	Actual minus Normative	Actual	Actual minus Normative
1947	39.89	2.25	30.92	0.89	9.58	-2.95	19.61	-0.20
1950	39.79	-9.40	30.44	7.83	9.58	1.31	20.19	0.26
1951	38.92	-8.89	30.24	6.82	10.18	1.77	20.66	0.31
1952	36.90	-14.36	28.74	4.32	13.90	4.82	20.46	5.23
1953	35.12	-16.88	28.24	2.09	16.97	8.79	19.67	6.00
1954	33.33	-18.58	27.73	1.61	19.31	11.07	19.63	5.90
1955	33.33	-18.67	27.21	1.33	20.28	11.99	19.18	5.35
1958	32.51	-14.81	30.36	-1.06	19.29	11.12	17.84	4.75
1959-61	32.51	-10.63	31.70	-1.93	19.09	9.68	16.70	2.87
1962-64	32.02	-8.87	30.59	-2.93	21.04	10.76	16.35	1.05
1966-67	31.91	-4.84	31.18	-3.41	21.09	9.49	15.64	-1.24
1968-70	31.57	-2.88	32.31	-3.17	20.54	8.73	15.58	-2.67
1971-73	31.52	-1.26	33.51	-0.95	19.92	6.09	15.05	-3.89
1974-76	25.00	-4.42	41.95	1.92	19.30	7.48	13.75	-4.98
1977	25.00	-3.24	43.30	3.39	17.60	5.37	14.10	-5.53
1978-79	25.00	-2.60	43.75	4.03	17.82	5.46	13.43	-6.89
1980-82	25.00	-0.82	47.19	9.63	17.12	3.23	10.69	-12.04
1983-85	25.00	-1.20	48.99	11.54	15.70	2.32	10.31	-12.67
1986-88	25.00	-0.31	49.33	12.46	15.07	2.03	10.60	-14.18
1989-91	25.00	-0.09	49.45	14.76	14.63	2.23	10.92	-16.90
1992-94	25.00	0.66	51.20	16.96	12.41	1.61	11.41	-19.23

Source–Actual assessment: CC Report and FC Report, 1st - 46th sessions, 1946-1991. Normative assessment: see appendix A.

Part II

Methodological Issues

International Comparisons of Prices, Output and Productivity
Edited by D.S. Prasada Rao and J. Salazar-Carrillo
1996 Elsevier Science B.V.

VAN IJZEREN'S METHOD OF INTERNATIONAL PRICE AND VOLUME COMPARISON : AN EXPOSITION

Bert M. Balk [1]
Department of Price Statistics
Netherlands Central Bureau of Statistics
AZ VOORBURG, The Netherlands

1. Introduction

This paper provides a brief introduction to Van IJzeren's (1956, 1983, and 1987) method of international comparison. Section 2 draws heavily on the more elaborate exposition of Balk (1989). Section 3 illustrates the various methods discussed in this paper with the help of a numerical example of Van IJzeren (1987).

The problem of international or interregional price and volume comparisons only superficially resembles that of intertemporal comparisons. There are at least three important differences.

1. It is desirable that international price and volume indexes be *transitive*, that is the price (volume) index of country 2 relative to country 1 times the price (volume) index of country 3 relative to country 2 equals the price (volume) index of country 3 relative to country 1. In other words, the country chosen as base acts only as a numeraire and can be replaced by any other country without affecting the results.

2. In addition to a system of volume indexes one desires a system of volume levels which can be *added* across countries and compared in a way consistent with the indexes. Values expressed in country-specific currencies should be revalued such that they can be added, for example in order to construct GDP figures for an aggregate of countries.

3. Unlike time periods, countries are not equally important (in an economic sense). It is undesirable that a country exerts more or less

[1] The views expressed in this paper are those of the author and do not necessarily reflect the policies of the Netherlands Central Bureau of Statistics.

influence on the results than is justified by its economic potential. This poses the problem of the appropriate *weighting* of countries.

The following notation is used. We assume that there are n countries that are to be compared. There are N commodities (goods and services) together constituting the GDP. The classification is identical for all countries. Ideally, each commodity is homogeneous so that it has a price and a (net) quantity. The price vector for country i expressed in its own currency is denoted by $p^i \equiv (p^i_1, ..., p^i_N) \in R^N_{++}$ for i=1,...,n. The corresponding quantity vector is $x^i \equiv (x^i_1, ..., x^i_N) \in R^N$.

Some quantities can be negative, for instance in the case of imports. However, we assume that $p^i.x^j \equiv \Sigma_{\ell=1}^N p^i_\ell x^j_\ell > 0$ for all i, j = 1,...,n.

2. The Van IJzeren method

Suppose we have a set of (scalar) purchasing power parties (alternatively called price level estimates, price deflators or currency converters) $P^1, ..., P^n$, determined up to a scalar multiple. Then

$$\begin{aligned} Q^i &\equiv (p^i.x^i/P^i)/(\Sigma_{j=1}^n p^j.x^j/P^j) \\ &= (\Sigma_{j=1}^n (p^j.x^j/p^i.x^i)(P^j/P^i)^{-1})^{-1} \end{aligned} \tag{1}$$

is the volume share of country i in the aggregate volume of all n countries. Note that $\Sigma_{i=1}^n Q^i = 1$. The volume index of country i relative to country j is

$$Q^i/Q^j = (p^i.x^i/p^j.x^j)/(P^j/P^i) \tag{2}$$

The ratio P^i/P^j is called the purchasing power parity of country i relative to country j. "International" prices and quantities are in full generality defined as

$$\pi = \Sigma_{i=1}^n g^i p^i/P^i \tag{3}$$

$$\chi = \Sigma_{i=1}^n g^i x^i/Q^i \tag{4}$$

where g^i, i=1,...,n are positive scalar country weights with $\Sigma_{i=1}^n g^i = 1$ Thus what is averaged are not price vectors p^i (quantity vectors x^i), but price *structure* vectors p^i/P^i (quantity *structure* vectors x^i/Q^i).

We link the price levels $p^j.\chi$ with the indexes P^i and the quantity levels $\pi.x^j$ with the indexes Q^j $(j = 1, ...n)$. Let

$$p^j.\chi = c^j \quad P^j \qquad\qquad (j = 1, ..., n) \tag{5}$$

$$\pi.x^j = c^j \quad Q^j$$

Combining both equations we obtain

$$p^j.\chi/P^j = \pi.x^j/Q^j \tag{6}$$

This is called the "balancing principle" : the value of "international quantities"in country j deflated prices equals the value of the country j deflated quantities in "international" prices. Substituting (2), (3) and (4) into (6) we obtain

$$\Sigma_{i=1}^n g^i P_L^{ij} P^i/P^j = \Sigma_{i=1}^n g^i P_L^{ji} P^j/P^i \tag{7}$$

where

$$P_L^{ij} \equiv p^j.x^i/p^i.x^i \tag{8}$$

is the Laspeyres price index of country j relative to country i. The system of equations (7) has a unique positive solution $P^1, ..., P^n$ (up to a scalar multiple), as is proved by Van IJzeren (1956). It is easy to show that when n = 2 the solution is

$$P^2/P^1 = P_F^{12} \equiv ((p^2.x^1/p^2.x^1)(p^2.x^2/p^1.x^2))^{1/2} \tag{9}$$

which is the Fisher price index of country 2 relative to country 1.

An expression for the factors c^j (j=1,...,n) can be found in Balk (1989). We also refer to this paper for a discussion of the relation between indexes for the GDP and indexes for subaggregates. It appears that the procedure is not consistent-in-aggregation, i.e., the results obtained for higher level subaggregates depend on whether they are obtained via lower level subaggregates or directly from individual commodities.

We note that the purchasing power parities $P^1, ..., P^n$, obtained as solution of (7), depend on all prices, all quantities, and all country weights. The expression $(p^j.x^j)/(P^j/P^i)$, occurring in (1), denotes the volume index of country j relative to country i. This index does not only depend on the country j and country i prices and quantities, but also on the prices and quantities of all other countries, in addition to the country weights. Hence, the present method can be considered as a multilateral generalization of the *own share system* proposed by Diewert (1986). We obtain the own share system when we replace $(p^j.x^j/(p^i.x^i))/(P^j/P^i)$, by the inverse of a bilateral quantity index for country i relative to country j, that is a quantity index only depending on p^i, p^j, x^i, x^j . Thus

$$Q_D^i \equiv (\Sigma_{j=1}^n (Q^{ij})^{-1})^{-1} \tag{10}$$

where Q^{ij}denotes a bilateral quantity index for country i relative to country j.

We now consider the relationship between the purchasing power parities according to Van IJzeren and those according to the *EKS method* (Eltetö and Köves 1964, Szulc 1964). Consider expression (7). Left hand and right hand part of (7) can be considered as weighted arithmetic average of "country reversal discrepancies". Replace the arithmetic averages by geometric averages, thus

$$\Pi_{i=1}^n (P_L^{ij} P^i / P^j)^{g^i} = \Pi_{i=1}^n (P_L^{ji} P^j / P^i)^{g^i} \qquad (j = 1, ..., n). \tag{11}$$

Rewriting this, we obtain

$$\Pi_{i=1}^n (P^j / P^i)^{g^i} = \Pi_{i=1}^n (P_F^{ij})^{g^i} \tag{12}$$

Dividing (12) by the analogous expression for $j' \neq j$, and recalling that $\Sigma_{i=1}^n g^i = 1$, we obtain

$$\begin{aligned} P^j / P^{j'} &= \Pi_{i=1}^n (P_F^{ij} / P_F^{ij'})^{g^i} \\ &= \Pi_{i=1}^n (P_F^{j'i} / P_F^{ij})^{g^i} \qquad (j, j' = 1, ...n; j \neq j') \end{aligned} \tag{13}$$

This is the weighted version of the EKS method.

Much use has been made of the *Geary (1958) - Khamis (1972) (GK) method* in international comparisons. Purchasing power parities according to the GK method are found by solving the following system of equations

$$\pi_\ell = (\Sigma_{i=1}^n p_\ell^i x_\ell^i / P^i)/\Sigma_{i=1}^n x_\ell^i \quad (\ell = 1, ..., N) \tag{14}$$

$$P^i = p^i.x^i/\pi.x^i \quad (i = 1, ..., n) \tag{15}$$

Note that (14) resembles (3) but is not a special case of it: the scalar country weights g^i in (3) are replaced by vectors with elements $x_\ell^i/\Sigma_{i=1}^n x_\ell^i$. Diewert (1986) shows that under a certain condition (14 and 15) has a unique (up to a positive scale factor) positive solution, $P^1, ..., P^n$.

Diewert (1986) developed a set of tests for multilateral comparisons. Balk (1989) modified these tests by incorporating country weights. He concluded that the Van IJzeren volume shares only fail to satisfy the (appropriately modified) proportionality test. This places the Van IJzeren system at least on equal footing with Diewert's own share system, which also fails to satisfy this test. The advantage of the Van IJzeren systems lies in the direct link between volume shares and quantity levels based on "international" prices, together with the aggregation and comparison possibilities they provide. Of course, it is possible to obtain volume shares and purchasing power parities via the own share system and then define "international" prices and quantities via (3) and (4). The point is, however, that we can not satisfy relations (5) in this case. Thus there is no intrinsic link between levels and indexes.

The GK system fails the proportionality test in a relatively spectacular manner, as shown by Diewert (1986) following Geary (1958). Replace the country k quantity vector x^k *by* λx^k *for* $\lambda > 0$ in (14) and then let λ tend to infinity. Then the GK volume indices and purchasing power parities for country i relative to country j tend to

$$Q^i/Q^j \rightarrow p^k.x^i/p^k.x^j \tag{16}$$

$$P^i/P^j \rightarrow P_P^{ki}/P_P^{kj} \tag{17}$$

where $P_P^{ki} \equiv p^i.x^i/p^k.x^i$ is the Paasche price index of country i relative to country k. Thus the limiting parity is a ratio of bilateral Paasche price indices.

With respect to the proportionality test the failure of the Van IJzeren method is not as "bad" as the failure of the GK system. Replacing x^k *by* λx^k *and* g^k *by* λg^k and taking limits as λ tends to infinity, we obtain from (7)

$$P_L^{kj} P^k / P^j = P_L^{jk} P^j / P^k \qquad (j = 1, ..., n) \tag{18}$$

The solution is

$$P^j / P^k = P_F^{kj} \qquad (j = 1, ..., n) \tag{19}$$

$$\text{or} \qquad P^i / P^j = P_F^{ki} / P_F^{kj} \tag{20}$$

which is reasonable from an economic viewpoint.

3. A numerical example

Van IJzeren (1987) constructed a useful data set, consisting of four artificial countries and six commodities. The basic ingredients are contained in Table 1. Country B is big, A is intermediate, C is small with "high" prices, and D is small. The matrix of inner products $p^i.x^j$ is given in Table 2. The main results are contained in Table 3. The first four rows contain bilateral index numbers. Row 1 contains the Laspeyres price index numbers, row 2 the Paasche price index numbers, row 3 the Fisher price index numbers, and row 4 the associated Fisher quantity index numbers. The remaining rows contain multilateral index numbers, which are transitive by construction. Row 5 contains the GK purchasing power parities. Rows 6 and 7 contain the Van IJzeren parities and the EKS parities respectively, both for the unweighted parities and the EKS parities respectively, both for the unweighted case (that is $g^i = 1/n$ for all i). Rows 8 and 9 contain the Van IJzeren parities and the EKS parities respectively, both for the case where $g^i = Q^i$ (The EKS result is obtained via an iterative procedure). As could be expected from the theoretical argument, the Van IJzeren results and the EKS results closely agree with each other. In the weighted case the differences are negligible. Finally, row 10 contains the volume index numbers according to the Diewert own share system. They are calculated from the bilateral Fisher quantity index numbers in row 4. Row 11 contains the associated purchasing power parities.

Table 1: The data set

Country	1		2		3		4		5		6	
	p	x	p	x	p	x	p	x	p	x	p	x
A	11	55	20	45	10	100	17	55	10	140	8	120
B	15	175	14	275	10	500	21	200	9	675	9	575
C	88	26	112	19	140	17	200	10	96	12	216	10
D	15	32	24	24	18	24	63	6	24	11	42	14

Table 2: The inner products $p^i.x^j$

	j=A	B	C	D
i=A	5800	27175	1206	1396
B	5950	26925	1234	1407
C	74240	345200	12108	14144
D	15570	71175	2490	2718

Table 3: Index numbers

Index	B/A	C/A	D/A	C/B	D/B	D/C
P_L	1.0259	12.8000	2.6845	12.8208	2.6435	0.2056
P_P	0.9908	10.0398	1.9470	9.8120	1.9318	0.1922
P_F	1.0082	11.3362	2.2862	11.2160	2.2598	0.1988
Q_F	4.6046	0.1842	0.2050	0.0401	0.0447	1.1292
P_{GK}	1.0166	10.3526	2.0387			
$P_y, g^i 1/n$	1.0098	11.3689	2.2769			
$P_{EKS}, g^i = 1/n$	1.0097	11.3698	2.2760			
$P_y, g^i = Q^i$	1.0084	11.3196	2.2792			
$PEKS, g^i = Q^i$	1.0084	11.3199	2.2791			
Q_D	4.4500	0.1783	0.1989			
P_D	1.0432	11.7083	2.3561			

References

Balk, B. M. (1989), "On Van IJzeren's Approach to International Comparisons and its Properties", *Statistical Papers/Statistische Hefte* 30, pp. 295-315

Diewert, W.E. (1986), *Microeconomic Approaches to the Theory of International Comparisons*, Technical Working Paper No. 53, National Bureau of Economic Research, Cambridge MA. Truncated version in Eichhorn (1988).

Eichhorn, W. (ed) (1988), *Measurement in Economics*, Physica-Verlag, Heidelberg.

Eltetö, O. and P. Köves (1964), "On an Index Computation Problem in International Comparisons" (in Hungarian), *Statisztikai Szemle* 42, pp. 507-518.

Geary, R.C. (1958), "A Note on Comparisons of Exchange Rates and Purchasing Power between Countries", *Journal of the Royal Statistical Society A 121*, pp. 97-99.

Khamis, S. H. (1972), "A New System of Index Numbers for National and International Purposes", *Journal of the Royal Statistical Society A 135*, pp. 96-121.

Szulc, B. (1964), "Index Numbers of Multilateral Regional Comparisons" (in Polish), *Przeglad Statysticzny* 3, pp. 239-254.

Van IJzeren, J. (1956), *Three Methods of Comparing the Purchasing Power of Currencies*, Statistical Studies No. 7, The Netherlands Central Bureau of Statistics/De Haan, Zeist.

Van IJzeren, J. (1983), *Index Numbers for Binary and Multilateral Comparison: Algebraical and Numerical Aspects*, Statistical Studies No. 34 The Netherlands Central Bureau of Statistics/ Staatsuitgeverij, The Hague.

Van IJzeren, J. (1987), *Bias in International Index Numbers: A Mathematical Elucidation* (Private edition).

Van IJzeren, J. (1988), "Weighting and Additivity Problems of Multilateral Comparison", in Eichhorn (1988).

International Comparisons of Prices, Output and Productivity
Edited by D.S. Prasada Rao and J. Salazar-Carrillo

CONSISTENCY IN AGGREGATION PRINCIPLE FOR MULTILATERAL COMPARISONS OF PURCHASING POWER PARITIES AND REAL PRODUCTS

Salem H. Khamis
Hemel Hempstead
United Kingdom

1. Introduction

International economic comparisons depend, *inter alia*, on the determination of appropriate international (average, regional or world) commodity prices expressed in a common currency unit and of corresponding purchasing power parties (PPPs) of national currency units. These enable the valuation of national aggregates such as consumption or output in terms of a common currency unit relevant to the measurement of these aggregates in real terms, e.g. real domestic product, and also enable the aggregation of such values over countries (e.g. world real product, real product of the European Union or of other regional or geographic economic areas). For this purpose, it is natural to impose a consistency condition on the international prices and PPPs which requires equality of the resulting aggregates obtained through the international prices and the corresponding aggregates obtained through PPPs. Under this equality the set of international prices is said to be consistent with the set of PPPs and vice versa. Such consistency is necessary for any meaningful relationship between the international prices and PPPs.

The main aim of this short paper is to illustrate the role of the *consistency in aggregation* principle as described above in the unique determination of the international prices and PPPs themselves and of the related indexes of PPPs and real product (volume indexes). Uniqueness here means that the same indexes are obtained regardless of whether they are calculated through the international prices or through deflation of the national aggregates by the corresponding PPP indexes.

2. Application of the Consistency Principle

For a set of N commodities and M countries we denote by p_{ij} and q_{ij} the national price and quantity of output of commodity i in country j with i = 1,2,...,N and j = 1,2,...,M. We also denote by e_j the reciprocal of the PPP of country j (with e_j measuring a type of "real exchange rate" for the currency unit of country j) and by P_i the "average" (regional, international) price of commodity i. The prices and quantities and the e_j all correspond to a given period of time. With this notation we note that there are two ways of valuating national consumption or output, one corresponding to the left hand side and one to the right hand side of the equation

$$e_j \sum_i p_{ij}\, q_{ij} \;=\; \sum_i P_i\, q_{ij}, \qquad j \;=\; 1, 2, ..., M \tag{1}$$

with equality being the requirement of the consistency principle. There is general acceptance of the set of the M equations in (1) regardless of the definitions of the "average" prices P_i and of the "real exchange rates" e_j as long as equality is attained. Equation (1) is the result of the application of the consistency principle to total national output (or expenditure). Applying the same principle to total output of (or expenditure on) commodity i, one obtains the relationship

$$P_i \sum_j q_{ij} \;=\; \sum_j e_j\, p_{ij}\, q_{ij}, \qquad i \;=\; 1, 2, ..., N \tag{2}$$

where the LHS and RHS correspond to the valuation through the "average" prices P_i and the "exchange rates" e_j respectively. The summations over i and j in (1) and (2) above are respectively over the whole set of commodities and countries. Although the sets of equations (1) and (2) are the necessary result of the consistency principle, some researchers still find it difficult to subscribe to equation (2) which is equivalent to the Geary definition

$$P_i \;=\; \frac{\sum_j e_j\, p_{ij}\, q_{ij}}{\sum_j q_{ij}}, \qquad i \;=\; 1, 2, ..., N \tag{3}$$

of "average" prices (Geary 1958).

3. Uniqueness

As noted by R. C. Geary, the summation of both sides of equation (1) over all j and that of both sides of equation (2) over all i lead to the same relationship

$$\sum_i \sum_j e_j \; p_{ij} \; q_{ij} \;=\; \sum_i \sum_j P_i \; q_{ij} \tag{4}$$

Obviously, equation (4) itself is also a direct result of the consistency in aggregation principle. The relationship in equation (4) is of fundamental importance as it guarantees the existence of solutions, other than the trivial ones, for the prices P_i and for the exchange rates e_j as defined by equations (1) and (2). The proof of the uniqueness of these solutions (apart from a constant scalar multiplier) and their positiveness first given by the author (Khamis,1970 and 1972) for non-negative quantities is equally applicable in cases where some of the quantities q_{ij} are negative (e.g. for the value added method of estimate gross domestic product) provided

$$\sum_i p_{ij} \; q_{ik} \;>\; 0 \tag{5}$$

for all pairs of values of j and k. The condition of non-negative quantities in that proof was introduced simply because the Geary-Khamis(GK) method defined by the equations (1) and (2), had originally been developed for the assessment of temporal changes in regional and world production of food and of agricultural commodities. Subject to the condition of equation (5), the same proof will apply with the necessary and sufficient condition for a unique positive solution being the irreducibility of the relevant matrix in the original proof. Thus, the GK method may then be applicable to the value added method of calculating real national product or real product by industrial origin.

The index Q_{ks} of real product of country s relative to country k is then given by

$$Q_{ks} \;=\; \frac{\sum_i P_i \; q_{is}}{\sum_i P_i \; q_{ik}} \tag{6}$$

or the equivalent formula

$$Q_{ks} \;=\; \frac{\sum_i p_{is} \; q_{is}}{\sum_i p_{ik} \; q_{ik}} \, / PPP_{ks} \tag{7}$$

where PPP_{ks} is the PPP index of country s relative to country k defined by

$$PPP_{ks} \;=\; \frac{PPP_s}{PPP_k} \;=\; \frac{e_k}{e_s} \tag{8}$$

for any pair of countries s, k. Equations (1) and (2) ensure the equality of the indexes obtained through either of the two equations (6) and (7), thus leading to unique indexes regardless of whether they are obtained through the average prices P_i directly or through the division of the nominal value index by the corresponding PPP index. In this connection, equation (7) shows that the well-known (restricted) factor test is inherently satisfied by the GK method as it is implied by equation (1). In other words, the factor test is also implied by the consistency in aggregation principle enunciated above. It is unfortunate that a number of highly able researchers have missed this intrinsic property of the GK method by asserting that it does not satisfy the factor test. (cf., e.g., Kurabayashi and Sakuma, 1990, note 7, p.157).

4. Additivity and Matrix Consistency

In addition to leading to the unique prices P_i, "real exchange rates", PPPs and volume and PPP indexes refered to above, the consistency in aggregation principle also guarantees the uniqueness of real product sub-aggregates and ensures their being equal to the sum of the real product of their sub-components. Had the price and quantity data on individual commodities been available this property would ensure the full additivity of the GK method. The non-availability of such detailed data restricts additivity to the smallest "commodity" heading for which data are available. This restricted additivity is also called "matrix consistency" (cf.Kurabayashi and Sakuma, 1990, and related references). These properties have been given very high priority for choice amongst available aggregation methods. While the International Comparisons Program (ICP) adopted the GK method from the start of the United Nations work (Kravis et al, 1975), the Statistical Office of the European Communities (EUROSTAT) used for their 1975 comparison the Gerardi method (Khamis and Prasada Rao, 1989) instead of the so-called EKS method specifically because of the non-additivity of the latter method (EUROSTAT 1988). For purposes of international co-ordination, the EUROSTAT for their next two quinquennial comparisons adopted the GK method although they were of the opinion that there was no sufficient reason to decide which of the two methods - GK or Gerardi - was more appropriate.

Beginning with 1990, the Organisation for Economic Co-operation and Development (OECD) and EUROSTAT, in addition to their GK based measurements of PPPs and real products, started also to use the EKS (based on Fisher's binary index) for the same purpose with the EUROSTAT using the latter PPPs as the official ones for the European Union. They give no explanation for the shift in the EURO-STAT preference from the Gerardi method used in 1975 to that of the EKS. Their sacrifice of the additivity property with its serious effect on the non-uniqueness of the resulting indexes and their related aggregates and sub-aggregates (arising from the unequal results from the equations (6) and (7)) is hardly justified. In fact their claim that the "EKS results are considered to be better suited for comparisons across countries of the prices and volumes of individual aggregates such as clothing and footwear..." (OECD 1992 p.4) is highly questionable because non-uniqueness does involve two different measures and the non-additivity is much more serious for sub-aggregates where the relative differences would be much higher (cf., e.g., the entries for Denmark, France, Germany and Greece in the numbered lines 23 to 29 for the aggregate Transport and communication and the corresponding totals of its components in Table 1.1 of OECD 1992). The arguments given for the property that the EKS method was nearest to the Fisher binary results also holds in the case of any other binary index satisfying the country reversal test. The so-called characteristicity property and Gerschenkorn effect do not introduce any new criterion as they are other linguistically equivalent terms implied by the well-known Laspeyres-Paasche spread. Such arguments are in the opinion of the author, an inadvertent transport of misconceptions prevalent in earlier literature on temporal national price and volume indexes not based on a fully acceptable theoretical foundation (cf. EUTOSTAT 1982 chapter III, and Khamis 1972, 1983, 1984, 1988 and 1993).

5. Concluding Remarks

The principle of consistency in aggregation as presented above is based on a short note presented at the 1992 Miami Seminar on "International Comparisons of Price Structures and their Influence on Productivity and Growth" held at Florida International University. As pointed out above, there is general agreement on the advantages of additivity which is a consequence of the consistency in aggregation principle. If the principle was to be carried to its logical conclusion the consequences of equations (1) and (2) would lead to a unique method for multilateral comparisons, namely the Geary-Khamis method.

The main argument advanced by those opposed to equation (2) is that the average prices implied by it (equation (3)) are dominated by those of the "richest" or highest consuming country leading to what they term a "bias" towards higher real product for the poorer (or less developed) countries. While the larger quantities of a "rich" country are expected to lead to larger weights in the average prices equation (3), the resulting effect is not necessarily as claimed because it is not the absolute magnitude of the average prices but rather their relative structure which is important. An inspection of e.g. the real product of countries covered by the ICP will show exceptions to the claimed "bias". In the absence of knowledge of the true indexes one cannot claim "bias" in one direction or another. Attempts to derive the ideal Fisher binary index through an axiomatic or test approach to index numbers (e.g. by Van IJzern, 1983, or by Diewert, 1992) and its related extensions to multilateral comparisons involved either vicious circular arguments (in the case of Van IJzern) or controversial assumptions (in the case of Diewert, although he himself was aware of these matters). There is yet no acceptable theoretical proof that the "true index" necessarily lies between the Paasche and Laspeyres indexes. On the other hand, attempts to derive through economic theory of living generally require theoretical assumptions which are unduly restrictive.

The author is of the opinion that the main alternative to the adoption of equation (2) is the provision of another meaningful definition of the average prices P_i that guarantees additivity or at least which leads to measurable limits to deviations from additivity that are small enough for the purposes of applied economic analysis and other uses of the resulting data.

References

Diewert, W.E. (1992): "Fisher Ideal Output, and Productivity Indexes Revisited", *J. Productivity Analysis*, Vol. 3.

EUROSTAT (1982): *Multilateral Measurement of Purchasing Power and Real GDP*, Luxembourg.

EUROSTAT (1988): *Purchasing Power Parities and Gross Domestic Product in Real Terms - Results 1985*, Luxembourg.

Khamis, S.H. (1970): "Properties and Conditions for the Existence of a New Type of Index Numbers", *Sankhya, Series B,* Vol. 32.

Khamis, S.H. (1972): "A New System of Index Numbers for National and International Purposes", *JRSS, Series A,* Vol. 135.

Khamis, S.H. (1983): "Application of Index Numbers in International Comparisons and Related Concepts", *Bull. Inter. Stat. Inst.,* Vol. 50.

Khamis, S.H. (1984): "On Aggregation Methods for International Comparisons", *Review of Income and Wealth,* Vol. 30.

Khamis, S.H. (1988): "Remarks on Some Criteria for Spatial Index Numbers", *Pre-proceedings, 1st Conference, Inter.Assoc. for Official Statistics,* International Statistical Institute.

Khamis, S.H. (1993): "On Some Aspects of the Measurement of Purchasing Power Parities", Contributed Papers, Book 2, *Bull. Inter. Stat. Inst,* 49th Session.

Khamis, S.H. and Prasada Rao, D.S. (1989): "On Gerardi Alternative for the Geary-Khamis Measurement of International Purchasing Powers and Real Product", *J. Office Statistics,* Vol. 5, No. 1, Sweden.

Kravis, I.B., Kenessey, Z., Henston, A.W. and Summers, R. (1975): *A System of Comparison of Gross Domestic Product and Purchasing Power,* John Hopkins University Press, Baltimore.

Kurabayashi, Y. and Sakuma, I. (1990): *Studies in International Comparisons of Real Product and Prices,* Kinokuniya Co. Ltd and Oxford University Press.

OECD (1992): Purchasing Power Parities and Real Expenditure, Vol. 1 (EKS Results), Paris.

Van IJzeren, J. (1983): Index Numbers for Binary and Multilateral Comparisons - Algebraical and Numerical Aspects, *Statist.Studies No. 34*, Central Statistics Bureau, Voorburg, Netherlands.

International Comparisons of Prices, Output and Productivity
Edited by D.S. Prasada Rao and J. Salazar-Carrillo

STOCHASTIC APPROACH TO INTERNATIONAL COMPARISONS OF PRICES AND REAL INCOME

D.S. Prasada Rao
University of New England
Armidale, Australia

and

E.A. Selvanathan
Griffith University
Brisbane, Australia

1. Introduction

The main purpose of this paper is to present some of the recent research concerning the development of suitable methods for international comparisons of prices and output using the stochastic approach developed in the early work of Theil(1965), Banerjee(1975), Balk(1980), Clements and Izan(1981) and Selvanathan(1987,1989). In contrast to the general approaches followed in the derivation of index number methods for aggregation of price and quantity data, e.g., Geary-Khamis, Van IJzeren and other methods, the stochastic approach uses simple regression techniques to measure the levels and changes underlying the observed price and quantity data over time and space.

The stochastic approach for international comparisons uses the basic idea that most of the indices, computed either directly or through the concept of purchasing power parities, are essentially measures of central tendency derived from observed changes in prices of a set of commodities. Until now the purchasing power parities, in the context of international comparisons of prices, have been usually computed and provided for use as definitive rather than some sort of estimates of the true purchasing power parities. It is indeed very rare that any kind of standard errors are published in conjunction with purchasing power parities. However, it is useful to provide standard errors for these index numbers which reflect the reliability of the index as a single numerical measure of change in a set of commodity prices as well as the precision which is influenced by the sampling aspects and errors in measurement.

The present paper focuses on the stochastic approach to index number construction, demonstrates the feasibility of deriving most of the well-known index numbers such as the Laspeyres, Paasche, Theil-Tornqvist index numbers and their standard errors. A description of the basic ideas underlying the stochastic approach and the models leading to some of the well known index number formulae are dealt with in Section 2. Section 3 deals with generalised Theil-Tornqvist indices for international comparisons, including the derivation of the Caves-Christensen-Diewert(1982) index and its generalisations provided in some recent work of Prasada Rao and Selvanathan (1991) and Selvanathan and Prasada Rao (1992). The stochastic specification of the Geary-Khamis is undertaken in Section 4. The paper is concluded with some remarks in Section 5.

2. The Stochastic Approach

In this section we outline the stochastic approach and show how some of the well-known index numbers and their standard errors can be derived using this approach. The standard errors are useful in assessing the precision as well as for constructing confidence intervals for the price indexes.

Under the stochastic approach, each price relative is taken to be equal to the underlying price index which measures the overall price changes between the current and base periods, plus other components which are random and nonrandom. If we have n prices, then the price index can be estimated by taking some form of average of the n price relatives.

The index number problem under stochastic approach can be viewed as a signal extraction problem. To illustrate, consider the simplest case whereby each of the price relatives is the sum of the underlying overall price index and an independent random component. Here, each observed price relative is a reading on the index of overall price changes 'contaminated' by the random term. The averaging of the price relatives serves to eliminate as much as possible of the contamination and leaves an estimate of the underlying signal, the index of overall price changes.

Now we show how the stochastic approach can be used to derive well-known price index numbers Laspeyres, Paasche and Theil-Tornqvist index numbers.

2.1 *Laspeyres Index*

Let p_{i0} and p_{it} be the price of commodity $i(i = 1, ..., n)$ in periods 0 and t. Then $p_{it}^0 = (p_{it}/p_{io})$ is the ith price relative. For each period, let each price relative be made up of a systematic part γ_t and a random component ϵ; that is

$$p_{it}^0 = \gamma_t + \epsilon_{it}, \quad i = 1, ..., n. \tag{1}$$

We assume that the random components having expectation zero and with covariance structure

$$E(\epsilon_{it}) = 0, \quad \text{Cov}(\epsilon_{it}, \epsilon_{jt}) = \frac{\lambda_t^2}{w_{i0}}\delta_{ij} \tag{2}$$

where λ_t^2 is a constant with respect to the commodities; $w_{i0} = p_{i0}q_{i0}/M_0$ is the budget share of i in period 0; and δ_{ij} is the Kronecker delta. Under (1) we have that the variance of price relative of i is λ_t^2/w_i and is inversely proportional to w_{i0}. This means that the variability of a price relative falls as the commodity becomes more important in the consumer's budget.

Now we develop the GLS estimator of γ_t. We multiply both sides of (1) by $\sqrt{w_{i0}}$ to give

$$y_{it} = \gamma_i x_{i0} + u_{it} \tag{3}$$

where $y_{it} = p_{it}^0\sqrt{w_{i0}}$; $x_{i0} = \sqrt{w_{i0}}$; and $u_{it} = \epsilon_{it}\sqrt{w_{i0}}$. It follows from (2) that $Cov[u_{it}, u_{jt}] = w_{i0}\,Cov[\epsilon_{it}, \epsilon_{jt}] = \lambda_t^2\delta_{ij}$. Therefore $Var[u_{it}] = \lambda_t^2$, which is common for all commodities. Thus we can now apply LS to (3) to get BLUE (GLS estimator) of γ_t,

$$\hat{\gamma}_t = \frac{\sum_{i=1}^n y_{it} x_{i0}}{\sum_{i=1}^n x_{i0}^2} = \sum_{i=1}^n w_{i0} \frac{p_{it}}{p_{i0}} = \frac{\sum_{i=1}^n p_{it} q_{i0}}{\sum_{i=1}^n p_{i0} q_{i0}}, \tag{4}$$

where we have used $\sum_{i=1}^n x_{i0}^2 = \sum_{i=1}^n w_{i0} = 1$. The estimator (4) is the Laspeyres price index.

The variance of $\hat{\gamma}_t$ is given by

$$Var(\hat{\gamma}_t) = \frac{\lambda_t^2}{\sum_{i=1}^n x_{i0}^2} = \frac{\lambda_t^2}{\sum_{i=1}^n w_{i0}^2} = \lambda_t^2. \tag{5}$$

The parameter λ_t^2 can be estimated unbiasedly by

$$\hat{\lambda}_t^2 = \frac{1}{n-1} \sum_{i=1}^n (y_{it} - \hat{\gamma}_t x_{i0})^2 = \frac{1}{n-1} \sum_{i=1}^n w_{i0} (p_{it}^0 - \hat{\gamma}_t)^2.$$

Equation (5) gives the variance of the Laspeyres price index.

2.2 *Paasche Index*

Now replace error covariance structure in (2) with the following specification:

$$E[\epsilon_{it}] = 0, \quad Cov[\epsilon_{it}, \epsilon_{jt}] = \frac{\lambda_t^2}{w_{i0}^t} \delta_{ij}, \tag{6}$$

where λ_t^2 is a constant with respect to commodities; and $w_{i0}^t = p_{i0} q_{it} / M_0^t$ is the budget share resulting from the purchase of current period quantities with base period prices and these budget shares satisfy $\sum_{i=1}^n w_{i0}^t = 1$; and $M_0^t = \sum_{i=1}^n p_{i0} q_{it}$ is the corresponding total expenditure. Equation (6) is the same as (2) except that base-period consumption q_{i0} in the former set of equations is replaced with current-period consumption. As before, by multiplying both sides of (1) by $\sqrt{w_{i0}^t}$, we obtain the GLS estimation of γ_t under error covariance structure (6) as

$$\gamma_t^* = \frac{\sum_{i=1}^n p_{it} q_{it}}{\sum_{i=1}^n p_{i0} q_{it}}, \tag{7}$$

which is the Paasche price index; and its estimated variance is

$$Var(\gamma_t^*) = \frac{1}{1-n} \sum_{i=1}^n w_{i0}^t (p_{it} - \gamma_t^*)^2. \tag{8}$$

2.3 *Theil-Tornqvist Index*

Now we derive another popular index number the Theil-Tornqvist index number using the stochastic approach. This index is well-known in the index number literature for its use in binary comparisons of cost of living, prices, real output and productivity of two regions within a country or two regions or two time periods.

Let $\{(p_{it}, q_{it}), i = 1, 2, ..., n\}$ and $\{(p_{is}, q_{is}), i = 1, 2, ..., n.\}$ be two pairs of price and quantity vectors corresponding to two time periods t and s (t and s can also denote either two regions or two countries). To derive the Theil-Tornqvist index, using the approach, we write the price log-change, $Dp_{its} = ln\, p_{it} - ln\, p_{is}$, in the price of commodity i over periods t and s in the form

$$Dp_{its} = \pi_{st} + u_{ist}, \quad i = 1, 2, ..., n. \tag{9}$$

In the above model, the parameter π_{st} can be interpreted as a measure of common trend in prices of all n commodities over the periods s and t.

We assume the following specification for the error structure of model (9):

$$E[u_{ist}] = 0;$$

$$Var[u_{ist}] = \frac{\sigma^2}{\bar{w}_{ist}}; \text{ and}$$

$$Cov[u_{ist}, u_{i's't'}] = 0 \text{ for all } i \neq i', s \neq s', t \neq t'. \tag{10}$$

where σ^2 is a constant.

Under (10), the GLS estimator of π_{st} in model (10) is given by

$$\hat{\pi}_{st} = \sum_{i=1}^{n} \bar{w}_{ist} Dp_{ist}. \tag{11}$$

Estimator (11) is identical to the additive form of the Theil-Tornqvist index.

The variance of $\hat{\pi}_{st}$ will be given by

$$Var(\hat{\pi_{st}}) = \sigma^2. \tag{12}$$

The parameter σ^2 can be estimated unbiasedly by

$$\hat{\sigma}^2 = \frac{1}{n-1} \sum_{i=1}^{n} \bar{w}_{ist}(Dp_{ist} - \hat{\pi}_{ist})^2.$$

2.4 *An Illustrative Application*

We now present an application of the Laspeyres price index. We use the private consumption expenditure data for many commodity groups (namely, food, beverages, clothing, housing, durables, medical care, transport, recreation and education, and miscellaneous) in the UK for the period 1977-1989 to compute the Laspeyres price index and its standard error with base year 1977. As can be seen, in most years the Laspeyres price index is significantly different from one.

Table 1
Estimates of Laspeyres Price Index and its Standard Errors;
United Kingdom, 1977-1989
(1977=1.00)

Year (1)	Laspeyres Price Index (2)	Standard error (3)
1978	1.0968	.0080
1979	1.2488	.0179
1980	1.4550	.0328
1981	1.6184	.0522
1982	1.7691	.0712
1983	1.8444	.0793
1984	1.9372	.0849
1985	2.0448	.0968
1986	2.1364	.1099
1987	2.2289	.1221
1988	2.3447	.1360
1989	2.4855	.1483

3. Index Numbers for Spatial Comparisons

In the last section we introduced the stochastic approach and showed how this approach can be used to derive various index numbers and their standard errors within a time-series context. In this section we demonstrate the use of the stochastic approach in deriving index numbers formulae for multilateral spatial comparisons.

3.1 *CCD Multilateral Index*

We re-label the Theil-Tornqvist index in multiplicative form for binary price comparisons of two countries j and k ($j = 1, 2, ..., M$;

M =number of countries; k =base country) and write

$$I_{kj}^{TT} = \prod_{i=1}^{n} \left[\frac{p_{ij}}{p_{ik}} \right]^{\bar{w}_{ikj}} \tag{13}$$

where $\bar{w}_{ikj} = \frac{1}{2}(w_{ik} + w_{ij})$, $w_{ij} = p_{ij}q_{ij} / \sum_{l=1}^{n} p_{lj}q_{lj}$ is the budget share of the ith commodity in the jth country.

In additive form (13) can be written as

$$\Pi_{kj}^{TT} = \sum_{i=1}^{n} \bar{w}_{ikj} dp_{ikj} \tag{14}$$

where $\prod_{kj}^{TT} = ln\, I_{kj}^{TT}$ and $Dp_{ikj} = ln\,(p_{ij}/p_{ik})$.

It is well-known that the TT index is 'exact' and 'superlative' but not transitive. As TT index is not transitive, it is not that much use in the context of multilateral comparisons. To overcome this difficulty, Caves, Christensen and Diewert (1982a) proposed a new index, (here onwards, we label it as 'CCD' index) which is a simple geometric mean of M indirect comparisons between j and k derived through a bridge country l $(l = 1, 2, ..., M)$, in the form

$$I_{kj}^{CCD} = \prod_{i=1}^{M} \left[I_{jl}^{TT} \,.\, I_{lk}^{TT} \right]^{1/M} \tag{15}$$

In additive form (13) becomes

$$\Pi_{kj}^{CCD} = \pi_j^* - \pi_k^*$$

where $\pi_{kj}^{CCD} = ln\, I_{kj}^{CCD}$; $\pi_j^* = \frac{1}{M} \sum_{l=1}^{M} \pi_{jl}^{TT}$ and $\pi_k^* = \frac{1}{M} \sum_{l=1}^{M} \pi_{lk}^{TT}$. It can be easily shown that the CCD index satisfies transitivity (i.e., $\pi_{kj} = \pi_{kl} + \pi_{lj}$) and country symmetry properties. An index π_{kj} satisfies transitivity if and only if there exists real numbers $\pi_1, \pi_2, ..., \pi_M$ such that $\pi_{kj} = \pi_j - \pi_k$. Now we show how the stochastic approach can be used to derive the CCD index and its standard error. We now replace the time subscript in (13) with country subscripts, to give

$$Dp_{ikj} = \pi_{kj} + u_{ikj}, \quad i = 1, 2, ..., n. \tag{16}$$

with

$$E(u_{ikj}) = 0; \quad Var(u_{ikj}) = \frac{\sigma^2}{\bar{w}_{ikj}} \text{ and}$$

$$Cov[u_{ikj}, u_{i'k'j'}] = 0 \text{ for all } i \neq i', \ j \neq j', \ k \neq k'$$

If we impose transitivity, then (16) takes the form

$$Dp_{ijk} = \pi_j - \pi_k + u_{ijk} \qquad \begin{array}{l} i = 1, 2, ..., n; \\ k = 1, 2, ..., M - 1; \\ j = k + 1, ..., M. \end{array} \tag{17}$$

Obviously model (17) is not identified. This can be seen by noting that an increase in π_k, $k = 1, ..., M - 1$ by any number c and an increase in π_j, $j = k = 1, ..., M$ by same c leaves the right-hand of (17) unaffected. To identify model (17), we set $\hat{\pi}_M = 0$ and solve for $\hat{\pi}_1, \hat{\pi}_2, ..., \hat{\pi}_{M-1}$ uniquely. The GLS estimator (17) in this case will be given by

$$\hat{\pi}_j = \frac{1}{M}\left[\sum_{k=1}^{M}\sum_{i=1}^{n} \bar{w}_{imk}\, ln\frac{p_{ik}}{p_{im}} + \sum_{k=1}^{M}\sum_{i=1}^{n} \bar{w}_{ijk}\, ln\frac{p_{ij}}{p_{ik}}\right] j = 1, 2, ..., M \tag{18}$$

$$\text{and } \hat{\pi}_M = 0$$

Thus the solution $\hat{\pi}_j$ may be interpreted essentially as a log-change index for country j with base country M. In multiplicative form (18) may be expressed for j and k as

$$I_{kj}^{CCD} = \prod_{l=1}^{M} \left[\prod_{i=1}^{n} \left[\frac{p_{il}}{p_{ik}} \right]^{\bar{w}_{ikl}} \prod_{i=1}^{n} \left[\frac{p_{ij}}{p_{il}} \right]^{\bar{w}_{ilj}} \right]^{1/M} \tag{19}$$

The index number formulae I_{kj}^{CCD} is the generalised TT index or CCD due to Caves, Christensen and Diewert which provides a multivariant generalisation of TT index. The CCD index satisfies the transitivity and country symmetry or base invariance properties. As I_{kj}^{CCD} is obtained from a regression model (17), it would be possible to compute the standard errors associated with I_{kj}^{CCD}.

Using (13) we can write (19) in the form

$$I_{kj}^{CCD} = \prod_{l=1}^{M} \left[I_{kl}^{TT} . I_{lj}^{TT} \right]^{1/M} \tag{20}$$

This shows that I_{kj}^{CCD} is a simple geometric mean of all the M indirect comparisons between countries k and j, where each indirect comparison is made through a country l using the binary formulae.

3.2 *Generalised CCD multilateral Index*

From (20) it can be easily seen that the CCD multilateral index for comparison between countries j and k is a simple geometric mean of all the indirect comparisons through a third country l. Obviously, assigning the same weight or equal importance to all countries is a problem with the CCD index. For example, if k refers to the USA and j refers to the UK, then an indirect comparison between the USA and UK through France would be more reliable than a comparison through India, suggesting a deferential weighting scheme.

To derive a weighted CCD multilateral index, in model (17) we replace the variance structure with

$$Var[u_{ikj}] = \frac{\sigma^2}{\bar{w}_{ikj}} d_{kj};$$

where d_{kj} is the economic distance between j and k defined as

$$\begin{aligned} d_{kj} &= \left| ln\left[\frac{E_j}{I_{lj}}\right] - ln\left[\frac{E_k}{I_{lk}}\right]\right| \\ &= |(ln\, E_j - \pi_j) - (ln\, E_k - \pi_k)| \end{aligned}$$

and E_j is the nominal per capita income in country j and E_j/I_{lj} is the converted per capita income of country j into the currency unit of country ℓ. The GLS estimators of $\pi_j,\ j = 1, 2, ..., M$ can be obtained as before. We denote the resulting generalised CCD indices (GCCD, for short) by I_{kj}^{GCCD}. Due to the complex structure of the new weighting scheme, simple expressions for I_{kj}^{GCCD} are not yet found. However, for the simpler case, when $M = 3$, it can be shown that the GCCD index in the multiplicative form can be written as

$$I_{31}^{GCCD} = \left[\sum_{i=1}^{n}\left[\frac{p_{i2}}{p_{i3}}\right]^{\bar{w}_{i23}} \sum_{i=1}^{n}\left[\frac{p_{i1}}{p_{i2}}\right]^{\bar{w}_{i12}}\right]^{\hat{d}_{23}/\alpha} \left[\sum_{i=1}^{n}\left[\frac{p_{i1}}{p_{i3}}\right]^{\bar{w}_{i13}}\right]^{(\hat{d}_{12}+\hat{d}_{23})/\alpha}$$

where $\alpha = \hat{d}_{12} + \hat{d}_{13} + \hat{d}_{23}$. In terms of binary Theil-Tornqvist indices this can be expressed as

$$I_{31}^{GCCD} = \left[I_{32}^{TT}.I_{21}^{TT}\right]^{\hat{d}_{13}/\alpha}.\left[I_{31}^{TT}\right]^{(\hat{d}_{12}+\hat{d}_{23})/\alpha}.$$

3.3 *Illustrative Application*

Now we present an application of TT index, CCD index, GCCD index using the price and quantity data from selected countries from the Phase IV of the International Comparison Project of the U.N. Statistical office (1987). The commodity list used here is eight highly aggregated commodity groups of private consumption expenditure, viz (I) food, beverages and tobacco (2) clothing and footwear, (3) rent and fuel, (4) house furnishing and operations, (5) medical care, (6) transport and communication, (7) recreation and education and (8) miscellaneous. The following table presents the results with the USA as the base country. Root mean squared errors are reported in parentheses. As can be seen, in most cases there is no appreciable difference between the three indices. However, a comparison of the RMST's show that, in general, the RMSE is relatively lower than the binary. This is also due to the large degrees of freedom which resulted in high precision associated with the multilateral indices relative to their binary counterparts. It is also worth noting that the differences between the RMSE's of multilateral indices are not significant.

Table 2
Theil-Tornqvist Binary and Multilateral Indices and their Standard Errors (Base Country USA)

Country	Binary	Multilateral	
	I_{ij}^{TT}	I_{ij}^{CCD}	T_{ij}^{GCCD}
USA	1.0000(-)	1.0000(-)	1.0000(-)
Canada	1.0184 (.1721)	1.0655 (.0267)	1.0344 (.0287)
France	5.3287 (.4380)	5.3769 (.1359)	5.3388 (.1378)
Germany	2.4580 (.1459)	2.4460 (.0618)	2.4286 (.0661)
Japan	241.8619 (27.5749)	257.8033 (6.5168)	249.5602 (6.9427)
UK	.4843 (.0526)	.4923 (.0124)	.4855 (.0138)
Brazil	32.4468 (4.3425)	30.9918 (.7834)	30.2018(2.1630)
Korea	418.7953 (101.8663)	416.6594 (10.5325)	407.6871(26.8041)
Philippines	2.8837(.5062)	2.9748 (.0752)	2.9090 (.0973)
India	3.3975 (.8327)	3.4153 (.0863)	3.3622 (.1161)
Indonesia	286.8827 (44.7682)	284.8609 (7.2008)	274.7606 (8.9106)

Root-mean-squares are in parenthesis

4. Stochastic Approach to the Geary-Khamis Method

In this section we deal with the Geary-Khamis index for international comparisons and demonstrate the feasibility of deriving the index using stochastic approach and then present GK parities and associated standard errors for selected countries of the Phase IV of the United Nations' International Comparisons Program. The Geary-Khamis method derives its name from the seminal work of Geary (1958) and that of Khamis (1970,1972,1984), and it is the most widely used method for international comparisons. It has been the main aggregation procedure employed in deriving purchasing power parities above the basic heading level. The versatility of the stochastic approach is demonstrated in this section by deriving the purchasing power parities and international prices. Let PPP_j represent the purchasing power parting for currency

j ($j = 1, ..., M$) and P_i denote the "international average" price of ith commodity ($i = 1, ..., N$). PPP_j represents the number of currency units of country j with the same purchasing power as one unit of a reference currency. This PPP_j is similar to the idea of an exchange rate. The reciprocal R_j,

$$R_j = 1/PPP_j$$

represents the number of reference currency units equivalent in purchasing power per unit of country j currency.

The Geary-Khamis method is defined in terms of PPP_j, R_j and P_i as

$$R_j = \frac{1}{PPP_j} = \frac{\sum_{i=1}^{N} P_i q_{ij}}{\sum_{i=1}^{N} p_{ij} q_{ij}} \text{ for all } j = 1, 2, ..., M; \tag{21}$$

and

$$P_i = \frac{\sum_{j=1}^{M} R_j p_{ij} q_{ij}}{\sum_{j=1}^{M} q_{ij}} = \frac{\sum_{j=1}^{M} p_{ij} q_{ij} / PPP_j}{\sum_{j=1}^{M} q_{ij}} \text{ for all } i = 1, 2, ..., N. \tag{22}$$

This system represents a set of $(M + N)$ linear homogeneous of equations in as many unknowns,R_j's and P_i's. This system, under very general conditions (Prasada Rao, 1971) provides a unique positive solution to the unknown parities and prices after setting one of the unknowns at an arbitrary positive level.

Most of the applied international comparisons work applies these formulae to appropriate price and quantity data and publish the resulting PPPs, UN (1987), FAO (1986) and Prasada Rao (1993) are typical examples of large scale application of this aggregation method without any mention of standard errors or measures of reliability or precision attached to these parities.

A close examination of equations (21) and (22) of the GK system shows that the international prices P_i, and parities R_j (or PPP_j)

can be interpreted as weighted averages. This gives rise to the possibility of a suitably defined regression model. Prasada Rao (1972) and Khamis (1984) use regression based interpretation to justify the definitions given in equations (21) and (22).

In the following two short sub-sections we describe the stochastic approach to the computation of purchasing power parities and international prices.

4.1 *Stochastic Approach to Purchasing Power Parities*

Given a set of international prices, $P_1, P_2, ..., P_N$, of commodities, all of them expressed in a common reference currency unit, a measure of purchasing power of currency is given by the ratio P_i/p_{ij} for i^{th} commodity. Thus we have different measures of the purchasing power parity. If these ratios are identical then R_j would be equal to the ratio. However in practice these ratios exhibit significant variation. In such an event we may consider R_j to be the expected value of the ratio P_i/p_{ij}.

Assuming the knowledge of the international prices P_i $(i = 1, 2, ..., N)$ (without loss of generality we may assume the values of P_i to be known as the solutions to the Geary-Khamis system are unique up to a factor of proportionality), we can postulate the following regression model.

$$\frac{P_i}{p_{ij}} = R_j + u_{ij} \tag{23}$$

with observations $i = 1, 2, ..., N$ for each j. As is standard for regression models, u_{ij} is a random disturbance term with zero mean and variance σ_{ij}^2 implying heteroskedastic disturbances for different commodities.

The following assumptions regarding the variances and covariances of disturbances u_{ij} (for $i = 1, 2, ..., N$) lead to the Geary-Khamis definition of R_j. These are

$$
\begin{aligned}
Var(u_{ij}) &= \sigma_u^2/p_{ij}q_{ij} \\
Cov(u_{ij}, u_{lk}) &= 0, \quad \text{for all } i, j, l, k \, \text{and} \, i \neq l, j \neq k
\end{aligned}
\tag{24}
$$

The variance specification can be written as

$$
Var(u_{ij}) = \frac{\sigma_u^2/M_j}{w_{ij}}
$$

where $M_j = \sum_{i=1}^{N} p_{ij}q_{ij}$ and $w_{ij} = p_{ij}q_{ij}$ is the value share of ith commodity. The variance specification used here suggests that variance is inversely related to the total value M_j in country j and the value share of the commodity. Note that this specification is somewhat similar to the specification used in deriving the Laspeyres and Paasche indices in Section 2.

The generalised-least squares estimator of R_j in equation (3), accounting for the variance of the disturbance term, is given by

$$
\hat{R}_j = \frac{\sum_{i=1}^{N} P_i q_{ij}}{\sum_{i=1}^{N} p_{ij}q_{ij}}
$$

which is the GK definition of $R_j = 1/PPP_j$. This implies that the purchasing power parity PPP_j can be estimated as:

$$
\widehat{PPP}_j = 1/\hat{R}_j
$$

The standard errors associated with $\hat{R}_j$ is given by

$$
SE(\hat{R}_j) = \left[\frac{\hat{\sigma}_u^2}{\sum_{i=1}^{N} p_{ij}q_{ij}} \right]^{1/2}
\tag{25}
$$

where $\hat{\sigma}_u^2$ is an estimate of σ_u^2 based on the generalised least squares residuals.

The standard errors associated with $\widehat{PPP}_j$ is approximated as

$$SE(\widehat{PPP}_j) = SE(1/\hat{R}_j) \simeq \frac{SE(\hat{R}_j)}{\hat{R}_j^2} \tag{26}$$

It is evident from the formulae for the standard errors that these are inversely related to the total value of the basket of goods associated with country j.

4.2 *Stochastic Approach to International Prices*

Now we turn to the second component of the GK system, the international prices, and describe the structure of a regression model underlying the international price P_i of ith commodity. Given that p_{ij} is the price of ith commodity in country j, expressed in national currency units, p_{ij}/PPP_j, converts the national price of ith commodity expressed in the reference currency unit.

Using price of ith commodity in different countries, we have M measures, p_{ij}/PPP_j $(j = 1, 2, ..., M)$ one from each country. In an ideal situation all the M values p_{ij}/PPP_j will be the same, the common value leading to international price P_i. In the absence of this we consider

$$P_i = E\left[\frac{p_{ij}}{PPP_j}\right]$$

This leads to the regression model of the form

$$\frac{p_{ij}}{PPP_j} = P_i + \epsilon_{ij} \tag{27}$$

where ϵ_{ij} is a random disturbance term. The following assumptions on the disturbance term lead to the GK definition of international prices.

$$E(\epsilon_{ij}) = 0$$

$$Var(\epsilon_{ij}) = \sigma_\epsilon^2, \text{ for all } j = 1, 2, ..., M;$$

$$Cov(\epsilon_{ij}, \epsilon_{lk}) = 0, \quad \text{for all } i, j, k, l, \text{ and } i \neq l, j \neq k.$$

This implies that variability in (p_{ij}/PPP_j) is inversely related to the quantity of ith commodity in j^{th} country.

Under this structure of heteroskedastic disturbances, the generalised least squares estimator of P_i for each i is given by

$$\hat{P}_i = \frac{\sum_{j=1}^{M} p_{ij} q_{ij} / PPP_j}{\sum_{j=1}^{M} q_{ij}} \tag{28}$$

with an associated standard error of

$$SE(\hat{P}_i) = \left[\hat{\sigma}_\epsilon^2 / \sum_{j=1}^{M} q_{ij} \right]^{1/2} \tag{29}$$

where $\hat{\sigma}_\epsilon^2$ is an estimator of the unknown σ_ϵ^2.

Equation (29) shows that the G-K definition of international price can be derived from the regression equation (28).

Thus we have established the feasibility of providing standard errors of the Geary-Khamis parities, PPP_j, and international prices P_i. These derivations make use of the fact the Geary-Khamis method leads to a unique solution for the parities. This result formed the basis for the separate regression equations for the parities and international prices.

4.3 *Numerical Illustration*

For the purposes of illustration and to examine the nature and extent of the standard errors, the ICP Phase IV data on the eight categories of private consumption expenditure have been used. Results are presented for a selection of countries, though the actual calculations have been performed for the full set of 60 countries. As this section is essentially based on the results in Prasada Rao and Selvanathan (1992) the numerical illustration is drawn from the complete set of results in the paper.

Table 3
Geary-Khamis Purchasing Power Parities
and their Standard Errors
(Base Country: USA)

Country	PPP	Standard Error
Canada	1.0130	0.1268
France	5.3866	0.2628
Germany	2.4457	0.1085
Japan	250.14	13.31
United Kingdom	0.4895	0.0183
Brazil	29.2547	2.7362
Korea	379.27	55.53
Philippines	2.9511	0.3515
India	3.3150	0.6577
Indonesia	275.88	35.17

The table suggests that the standard errors associated with the purchasing power parities are generally low. The standard errors are relatively low for developed countries, generally around 5 percent of the parities, but for most of the developing countries this percentage is over 10 percent and for India the standard error is nearly 20 percent. Another point that emerges from Tables 2 and 3 is that once the standard errors are taken into account the differences in results are no longer significant. For example, in the case of India the CCD and GK parities are, respectively, 3.4153 and 3.3150 with associated standard errors of 0.0863 and 0.6577. Therefore it is quite useful to keep the standard errors in perspective while assessing differences in results derived from different methods.

Now we turn to the Geary-Khamis international price P_i and the standard errors associated with each of the prices. These are presented below in Table 4.

Table 4
International Prices and their Standard Errors

Commodity	International Price	Standard Error
Food, beverages and tobacco	0.9951	0.0218
Clothing and footwear	0.9946	0.0326
Rent and fuel	1.0252	0.0399
Housing furnishings and operation	1.0014	0.0296
Medical care	0.8987	0.0374
Transport and communication	1.0900	0.0297
Recreation and education	1.0300	0.0393
Miscellaneous	0.9230	0.0212

International prices in Table 4 are computed with United States as the base country so that the price level of private consumption expenditure is set to 1 and, therefore, the international prices show the prices relative to the purchasing power of the US dollar set at 1 for the total aggregate. The table shows that international average prices for food, clothing, medical and miscellaneous items are relatively cheaper than rent and fuel; and housing furnishings; transport and communication; and recreation and education. The standard errors associated with different commodity groups are uniformly low across the eight groups; higher standard errors indicate more variability in relative prices across countries for a given commodity group.

5. Concluding Remarks

In this paper we have briefly described principal aspects of the *stochastic approach* to comparisons of prices and real income. The paper provided a description of the approach and then an illustration of the versatility of the stochastic approach in dealing with the problem of binary as well as multilateral price comparisons. Sections 3 and 4 establish that the Geary-Khamis and Caves-Christensen-Diewert formulae can be derived through the application of stochastic approach. Derivation of various formulae through regression equations provides a framework to utilise the information contained in the price and quantity structures observed. In Section 3 we have demonstrated the possibility of weighted CCD indices which preserve characteristicity of comparisons between countries at similar levels of development. Further research is underway to extend the results presented here in order to develop a more wholesome approach to the construction of index numbers for international comparisons.

References

Balk, B.M. (1980). 'A Method for Constructing Price Indices for Seasonal Commodities,' *Journal of the Royal Statistical Society, Series A*, 142, part I: 68-75.

Banerjee, K.S. (1975). *Cost of Living Index Numbers - Practice, Decision and Theory.* New York: Marcel Dekker.

Caves, D.W., Christensen, L.R. and Diewert, W.E. (1982a). 'Multilateral Comparisons of Output, Input and Productivity Using Superlative Index Numbers,' *Economic Journal* 92: 73-86.

Caves, D.W., Christensen, L.R. and Diewert, W.E. (1982b). 'The Economic Theory of Index Numbers and the Measurement of Input, Output and Productivity,' *Econometrica* 50: 1393-1414.

Clements, K.W. and Izan, H.Y. (1981). 'A Note on Estimating Divisia Index Numbers,'*International Economic Review* 22: 745-47. *Corrigendum* 23 (1982): 499.

Food and Agricultural Organization (1986). *Inter-country Comparisons of Agricultural Production Aggregates* (Economic and Social Development Paper No. 61), Rome: FAO.

Khamis, S.H. (1969). 'Neoteric Index Numbers,' Technical Report, Indian Statistical Institute, Calcutta.

Khamis, S.H. (1970). 'Properties and Conditions for the Existence of a New Type of Index Numbers,' Sankhȳa, *The Indian Journal of Statistics, Series B* 32: 81-98.

Khamis, S.H. (1972). 'A New System of Index Numbers for National and International Purposes,' *Journal of the Royal Statistical Society, Series A* 135, Part I: 96-121.

Khamis, S.H. (1984). 'On Aggregation Methods for International Comparisons,' *Review of Income and Wealth* 30: 185-205.

Kravis, I.B., Heston, A. and Summers, R. (1982). *World Product and Income: International Comparisons of Real Gross Product*, Baltimore: The John Hopkins University Press.

Prasada Rao, D.S. (1971). 'Existence and Uniqueness of a New Class of Index Numbers,' *Sankhȳa Series B* 33: 341-354.

Prasada Rao, D.S. (1972). *Contributions to Methodology of Construction of Consistent Index Numbers*, Ph.D. Thesis, Indian Statistical Institute, Calcutta, India.

Prasada Rao, D.S. and Selvanathan, E.A. (1991), 'A Log-Change Index Number Formula for Multilateral Comparisons,' *Economics Letters* 35: 297-300.

Prasada Rao, D.S. and Selvanathan, E.A. (1992a). 'Uniformly Minimum Variance Unbiased Estimators of Theil-Tornqvist Index Numbers,' *Economics Letters* 39: 123-7.

Prasada Rao, D.S. and Selvanathan, E.A. (1992b). 'Computations of Standard Errors for Geary-Khamis Parities and International Prices,' *Journal of Business and Economics Statistics* 10(1): 109-15.

Selvanathan, E.A. (1987). *Explorations in Consumer Demand*, Ph.D. Thesis, Murdoch University, Western Australia.

Selvanathan, E.A. (1989). 'A Note on the Stochastic Approach to Index Numbers,' *Journal of Business and Economic Statistics* 7(4): 471-474.

Selvanathan, E.A. (1991). 'Standard Errors for Laspeyres and Paasche Index Numbers,' *Economics Letters* 35: 35-38.

Selvanathan, E.A. (1993). 'More on Laspeyres Price Index,' *Economics Letters*, forthcoming.

Selvanathan, E.A. and Prasada Rao, D.S. (1992). 'An Econometric Approach to the Construction of Generalized Theil-Tornqvist Indices for Multilateral Comparisons', *Journal of Econometrics* 54: 335-46.

United Nations (1987). *World Comparison of Purchasing Power and Real Product for 1980* New York: United Nations.

International Comparisons of Prices, Output and Productivity
Edited by D.S. Prasada Rao and J. Salazar-Carrillo

STRUCTURE OF INTERNATIONAL PRICES: A PRODUCTION-BASED APPROACH

Yoshimasa Kurabayashi
Faculty of Social Sciences
Toyo Eiwa Women's University
Yokohama, Japan

1. Introduction

In a paper which was a revised version of their paper included in Salazar Carrillo and D.S. Prasada Rao,(1988), and published later in Kurabayashi and Sakuma(1990), Kurabayashi and Sakuma proposed an approach to measurements of real value added and its price for international comparisons. The paper was founded on the premises: (a) a model of international price formation is required for meaningful comparisons of real product; (b) such a model could be obliged to differ according to economic conditions of different groups of countries; and (c) a stable structure of international wage differential could result from unequal exchanges between developed and developing countries under the conditions of free mobility of capital and international migration of labour. The thrust of our approach is significantly motivated by the insights and observations which were incorporated in a paper by P.N. Mathur(1988). His ideas were further developed and reached to the culmination that his theory has been fully expounded in P.N. Mathur(1991). In this note I intend to reconsider the standpoint of our approach in the light of the insights provided in Mathur's work. It is my great regret that his untimely death has deprived me of his further thoughtful comments on this note. Thus this note is dedicated to his memory and is intended to pay homage to a great economist, Professor P.N. Mathur.

2. Determination of International Price Structures

As those who have worked in the past two decades and more with the International Comparison Project (now Program) jointly carried out by the United Nations, O.E.C.D. and the European Union have familiarized themselves, the structure of international prices by commodity has been solved by the theoretical framework structured by the Geary-Khamis method. The method is primarily concerned with a simultaneous solution of a system of equations consisting of the exchange rates between countries and the international prices by commodity measured in international currency units, where the international prices by commodity are constituted by the final expenditure items. Thus it naturally follows from this methodology that from the outset the approach adopted by the ICP has been oriented by working with disaggregation of GDP with respect to final expenditures. In contrast, our approach attempts to unravel the determination of the structure of international prices of GDP in terms of real value added originating from different production sectors. In carrying out this exercise we rely, in essence, on the Sraffa-Leontief model. The idea of using the Sraffa-Leontief model has originated from Mathur's observations collected from the ICP data in Mathur(1991). Reflections on his observations suggest that the relative prices of tradable goods would not be supposed to be the same in different countries.

As Mathur proposes, in his book, a system of equations which enables one to determine the structure of internal prices of commodities for a given level of the value added by production sector on the basis of the Leontief model of input-output relations, it is worth summarizing here the essence of his approach.

In the determination of internal commodity prices, Mathur follows, in essence, Hicksian 'fix-price' approach, the commodity prices being equal to the cost of production of the marginal producer. It is true that some conditions need to be met if the Hicksian 'fix-price' approach should be satisfactorily implemented. But, for the sake of simplification, the consideration for the necessary conditions is left out of this note.

Let A be the domestic flow coefficient input-output matrix, m and ℓ be import and labour coefficient row vectors. Moreover, let P be the row vector of commodity prices, w being the wage rate. Then

$$P = [w\ell(I + \lambda) + m](I - A)^{-1} \tag{1}$$

Here, λ is the diagonal matrix of the proportion of the non-wage income to the wage income by production sector. Thus it is noted that the diagonal matrix which stands for the profit share be expressed by

$(\hat{w}\ell)(I+\lambda)^{-1}$.

Two points on Mathur's model should be made for further clarifications. In the first place, as (1) gives only (n-1) equations, where n stands for the number of production sectors, the model is supplemented by the following equation

$$w = y^*/[l^*(1+\lambda_c)] \tag{2}$$

where, y^* stands for the direct and indirect value added in the production of the export commodity, whereas l^* indicates direct and indirect labour used in the production of the export commodity. Note that λ_c, is the proportion of non-wage income to wage income in the direct and indirect value added by the production of the export commodity. Thus, for the value added in the production of the export commodity sets the standard for the rest of the economy. These n independent equations together determine the purchasing power parity in terms of the export commodity. If there is more than one export commodity, the one giving the lowest wage rate will be effective in making n independent equations. In this case, the export of other commodities will generate profits for the exporters.

In the second place, as ℓ or $\rho\lambda$ is expressed by a vector, the profit share can differ according to different production sectors. It is implied by the fact that the determination of n variables by (1) and (2) makes much difference in the treatment of Sraffa's "standard commodity" approach. It is well known that in Sraffa's "standard commodity" there exists a relation

$$\rho = 1/(1+r) = 1/(1+g) \tag{3}$$

where, r is the profit rate which is assumed to be equalized by perfect competition and g stands for the Von Neumann maximal growth rate, whereas ρ expresses the unique, positive, characteristic root of A. Hence, letting M = 0 for simplification, (1) is reduced to

$$P = w\ell + (1+r)PA \tag{1'}$$

if for each i-th production sector (i=1,2,...,n)

$$(\lambda)(w\ell)(PA)^{-1} = r \tag{4}$$

It is immediate to see that the structure of prices in Mathur's approach is translated into the case of Sraffa's "standard commodity" if (3) and (4) are met. Note that the profit rate is equalized across all production sectors by (4) for some or other reasons. Needless to say that in Sraffa's "standard commodity" the unique profit rate across all production sectors is ensured by the existence of perfect competition. Thus, the theory that the structure of prices should be linked to the international price level by the prices of the export commodity and that the determination of the structure of prices can be translated into the model of Sraffa's "standard commodity" subject to some necessary conditions underlies the ingenuity of Mathur's approach.

Again, it should be stressed that in Mathur's approach the structure of prices is determined by the Hicksian "fix-price" approach. By contrast, the conventional methods for measuring the structure of prices and their purchasing powers have insufficient functional theories that can explain their determination, although such attempts by Prasada Rao and others to present the theories have been made, as we have pointed out in our book referred above. A caution to these conventional methods for international comparisons attempted by ICP has been given by Seton and deserves to be quoted here at some length.

"In all cases, the method suffers from an escapable ambiguity, as the results of comparing countries A and B give sharply different, and often conflicting, verdicts according to which of the two countries is chosen to furnish the uniform price basis. It may be concluded that such "transplants" or organically alien valuations can at best eliminate the bias arising from differential pricing, but cannot escape the residual bias inherent in any one country- or time-specific price structure *per se*. .... To cast the "world as a whole" in the role of the third country appears to inject an element of objectivity by restricting arbitrary choice, but hides other assumptions of doubtful validity, such as the notion that the appropriateness of a country's price system as a universal yardstick is proportional to its size, population, prosperity, or whatever furnishes the weight with which it figures as a constituent of "the world" in international statistics." [Seton(1985), pp.8-9]

3. The International Prices and the Specialization Frontier

In our formulation and application of the Sraffa-Leontief system for exploring the problem how international prices of commodities and their purchasing powers are determined, the role of international trade is implicit to the effect that it is reflected back in the specialization frontier of the commodity which is internationally traded. For the sake of simplification, a two-commodity and two-country case of the international trade which has been discussed in Kurabayashi and Sakuma(1990), is also considered.

Suppose trade of two commodities between two countries is proposed. Assuming that in each country the wage rates are kept to be same no matter how each country is in the autarkic or in the trading regime and that the economy of each country has only one technique, with trade it is possible that each country specializes in the production of one commodity which uses a single technique and is supported by imported inputs of the other commodity. The possibility of the trade provides an economy with two alternative techniques each of which consists of a single activity. In the Sraffa-Leontief system of production, the alternative techniques are represented in the wage-profit trade-off relations when an economy specializes in the production of one of commodities. Each of the trade-off relations is termed here the specialization frontier with respect to a particular commodity.

Adopting the same notations which are used in the preceding section, the specialization frontier with respect to the commodity 1 can be expressed by

$$p_1 = w\ell_1 + (1+r)PAe_1^{'} \tag{5}$$

whereas the specialization frontier with respect to the commodity 2 can be written by

$$p_2 = w\ell_2 + (1+r)P_Ae_2^{'} \tag{6}$$

Here, $\ell = (\ell_1, \ell_2)$, $\ell_i (i = 1, 2)$ being the labour input coefficient for the production of the i-th commodity; $P = (p_1, \ell)$, P being a row vector whose elements stand for the normalized price of each commodity, the price of the commodity 2 being unity; $e_1 = (1,0)$ and $e_2 = (0,1)$ respectively. Let ρ^f stand for the Frobenius root of the matrix A. The normalized price vector which corresponds to the Frobenius root of A can be represented by p^f , whose first element being p_1^f. Then, we have

$$p_1^f = w\ell_1 + (1+r)p^f A e_1 \tag{7}$$

and

$$p_2^f = w\ell_2 + (1+r)p^f A e_2 \tag{8}$$

As Seton has once suggested p_1^f, might be used for a yardstick which allows us to compare international commodity prices. In order to carry out the comparison, we have to consider two possibilities of trade between two countries. They are (i) the Ricardian case of trade and (ii) the case of trade with unequal exchange.

First, let us consider the Ricardian case of trade. As the trade of one country with an other country is motivated by the efforts that relevant countries endeavour to attain a superior wage-profit relation in the production possibility, the international price of commodities should be in the domain whose boundary is formed by the lower and upper limit of prices of the relevant commodity produced by two countries under the autarkic regime. Indeed, letting A and B stand for the two countries in question and p_1^* represent the international price of the commodity l, in the Sraffa-Leontief system of production the international price is settled by the wage-profit relation. Suppose the price of the commodity l produced by country A (p_1^A) is less than p_1^*, country A will specialize in the production of the commodity l and export the commodity. But p_1^* will not exceed the price of the commodity l produced by country B, otherwise country B will necessarily specialize in the production of the commodity l. Thus, for the case of Ricardian trade

$$p_1^A < p_1^* < p_1^B \tag{9}$$

But, it is readily seen by recalling $(1)'$ that for the Frobenius root of A

$$1 + r_{max} = 1/\rho^f \tag{10}$$

In (10) r_{max} represents the maximum profit rate. Suppose the profit rates which correspond to p_1^A, p_1^B, and p_1^* are expressed by r^A, r^B and r^* respectively. In line with (9) we shall have

$$r^B < r^* < r^A \tag{11}$$

Reflections on (10) suggests that r_{max} can approach as much close as r^A and is far grater than r^*. The limiting case is, of course.

$$r_{max} = r^A \tag{12}$$

If r_{max} hits the limiting case of (12) we can see that the Sraffa-Leontief system of production is transformed into the well-known "standard commodity" case. It is also seen that p_1^f is far less than p_1^* and that in the limiting case approximates to p_1^A.

Next, we have to turn our attention to the trade with unequal exchange. While, under the trade with unequal exchange, the wage rates differ between countries, the profit rate is equalized across countries to such level (r^*) that the specialized technique in a higher wage country attains. Suppose country A specialized in the production of the commodity 1. A variety of specialization patterns, some of which were discussed in our book, would arise for the two countries. The characteristics of the specialization patterns under the trade with unequal exchange which we unravelled in the book are summed up below.

(1) r^* is contained in r^A and r^B in the same order of the case of Ricardian trade as (11).

(2) But p_1^* lies outside of the domain set by p_1^A and p_1^B and the order of the magnitude can be either

$$p_1^A < p_1^B < p_1^* \tag{13}$$

or

$$p_1^* < p_1^B < p_1^A \tag{14}$$

In the possibilities of either (13) or (14) the specialization frontier should be reformulated. I would conjecture that (7) or (8) might be transformed into a more general expression such that

$$P = w\ell + (1+r)PA\Omega \tag{15}$$

where Ω stands for a matrix which specifies the specialization patterns for the two countries. Because the Frobenius root and its value of $A\Omega$ play a crucial role, the further elaborations and analysis for them far exceed the scope of this note. However, in this regard it should be noted that $A\Omega$ can be regarded as a generalized expression in a matrix form by which e_1 and e_2 in (7) and (8) are replaced. Moreover, it is expected that the role of the export commodity which has played an essential role in Mathur's approach be duly reflected in the formulation of $A\Omega$.

4. Concluding remarks

In concluding this short note I cannot help referring to an important work by Velupillai(1993) who has elaborated the theoretical aspects of production-based indicators and their purchasing power. In that paper he has given a number of extremely valuable comments and observations to our work. In particular, he has carefully examined our approach to the case of Ricardian trade and indicated some important problems that are inherent in our approach. Moreover, in the work, he has proposed an alternative approach that attempts a synthesis of what has been proposed by Seton and our approach. Several remarks which have been made by him from the alternative approach are quite useful for clarifying, though difficult, but highly challenging aspects of genuine intersystem and interspatial comparisons giving a synthesis of the production based Seton and K-S approach with the traditional ICP approach. The task will be a topic for future research.

References

Kurabayashi, Yoshimasa and Sakuma, Itsuo (1990), *Studies in International Comparisons of Real Product and Prices*, Kinokuniya Company LTD., Tokyo.

Marglin, Stephen A. (1984), *Growth, Distribution and Prices*, Harvard University Press, Cambridge, Massachusetts and London, England.

Mathur, P., (1991), *Why Developing Countries Fail to Develop, International Economic Framework and Economic Subordination*, Macmillan, London.

Salazar-Carrillo J., and D.S. Prasada Rao(eds.)(1988), *World Comparison of Income, Prices and Product*, North-Holland Publishing Company, Amsterdam.

Seton, Francis (1985), *Cost, Use, and Value, The Evaluation of Performance Structure and Prices across Time, Space, and Economic Systems*, Clarendon Press, Oxford.

Velupillai, Kumaraswamy (with Stefano Zambelli), (1993), *The Economics of Production Based Indicators and the Purchasing Power of Currencies for International Economic Comparisons*, A Paper for the World Bank, Socio-Economic Data Division, International Economics Department.

International Comparisons of Prices, Output and Productivity
Edited by D.S. Prasada Rao and J. Salazar-Carrillo

A RECONSIDERATION OF LOG-CHANGE INDEX NUMBERS FOR INTERNATIONAL COMPARISONS

D. S. Prasada Rao
University of New England
Armidale, Australia

and

Jorge Salazar-Carrillo
Florida International University
Miami, U.S.A.

1. Introduction

Since the seminal work of Milton Gilbert, in the early 1950 s, and subsequent research of Gilbert and Kravis, the last three decades have witnessed many developments in the area of international comparisons of prices, purchasing powers of currencies and real product. Research in this area has been supported by a number of international organizations such as the World Bank, Statistical Offices of the United nations and the European Union and the Food and Agriculture Organization.

A natural by-product of such a healthy interest in international comparisons is the proliferation of a large number of index number methods for purposes of aggregation. The most-widely used method is the Geary-Khamis method which is the main aggregation procedure used in various phases of the International Comparisons Program (ICP) of the United Nations (see Kravis et.al.1978 and 1982 for details). Despite the emphasis placed on the Geary-Khamis method, a number of alternative methods have been applied in the context of international comparisons. Salazar-Carrillo (1978), Prasada Rao (1990), Caves, Christensen and Diewert (1982), Prasada Rao and Sheperd (1983), Prasada Rao and Banerjee (1986) provide an array of such alternatives. A subset of the available methods are based on geometric averaging procedure, and are essentially log-change index numbers in character. As most of the log-change index numbers in the literature due to Theil-Kloek (1965), Theil (1973) and Sato (1976), are essentially binary index numbers, this paper focuses on multilateral log-change index numbers and examines the theoretical underpinnings of the methods involved.

Section 2 provides a brief description of the aggregation problem in the context of multilateral comparisons and describes a number of log-change index numbers that are presently in use; Section 3 examines some of the mathematical and economic theoretic issues underlying these methods. The final section provides some conclusions and directions for further research.

2. Definitions and Alternative Multilateral Methods

Let p_{ij} *and* q_{ij} (i=1,2,...,N and j=1,2,...,M) represent respectively price and quantity of i-th commodity in j-th country [1] with M > 2. We assume, without loss of generality, that: (i) $p_{ij} > 0$ for all i and j - and (ii) $q_{ij} \geq 0$ for all i and j, for each i, $q_{ij} > 0$ for at least one j and for each j, $q_{ij} > 0$ for each i.

The problem of consistent multilateral comparisons is essentially one of finding index numbers I_{jk} (j,k = 1,2,....M), index number for country k with j-th country as the base, such that the resulting index numbers are:

(i) transitive, i.e., for any triplet of countries j, k and ℓ
$I_{jl}.I_{lk} = I_{jk}$; and

(ii) the index numbers I_{jk} are base invariant.

These properties are considered as essential in the context of multilateral-spatial comparisons. There are a number of other properties which are considered desirable, but these two are the most important requirements. These two properties have certain implications for the characteristics of suitable methods for multilateral comparisons. The transivity property implies that computing index numbers I_{jk} is equivalent to finding real numbers $\pi_1, \pi_2, ..., \pi_M$ such that

$$I_{jk} = \frac{\pi_k}{\pi_j}$$

[1] For ease of exposition we use countries instead of regions within a country or time periods.

These π's may be interpreted as 'general price levels' in different countries. If R_j represents the reciprocal of π_j, then R_j may be interpreted as the purchasing power of currency in j-th country in which case I_{jk} may be expressed as

$$I_{jk} = \frac{R_j}{R_k}$$

In fact, all the index number formulae for multilateral comparisons fall roughly into two categories. The first consists of all those methods that define the indices directly as functions of observed price-quantity data; and the second group consists of all those methods that define either the general price levels π_j or the purchasing power parities R_j first and the necessary indices are then defined indirectly.

In this paper we consider two log-change index numbers for multilateral comparisons, one from each category mentioned above. The methods considered here are the Geometric-Walsh and Rao methods for multilateral comparisons. These indices are briefly described below.

Geometric-Walsh method

This method due to Walsh is described in detail in Ruggles (1967), and has been in use as the main aggregation procedure for Latin American comparisons (see Salazar-Carrillo, 1973 and 1978). The Geometric-Walsh price index numbers are defined by:

$$I_{jk} = \Pi_{i=1}^{N} \left[\frac{p_{ik}}{p_{ij}}\right]^{w_i} \tag{1}$$

where

$$w_i = \frac{\Pi_{j=1}^{M} (v_{ij})^{\frac{1}{M}}}{\Sigma_{i=1}^{N} \left[\Pi_{j=1}^{M} (v_{ij})^{\frac{1}{M}}\right]}$$

and v_{ij} represents the value-share of i-th commodity in j-th country. In the form of a log-change index number I^*_{jk}, we have

$$I^*_{jk} = \sum_{i=1}^{N} w_i log(\frac{p_{ik}}{p_{ij}}) \tag{2}$$

which is a weighted average of the logarithm of the price relatives.

Rao method

This method was first described in Prasada Rao (1972) but a number of properties are expounded in Prasada Rao (1990). This method defines the index numbers through the purchasing power parities R_j which are first defined using the observed price-quantity data. The parities R_j are defined by, for each j,

$$R_j = \Pi_{i=1}^{N} \left[\frac{P_i}{p_{ij}}\right]^{v_{ij}} \tag{3}$$

where P_i is an international average price of i-th commodity given by

$$P_i = \Pi_{j=1}^{M} [R_j p_{ij}]^{w^*_{ij}} \tag{4}$$

where

$$w^*_{ij} = \frac{v_{ij}}{\Sigma_{j=1}^{M} v_{ij}}$$

The purchasing power R_j measures the general level of prices in country j, vis-a-vis the international average price level. This method is essentially characterised by a system of (M+N) log-linear equations in as many unknowns. Existence and uniqueness of solutions and other properties are discussed in Prasada Rao (1990). This method is very useful when detailed price-quantity data are not available, and it is extensively used in Australia-U.K. comparisons (see Shepherd and Prasada

Rao (1981) and Prasada Rao and Shepherd(1983)).

This method defines R_j as a geometric mean of price relatives $(\frac{P_i}{p_{ij}})$ and a log-change parity R_j^* may be defined as

$$R_j^* = \sum_{i=1}^{N} v_{ij} log(\frac{P_i}{p_{ij}}) \qquad (5)$$

This is similar to the Tornqvist-type log-change index numbers considered in Kloek and Theil (1965).

3. Mathematical and Economic-Theoretic Properties

The two index number systems described in section 2 are essentially multilateral in character and they satisfy the twin requirements of transitivity and base invariance. In order to examine their properties vis-a-vis the properties of some of the well-known log-change index numbers it is necessary to consider the binary forms of the indices for the special case where number of countries, M, reduces to 2.

The Geometric-Walsh index in the binary case reduces to

$$I_{12} = \Pi_{i=1}^{N} \left[\frac{p_{i2}}{p_{i1}}\right]^{\frac{(v_{i1}v_{i2})^{\frac{1}{2}}}{\Sigma_i (v_{i1}v_{i2})^{\frac{1}{2}}}} \qquad (6)$$

and in the form of the log-change index

$$I_{12}^* = \sum_{i=1}^{w} \frac{(v_{i1}v_{i2})^{\frac{1}{2}}}{\Sigma(v_{i1}v_{i2})^{\frac{1}{2}}} log(\frac{p_{i2}}{p_{i1}}) \qquad (7)$$

The Rao index for the case M = 2 reduces to

$$I_{12} = \Pi_{i=1}^{N} \left[\frac{p_{i2}}{p_{i1}}\right]^{\frac{\frac{v_{i1}v_{i2}}{v_{i1}+v_{i2}}}{\Sigma_i \frac{v_{i1}v_{i2}}{v_{i1}+v_{i2}}}} \qquad (8)$$

These two binary indices may be compared to some of the well-known log-change index numbers. The Theil-Tornqvist index for binary comparisons is

$$I_{12} = \Pi_{i=1}^{N} \left[\frac{p_{i2}}{p_{i1}}\right]^{\frac{v_{i1}+v_{i2}}{2}}$$

$$= \Pi_{i=1}^{N} \left[\frac{p_{i2}}{p_{i1}}\right]^{\frac{v_{i1}+v_{i2}}{\Sigma(v_{i1}+v_{i2})}} \tag{9}$$

Theil (1973) suggests an index of the form

$$I_{12} = \Pi_{i=1}^{N} \left[\frac{p_{i2}}{p_{i1}}\right]^{w_i} \tag{10}$$

where

$$w_i = \frac{\left[\frac{v_{i1}+v_{i2}}{2} v_{i1} v_{i2}\right]^{\frac{1}{3}}}{\Sigma_i \left[\frac{v_{i1}+v_{i2}}{2} v_{i1} v_{i2}\right]^{\frac{1}{3}}}$$

In addition to those two formulae, Sato (1974) and Sato (1976) provide additional log-change index number formulae. In what follows we briefly describe a number of properties attributable to the Geometric-Walsh and Rao indices in equations (1) and (2), and their multilateral versions.

Property 1: The Geometric-Walsh and Rao indices provide multilateral generalizations of simple log-change index numbers of the form given in equations (6) and (7).

This property shows the versatility of the two index number formulae. Similar generalizations of the Kloek-Theil and Theil (1973) indices in equations (8) and (9) are not available. The only known way to generalize these two indices for the multilateral case is pursued in Prasada Rao and Banerjee (1986), but the generalizations suggested there do not result in multilateral index numbers in a log-change form.

Property 2: All the index numbers presented here are based on log-changes, in prices of commodities, which are symmetric, additive and normed.

This property is often overlooked by empirical workers. The reader is referred to an excellent exposition of this material in Tornqvist, Vartia and Vartia (1985) where the issues concerning the relative price measurements are forcefully discussed with great simplicity. In view of the results contained there in, use of log-change index numbers must be made more popular. The Rao multilateral system, in equation (3) and (4), consists of a system of log-linear equations where relative changes are all measured using logarithms of price ratios.

Property 3: The binary forms of the Geometric-Walsh and Rao index numbers, in equation (6) and (7), satisfy the factor reversal test to the third order of smallness.

Proof of this property follows from the main result contained in Sato(1974)'s paper[2]. Factors reversal test is a well-known requirement which stipulates that the product of price and quantity index numbers based on the same index number formula should be equal to the value ratio. Since the formulae considered here are based on log-changes, the factor reversal test is never exactly satisfied. But property 3 ensures that any discrepancy that exists is very small. All formulae, in equations (6) to (10), possess this property and the formula in equation (10) suggested in Theil(1973) satisfies the factor reversal test to the fifth order of smallness.

While these properties are essentially mathematical and statistical in nature, the following property is based on economic-theoretic considerations. The discussion below uses a number of concepts and results based on Diewert's work and a good reference is Diewert (1981).

Property 4: The Geometric-Walsh and Rao binary indices, in equations (6) and (7), are exact for a Cobb-Douglas utility function of the form $f(q) = \alpha_0 \prod_{i=1}^{N} q_i^{\alpha i}$

$where\ \alpha_0 > 0,\ \alpha_i > 0\ for\ all\ i\ and\ \sum_i \alpha_i = 1.$

Proof of this statement follows from Theorem 21 of Diewert (1981). Infact this result encompasses all the formulae where the

[2]proofs of properties (1) and (4) are available from the authors upon request. These proofs have been omitted to keep the length of the paper short.

weights satisfy a simple requirement. In fact the Theil-Tornqvist index in equation (9) has an additional property that it is a *superlative* formula in that it is exact for a translog unit cost function (see Theorem 24 in Diewert (1981)). The Geometric-Walsh and Prasada Rao indices do not appear to be superlative but these formulae would be in close proximity to the Theil-Tornqvist index due to the nature of the formulae. It would be an interesting exercise to examine if these indices satisfy any other economic-theoretic properties.

Property 5 : The Rao multilateral Index number system provides a geometric variant of the Ikle$'$(1972) method. The volume shares of the Rao method satisfy a number of tests including: positivity and continuity; identity test; and proportionality test. However, it fails to satisfy the country partitioning test and the irrelevance of tiny countries test.

Proof of this property is provided in a recent paper by Balk(1995). This proposition establishes a link between Rao method and yet another well-known Ikle$'$ method.

4. Conclusions

This paper considered some of the mathematical, statistical and economic theoretic properties possessed by the two multilateral systems, viz., geometric-Walsh and Rao index number systems. While some of the well-known systems such as the Geary-Khamis system were studied in great detail, no systematic attempt has been made to examine the properties of log-change multilateral systems. In fact it would be a simulating exercise to establish other properties of these formulae.

References

Balk, B.M., (1995), " A Comparison of ten Methods for Multilateral International Price Comparisons", *mimeographed.*

Diewert, W.E., (1981), "The Economic Theory of Index Numbers: A Survey", in *Essays in Theory of Measurement of Consumer Behavior*, Ed. A. Deaton, Cambridge University Press.

Ikle′, D.M., (1972), " A New Approach to the Index Number Problem", *Quarterly Journal of Economics*, 86, 188-211.

Kloek, T. and H. Theil, (1965), "International Comparison of Prices and Quantities Consumed", *Econometrica*, 33, 535-556.

Kravis, I.B., A.W. Heston, and R. Summers, (1978), *International Comparison of Real Product and Purchasing Power*, Baltimore, The Johns Hopkins University Press.

Kravis, I.B., A.W. Heston, and R. Summers, (1982), *World Product and Income: International Comparison of Real Gross Product*, Baltimore, The Johns Hopkins University Press.

Prasada Rao, D.S., (1972), *Contribution to Methodology of Construction of Consistent Index Numbers*, Ph.D. Dissertation, I.S.I., Calcutta.

Prasada Rao, D.S., (1990), " A System of Log-change Index Numbers for Multilateral Comparisons", in J.Salazar-Carrillo and D.S. Prasada Rao(eds.). *Comparisons of Prices and Real Products in Latin America*, North-Holland, Amsterdam.

Prasada Rao, D.S., and K.S. Banerjee, (1986), " A Multilateral Index Number System Based on the Factorial Approach", *Statistische Hefte*, 27, 297-313.

Prasada Rao D.S., and W.F. Shepherd, (1983), " A Comparison of Pound Sterling-Australian Dollar Purchasing Power Parities for Selected Population Subgroups in Australia and the United Kingdom", *Review of Income and Wealth*, 29,4, 445-455.

Ruggles, R., (1967), " Price Indexes and International Price Comparisons", *Ten Economic Studies in the Tradition of Irving Fisher*, John Wiley, New York.

Salazar-Carrillo, J., (1973), " Price, Purchasing Power and Real Product Comparison in Latin America", *Review of Income and Wealth*, Series No. 19,1.

Salazar-Carrillo, J., (1978), *Prices and Purchasing Power Parities in Latin America 1960-1972*, Washington, D.C.: Organization of the American States.

Sato, K., (1974), "Ideal Index Numbers that almost Satisfy the Factor Reversal Test", *Review of Economics and Statistics*, 54, 549-552.

Sato, K., (1976), "The Ideal Log-Change Index Number", *The Review of Economics and Statistics*, 58, 223-228.

Shepherd, W.F., and D.S. Prasada Rao, (1981), " A Comparison of Purchasing Power Parity between the Pound Sterling and the Australian Dollar in 1979", *Economic Record*, 57, 215-223.

Theil, H., (1973), "A New Index Formula", *Review of Economics and Statistics*, 55, 498-502.

Tornqvist, Leo, P. Vartia, and Y.O. Vartia, (1985), " How Should Relative Change be Measured?", *The American Statistical Association*, 39, 43-46.

International Comparisons of Prices, Output and Productivity
Edited by D.S. Prasada Rao and J. Salazar-Carrillo

REGRESSION ESTIMATES OF PER CAPITA GDP BASED ON PURCHASING POWER PARITIES [1]

Sultan Ahmad
Socio-Economic Data Division
International Economics Department
The World Bank
Washington, D.C.

1. Introduction

The estimates of gross national product (GNP) per capita in US dollars published in the *World Bank Atlas* are used throughout the world for comparing relative levels of income across countries. The *Atlas* method of calculating per capita GNP is designed to smooth effects of fluctuations in prices and exchange rates and consists of converting local currency values to US dollars by a form of average exchange rates[2]. Since exchange rates do not measure relative purchasing powers of currencies in domestic markets, the *Atlas* estimates can often show changes in the relative ranking of two countries from one year to the next even if there are no changes in real growth rates but if there are changes in exchange rates which are not in line with relative price changes. Improved estimates can be obtained if purchasing power parities (PPP)[3] rather than exchange rates are used as conversion factors. However, PPP-based estimates of per capita income, usually associated with late Professor Irving Kravis of the University of Pennsylvania, and UN International Comparison Program (ICP)[4], are yet to cover all countries

[1]D. C. Rao, John O'Connor, Jitendra Borpujari and Adnan Mazarei made helpful comments on the paper; Nam Pham and Taranjit Kaur helped with the statistical work. However, the opinions expressed and any errors are the author's own.

[2]The *Atlas* method consists of converting current price local currency GNP to US dollars by a three-year average exchange rate. The average is computed as follows: the current year exchange rate is added to those of the previous two years after they have been extrapolated to the current year by relative rates of inflation between the country and US, and divided by three.

[3]PPP is defined here as the number of units of a country's currency required to purchase the same amounts of goods and services in the country as one dollar would buy in the United States.

[4]The ICP conducts benchmark surveys and publishes results in phases. So far

and all years needed in the *Atlas*. There have been attempts in the past to fill the gaps by short-cut estimates using regression techniques or by using a reduced set of information. In an attempt to fill these gaps, the World Bank has used regression estimates of its own and published them in the World Development Indicators (WDI)[5]. This paper describes how these estimates are made.

Sections 2 and 3 deal with choice of methods and explanatory variables. Section 4 presents selected regressions and section 5 analyses the results. Section 6 compares the results with those of the Penn World Tables, version 5 (PWT5)[6] , the latest such estimates available in the public domain. Section 7 contains concluding remarks and directions for further work.

2. Methods

A preferred approach to making quick estimates for countries for which ICP benchmark estimates are not available is to collect prices for a reduced sample of carefully selected items and make ICP type calculations for GDP and a small number of its components. Such a method, termed "the reduced information method"[7] , requires surveys and is not pursued here.

The paper follows the conventional method of making shortcut estimates which uses regression techniques, and offers a plausible rationale for explaining deviations between ICP and exchange rate based estimates of GDP. This involves developing an estimating equation linking ICP estimates of GDP per capita and a selection of easily observable explanatory variables for countries for which ICP estimates are available and using the equation to estimate ICP-type values for non-ICP countries[8]. Estimates made for a reference year (1985) are extrapo-

---

five phases have been completed as follows: Phase I for 1970 (ten countries), Phase II for 1973 (sixteen countries), Phase III for 1975 (thirty four countries), Phase IV for 1980 (sixty countries) and Phase V for 1985 (about 62 countries). Phase VI for 1990 have been completed for the OECD and several East European countries; surveys in Africa, Asia and Latin America are underway.

[5] See *World Development Report 1992*

[6] Summers and Heston (1991); these data have been updated in version 5.5 which is available from the authors on request.

[7] Ahmad (1980, 1988)

[8] See Ahmad (1980); Beckerman (1966); Beckerman and Bacon (1966); Clague

lated to other years by real growth rates and adjusted for US inflation in order to bring them to current dollars.

3. Selection of variables

In making regression estimates of ICP type per capita GDP, the choice of variables was dictated by considerations of analytical relevance and availability of information for a large number of countries, especially those reported in WDI tables.

In general, per capita GDP converted at PPP tends to be higher for a poorer country than the corresponding exchange rate converted value. Two empirical facts stand out in this regard:

(a) the divergence grows inversely with per capita GDP; and (b) the noise around this relationship increases inversely with income levels.

This is confirmed by Chart 1 which shows the deviations between ICP and exchange rate converted estimates of per capita GDP by plotting the price level (ratio of PPP to exchange rate, which is the same thing as the ratio of *Atlas* GNP to ICP GDP)[9] against *Atlas* GNP per capita for 1985. The data refer to 76 ICP countries; for countries not in 1985 ICP, the figures are extrapolations of the latest year data available. If ICP and *Atlas* estimates of income were the same, PPP would be equal to the *Atlas* exchange rate, and the scatter would be on the 100 mark, the US value, on the Y-axis. The chart shows that the vertical distance of a data point from 100 tends to increase as one moves from right (high income) to left (low income) on the X-axis, and that the cluster is much more dispersed vertically at the lower end of the income scale than at the higher.

(1986); Clague and Tanzi (1972); Isenman (1980); Kravis, Summers and Heston (1978); Summers and Heston (1984, 1988 and 1991). etc.

[9]The deviation between PPP converted and exchange rate converted values has been described in the literature in two ways: (1) the ratio of PPP to exchange rate (ER) called *price level* or (2) the ratio of ER to PPP, popularly known as *exchange rate deviation index* or ERDI, which is the reciprocal of price level. Note that price level can also be measured by the ratio of exchange rate converted GDP to PPP converted GDP as follows: Price level = (GDP/ER)/(GDP/PPP) = PPP/ER, and its reciprocal, ERDI = (GDP/PPP)/(GDP/ER) = ER/PPP.

CHART 1

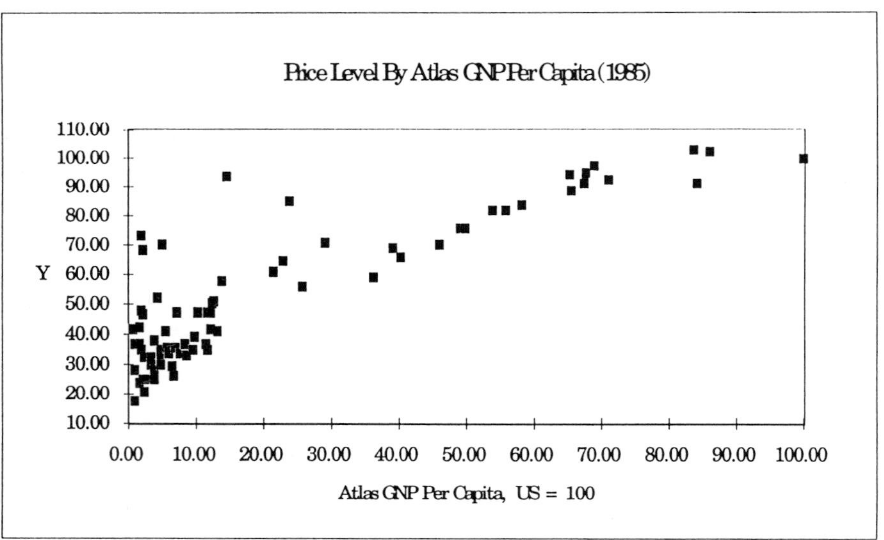

CHART 2

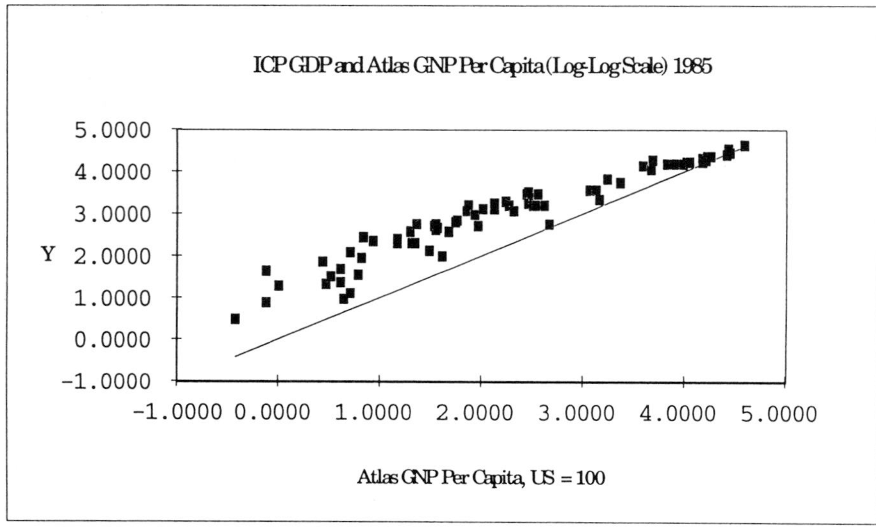

The relationship can also be pictured in another way as in Chart 2 which plots on a log-log scale *Atlas* GNP per capita on the X axis and ICP GDP per capita on the Y axis, both expressed as US = 100. Here the distance from the 45 degree line is the measure of deviation between the two estimates. Chart 2 shows that ICP estimates tend to be higher than *Atlas* estimates (indicated by points above the 45 degree line), that the difference between the two estimates increases as one moves from higher to lower end of the income scale, and that deviations tend to be more dispersed at the lower end of the income scale than at the higher.

Explanatory Variables

The list of candidate variables, therefore, includes *Atlas* estimates of per capita GNP to place countries on an income scale and others that would explain the noise around the broad trend set by *Atlas* estimates.

It is observed that generally price levels are relatively lower in poorer countries, and the divergence is more pronounced in services than in commodities. For instance, if the 1975 price index (PPP/ER) for the US is assumed to be 100 for total GDP, then it was 41 for the poorest group of countries and 108 for the richest. The price indices for commodities (defined here as all final product commodities excluding construction) and services (defined here as final product services and construction) were respectively 60 and 25 for the poorest group and 119 and 97 for the richest group[10] . Thus while commodity prices in poorer countries are approximately 50 percent (60/119) of those of the richer countries, service prices are only about 25 percent (25/97). In nominal terms, services account for nearly 30 percent of GDP for low income countries compared with about 50 percent in high income countries [11]. The effect of PPP conversion is to raise this share to levels comparable to those of richer countries. Since exchange rates are at best affected by relative prices of tradeables (commodities excluding construction), and since PPP measures relative prices of all goods and services, non-tradeable as well as tradeable, any explanation of the difference between PPP and exchange rate must include factors which relate to differences in price levels, especially those of services.

We hypothesize that the discrepancy between ICP and *Atlas* esti-

[10] Kravis and Lipsey (1983), p.12.

[11] *World Development Report 1991,* Table 3.

mates reflects persistence of differences in factor productivity and wage differentials among nations due to constraints on international mobility of labor[12] . Richer countries have higher labor productivity. Within a country, higher productivity in the trading sectors leads to higher wages in these sectors and competition tends to spread these wages to service sectors. Primarily because of the lack of labor mobility, wage differentials persist across international frontiers. Compared with poorer countries, richer countries, therefore, will tend to have higher prices of services, higher price levels (ratio of PPP to exchange rate) and lower deviation between PPP converted and exchange rate converted GDP[13]. Therefore, regression equations, *apriori*, should include variables that can capture differences in labor productivity.

Among the variables considered here are indicators of natural resources, human capital, structure and openness of the economy, and price and exchange regimes.

Natural resources: Two countries with similar technology and capital stock but different natural resources could have different labor productivity and wage levels. However, reliable and consistent measures of natural resources for a large number of countries are not available.

Human capital: Indicators of human capital or labor skills include education variables, demographic variables and variables relating to health and nutrition. Among the education variables are index of education attainment or mean years of schooling, and school enrolment. Education attainment is a more appropriate measure of human capital than enrolment. While there is no uniform definition of education attainment, a proper measure of education attainment would have to include the number of graduates by levels of education and their quality. Such measures are not available on a consistent basis except for a handful of countries. One measure of education attainment, reported in the Bank's *Social Indicators of Development*, is mean years of schooling embodied in the labor force. This is based on population censuses and is available at ten-year intervals. Since data were not available for many developing countries, this variable was not used. Another

[12]Bel Balassa (1964); Paul Isenman (1980)

[13]A recent study using data for developed countries has found confirmation of the productivity differential hypothesis. It concludes that "there is a long-run equilibrium relation between the productivity differentials and the deviation of purchasing power parity from the equilibrium exchange rate.." Mohsen Bahmani-Oskooee (1992).

measure is simply mean years of schooling of the population. This is available for a larger number of countries and was included. Following Isenman (1980), secondary school enrolment ratios was also used as a proxy variable for educational attainment.

Among the demographic variables that are expected to be closely associated with productivity differentials (levels of living) are life expectancy and infant mortality rates. As these variables contain model estimates based on income levels, they were tried but not chosen.

Supply of calories as percent of requirement is a good indicator of health which promotes productivity. However, since data on calories as percent of requirements are no longer available, gross supply of calories per person per day was used. Number of population per doctor as an indicator of access to health care is expected to be correlated with productivity. But it was not used because data for the base year were not available.

The Human Development Index (HDI) published by the United Nations Development Program (UNDP) was also expected to be highly correlated with human capital. However, since the PPP-based estimate of per capita GDP was a component of this index, it was not retained in the final runs.

A more direct measure of productivity differential would have been hourly output per worker in manufacturing. However, such data are not available on the scale needed for this exercise.

Structure and openness of the economy: A country having a large manufacturing sector (or a small agricultural sector) or succeeding in exporting a large proportion of its manufactures, is likely to have high productivity and high wages. To capture these, we considered variables such as share of manufactures in exports and share of manufactured exports in value added in manufactures. Since data for exports of manufactures were not available except for a handful of countries, these variables could not be used. Share of agriculture in GDP is usually inversely related to level of development, productivity and wages, and was included in the exercise. Openness of the economy measured by exports plus imports as share of GDP is usually associated with higher prices (Kravis and Lipsey, 1983) and was included in the list of variables.

Price and exchange rates: One reason for differences in PPP and exchange rate could be that countries with trade and payments restrictions would not allow exchange rates to adjust to price changes and would maintain an overvalued currency. As an indicator of currency overvaluation, we included the ratio of black market rate to official exchange rate. As a proxy for price differentials, we also included UN post adjustment index as one of the explanatory variables.

Thus, to summarize, the variables not used for lack of sufficient data were: natural resources, school attainment, hourly output per worker in manufacturing, exports of manufactures as proportion of either total exports or of value added in manufacturing, and population per doctor; those not used on a-priori reasons were : life expectancy, infant mortality and HDI.

A whole array of the so-called *physical indicators* popularized by Beckerman and Bacon[14] was not included because in past studies they were found to be highly inter- correlated and not much could be gained in explanatory power by including them. These are miles of roads, per capita consumption of electricity, energy, steel, milk, meat, newsprint, or numbers of radios, telephones, televisions or automobiles per capita.

Listed below are the explanatory variables that were used in the exercise:

(1) ATLAS = *Atlas* GNP per capita;

(2) MNSKL = mean years of schooling;

(3) ENROL = secondary school enrollment ratio;

(4) CALOR = supply of calories per person per day;

(5) AGR = value added in agriculture as proportion to GDP;

(6) OPEN = openness: sum of exports and imports as proportion of GDP;

(7) BLKRTO = black market exchange rate as a ratio to official rate; and

[14]Wilfred Beckerman (1966); Wifred Beckerman and R. Bacon (1966).

(8) UNADJ = UN post adjustment index.

Dependent variable:

The dependent variable of the regression could take one of two forms: either (a) the deviation between ICP and *Atlas* estimates of per capita income (i.e., price level or ERDI as in Chart 1) or (b) ICP GDP per capita. It is more interesting to investigate why PPP differs from the exchange rate and use form (a) as the dependent variable. However, since the purpose of this paper is to estimate ICP-based numbers when such numbers are not available, form (b) as depicted in Chart 2 is more appropriate here. It has to be noted though that since in this formulation the same GDP data in local currency underlie the figures on both sides of the equation (in ICP estimates on the left hand side and *Atlas* estimates on the right), the coefficient of correlation will tend to be higher than in the other formulation. We try both variants and report on (b) to facilitate comparison with estimates in PWT5 which uses the same dependent variable.

Since ICP GDP per capita was available for a different set of countries in different phases, it was extrapolated to the reference year by the country's real growth rate and scaled up by US inflation. However, a choice had to be made whether to use the average of all available estimates for a country or only the latest. We concentrated on the latest. Thus the variants of dependent variable considered were the following:

(a) PL = Price level (ratio of *Atlas* to ICP estimates); and

(b) ICPL = ICP GDP per capita, latest available year extended to reference year by real growth rate and US inflation.

4. Regressions

All variables (except BLKRTO, ratio of black market to official exchange rate) were first expressed as indices with US=100 and then converted to natural logs. The functional form of the equation was:

$$lnY = f(lnx_1, lnx_2, ...lnx_k); \qquad (1)$$

where Y is ICPL and the X's are the various independent variables.

First, "leaps and bounds"[15] procedures were run to identify best subset regressions based on adjusted R-squares. Regressions were run separately for different data sets to check on the stability of the equations. The data sets related to different phases of ICP: 1975 with 34 countries, 1980 with 60 countries and 1985 with 56 countries[16]. These data were also pooled, with regional dummy variables for Europe and Africa and time dummy variables for 1975 and 1980 in order to separate the effects of regions or time periods on the overall estimates. Another sample was all countries that ever participated in ICP, with 1985 as the base year, consisting of actual phase V (1985) numbers for countries participating in phase V and extrapolations of earlier phase data for others. Separate regressions were also run for sub-samples of low income (less than $1,000 of *Atlas* GNP per capita in 1985) and high income countries. In order to minimize the effect of extrapolations, 1985 was adopted as the base year. The best subset regression was picked on the basis of goodness-of-fit statistics and stability of the regression over various sub-samples, and the estimating equation was obtained from the sample of 76 ICP countries for which data for the chosen independent variables were available. The final estimating equation was:

$$ln(ICPL) = \underset{(.0319)}{.5726} ln(ATLAS) + \underset{(.0540)}{.3466} ln(ENROL) + \underset{(.1579)}{.3865} \qquad (2)$$

RMSE = .2240 Adj.R-sq = .9523 N = 76.

The variables in the regression performed well in all data subsets consisting of different phases of ICP run separately as well as pooled; the coefficients are robust (with low standard errors) and the adjusted R-square (.952) and RMSE (.224) are no worse than those of PWT5 equations which have adjusted R-squares ranging from .926 to .976 and RMSE from .263 to .159 (see Table 4). The equation can be interpreted to support the hypothesis that the differences between exchange rate converted and PPP converted GDP can be explained reasonably well

[15] Leaps-and-bounds method of picking best subset regressions is, unlike step-wise regression, independent of the order in which the variables are introduced in the equation.

[16] In all 63 countries participated in ICP Phase V for 1985 (no Latin American country was included); data for seven Caribbean countries were not available at the time of performing these calculations. The remaining 56 countries participated in several regional exercises. The data reported here for these countries are likely to be revised when the regional estimates are officially linked together to form a global comparison. As mentioned earlier, data for 1990 for 30 OECD and other Eastern European countries have not been included in this study.

by productivity differentials as they are measured by secondary school enrolment ratios.

Although the equation with ATLAS and ENROL was chosen, there were close contenders. Combinations of ATLAS, ENROL and CALOR performed well in all data subsets. Other regression with ATLAS and CALOR or with ATLAS, ENROL and CALOR offered equally attractive alternatives. These other regressions are:

$$\underset{}{ln(ICPL)} = \underset{(.0405)}{.6396 ln(ATLAS)} + \underset{(.2689)}{.7728 ln(CALOR)} - \underset{(1.087)}{1.7782} \qquad (3)$$

RMSE = .2655 Adj.R-sq = .9329 N = 76.

$$\begin{aligned} ln(ICPL) = \; & \underset{(.0385)}{.5280 ln(ATLAS)} + \underset{(.2289)}{.4552 ln(CALOR)} \\ & + \underset{(.0545)}{.3211 ln(ENROL)} - \underset{(.9014)}{1.3802} \end{aligned} \qquad (4)$$

RMSE = .2196 Adj.R-sq = .9541 N = 76.

V. Results

Table 1 summarizes the results of regression estimates along with those of *World Bank Atlas* and Penn World Tables, Mark 5 (PWT5) for the year 1985. The numbers in a given column are a mixture of actual and estimated. The regression estimates are used only to fill gaps; they are tagged by footnote d. The rest of the countries for which ICP numbers are available show the latest such numbers extrapolated to 1985. These numbers have been presented in columns (3) and (4), termed ICP/REG (REG stands for regression estimates); these numbers and their extrapolations to 1990 have been presented in the WDI. The regression estimates in columns (3) and (4) are based on equation (2) above consisting of ATLAS and ENROL as explanatory variables. Columns (5) and (6), marked ICP/REG(2) (REG(2) is a second version of REG), presents an alternative set of estimates derived by equation (4) above which uses CALOR in addition to ATLAS and ENROL as explanatory variables. Columns (7) and (8) are PWT5 estimates. *Atlas* estimates are GNP, while those from ICP are GDP (ICP preferred to work with GDP rather than GNP). The table presents only those countries for which estimates are available from all three sources - *Atlas*, PWT5 and ICP/REG.

As expected, the numbers in columns showing ICP and regression estimates are invariably higher than those of *Atlas* except for one country (with the highest per capita income in *Atlas*), the differences being larger at the lower end of the income scale. Thus comparing absolute values is not meaningful since PPP-based numbers have a different scale or meaning as they are based on "international" average rather than national average prices. Comparing ranks is more meaningful.

A comparison of ranks is presented in Table 2. When considering the entire array, changes in ranks from one measure of per capita income to another are not significant on the average as demonstrated by high degrees of rank-order correlation. The correlation between *Atlas* and PWT5 is .971; between *Atlas* and REG is .975; and between PWT5 and REG is .983. However, the average hides some very big differences as shown in Table 3.

Table 3 lists all countries which changed ranks ten places or more between REG and *Atlas*, PWT5 and *Atlas*, and between PWT5 and REG. Several observations can be made for these outliers. First, big changes are concentrated among low income countries. Sixteen of the 28 countries in the table are ICP participants; these are the countries that show the largest changes in ranks between *Atlas* and ICP. Fourteen of these sixteen countries show up under the REG-*Atlas* column which means that REG for non-ICP countries has not had a big influence on the rankings vis-a-vis *Atlas*. Secondly, due to the influence of ATLAS, which alone accounts for about 90 percent of the variance and has greater weight in the equation, REG estimates are likely to be closer to the corresponding *Atlas* numbers than those estimated without ATLAS. For Gabon, which shows a big change in rank, it seems that oil prices keep the exchange rate strong resulting in a relatively high *Atlas* estimate, while low enrolment ratio signifies a considerably low level of human capital and low estimate under REG. Comments on the differences with PWT5 are made in the next section.

One note of caution while using the regression estimates. Since the table presents a mixture of actual ICP for some countries and regression estimates for others, it is possible that two countries with comparable levels of *Atlas* and enrolment values may show very different results - in level as well as rank - just because one shows the actual and the other the fitted value. This is to be expected because the regression estimates of some countries in the sample can have large residuals. It is sometimes suggested that to avoid these situations, one should present only the estimated values. That would solve the problem of comparability but ignore the known residuals. To throw away actual observations and replace them by fitted values is, however, not an accepted practice in econometric estimation.

Alternative Regression Estimates

To underscore the approximate nature of the regression estimates, the paper presents a second set of estimates which compared with REG are more or less equally plausible. These estimates, presented in Table 1, Columns (6) and (7) under ICP/REG(2) are made using the regression equation (4) above which uses CALOR in addition to ATLAS and ENROL as independent variables. Although equation (4) has a higher adjusted R-square and lower RMSE, equation (2) was picked as the preferred equation because the latter was more stable from sample to sample. These alternative estimates are quite close to those of REG but are different for some countries. As can be seen in Table 2, column (8), some 27 out of 106 countries change ranks although the biggest change is only 5 places (for Ghana, for instance).

Finally, it is worthwhile reminding that large values of coefficients of determination are the result of placing GNP/GDP values on both sides of the equation; as mentioned earlier, they would be significantly lower if the equations were formulated with the ratio of PPP to exchange rate (PL) on the left hand side, and if the sample as restricted to low income countries.

6. Comparison of REG and PWT5 Estimates

PWT5 provides estimates of PPP-based national accounts for 138 countries and for the period 1950-1988. It provides estimates of per capita GDP in several forms (at current prices, constant 1985 prices, constant chain linked prices, and at constant prices adjusted for changes in terms of trade) and its three major components (consumption, investment and government). In addition, it provides data on relative prices, within and between countries, and demographic data and capital stock estimates as well. Since these data are available in electronic form, these are being used widely in research and have somewhat overshadowed the actual benchmark ICP numbers.

The PWT5 follows the earlier work of Summers and Heston on making regression estimates of ICP-type per capita GDP using various physical and monetary indicators[17] Unlike in earlier efforts, the authors do not use exchange rate converted per capita GDP as an explanatory variable in PWT5. Instead, they take various post adjustment (PA) price indices to estimate price relatives, relate the dollar estimates of per capita GDP based on these price relatives to those of ICP, and use these relationships to estimate ICP-type values for countries for which PA data are available but ICP data are not. For each country, two estimates are made for 1985 and averaged, one based mainly on 1985 data and another on 1980 data. Extrapolations of benchmark data are made on the basis of "consistentized" growth rates which are obtained by adjusting both SNA and ICP growth rates to make them consistent with each other.

The PWT5 results for 1985 are presented in Table 1 columns (8) and (9). As in REG, actual ICP numbers (or, if necessary, extrapolations) are shown for ICP countries and regression estimates only for non-ICP countries. Consequently, for ICP countries, the values in PWT5 should be the same as those in REG. But they differ because ICP data used by PWT5 are their own estimates which are potentially different from those in the public domain (and used in REG) in three respects: (a) PWT5 uses current vintage national accounts data, (b) it re-estimates Geary-Khamis without maintaining "fixity"[18] ; and (c) uses "consistentized" growth rates for extrapolations.

Compared with *Atlas*, PWT5 has only four more countries than REG with ranking differences of ten or more shown in Table 3. The biggest differences between REG and PWT5 are for low income non-ICP countries, some ranked higher in PWT5 (Somalia, Mozambique, China, Sierra Leone) and others lower (Uganda, Togo, Zaire, Ghana, Jordan, Algeria) than in REG. For most of the other countries in Table 3, REG and PWT5 are quite close to each other but both differ significantly from the *Atlas*. In order to highlight the patterns in these

[17] Summers and Heston (1984, 1988).

[18] "Fixity" refers to the practice of keeping the relative positions of countries in the European Communities (EC) in the regional comparison fixed or unchanged when they are linked with other regional comparisons to form a global comparison. A global comparison, which uses a global average price structure, would normally alter relative positions observed in regional comparisons based on regional average prices. Thus "fixity" introduces an element of incomparability between EC and other countries. In order to correct this incomparability, PWT5 re-estimates PPPs globally without maintaining "fixity", making the estimates potentially different from those published.

differences, Table 3 presents the countries in several groups, those at top of table having much higher ranks in REG than in PWT5, those at bottom of table showing the opposite tendency (PWT5 ranks much higher than those of REG), and the rest in the middle of the table which show quite close ranks between REG and PWT5 but both having large differences with the *Atlas* ranks.

While comparing PWT5 numbers with others, it has to be remembered that PWT5 authors have given quality ratings for all their estimates varying in descending order from A to D. Generally, countries with ICP experience rank higher than those without, although many ICP countries have been given low ratings. These quality ratings for countries in Table 3 are shown in the last column. Sixteen of the 29 countries in the table have a quality rating of D, meaning that the PWT5 authors do not have much confidence in the accuracy of these numbers.

Except for Iran, countries at the top of the table did not participate in ICP. The REG numbers are closer to *Atlas* because of the influence of *Atlas* numbers in the estimating equation. The national accounts of Zaire and Uganda have gone through major revisions, and much of the difference can be attributed to differences in the vintage of national accounts data used in these estimates. PWT5 ranks for Uganda and Togo are quite close to those of *Atlas*, but because they have relatively low enrolment ratios, their REG estimates are also relatively low. For Jordan, a potential source of difference could be the treatment of population. *Atlas* estimates are based on East Bank only data, while the earlier data base had an anomaly - Jordan showed population for both East and West Bank but GDP for East Bank only. Algeria and Iran (also Gabon), because of oil, have over-valued currencies (with high black-market premiums) raising *Atlas* estimates but high domestic prices lowering PWT5 values.

Countries in the middle of Table 3 are all ICP participants (except for Gabon) and not surprisingly the REG and PWT5 numbers agree with each other but differ from the *Atlas*. This is because for these countries both PWT5 and REG show actual ICP numbers. The differences in the ICP numbers themselves are due to the factors described in above.

Except for Syria, all the countries at the bottom of the table are non-ICP countries. REG ranks Mozambique, Somalia, and China quite close to *Atlas* but PWT5 ranks them relatively higher. The China numbers in PWT5 are based on Kravis (1980), estimates which are widely regarded as too high. For Somalia and Mozambique, there is considerable uncertainty about national accounts, appropriate exchange rates and prices paid by UN staff so that both *Atlas* and PWT5 numbers are of poor quality. It is not apparent why the ICP estimate for Sierra Leone in PWT5 is so much higher than that in REG.

Which set of estimates is better? Based on the goodness-of-fit statistics, the choice is not clear (see Table 4). Among the twelve equations used in PWT5, adjusted R-square varies between .926 and .976 and RMSE between .263 and .159. Compare those with REG: adjusted R-Square of .95 and RMSE of .224. The judgment has to be based on an evaluation of underlying assumptions, reliability of information used and, for Bank purposes, ease of updating the estimates.

PWT5 estimates are based on empirical evidence. It assumes that post adjustment prices differ from national price patterns uniformly in every country. Intuitively, this is hard to accept because post adjustment data refer to a fixed basket of mostly goods consumed by foreigners living in a capital city and not adjusting to local conditions. Empirically, however, the relationship is quite strong. REG, on the other hand, assumes that the average exchange rates underlying *Atlas* estimates equate prices of tradeable goods, and that secondary school enrolment explains the difference between PPP and *Atlas* exchange rate. The choice of school enrolment (or calorie) as an explanatory variable is supported by an analytical reasoning. Although, empirically, exchange rates do not usually equate prices of tradeable goods especially in the short run and although not everybody is convinced of the analytical reasoning behind including enrolment as proxy for human capital, the relationship computed from available data and depicted by the REG equation is quite robust.

The advantage of PWT5 is that it is more comprehensive than REG. It has estimates for other concepts of income and several components of GDP (the table has estimates for twenty seven variables); REG has only one - GDP per capita. PWT5 numbers are estimated on the basis of observed differences in exchange rate and actual (post adjustment) prices and should have an advantage over REG which seeks to estimate that difference indirectly through proxy variables. Since enrolment ratios (or calorie supply) are slow to change over time, changes in the regression estimates from time to time will more or less follow the pattern in the *Atlas* estimates. PWT5 numbers, on the other hand, could conceivably be more sensitive to actual price movements.

However, the Bank will not be able to update the PWT5 numbers at the same time it updates other GNP numbers because all the adjustments made to the post adjustment data for PWT5 estimates are not known. Also, PWT5 estimates do not advance our goals for integrating ICP with national statistical data base as the post adjustment data are "foreign" to national statistical offices.

7. Conclusions and directions for further work

The REG procedure attempts to explain why PPP and exchange rates differ - a procedure attempted earlier but not pursued in more recent studies[19]. There are doubts about the validity of the statements that (a) *Atlas* exchange rates equate prices of tradeable goods, primarily because capital movement based on differential interest rates, political security, etc have greater influence on exchange rates in the short run than relative prices, or that (b) enrolment (or calorie supply) is a good proxy for human capital; but the goodness-of-fit statistics are quite robust. However, the method can produce different but more or less equally defensible results depending on the choice of explanatory variables, so that these estimates should be used for broad tendencies for groups of countries; estimates of individual countries should be used with caution.

Further work in this area could take the form of introducing new variables (e.g., cost of basic sustenance instead of ATLAS, averaging enrolment for a number of years, physical capital as contributing to productivity); finding a better explanation at the lower end of income scale, and may be choosing different variables for different income or regional groups. However, based on past experience, this line of investigation is unlikely to bring dramatically different results because very little variance is left to be explained.

A much more reliable procedure would be to use reduced information techniques to survey a small number of prices and come up with estimates at regular intervals.

[19] Summers and Heston (1984, 1988); Clague (1986)

The most rewarding direction of further work, however, has to be to make ICP benchmark surveys regular and universal, and improve the quality of the estimates. To do this we have to integrate ICP with regular national statistical work, make detailed data accessible to all users, and demonstrate the relevance of the data for country policy work. The World Bank is pursuing these goals vigorously in cooperation with United Nations and other international organizations.

References

Ahmad, Sultan. (1988), "International Real Income Comparisons with Reduced Information". In *World Comparisons of Incomes, Prices and Product,* ed. J. Salazar-Carrillo and D. S. Prasada Rao. North Holland: Elsevier Science Publishers.

Ahmad, Sultan. (1980), *Approaches to Purchasing Power Parity and Real Product Comparison Using Shortcuts and Reduced Information.* World Bank Staff Working Paper 418.

Balassa, Bela. (1964), "The Purchasing Power Parity Doctrine: A Reappraisal".*Journal of Political Economy.* LXXII (December), pp.584-590.

Bahmani-Oskooee, Mohsen. (1992), "A Time-Series Approach of Test the Productivity Bias Hypothesis in Purchasing Power Parity". *KYKLOS.* Vol. 45, pp. 227-236.

Beckerman, Wilfred. (1966), *International Comparisons of Real Incomes.* Paris: Development Center, Organization for Economic Cooperation and Development.

Beckerman, Wilfred. (1984), Updating Short-cut Methods for Predicting "Real" Per Capita GDP. A report to the World Bank (mimeo). September.

Beckerman, Wilfred and R. Bacon. (1966), "International Comparisons of Real Income Levels: A Suggested New Measure". *The Economic Journal.* 76 pp. 519-536.

Bhagwati, Jagdish N. (1984), "Why Are Services Cheaper in Poor Countries?" *Journal of International Economics.* 94.

Clague, Christopher. (1986), "Short Cut Estimates of Real Income". *Review of Income and Wealth* : 313-31.

Clague, Christopher and Vito Tanzi. (1972), "Human Capital, Natural Resources and the Purchasing Power Parity Doctrine: Some Empirical Results". *Economia Internazionale.* 25, No.1 , pp.3-16.

David, Paul A. (1972), "Just How Misleading Are Official Exchange Rate Conversions?" The *Economic Journal.* 82, pp. 979-90.

Heston, Alan W. (1973), "A Comparison of Some Short-Cut Methods of Estimating Real Product Per Capita". *Review of Income and Wealth* 19(1): 79-104.

Isenman, Paul. (1980), "Inter-Country Comparisons of "Real" (PPP) Incomes: Revised Estimates and Unresolved Questions". *World Development* 8(1).

Kravis, Irving B. (1980), An Approximation of the Relative Real Per Capita GDP of the People's Republic of China. Appendix in *Report of the CSCPRC Economics Delegation to the People's Republic of China*, October 1979. Washington, DC: National Academy of Sciences.

Kravis, Irving B. (1984), "Comparative Studies of National Incomes and Prices".*Journal of Economic Literature 22.*

Kravis, Irving B. , Alan W. Heston, and Robert Summers. (1978), "Real GDP Per Capita for More Than One Hundred Countries". *Economic Journal* 88(350): 215-42.

Kravis, Irving B. (1981), "New Insights into the Structure of the World Economy". *The Review of Income and Wealth* 27(4): 339-355.

Kravis, Irving B., (1982), *World Product and Income: International Comparisons of Real GDP.* Baltimore: John Hopkins University Press.

Kravis, Irving B. and Robert E. Lipsey. (1983), *Toward an Explanation of National Price Levels.* Princeton Studies in International Finance, No.52 (November).

Kravis, Irving B. and Robert E. Lipsey. (1991), International Comparison Program: Current Status and Problems. In *International*

Economic Transactions: Issues in Measurement and Empirical Research, ed. Peter Hooper and J. David Richardson. National Bureau of Economic Research, Studies in Income and Wealth, Vol.55. Chicago: University of Chicago Press.

Summers, Robert, and Alan W. Heston. (1984), "Improved International Comparisons of Real Product and Its Composition", 1950-80. *Review of Income and Wealth* 30(2) : 207-62.

Summers, Robert, and Alan W. Heston. (1988), "A New Set of International Comparisons of Real Product and Prices Levels: Estimates for 130 Countries", 1950-1985. *Review of Income and Wealth* 34(1) : 1-25.

Summers, Robert, and Alan W. Heston. (1991), "The Penn World Tables (Mark V): An Expanded Set of International Comparisons",1950-88. *Quarterly Journal of Economics*: 327-68.

World Bank. *World Bank Atlas.* Various issues. Washington, D.C.:World Bank.

World Bank. (1990), *Social Indicators of Development 1990.* Baltimore: Johns Hopkins University Press.

World Bank. (1991), *World Development Report 1991: The Challenge of Development.* London: Oxford University Press.

World Bank. (1992), *World Development Report 1992: Development and the Environment.* New York: Oxford University Press.

TABLE 1

Comparison of Atlas and Regression Estimates of PPP-Based per Capita GDP, 1985

	COUNTRY	ATLAS(GNP)		ICP/REG			PRICE LEVEL	ICP/REG, 1990			ICP/REG(2)			PWT5	
		$$ (1)	US=100 (2)	$$ (3)	US=100 (4)		US=100 (5)	$$ (1)	US=100 (1)		$$ (6)	US=100 (7)		$$ (8)	US=100 (9)
1	Ethiopia	110	0.7	260	1.6		41.6	310	1.45		260	1.6		320	1.9
2	Chad	150	0.9	400	2.4	d	..	440	2.06	d	379	2.3	d	511	3.1
3	Mali	150	0.9	400	2.4		36.9	560	2.62		400	2.4		477	2.9
4	Somalia	150	0.9	510	3.1	d	..	540	2.53	d	496	3.0	d	828	5.0
5	Bangladesh	160	1.0	830	5.0		19.0	1,050	4.92		830	5.0		688	4.2
6	Nepal	160	1.0	740	4.5	d	..	950	4.45	d	706	4.3	d	716	4.3
7	Malawi	170	1.0	590	3.6		28.3	670	3.14		590	3.6		564	3.4
8	Mozambique	180	1.1	500	3.0	d	..	620	2.90	d	451	2.7	d	816	5.0
9	Burkina Faso	190	1.1	460	2.8	d	..	560	2.62	d	436	2.6	d	501	3.0
10	Niger	230	1.4	550	3.3	d	..	590	2.76	d	565	3.4	d	615	3.7
11	Uganda	230	1.4	650	3.9	d	..	800	3.75	d	642	3.9	d	422	2.6
12	Burundi	250	1.5	500	3.0	d	..	600	2.81	d	494	3.0	d	531	3.2
13	Togo	250	1.5	890	5.4	d	..	990	4.63	d	861	5.2	d	653	4.0
14	Zaire	260	1.6	910	5.5	d	..	950	4.45	d	877	5.3	d	351	2.1
15	Central African Rep.	270	1.6	840	5.1	d	..	900	4.21	d	773	4.7	d	686	4.2
16	Rwanda	270	1.6	630	3.8		42.1	610	2.86		630	3.8		719	4.4
17	Benin	280	1.7	1,070	6.5		25.7	1,130	5.29		1,070	6.5		1,083	6.6
18	India	280	1.7	750	4.5		36.7	1,150	5.38		750	4.5		684	4.2
19	Kenya	310	1.8	870	5.3		35.0	1,120	5.24		870	5.3		831	5.0
20	Madagascar	310	1.8	640	3.9		47.6	740	3.46		640	3.9		665	4.0
21	Haiti	320	1.9	950	5.8	d	..	960	4.49	d	911	5.5	d	909	5.5
22	Tanzania	320	1.9	430	2.6		73.2	540	2.53		430	2.6		472	2.9
23	China	330	2.0	1,260	7.6	d	..	1,950	9.13	d	1,311	7.9	d	1,850	11.2
24	Pakistan	340	2.0	1,340	8.1		24.9	1,770	8.29		1,340	8.1		1,426	8.7
25	Sierra Leone	340	2.0	490	3.0		68.2	580	2.72		490	3.0		999	6.1
26	Ghana	370	2.2	1,390	8.4	d	..	1,720	8.05	d	1,296	7.9	d	838	5.1
27	Sudan	370	2.2	1,090	6.6	d	..	1,180	5.52	d	1,043	6.3	d	930	5.6
28	Zambia	370	2.2	780	4.7		46.6	810	3.79		780	4.7		749	4.5
29	Senegal	380	2.3	1,150	7.0		32.5	1,360	6.37		1,150	7.0		1,136	6.9
30	Lesotho	390	2.3	1,180	7.2	d	..	1,700	7.96	d	1,179	7.2	d	1,215	7.4
31	Sri Lanka	390	2.3	1,850	11.2		20.7	2,370	11.10		1,850	11.2		1,928	11.7
32	Mauritania	410	2.4	1,050	6.4	d	..	1,240	5.81	d	1,040	6.3	d	910	5.5
33	Bolivia	430	2.6	1,712	10.4	c	..	1,910	8.94		1,712	10.4	c	1,539	9.3
34	Liberia	470	2.8	1,330	8.1	d	..	..	..		1,319	8.0	d	927	5.6
35	Philippines	540	3.2	1,790	10.9		29.7	2,320	10.86		1,790	10.9		1,718	10.4

TABLE 1 - continued

	COUNTRY	ATLAS(GNP)		ICP/REG			PRICE LEVEL	ICP/REG, 1990		ICP/REG(2)			PWT5	
		$$ (1)	US=100 (2)	$$ (3)	US=100 (4)		US=100 (5)	$$ (1)	US=100 (1)	$$ (6)	US=100 (7)		$$ (8)	US=100 (9)
36	Indonesia	550	3.3	1,637	9.9	c	..	2,350	11.00	1,637	9.9	c	1,675	10.2
37	Morocco	620	3.7	2,160	13.1		28.2	2,670	12.50	2,160	13.1		1,977	12.0
38	Zimbabwe	630	3.8	1,630	9.9		38.0	1,970	9.22	1,630	9.9		1,410	8.6
39	Egypt, Arab Rep.	660	3.9	2,610	15.8		24.9	3,100	14.51	2,610	15.8		1,898	11.5
40	Cote D'Ivoire	670	4.0	1,680	10.2		39.2	1,540	7.21	1,680	10.2		1,423	8.6
41	Honduras	740	4.4	1,388	8.4	c	..	1,610	7.54	1,388	8.4	c	1,219	7.4
42	Papua New Guinea	740	4.4	1,358	8.2	c	..	1,500	7.02	1,358	8.2	c	1,641	10.0
43	Nicaragua	760	4.5	2,075	12.6	d	..	1,710	..	1,905	11.6	d	1,857	11.3
44	Dominican Rep.	790	4.7	2,470	15.0	c	..	2,860	13.39	2,470	15.0	c	2,065	12.5
45	Thailand	800	4.8	2,630	15.9		29.9	4,610	21.58	2,630	15.9		2,472	15.0
46	Cameroon	810	4.8	2,310	14.0		34.5	2,020	9.46	2,310	14.0		1,761	10.7
47	El Salvador	840	5.0	1,595	9.7	c	..	1,890	8.85	1,595	9.7	c	1,736	10.5
48	Nigeria	850	5.1	1,190	7.2		70.2	1,420	6.65	1,190	7.2		1,047	6.4
49	Jamaica	910	5.4	2,188	13.3	c	..	3,030	14.19	2,188	13.3	c	2,340	14.2
50	Botswana	960	5.7	2,660	16.1		35.5	4,300	20.10	2,660	16.1		2,511	15.2
51	Peru	980	5.8	2,845	17.3	c	..	2,720	12.73	2,845	17.3	c	2,683	16.3
52	Congo, People's Rep.	1,040	6.2	2,710	16.4		37.7	2,690	12.60	2,710	16.4		2,600	15.8
53	Turkey	1,080	6.4	3,600	21.8		29.5	5,020	23.50	3,600	21.8		3,150	19.1
54	Mauritius	1,100	6.6	4,090	24.8		26.4	6,500	30.43	4,090	24.8		3,690	22.4
55	Tunisia	1,170	7.0	3,270	19.8		35.2	3,979	18.63	3,270	19.8		3,051	18.5
56	Ecuador	1,180	7.0	3,271	19.8	c	..	3,720	17.42	3,271	19.8	c	2,727	16.5
57	Colombia	1,270	7.6	3,717	22.5	c	..	4,950	23.17	3,717	22.5	c	3,244	19.7
58	Costa Rica	1,400	8.3	3,729	22.6	c	..	4,870	22.80	3,729	22.6	c	3,549	21.5
59	Chile	1,420	8.5	4,267	25.9	c	..	6,190	28.98	4,267	25.9	c	3,697	22.4
60	Uruguay	1,580	9.4	4,459	27.0	c	..	6,000	28.09	4,459	27.0	c	4,442	26.9
61	Brazil	1,630	9.7	4,107	24.9	c	..	4,780	22.38	4,107	24.9	c	3,926	23.8
62	Syrian Arab Rep.	1,740	10.4	3,565	21.6	c	..	4,110	19.24	3,565	21.6	c	4,931	29.9
63	Jordan	1,880	11.2	4,410	26.7	d	..	4530.0	20.40	4,177	25.3	d	2,685	16.3
64	Hungary	1,930	11.5	5,150	31.2		36.9	6,190	28.98	5,150	31.2		5,081	30.8
65	Malaysia	1,970	11.7	4,119	25.0	c	..	5,900	27.62	4,119	25.0	c	4,668	28.3
66	Portugal	1,970	11.7	5,570	33.8		34.8	7,950	37.22	5,570	33.8		4,457	27.0
67	Yugoslavia	2,040	12.2	4,820	29.2		41.6	5,090	23.83	4,820	29.2		4,408	26.7
68	Panama	2,060	12.3	4,266	25.9	c	..	4,120	19.29	4,266	25.9	c	3,592	21.8
69	Poland	2,080	12.4	4,040	24.5		50.6	4,530	21.21	4,040	24.5		3,751	22.8
70	Argentina	2,130	12.7	4,091	24.8	c	..	4,680	21.91	4,091	24.8	c	3,913	23.7

TABLE 1 - continued

	COUNTRY	ATLAS(GNP)		ICP/REG			PRICE LEVEL	ICP/REG, 1990			ICP/REG(2)			PWT5	
		$$ (1)	US=100 (2)	$$ (3)	US=100 (4)		US=100 (5)	$$ (1)	US=100 (1)		$$ (6)	US=100 (7)		$$ (8)	US=100 (9)
71	Mexico	2,180	13.0	5,258	31.9	c	..	5,980	28.00		5,258	31.9	c	5,241	31.8
72	South Africa	2,210	13.2	4,910	29.8	d	..	5,500	25.70		4,909	29.8	d	4,330	26.3
73	Korea, Rep.	2,320	13.8	3,970	24.1		57.5	7,190	33.66		3,970	24.1		3,791	23.0
74	Paraguay	2,440	14.5	2,569	15.6	c	..	3,120	14.61		2,569	15.6	c	2,305	14.0
75	Algeria	2,590	15.4	4,590	27.8	d	..	4,680	21.91	d	4,337	26.3	d	3,155	19.1
76	Gabon	3,560	21.2	3,928	23.8	d	..	4,590	21.50		3,725	22.6	d	4,137	25.1
77	Greece	3,610	21.5	5,880	35.7		60.3	7,340	34.36		5,860	35.5		5,613	34.0
78	Venezuela	3,830	22.8	5,838	35.4	c	..	6,740	31.55		5,838	35.4	c	5,562	33.7
79	Iran, Islamic Rep.	3,990	23.8	4,610	28.0		85.1	4,360	20.41		4,610	28.0		3,496	21.2
80	Spain	4,330	25.8	7,590	46.0		56.1	10,840	50.75		7,590	46.0		6,322	38.3
81	Ireland	4,680	27.9	6,700	40.6		68.7	9,130	42.70		6,750	40.9		5,903	35.8
82	Hong Kong	6,090	36.3	10,190	61.8		58.8	16,230	75.98		10,190	61.8		10,008	60.7
83	Trinidad and Tobago	6,130	36.6	8,684	52.7	d	..	8,510	39.84	d	8,256	50.1	d	7,350	44.6
84	Israel	6,570	39.2	9,351	56.7	c	..	11,940	55.90		9,351	56.7	c	9,134	55.4
85	New Zealand	6,740	40.2	10,050	60.9		66.0	11,560	54.12		10,050	60.9		9,963	60.4
86	Singapore	7,120	42.5	9,260	56.2	d	..	14,920	69.85	d	9,301	56.4	d	10,237	62.1
87	Oman	7,550	45.0	7,290	44.2	d	..	.	..		7,009	42.5	d	9,663	58.6
88	Italy	7,720	46.0	10,830	65.7		70.1	14,550	68.12		10,820	65.6		10,402	63.1
89	Belgium	8,230	49.1	10,670	64.7		75.8	12,950	60.60		10,670	64.7		10,278	62.3
90	United Kingdom	8,360	49.9	10,900	66.1		75.4	14,960	70.04		10,900	66.1		10,494	63.6
91	Germany	8,620	51.4	12,170	73.8		69.6	16,290	76.26		12,170	73.8		11,446	69.4
92	Saudi Arabia	8,640	51.5	8,560	51.9	d	..	.	..		7,926	48.1	d	9,376	56.9
93	Austria	9,040	53.9	10,900	66.1		81.6	14,750	69.05		10,900	66.1		10,113	61.3
94	Netherlands	9,360	55.8	11,260	68.3		81.7	14,600	68.30		11,250	68.2		10,748	65.2
95	France	9,750	58.1	11,440	69.3		83.9	15,200	71.16		11,430	69.3		11,180	67.8
96	Finland	10,970	65.4	11,460	69.5		94.1	15,620	73.13		11,460	69.5		11,032	66.9
97	Denmark	11,310	67.4	12,240	74.2		90.9	15,380	72.00		12,240	74.2		11,774	71.4
98	Japan	11,350	67.7	11,800	71.5		94.7	16,950	79.35		11,800	71.6		10,595	64.3
99	Australia	11,580	69.1	11,720	71.1		97.1	15,010	70.27		11,720	71.1		12,333	74.8
100	Sweden	11,940	71.2	12,680	76.9		92.6	16,000	74.91		12,680	76.9		12,168	73.8
101	Canada	14,140	84.3	15,260	92.5		91.1	19,650	91.99		15,260	92.5		14,754	89.5
102	Norway	14,450	86.2	13,910	84.4		102.1	17,220	80.62		13,920	84.4		13,261	80.4
103	Kuwait	15,010	89.5	15,060	91.3	d	..	.	..		13,797	83.7	d	12,465	75.6
104	Switzerland	16,240	96.8	16,600	100.7	d	..	21,690	101.60		16,061	97.4	d	14,142	85.8
105	United States	16,770	100.0	16,490	100.0		100.0	21,360	100.00		16,490	100.0		16,490	100.0
106	United Arab Emirates	22,220	132.5	16,350	99.2	d	..	16,590	77.70		15,399	93.4	d	20,176	122.4

Sources: Col (1),(2): World Bank
Col (3),(4): ICP and regression estimates
Col (5) : Price level, col(2)/ col(4), for ICP participants only
Col (6),(7): ICP and regression estimates by a second equation
Col (8),(9): Penn World Tables, Mark 5: QJE, May 1991

Note: c. Extrapolated from earlier years; d. regression estimates.

TABLE 2

Comparison of Atlas and Regression Estimates of PPP-Based per Capita GDP, 1985

	COUNTRY	Rankings				Difference in Ranks											
		ATLAS (1)	REG (2)	PWT (3)	REG2 (4)	REG-ATL (5)	PWT-ATL (6)	PWT-REG (7)	REG2-REG (8)	ATLAS (9)	REG (10)	PWT (11)	REG2 (12)	REG-ATL (13)	PWT-ATL (14)	PWT-REG (15)	REG2-REG (16)
1	Ethiopia	1	1	1	1	0	0	0	0	1	1	1	1	0	0	0	0
2	Chad	2	2	7	2	0	5	5	0	1	1	1	1	0	0	0	0
3	Mali	3	3	5	3	0	2	2	0	1	1	1	1	0	0	0	0
4	Somalia	4	9	20	9	5	16	11	0	1	1	1	1	0	0	0	0
5	Bangladesh	5	18	15	19	13	10	-3	1	1	1	1	1	0	0	0	0
6	Nepal	6	15	16	15	9	10	1	0	1	1	1	1	0	0	0	0
7	Malawi	7	11	9	11	4	2	-2	0	1	1	1	1	0	0	0	0
8	Mozambique	8	8	19	6	0	11	11	-2	1	1	1	1	0	0	0	0
9	Burkina Faso	9	5	6	5	-4	-3	1	0	1	1	1	1	0	0	0	0
10	Niger	10	10	10	10	0	0	0	0	1	1	1	1	0	0	0	0
11	Uganda	11	14	3	14	3	-8	-11	0	1	1	1	1	0	0	0	0
12	Burundi	12	7	8	8	-5	-4	1	1	1	1	1	1	0	0	0	0
13	Togo	13	21	11	20	8	-2	-10	-1	1	1	1	1	0	0	0	0
14	Zaire	14	22	2	22	8	-12	-20	0	1	1	1	1	0	0	0	0
15	Central African Rep.	15	19	14	17	4	-1	-5	-2	1	1	1	1	0	0	0	0
16	Rwanda	16	12	17	12	-4	1	5	0	1	1	1	1	0	0	0	0
17	Benin	17	25	29	26	8	12	4	1	1	1	1	1	0	0	0	0
18	India	18	16	13	16	-2	-5	-3	0	1	1	1	1	0	0	0	0
19	Kenya	19	20	21	21	1	2	1	1	1	1	1	1	0	0	0	0
20	Madagascar	20	13	12	13	-7	-8	-1	0	1	1	1	1	0	0	0	0
21	Haiti	21	23	23	23	2	2	0	0	1	1	1	1	0	0	0	0
22	Tanzania	22	4	4	4	-18	-18	0	0	1	1	1	1	0	0	0	0
23	China	23	30	42	31	7	19	12	1	1	1	2	1	0	1	1	-1
24	Pakistan	24	32	35	33	8	11	3	1	1	1	2	1	0	1	1	-1
25	Sierra Leone	25	6	27	7	-19	2	21	1	1	1	1	1	0	0	0	0
26	Ghana	26	35	22	30	9	-4	-13	-5	1	1	1	1	0	0	0	0
27	Sudan	27	26	26	25	-1	-1	0	-1	1	1	1	1	0	0	0	0
28	Zambia	28	17	18	18	-11	-10	1	1	1	1	1	1	0	0	0	0
29	Senegal	29	27	30	27	-2	1	3	0	1	1	1	1	0	0	0	0
30	Lesotho	30	28	31	28	-2	1	3	0	1	1	1	1	0	0	0	0
31	Sri Lanka	31	42	45	42	11	14	3	0	1	2	2	2	1	1	0	0
32	Mauritania	32	24	24	24	-8	-8	0	0	2	1	1	1	-1	-1	0	0
33	Bolivia	33	40	36	40	7	3	-4	0	2	2	2	2	0	0	0	0
34	Liberia	34	31	25	32	-3	-9	-6	1	2	1	1	1	-1	-1	0	0
35	Philippines	35	41	39	41	6	4	-2	0	2	2	2	2	0	0	0	0

TABLE 2 - continued

	COUNTRY	Rankings ATLAS (1)	REG (2)	PWT (3)	REG2 (4)	Difference in Ranks REG-ATL (5)	PWT-ATL (6)	PWT-REG (7)	REG2-REG (8)	ATLAS (9)	REG (10)	PWT (11)	REG2 (12)	REG-ATL (13)	PWT-ATL (14)	PWT-REG (15)	REG2-REG (16)
36	Indonesia	36	38	38	38	2	2	0	0	2	2	2	2	0	0	0	0
37	Morocco	37	44	46	44	7	9	2	0	2	2	2	2	0	0	0	0
38	Zimbabwe	38	37	33	37	-1	-5	-4	0	2	2	2	2	0	0	0	0
39	Egypt, Arab Rep.	39	49	44	49	10	5	-5	0	2	3	2	3	1	0	-1	1
40	Cote D'Ivoire	40	39	34	39	-1	-6	-5	0	2	2	2	2	0	0	0	0
41	Honduras	41	34	32	35	-7	-9	-2	1	2	1	1	1	-1	-1	0	0
42	Papua New Guinea	42	33	37	34	-9	-5	4	1	2	1	2	1	-1	0	1	-1
43	Nicaragua	43	43	43	43	0	0	0	0	2	2	2	2	0	0	0	0
44	Dominican Rep.	44	47	47	47	3	3	0	0	3	3	2	3	0	-1	-1	1
45	Thailand	45	50	50	50	5	5	0	0	3	3	3	3	0	0	0	0
46	Cameroon	46	46	41	46	0	-5	-5	0	3	3	2	3	0	-1	-1	1
47	El Salvador	47	36	40	36	-11	-7	4	0	3	2	2	2	-1	-1	0	0
48	Nigeria	48	29	28	29	-19	-20	-1	0	3	1	1	1	-2	-2	0	0
49	Jamaica	49	45	49	45	-4	0	4	0	3	2	3	2	-1	0	1	-1
50	Botswana	50	51	51	51	1	1	0	0	3	3	3	3	0	0	0	0
51	Peru	51	53	53	53	2	2	0	0	3	3	3	3	0	0	0	0
52	Congo, People's Rep.	52	52	52	52	0	0	0	0	3	3	3	3	0	0	0	0
53	Turkey	53	57	57	57	4	4	0	0	3	3	3	3	0	0	0	0
54	Mauritius	54	63	63	63	9	9	0	0	3	4	3	4	1	0	-1	1
55	Tunisia	55	54	56	54	-1	1	2	0	3	3	3	3	0	0	0	0
56	Ecuador	56	55	55	55	-1	-1	0	0	3	3	3	3	0	0	0	0
57	Colombia	57	58	59	58	1	2	1	0	3	3	3	3	0	0	0	0
58	Costa Rica	58	59	61	60	1	3	2	1	3	3	3	3	0	0	0	0
59	Chile	59	68	64	69	9	5	-4	1	3	4	3	4	1	0	-1	1
60	Uruguay	60	70	72	71	10	12	2	1	3	4	4	4	1	1	0	0
61	Brazil	61	65	68	65	4	7	3	0	3	4	4	4	1	1	0	0
62	Syrian Arab Rep.	62	56	75	56	-6	13	19	0	4	3	4	3	-1	0	1	-1
63	Jordan	63	69	54	67	6	-9	-15	-2	4	4	3	4	0	-1	-1	1
64	Hungary	64	75	76	75	11	12	1	0	4	4	4	4	0	0	0	0
65	Malaysia	65	66	74	66	1	9	8	0	4	4	4	4	0	0	0	0
66	Portugal	66	77	73	77	11	7	-4	0	4	4	4	4	0	0	0	0
67	Yugoslavia	67	73	71	73	6	4	-2	0	4	4	4	4	0	0	0	0
68	Panama	68	67	62	68	-1	-6	-5	1	4	4	3	4	0	-1	-1	1
69	Poland	69	62	65	62	-7	-4	3	0	4	4	3	4	0	-1	-1	1
70	Argentina	70	64	67	64	-6	-3	3	0	4	4	4	4	0	0	0	0

TABLE 2 - continued

	COUNTRY	Rankings				Difference in Ranks											
		ATLAS (1)	REG (2)	PWT (3)	REG2 (4)	REG-ATL (5)	PWT-ATL (6)	PWT-REG (7)	REG2-REG (8)	ATLAS (9)	REG (10)	PWT (11)	REG2 (12)	REG-ATL (13)	PWT-ATL (14)	PWT-REG (15)	REG2-REG (16)
71	Mexico	71	76	77	76	5	6	1	0	4	4	4	4	0	0	0	0
72	South Africa	72	74	70	74	2	-2	-4	0	4	4	4	4	0	0	0	0
73	Korea, Rep.	73	61	66	61	-12	-7	5	0	4	4	3	4	0	-1	-1	1
74	Paraguay	74	48	48	48	-26	-26	0	0	4	3	3	3	-1	-1	0	0
75	Algeria	75	71	58	70	-4	-17	-13	-1	4	4	3	4	0	-1	-1	1
76	Gabon	76	60	69	59	-16	-7	9	-1	5	4	4	3	-1	-1	0	-1
77	Greece	77	79	79	79	2	2	0	0	5	5	4	5	0	-1	-1	1
78	Venezuela	78	78	78	78	0	0	0	0	5	5	4	5	0	-1	-1	1
79	Iran, Islamic Rep.	79	72	60	72	-7	-19	-12	0	5	4	3	4	-1	-2	-1	1
80	Spain	80	82	81	82	2	1	-1	0	5	5	5	5	0	0	0	0
81	Ireland	81	80	80	80	-1	-1	0	0	5	5	5	5	0	0	0	0
82	Hong Kong	82	88	87	88	6	5	-1	0	5	5	5	5	0	0	0	0
83	Trinidad and Tobago	83	84	82	84	1	-1	-2	0	5	5	5	5	0	0	0	0
84	Israel	84	86	83	86	2	-1	-3	0	5	5	5	5	0	0	0	0
85	New Zealand	85	87	86	87	2	1	-1	0	5	5	5	5	0	0	0	0
86	Singapore	86	85	89	85	-1	3	4	0	5	5	5	5	0	0	0	0
87	Oman	87	81	85	81	-6	-2	4	0	5	5	5	5	0	0	0	0
88	Italy	88	90	91	90	2	3	1	0	5	5	5	5	0	0	0	0
89	Belgium	89	89	90	89	0	1	1	0	5	5	5	5	0	0	0	0
90	United Kingdom	90	92	92	92	2	2	0	0	5	5	5	5	0	0	0	0
91	Germany	91	98	97	98	7	6	-1	0	5	5	5	5	0	0	0	0
92	Saudi Arabia	92	83	84	83	-9	-8	1	0	5	5	5	5	0	0	0	0
93	Austria	93	91	88	91	-2	-5	-3	0	5	5	5	5	0	0	0	0
94	Netherlands	94	93	94	93	-1	0	1	0	5	5	5	5	0	0	0	0
95	France	95	94	96	94	-1	1	2	0	5	5	5	5	0	0	0	0
96	Finland	96	95	95	95	-1	-1	0	0	5	5	5	5	0	0	0	0
97	Denmark	97	99	98	99	2	1	-1	0	5	5	5	5	0	0	0	0
98	Japan	98	97	93	97	-1	-5	-4	0	5	5	5	5	0	0	0	0
99	Australia	99	96	100	96	-3	1	4	0	5	5	5	5	0	0	0	0
100	Sweden	100	100	99	100	0	-1	-1	0	5	5	5	5	0	0	0	0
101	Canada	101	103	104	103	2	3	1	0	5	5	5	5	0	0	0	0
102	Norway	102	101	102	102	-1	0	1	1	5	5	5	5	0	0	0	0
103	Kuwait	103	102	101	101	-1	-2	-1	-1	5	5	5	5	0	0	0	0
104	Switzerland	104	106	103	105	2	-1	-3	-1	5	5	5	5	0	0	0	0
105	United States	105	105	105	106	0	0	0	1	5	5	5	5	0	0	0	0
106	United Arab Emirates	106	104	106	104	-2	0	2	0	5	5	5	5	0	0	0	0
	Rank Correlation					98.5%	98.3%	99.0%	100.0%								

TABLE 3
Comparison of Atlas and Regression Estimates of PPP-Based Per Capita GDP, 1985
Countries with big differences in ranks

	COUNTRY	ATLAS(GNI	Rankings				Difference in Ranks							PWT5 Grade
		$$	ATLAS	REG	PWT	REG2	REG-ATL		PWT-ATL		PWT-REG		REG2-REG	
		(1)	(2)	(3)	(4)	(5)	(6)		(7)		(8)		(9)	(10)
14	Zaire	260	14	22	2	22	8		-12	**	-20	**	0	D
63	Jordan	1,880	63	69	54	67	6		-9		-15	**	-2	D
26	Ghana	370	26	35	22	30	9		-4		-13	**	-5	D
11	Uganda	230	11	14	3	14	3		-8		-11	**	0	D
13	Togo	250	13	21	11	20	8		-2		-10	**	-1	D
75	Algeria	2,590	75	71	58	70	-4		-17	**	-13	**	-1	D
79	Iran, Islamic Rep.	3,990	79	72	60	72	-7		-19	**	-12	**	0	C-
39	Egypt, Arab Rep.	660	39	49	44	49	10	**	5		-5		0	D+
66	Portugal	1,970	66	77	73	77	11	**	7		-4		0	A-
5	Bangladesh	160	5	18	15	19	13	**	10	**	-3		1	C-
48	Nigeria	850	48	29	28	29	-19	**	-20	**	-1		0	D+
22	Tanzania	320	22	4	4	4	-18	**	-18	**	0		0	C-
74	Paraguay	2,440	74	48	48	48	-26	**	-26	**	0		0	C
64	Hungary	1,930	64	75	76	75	11	**	12	**	1		0	B
6	Nepal	160	6	15	16	15	9		10	**	1		0	D+
28	Zambia	370	28	17	18	18	-11	**	-10	**	1		1	D+
60	Uruguay	1,580	60	70	72	71	10	**	12	**	2		1	C-
24	Pakistan	340	24	32	35	33	8		11	**	3		1	C-
31	Sri Lanka	390	31	42	45	42	11	**	14	**	3		0	C-
47	El Salvador	840	47	36	40	36	-11	**	-7		4		0	C
17	Benin	280	17	25	29	26	8		12	**	4		1	D+
73	Korea, Rep.	2,320	73	61	66	61	-12	**	-7		5		0	B-
76	Gabon	3,560	76	60	69	59	-16	**	-7		9		-1	D
8	Mozambique	180	8	8	19	6	0		11	**	11	**	-2	D
4	Somalia	150	4	9	20	9	5		16	**	11	**	0	D
23	China	330	23	30	42	31	7		19	**	12	**	1	D
62	Syrian Arab Rep.	1,740	62	56	75	56	-6		13	**	19	**	0	C-
25	Sierra Leone	340	25	6	27	7	-19	**	2		21	**	1	D+

Source: Table 2.

Note: PWT5 places quality ratings against its estimates for each country from highest A to lowest D (Col.10). Rating A is usually reserved for OECD countries; B and C are applied to countries with ICP experience, although there are many ICP countries with D; and D is generally applied to countries without ICP experience.

** indicates change of ten or more ranks.

TABLE 4
Comparison of Goodness-of-fit Statistics of PWT5 and IECSE Equations

PWT5 EQUATIONS

						RMSE	R-Sq Adj)
	For 1985 based on 1985 benchmark						
1	ln (r)	= f(ln [r(UN)])				0.263	0.926
2	ln (r)	= f(ln [r(ECA)])				0.199	0.957
3	ln (r)	= f(ln [r(USS)])				0.219	0.950
4	ln (r)	= f(ln [r(UN)],	ln [r(ECA)])			0.204	0.954
5	ln (r)	= f(ln [r(UN)],	ln [r(USS)])			0.228	0.944
6	ln (r)	= f(ln [r(USS)],	ln [r(ECA)])			0.193	0.960
	For 1985 based on 1980 benchmark						
7	ln (r)	= f(ln [r(UN)],	AD			0.231	0.948
8	ln (r)	= f(ln [r(ECA)],	AD			0.166	0.974
9	ln (r)	= f(ln [r(USS)],	AD			0.186	0.968
10	ln (r)	= f(ln [r(UN)],	ln [r(ECA)],	AD		0.168	0.972
11	ln (r)	= f(ln [r(UN)],	ln [r(USS)],	AD		0.194	0.963
12	ln (r)	= f(ln [r(USS)],	ln [r(ECA)],	AD		0.159	0.976

IECSE EQUATIONS

			RMSE	R-Sq Adj)
1	ln (r)	= f(ln (ATLAS), ln (ENROL), AD)	0.171	0.973
2	ln (r)	= f(ln (ATLAS), ln (ENROL))	0.213	0.965
3	ln (r)	= f(ln (ATLAS), ln (ENROL))	0.203	0.957
4	ln (r)	= f(ln (ATLAS), ln (ENROL))	0.224	0.952
5	ln (r)	= f(ln (ATLAS), ln (ENROL). ln (CALOR))	0.220	0.954

Where

r	= percapita GDP based on ICP PPP and expressed as US=100
r(UN)	= r but based on PPP computed from UN's cost of living index of of expatriates living in capital cities
r(ECA)	= same as r(UN) except the expatriates' cost of living data are from Economic Conditions Abroad (ECA)
r(USS)	= same as r(UN) except the expatriates cost of living data are from US State Department
AD	= Dummy variable for Africa
p	= price level as measured by the ratio of PPP to exchange rate, US=100
ATLAS	= per capita GNP estimated by the World Bank Atlas method.
LIFEX	= Life expectancy, US=100
IMR	= Infant mortality rate, US=100
ENROL	= Secondary school enrolment ratio, US = 100
CALOR	= Supply of calorie per person per day, US = 100

Note:

1 PWT equations 1-6 refer to 1985 based on 1985 benchmark data for 57 countries in 1985 benchmark plus 20 countries from 1975 and 1980 that did not participate in 1985, brought up to 1985 by 'consistentized' growth rates and US inflation.

2 PWT equations 7-12 refer to 1985 based on 1980 benchmark data for 60 countries in ICP phase IV, brought up to 1985 by consistentized growth rates and US inflation, and six countries that participated in Phase V for the first time.

3 IECSE equations refer to different country samples as noted against each equation. Estimates using equation (4) are presented in the paper under REG and in WDI; those using equation (5) are presented in the paper as alternative estiamtes under REG(2).

4 PWT5 estimates are weighted averages of two estimates for each country based on 1980 and 1985 data.

International Comparisons of Prices, Output and Productivity
Edited by D.S. Prasada Rao and J. Salazar-Carrillo

THE PPP DOCTRINE, LONG TERM EXCHANGE RATES AND A NEW METHOD TO ESTIMATE REAL GROSS DOMESTIC PRODUCTS

Elio Lancieri[1]
Banca Nazionale del Lavoro
Rome, Italy

1. Introduction

There has always been a need to compare the countries of the world by their economic weight - and therefore by their gross domestic or national product, GDP or GNP. Besides the obvious scientific interest in these comparisons, there are various commercial, social, and political implications, not to mention the military ones. The economic size of countries is a basic element for world demand studies, for planning and marketing decisions of multinational firms, and per capita income, together with other data on real wages, productivity, etc., is used to assess the economic performance of countries, their level of development, and, approximately, their standard of living.

International organizations, in particular, need comparable output figures for countries. They make use of GDP figures in the preparation of their budgets, as a criterion for deciding member countries' share in the maintenance of the organization itself; and the dollar per capita GDP has become an operational indicator for project development.

Statistically, since national income figures of countries are expressed in different currencies, the core problem of international economic comparability has always been that of how to convert data of various provenance into a single currency, which then constitutes the common numeraire. Traditionally, the currency used is the US dollar, also because most international trade and financial transactions

[1]After many years in the commodities Division of FAO, the author is presently with the Economic Research Department of Banca Nazionale del Lavaro (BNL) in Rome: his views do not necessarily reflect those of BNL. He is grateful to Michael Ward, Prasada Rao and his colleagues for the stimulating criticism and helpful suggestions received for this paper.

are carried out and recorded in dollars at their origin. The dollar's exchange rate, therefore, has become of crucial importance for income comparisons.

It has always been known that official exchange rates seldom give a realistic picture of countries' economies; until 1980, however, GDP/GNP figures converted at official exchange rates continued to be used without much complaint. Then, since 1981, international economic comparisons have been completely disrupted. In that year, for instance, when both countries had shown some real growth, the dollar GDP of Germany fell to $682 billion, from the $814 bn. of 1980, that of Japan, instead, rose from $1,059 bn. to $1,167 bn. In the following years, most countries' dollar GDPs continued to go down; between 1985 and 1988, then, they all rose again.

It is obvious that, in these conditions, rankings of countries, either by their total or per capita GDP, are radically altered. With regard to developing countries, in particular, the enormous fluctuations in their dollar GDPs create many difficulties in country risk analysis, which requires stable and updated GDP estimates more than any other analysis, because of the many ratios which are used in risk assessments, and are based on the dollar GDP (or GNP) of countries. Fluctuations in the values of GDPs distort the ratios, and make the analysis nearly impossible. At official exchange rates, for instance, Mexico's GDP was $186 bn. in 1980, jumped up to $240 bn. in 1981, and then sank again to $162 bn. in 1982, invalidating any economic assessment of the country, in the very year of its big debt crisis.

Country risk analysis also calls for GDP figures to be updated quickly from year to year. If, for instance, a certain risk assessment is to be carried out at the end of 1994 in order to guide lending operations during 1995, the ratio of debt to GDP would be most meaningful if the GDP considered was that of 1994; exceptionally, figures for 1993 could be accepted, but anything older than that would clearly endanger the quality of the scrutiny, and, particularly, its comparative indications with regard to different countries. In fact, the question of how long an economist has to wait for the estimates he needs is more serious than it may appear, and becomes of crucial importance in many exercises of applied economics.

If one considers the basic characteristics that a good estimation method should have, the first one is certainly that estimates would show realistic, plausible GDP levels, i.e., compatible with other economic information available on, for instance, industrial output and exports, imports and the consumption patterns of the population, etc. The three other features are that: 2) estimates could be made rapidly available; 3) that they should remain unaffected by nominal disturbances year by year, allowing comparisons in real terms, over time and across countries; and 4) that the method could be applied to a vast number of countries, in particular the developing ones.

With a view to fulfilling the four conditions outlined above, the aim of this paper is, first to discuss the characteristics of available methods (Section 2), then to analyse the purchasing power parity doctrine and the definition of the long term exchange rate (Section 3). Then (Section 4), a new estimation method based on the latter is presented, with proofs of its main statistical properties. Empirical results are discussed in Section 5 (figures for 20 countries are presented in the Statistical Appendix), conclusions are drawn in Section 6.

2. An Assessment of Available GDP Estimation Methods

Looking for a solution to the problem of GDP comparisons, the economic literature has been examined. Basically, four different approaches to dollar GDP estimation have been found: two quantitative ones (one by the Economic Commission for Europe (ECE), and one by Angus Maddison), the methods used by the World Bank, and an other based on purchasing power parities.

The approach of the ECE is based on a relatively small (30) number of physical indicators, which represent inputs for single regression analyses, and refer to 9 major categories of products and services. For industry, indicators like steel-, energy-consumption per head are used; for agriculture, animal protein per day, etc. Three products only are considered for consumer durables, that is passenger cars, television sets and radios. Other categories examined are education, health and communications. As published in 1980, the study by the ECE included results for 105 countries for 1970, and for 30 countries for 1973. In an overall assessment of this procedure, one should note that:

1. given the indicators used, the method is rather approximate, and unable to capture quality differences; obviously, indicators like

"animal protein per day", do not allow quality assessments;

2. most of the indicators appear outdated, considering the revolution which has taken place in industrial materials in the last 20 years: a high consumption of steel, for instance, is no longer an indicator of wealth at the world level, when most advanced countries have switched to lighter materials; and

3. implicit in the ECE approach is the hypothesis that in eastern European countries the efficiency of investment and consumption is equal to that in the West; by assuming that to same quantities used correspond same real incomes, important phenomena like waste, delays, etc. remain excluded. The systematic upward bias which can be noted in ECE results is in fact particularly striking for eastern European countries.

Angus Maddison first used his "production approach" in 1970 for 29 countries with reference to 1965. More recently in Maddison (1983), he updated the results for 19 countries to 1980. Statistically more wide-ranging, though similar to the ECE's, the Maddison approach produces estimates which appear realistic; they

"represent levels of net output for five sectors of the economy, using 80 indicators of output in agriculture, 70 for industry, and estimates for services based on employment data and relative productivity assumptions. They were made quite independently of the national accounts estimates for all countries except the United States" (Maddison, 1983, page 29).

Since 1966, and mostly with regard to per capita GNP, the World Bank has been using a "special Atlas method" which:

"applies a conversion factor that averages the exchange rate for a given year and the two preceding years, adjusting for differences in rates of inflation between the country and the United States. The resulting estimate is divided by the midyear population to obtain the per capita GNP in current US dollars." (World Bank, 1993, page 33).

From the above, the aim of the World Bank i.e., clearly one of dampening exchange rate fluctuations in order to present more "stable", and therefore more "reliable" statistics. Doubts, however, must be raised on the results obtained. Particularly striking is the US/Japan comparison over 1988-1990. With the American per capita GNP in 1988 at $19,820, the World Bank's estimate for Japan - $20,960 - is $1140 higher, while most economists doubt that, in real terms, the Japanese per capita income would have overcome the US income. For 1989, the World Bank's estimate for Japan goes up again by 16%, to $24,240, then increasing further to $25,430 for 1990. Not only these estimates are so much higher than the US per capitas (respectively, $20,850 and $21,700) but they turn out to be even higher than the Japanese per capita incomes calculated at official exchange rates, $23,490 in 1989 and $23,960 in 1990. Clearly, the World Bank's approach is too sensitive to nominal disturbances: not only it does not succeed in dampening exchange rate fluctuations, but even leads, in some cases, to bigger distortions, with the consequence that rankings of countries are disrupted year after year.

The fourth approach examined, i.e. purchasing power parities, represents an interesting but complex methodology, which requires a great deal of resources for implementation. So far, the largest research project in this field has been the U.N.'s International Comparison Program (ICP). In another paper, (Lancieri, 1990), it was shown, however, that its results have been disappointing, particularly with regard to the GDP estimates for the 60 countries analyzed. The major weaknesses noted in the PPP methodology were the following:

1. The implicit assumption of "the existence in the country of a single, homogeneous labour market" comprising the agricultural, industrial and services sector (Lancieri, 1990, p 18).

   In the realm of the tradeables/nontradeables argument, this is the necessary condition for the transmission of price signals and competitivity between the export sector (and the foreign markets) and the rest of the economy: the paper's conclusion, on the contrary, was that in developing countries we generally find the separation of labour markets.

2. The inability of PPPs to register that, "especially in large countries, there is often a pronounced dualism in the industrial sector, part of it being focused on exports, and therefore in line with world market prices and productivity, and another part domestic-

oriented, with a much lower productivity because it is not exposed to international competition" (Lancieri, 1990, p 19).

3. The fact that "PPPs take no account of capital and interest flows" (Ward, 1985, page 36), and that "by disregarding the capital market, they produce another distortion in favour of low income countries, which are the least endowed with capital and have undeveloped financial markets" (Lancieri, 1990, page 42);

4. Finally, that, while for industrial countries PPPs are updated by OECD each year, the elaboration of PPP estimates for developing countries takes so long that those available (in 1990) only referred to 1980, something which greatly reduces their usefulness. (The situation has not changed much: the new PPPs issued in 1993 refer to 1985!)

A general feature of ICP-IV is the excessive "revaluation" of the GDPs of most poor countries. A good example is the per capita GDP of Sri Lanka, estimated at $1,226 for 1980, i.e. more than four times the level of $280 indicated by exchange rates. Among the reasons found for such excessive revaluation, there were the hypotheses made in the ICP with regard to developing countries' productivity levels in the education and health sectors, and generally in the civil service. The consequence was an increase in the PPPs of these sectors of up to +800%, +900%, which substantially inflated the overall GDP estimates.

This was confirmed by Maddison, in comparing his results (1983), with the PPPs of ICP-III (Kravis, Heston and Summers, 1982), where basically the same methodology was applied as in ICP-IV. For 10 developing countries for which estimates were also available from his method, Maddison found that, while his results were on average 43% higher than GDPs at exchange rates, ICP estimates involved an average upward valuation of as much as +104%. Maddison reviewed their and his assumptions about productivity and quality levels in the services sector of developing countries, and showed that ICP had assumed in most cases the same levels as in advanced countries (levels, therefore, which often were four times higher than according to his assumptions). He concluded that "the Kravis-Heston-Summers expenditure-type comparison may well tend systematically to overvalue developing country real product levels because of its treatment of comparison-resistant and disguised services. This bias does not appear to operate in comparisons for developed countries" (1983, page 37).

With regard to the problem of the long delays in the availability of PPP estimates for developing countries, an attempt was made by Summers and Heston (1988) to extend and update ICP results till 1985. Notwithstanding the prestige of both the authors, it really seems that they have added new distortions to the biases already present in the ICP. For 1985, for instance, \$1,539 were attributed to Sri Lanka, \$3,056 to South Korea, \$750 to India, \$2,444 to China, figures which are all implausible, considering the other economic information available on the countries. While the estimates for Sri Lanka and India are already too high, what really appears to be an indefensible exaggeration is the per capita GDP attributed to China. By that, the total GDP of China would be the second largest in the world, and much bigger than Japan's. Obviously, if this was true, the world would already be aware of it.

With regard to purchasing power parities, in conclusion, it must be said that, while useful for sectoral analysis, they have a major problem in the levels of their GDP estimates. Then, it should not come as a surprise that even the Statistical Commission of the United Nations, on the results of Phase IV of the ICP, concluded that:

"more experience needs to be gained and further methodological improvement attained before the ICP results can be accepted for policy purposes at the world level" (U.N. and Eurostat, 1986/87, page iii).

3. The Purchasing-Power-Parity Doctrine and Long-Term Exchange Rates

With a distinct point of view from the methods analysed so far, in the last decades the theories of the determination of exchange rates - as well as that stream of the literature focusing on the "cointegration" of the latter - have tried to explain why do exchange rates move, and what are the linkages between exchange rate movements and changes in relative prices. To that end, but on a different plane from the purchasing power parities mentioned before, an explanation is supplied by:

"... the purchasing power parity doctrine (PPP). That doctrine in its "absolute version" states that the equilibrium exchange rate between domestic and foreign currencies equals the ratio of domestic to foreign price levels. The "relative version" of the doctrine relates equilibrium changes in exchange rates to changes in the ratio of domestic to foreign prices". (Frenkel, 1981, page 145).

Previously in Frenkel (1976), he had also noted that:

"PPP should be viewed as a long run equilibrium relationship between relative prices and exchange rates, rather then as a theory of exchange rate determination".

In fact, the empirical analysis which in the past has been testing for the PPP doctrine in a short-term context (exemplified by, among other things, the usage of quarterly or monthly data of exchange rates) has produced mostly unfavourable results. See, for instance, Frenkel (1981), Baillie and Selover (1987), Boothe and Glassman (1987), Enders (1988) and Taylor (1988). A relevant explanation is supplied by Edison (1987, p. 376):

"The economic rationale for the failure of PPP to hold in the short-run is that the economy is never observed in equilibrium, and over short periods large shocks or structural changes occur that disturb exchange rates from their long-run equilibrium position."

Here, the hypothesis is made that these changes, while certainly causing strong, sudden fluctuations of the nominal exchange rate in the short run, end up producing small or no variations in the long-run equilibrium position. Equilibrium is not intended with respect to the balance of payments, money markets, or interest rates, but to the ratio of domestic to foreign prices, according to the PPP doctrine in its "relative" version. Insulated from short-term price disturbances, this long-run equilibrium position of the exchange rate can be used for GDP comparisons. In fact, if the nominal fluctuations of official exchange rates are avoided and a constant long-term real exchange rate is adopted, then comparisons in real terms are possible.

The main aim of this paper, therefore, becomes that of setting up an empirical definition of such long-term rate which can be used for estimating GDPs in dollars. And it is of encouragement that some recent studies on real exchange rates and cointegration have provided new evidence that PPP may well hold in the long run. See, Rush and Husted (1985), Edison (1987), Dornbusch and Vogelsang (1992).

Looking in the literature for definitions of the long-term exchange rate – which is considered by most people the same thing as relative PPP – in Dornbusch and Vogelsang(1992), for instance, we find (p. 13):

"The absolute version of PPP states that the real exchange rate is equal to one at every point in time. The modern view of PPP takes several qualifications to such strict view of PPP. First, since price indices are observed, but actual price levels are not, we can only test a relative version of PPP which states that r must be a constant, but places no restriction on its level."

Few authors have pointed out at a crucial aspect of such definition, that is the presence of a constant term, or of a base-year, on which annual changes of PPP exchange rates should be anchored. Among them, Officer (1976, p.2):

"The [relative] purchasing power parity between two countries is defined as the product of the exchange rate in a base period and the ratio of the countries' price indices. Let A and B be two countries, t the current time period, and o a base period. Then by definition:

$$PPP_t^{rel} = R_o \frac{P_t^B}{P_t^A}$$

where

R_t = actual exchange rate in period t (number of units of country B's currency per unit of country A's currency)

PPP_t^{rel} = relative PPP in period t (number of units of country B's currency per unit of country A's currency)

P_t^i = price index in country i in period t with base period o.

However, as Rush and Husted have noted (1985, p.138):

"Basically, they [Officer and Gailliot] assume PPP holds during a base period and then use this assumed relationship to determine if PPP has continued to hold during (selected) succeeding years."

Since, unavoidably, in any approach the choice of a base year would always remain arbitrary, here procedures have been set out to simultaneously define both the long-term exchange rate and its (theoretical) base, constructed according to an accepted criterion. The aim is to establish a constant, long-term exchange rate which is an expression of the entire period analysed, and which can be confidently used for GDP comparisons. That such rate should be constant, however, is not generally accepted in the literature. Dornbusch and Vogelsang, for instance, have been asking (1992, p.1):

"The question whether national price levels are substantially invariant over time, as the purchasing power parity (PPP) doctrine would assert or on the contrary show a trend, continues to be a lively and fruitful research topic." In the end, their answer is (p.19):

"If structural changes occur often in the real exchange rate series, then we would find it difficult to conclude that any meaningful version of PPP could be postulated......If, on the other hand, such structural changes are infrequent, we can still postulate a meaningful "qualified" version of PPP, i.e. PPP holds except, say, for a one time shift in the mean level of the real exchange rate." On the same line, and pointing out at "changes in productivity and tastes", "shifts in comparative advantage", etc. are Baillie and Selover (1987), and Edison (1987). Of the opposite view, and hinting at a constant rate, seem to be Huizinga (1987), and Officer (1976). Here, the view is that, when dealing with national accounts, only a constant, long-term concept of the exchange rate is appropriate. The reasons why will be explained with an example. Looking at US GNP figures, it can be seen that product accounts are also available for each of the 50 states. Each state represents a separate economic area, with a different level of prices, wages, etc.; then, by applying an implicit regional weighting system, state accounts are reconciled with national totals, with state weights being updated every five years. Naturally, with time, structural changes take place in some states, in others prices move faster (or slower) than the national average; productivity goes down in depressed areas, etc. These phenomena are always dealt with by simply applying national accounting techniques, and one need not lament over particular biases or distortions. Now, if we ask what is, within the US, the exchange rate applied to each state, since we are in the realm of the same currency, the obvious answer is 1. In this case, state weights fulfill the role of exchange rates, and they are constant. In Table 1, growth rates and deflators for 20 selected states of the US are shown over 1977-1989, per capita GDPs for 1989.

Table 1
Average Real Rates of Growth and GDP Deflators for 20 Selected States in USA, 1977-1989; Per Capita GDPs for 1989

STATE	Real Growth	STATE	GDP Deflator	STATE	Per Capita GDP,1989
	%		%		$
New Hampshire	6.9	New Mexico	6.2	Alaska	35,800
Nevada	5.9	Louisiana	6.2	Nevada	24,590
Florida	5.3	Wyoming	5.9	New York	24,530
Arizona	5.2	Nevada	5.8	Wyoming	24,270
California	4.4	Hawaii	5.8	California	23,870
Alaska	4.1	Colorado	5.8	Hawaii	23,520
Washington	3.3	Oklahoma	5.8	New Hampshire	22,180
Hawaii	3.2	New York	5.6	Colorado	20,190
Utah	2.9	Florida	5.5	Washington	20,070
Colorado	2.7	Arizona	5.4	Nebraska	19,760
New York	2.6	Washington	5.2	Michigan	19,650
Missouri	2.4	Missouri	5.1	Missouri	19,640
Nebraska	1.9	Michigan	5.1	Indiana	19,070
Indiana	1.8	Nebraska	5.0	Iowa	18,970
New Mexico	1.6	Utah	4.9	Louisiana	18,610
Iowa	1.1	New Hampshire	4.8	Arizona	18,030
Michigan	1.0	Indiana	4.8	Florida	17,960
Oklahoma	1.0	Iowa	4.6	New Mexico	16,900
Wyoming	0.1	California	4.2	Oklahoma	16,620
Louisiana	-0.2	Alaska	3.9	Utah	14,730

Source: US Department of Commerce, Bureau of Economic Analysis.

It becomes apparent that, since each state also has a different rate of inflation (differences are even higher from year to year), in certain respects it is like having different currencies in different countries. With regard to per capita income, then, it can be noted that, while Alaska has the very high GDP typical of oil exporters with a small population (600 thousand), New York and California can be compared, for their economic structure, to high income industrialized countries like Switzerland and Sweden. In conclusion, while it is obvious that structural changes, as much as capital flows, "news", etc., affect short-term exchange rates, in dealing with GDP comparisons it is the long-term real exchange rate which one should be looking for, a rate which must be conceived as constant. Only a constant rate, in fact, allows comparisons which are conceptually on the same plane as those made in the realm of the same currency, and, for this same reason, are consistent in real terms.

4. A New Method

Given two countries A and B, we observe that from their GDP deflators, and ensuing inflation differentials, the size and direction of movement of inflation-adjusted exchange rates, year by year, are easily established for each country. Taking as base any nominal exchange rate of the period, $E_{\bar{t}}$, from equation(1), n different series of adjusted exchange rates can be obtained, for t = 1,2,...,n

$$\begin{aligned} \hat{\eta}_{\bar{t}-i}^{A,B} &= \frac{\hat{\eta}_{\bar{t}-i+1}^{A,B}}{\left(\frac{1+P_{\bar{t}-i+1}^{A}}{1+P_{\bar{t}-i+1}^{B}}\right)} & i &= 1,...,\bar{t}-1 \\ \hat{\eta}_{i}^{A,B} &= E_{i}^{A,B} & i &= \bar{t} \\ \hat{\eta}_{i}^{A,B} &= \hat{\eta}_{i-1} \times \left(\frac{1+P_{i}^{A}}{1+P_{i}^{B}}\right) & i &= \bar{t}+1,...,n \end{aligned} \tag{1}$$

where

$E_{t}^{A,B}$ is the nominal exchange rate of A's currency with respect to B's (e.g. the dollar);

P_{t}^{A} is A's price index (or GDP inflator);

P_{t}^{B} is B's (e.g. the U.S.) price index, or GDP inflator; and

$D_{t}^{A,B} = \frac{1+P_{t}^{A}}{1+P_{t}^{B}}$ is the inflation differential between A and B.

What is applied here is the relative PPP condition, since the constructed exchange rate series reflect the information about inflation differentials. Essentially, our problem is how to obtain an estimate of the long term exchange rate E*, given data only for nominal rates. Since the assumption is that nominal rates constantly fluctuate around a stable, long term equilibrium path, obviously the value of E* should be "central" to nominal rates. Such value - which may not coincide with any of the nominal exchange rates observed year by year - taken as base of the adjusted rates, would indicate one point of equilibrium; at the same time, by means of the whole adjusted series, it would also define the entire equilibrium path.

A tentative solution would be to simply draw the line which best fits the data for nominal exchange rates, by minimizing over the period the distances, year by year, between all the adjusted rates coming from each series constructed to different bases, and the nominal rates:

$$\sum_{t=1}^{n} \mid E_t^{A,B} - \hat{\eta}_t^{A,B} \mid = min \tag{2}$$

Such iterative procedure would be continued until, simultaneously, the minimum of the distances and the base E* would be found. This would amount to finding the balance of the distribution of positive and negative fluctuations of nominal exchange rates, fluctuations which have always an economic meaning "ex post", even when there have been non-economic factors at their origin. Minimization as in (2), however, would give rise to distortions; if not for other reasons, because nominal exchange rates increase enormously in periods of inflation, obviously influencing absolute distances.

In considering alternative approaches, the sum of the squares of the deviations was rejected, because it was disproportionally affected by the most pronounced differences; the geometric mean, on the contrary, was over sensitive to the smallest deviations. Finally, the objective function chosen was the sum of logarithmic differences. Taking as operational range of the procedure that one established by the exchange rates recorded in the period, such sum becomes zero when E* is found, and vice versa:

$$\sum_{t=1}^{n} log \frac{E_t^{A,B}}{\hat{\eta}_t^{A,B}} = 0 \tag{3}$$

Since the logarithm is a monotone increasing function, a unique solution for (3) exists, and can be computed numerically. Once the solution for E^* is found by using (1) and (3), the entire series of theoretically constructed, "best-adjusted", real, long-term exchange rates is obtained.

Two basic questions now emerge. Is there symmetry in this approach, in the sense that, by analysing country B referred to country A, the "best-adjusted" exchange rate would be the inverse of what is found by analysing A referred to B?

Moreover, is there transitivity in the system, so that the adjusted GDP of country A turns out at the same level, whether it has been estimated in relation to country B, or C, D, etc.?

To answer the first question, let us reconsider some previous definitions given for (1). Also, let us note that, for any pair of countries, exchange markets determine simultaneously two rates, each rate pertaining to one country and being the inverse of the other. Therefore:

$$E_t^{B,A} = \frac{1}{E_t^{A,B}}$$

$$D_t^{B,A} = \frac{1+P_t^B}{1+P_t^A} = \frac{1}{D_t^{A,B}}$$

From (1) we will have:

$$\hat{\eta}_{\bar{t}+1}^{B,A} = \frac{1}{\hat{\eta}_{\bar{t}-i+1}^{A,B}} \Big/ \frac{1}{D_{\bar{t}+i}^{A,B}} = \frac{1}{\hat{\eta}_{\bar{t}-i}^{A,B}} \qquad i = 1, ..., \bar{t}-1 \qquad (4)$$

$$\hat{\eta}_i^{B,A} = \frac{1}{E_i^{A,B}} = E_i^{B,A} = \frac{1}{\hat{\eta}_i^{A,B}} \qquad i = \bar{t}$$

$$\hat{\eta}_i^{B,A} = \frac{1}{\hat{\eta}_{i-1}^{A,B}} \times \frac{1}{D_i^{A,B}} \qquad i = \bar{t}+1, ..., n$$

From (3) we obtain:

$$0 = \sum_{t=1}^{n} log \frac{E_t^{A,B}}{\hat{\eta}_t^{A,B}} = -\sum_{t=1}^{n} log \frac{\hat{\eta}_t^{A,B}}{E_t^{A,B}} = -\sum_{t=1}^{n} log \frac{E_t^{B,A}}{\hat{\eta}_t^{B,A}} \qquad (5)$$

Since $E_t^{B,A} = 1/E_t^{A,B}$, and this is true for nominal exchange rates for any real t, even when t does not correspond to some year of the period, then the solution for (3) is:

$$E^{*A,B} = \frac{1}{E^{*A,B}}$$

With regard to transitivity, it must be observed that all currencies traded in exchange rate markets - more so since the progress made by the liberalization of international capital markets - are connected among each other through their cross rates. Quotations for all countries are given only with respect to the dollar; certain groups of currencies (e.g. the European, the Asian ones) are also quoted vis-a-vis the D-mark, the yen, etc. Though often not officially quoted, cross-rates are constantly calculated by traders, guiding operations on the markets. Exchange rates may show divergences from their cross-rates, but only for a short time, because as soon as traders become aware of this, speculative activity immediately takes place and such divergences disappear. Therefore, for instance,

$$\frac{Y}{\$} = \frac{Y}{DM} \times \frac{DM}{\$}, \quad \frac{DM}{\$} = \frac{DM}{£} \times \frac{£}{\$}$$

Consequently, we have that

$$E_t^{A,C} = E_t^{A,B} E_t^{B,C}$$

which is true for all real t.

From (3) we will have:

$$\begin{aligned} 0 = \sum_{t=1}^{n} log \frac{E_t^{A,C}}{\hat{\eta}_t^{A,C}} &= \sum_{t=1}^{n} log \frac{E_t^{A,B} E_t^{B,C}}{\hat{\eta}_t^{A,B} \hat{\eta}_t^{B,C}} \\ &= \sum_{t=1}^{n} log \frac{E_t^{A,B}}{\hat{\eta}_t^{A,B}} + \sum_{t=1}^{n} log \frac{E_t^{B,C}}{\hat{\eta}_t^{B,C}} \end{aligned} \quad (6)$$

The solution to these equations is $E^{*A,C}$, which, by the identity $E_t^{A,C} = E_t^{A,B} E_t^{B,C}$, is true for any real t, implies that:

$$E^{*A,C} = E^{*A,B} E^{*B,C}$$

The combination of the adjusted exchange rates for the A/B, and for the B/C comparison, is an equivalent solution to that given by the direct comparison of country A with country C.

5. Empirical Results

The method is now applied to Japan, over 1973-1993. In the first two columns of Table 2, basic data for inflation differentials vis-a-vis the United States (calculated year by year from GDP deflators) and official exchange rates are reported. From equation (1), twenty-one "adjusted" exchange rate series have been calculated, all covering the entire period 1973-1993, but each one anchored to the level of the official exchange rate of a different year of the period. The highest, the 1993-based, and lowest, the 1985-based, series are singled out, and reported in columns 3 and 4. The distance between these two series is taken as the range of operation of the system. Then from equation (3), iteratively applied to all the intermediate values of the range, an estimate of the "best-adjusted", real, long-term exchange rate is obtained (column 5). By observing (in columns 3b, 4b and 5b) the deviations between "adjusted" and official series, it can be noted that for the highest (1993-based) series, the most pronounced logarithmic difference is that for 1985 – 0.59, i.e. +80.4% – and the average is 0.34, i.e. +40.5% a year. For the lowest (1985-based) series, the largest difference is -0.59. The "best-adjusted" series, when compared to the other series, shows systematically smaller positive and negative differences: its average, as desired, is 0.00. The overall symmetry of the method can be well observed in Graph 1, where all the "adjusted" series appear to be (as expected) strictly parallel to each other, for the entire period.

In conclusion, the "best-adjusted" long-term exchange rate for Japan in 1993 is 155 yen to the dollar, and the actual rate 111.2 turns out to be overvalued by 40%. By correcting for such overvaluation, the Japanese GDP for 1993 is estimated at $3,020 bn., instead of $4,227 bn., the per capita GDP $24,170 instead of $33,800. Conversely, the "best-adjusted" Japanese GDP for 1985 turns out much higher: $1,745 bn. instead of $1,348 bn..

In the Statistical Appendix to this paper, a full set of results 1973- 1993 is supplied for 20 countries, and given their diversity, much analysis becomes possible through the data. Two questions, however, need to be asked:

1) can this approach cope with hyperinflation?

2) how does the system react to new data added year by year?

The results for Bolivia - a country where inflation rose to 13,650% in 1985, then fell to 220% in 1986, and to 11% in 1987 - are a good answer to the first question. Long term exchange rates over 1973-1993 have been estimated without difficulties, and the "best-adjusted" GDP

Table 2
"Adjusted" and "Best-Adjusted" Dollar Exchange Rates
Japan 1973-1993

YEAR	(1)	(2)	(3)	(4)	(5)	(3b)	(4b)	(5b)
1973	6.3	272	162	294	227	0.52	-0.08	0.18
1974	10.2	292	179	324	250	0.49	-0.10	0.16
1975	-2.1	297	175	317	245	0.53	-0.07	0.19
1976	1.6	297	178	322	249	0.51	-0.08	0.18
1977	-0.3	269	177	321	248	0.42	-0.18	0.08
1978	-2.7	210	173	313	241	0.20	-0.40	-0.14
1979	-5.3	219	163	296	229	0.29	-0.30	-0.04
1980	-4.6	227	156	283	218	0.37	-0.22	0.04
1981	-5.7	221	147	266	206	0.41	-0.19	0.07
1982	-4.2	249	141	255	197	0.57	-0.02	0.23
1983	-2.2	238	138	250	193	0.55	-0.05	0.21
1984	-2.1	238	135	244	189	0.57	-0.03	0.23
1985	-2.4	239	132	239	184	0.59	0.00	0.26
1986	-1.0	169	130	236	182	0.26	-0.34	-0.08
1987	-3.1	145	126	229	177	0.14	-0.46	-0.20
1988	-3.3	128	122	221	171	0.05	-0.55	-0.29
1989	-2.6	138	119	216	167	0.15	-0.45	-0.19
1990	-1.7	145	117	212	164	0.21	-0.38	-0.12
1991	-2.0	135	115	208	160	0.16	-0.43	-0.17
1992	-0.6	127	114	206	159	0.11	-0.49	-0.23
1993	-2.3	111	111	202	156	0.00	-0.59	-0.34
Average	-1.4	208	143	260	201	0.34	-0.26	0.00

Column(1) = Inflation differentials, in percentage.
Column(2) = Official exchange rates.
Column(3) = "Adjusted" exchange rates, based on the official 1993 level.
Column(4) = "Adjusted" exchange rates, based on the official 1985 level.
Column(5) = "Best-adjusted" exchange rates.
Column(3b, 4b and 5b) = Logarithmic differences between "adjusted"

for Bolivia in 1993 has turned out to be $7.58 bn., instead of $5.44 bn. at official exchange rates. With regard to the second question, it must be said that the system is extremely stable. In a vast majority of cases, the new data added year by year lead at changes of 1-2%. The GDP of Germany for 1990, for instance, (estimated at $1,305 bn with data over the period 1973-90) rises by 0.5% when estimated with additional figures for 1991, rises again by 1.1% adding 1992, by 0.8% adding 1993. For Bolivia, variations shown from 1991 onwards are -1.9%, -1.7%, -1.7%; for Japan +1.3%, +1.4%, +1.7%.

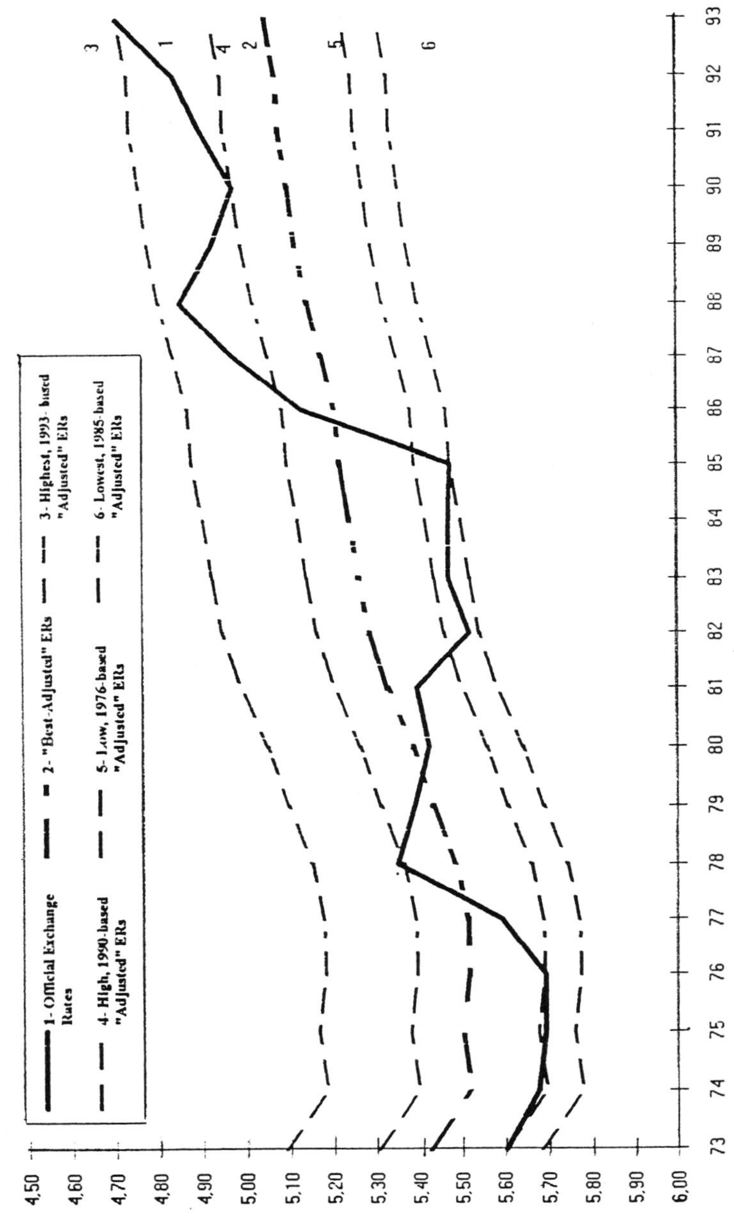

GRAPH 1 - "ADJUSTED" AND OFFICIAL DOLLAR EXCHANGE RATES (Logs) : JAPAN 1973-1993

Something which should not be forgotten, on the other hand, is that these variations always apply to the entire set of estimates. When the "best-adjusted" German GDP for 1990 is revised upwards by 1%, so is the GDP for 1989, 1988, etc., and consequently real relationships between one year and another remain unaltered. On the whole, this new approach seems to fulfill the four conditions outlined in the introduction, by which a good method should have been able to supply realistic estimates, which could be rapidly updated from year to year, which could be calculated for a vast number of countries, and which, most of all, would remain unaffected by nominal disturbances.

Now that the basic properties and the functionality of the system have been explored, a question comes to the fore: can "adjusted" long-term exchange rates be related theoretically to the concept of purchasing power parity, and how do they compare with ICP-type parities? Here, the long-term exchange rate has been defined on the basis of the "relative" PPP doctrine, and therefore it incorporates the concept of relative PPP. There is, however, one major difference between the two: while the long-term exchange rate is sensitive to capital - in the sense that it also reflects the international position of the capital sector of a country - purchasing power parity is not, as was first noted by Michael Ward (1985).

Capitalwise, both with regard to current flows and cumulated stocks, countries differ for three main factors: 1) The ratio of savings to GDP in the economy, which makes for an abundant or scarce supply of capital domestically; 2) Investment made abroad - both portfolio and direct investment - versus the foreign investment realized in the country; 3) The flow, in the current account of the balance of payments, of net factor income from abroad, which is the result of past investment. When these factors are favorable, there are two consequences, a low cost of capital and a "high standing", internationally, of the currency. That is, a permanent appreciation of the currency in excess of what the domestic price level and other conditions would entail, because capital markets trust this currency to be a good tool for international transactions.

Besides having a financial meaning, these two results lead also to real income effects, and long-term exchange rates, by reflecting these effects, are a better instrument for GDP comparisons. While purchasing power parities only refer to consumers and investors, and their expenditure on goods and services within the strict boundaries of conventional GDP calculations, the long-term exchange rate refers to the wider and more modern concept of the national income, and to its allocation in a fully international context. Residents are not seen only as consumers and international travellers, but also as international investors, and when they come from a capital rich country, their real income can be higher than their PPP. Obviously, the reverse is true for capital scarce countries.

In conclusion, while purchasing power parities only allow for a partial assessment of countries' annual economic transactions, GDP estimation through "Adjusted" Long-Term Exchange Rates (ALTER) gives a more complete and meaningful assessment of each country's economic position in the world.

6. Conclusions

The aim of this paper has been that of finding a dollar GDP estimation method that would allow international comparisons of countries overtime where consistency in real terms could be maintained, and disruptions from exchange rate fluctuations could be avoided. Therefore, after illustrating why stable and recent GDP comparisons are needed, the main approaches used in the last 20-30 years have been examined.

Quantitative methods, in particular the one by the ECE of Geneva, turned out to be somewhat outdated; and, also, too slow in supplying their results (7-8 years). Surprisingly, the GNP estimates presented in the World Bank Atlas and Development Report demonstrated to even exaggerate the violent fluctuations already present in official exchange rates. Purchasing power parities from the different phases of ICP have shown again an excessive "revaluation" of the GDPs of most poor countries (this aspect was extensively illustrated in a previous study), while the time span necessary to supply the estimates has remained of about 8 years. On the other hand, the extrapolations from ICP results made by Summers and Heston for the Penn World Tables appear to have often amplified and made worse the biases already noted in the ICP.

At this stage, the literature on long term exchange rates and the "relative" PPP doctrine has been examined, coming to the conclusion that the concept of the long term exchange rate – taken to be constant, as a number of authors do – can be an appropriate instrument for GDP comparisons. Therefore, having set up a statistical definition of the long term exchange rate where such rate: 1) perfectly compensates year by year for the inflation differential between two countries, as postulated by the "relative" PPP doctrine; and 2) avoids having a base-year but, on the contrary, is the expression of the entire period analysed – something which makes this exchange rate truly long term – a new GDP estimation method has been presented, and its equations illustrated.

Further, the algebraic proofs have been given that this theoretically constructed, "Adjusted" Long Term Exchange Rate (ALTER) is symmetrical in bilateral comparisons – alternatively taking as reference one or the other country and currency – and, when three or more countries and currencies are involved, is fully transitive as well. By analysing and discussing the main features of the results, it has been seen, too, that the system can cope with any degree of hyper-inflation (as Bolivia's 14,000 per cent, for instance), and that it is extremely stable when new data are added year by year. In the Statistical Appendix, a full set of estimates has been presented, for 20 countries over 1973-1993.

On the whole, main conclusions are the following: Firstly, this new field of enquiry seems to have a vast potential for further research: among other things, the first seeds are discernible for the construction of a World Model of Exchange Rates, which could also be used for forecasts on exchange rates. Secondly, according to the current availability of data, about 150 countries could be analyzed, and ALTER could really represent an alternative to the various methods used so far. Given the wide coverage of countries, estimates for the world gross product could also be prepared. Thirdly, average, real rates of growth for the world economy, and for regional areas as well, could be calculated with more precision than now, unhindered by the problem – which has never been solved – of how to attribute, to the different countries, weights for the regional averages which are not affected by exchange rate fluctuations. Finally, from the "adjusted" rates estimated over the period 1973-1993, extrapolations to 1950, and projections to 2000-2020, could be prepared. While the historical analyses of the world economy would benefit from the stability of the data, projections could rely on a more dependable base, especially with regard to each country's weight attributed at the beginning of the projection period.

References

Baillie, R.T. and Selover, D.D. (1987), "Cointegration and Models of Exchange Rate Determination", *International Journal of Forecasting*, 3.

Boothe, P. and Glassman, D. (1987) , "Off the Mark: Lessons for Exchange Rate Modelling",*Oxford Economic Papers*, 39.

Davutyan, N. and Pippenger, J. (1990) , "Testing Purchasing Power Parity: Some Evidence of the Effects of Transaction Costs", *Econometric Review*, 9(2).

Diebold, F.X., Husted, S. and Rush, M.(1991), "Real Exchange Rates Under the Gold Standard", *Journal of Political Economy*, 99, No. 6.

Dornbusch, R. and Vogelsang, T. (1992), "Real Exchange Rates and Purchasing Power Parity", in J. de Melo and A. Sapir (eds) *Trade Theory and Economic Reform: North, South and East.* Essays in Honour of Bela Belassa.

ECE (1980), *Economic Bulletin for Europe: Comparative GDP Levels, Vol. 31, No. 2*, New York, United Nations, 1980.

Edison, Hali, J. (1987), "Purchasing Power Parity in the Long-Run: A Test of the Dollar/Pound Exchange Rate 1890-1978", *Journal of Money, Credit and Banking*, Vol. 19, No. 3.

Enders, Walter (1988), "Arima and Cointegration Tests of PPP under Fixed and Flexible Exchange Rate Regimes", *The Review of Economics and Statistics.*

Frenkel, Jacob, A. (1976), "A Monetary Approach to the Exchange Rate: Doctrinal Aspects and Empirical Evidence", *Scandinavian Journal of Economics*, 78.

Frenkel, Jacob, A. (1981), "The Collapse of Purchasing Power Parities during the 1970s", *European Economic Review*, 16.

Gubitz, Andrea (1988), "Collapse of the Purchasing Power Parity in the Light of Co-Integrated Variables?", *Welt-Wirtschaftliches Archiv*, Heft 4.

Holden, Merle (1991), "Real Exchange Rates and Their Measurement", *The South African Journal of Economics*, 59, No. 1.

Huizinga, John (1987), "An Empirical Investigation of the Long-Run Behavior of Real Exchange Rates", *Carnegie Rochester Conference Series on Public Policy* 27, North Holland, Amsterdam.

Kravis, I., Heston, A. and Summers, R. (1982), *World Product and Income*. The John Hopkins U.P., Baltimore.

Lancieri, Elio (1990), "Purchasing Power Parities and Phase IV of the ICP: Do They Lead to "Real" Estimates of GDP and its Components?", *World Development*.

Maddison, Angus (1970), *Economic Progress and Policy in Developing Countries*. New York.

Maddison, Angus (1983), "A Comparison of the Levels of GDP Per Capita in Developed and Developing Countries, 1700-1980", *The Journal of Economic History*.

Manzur, Meher (1991), "Purchasing Power Parity and Relative Price Variability: the Missing Link?", *Australian Economic Papers*, 30.

McNown, R., and Wallace, M.S. (1990), "Cointegration Tests of Purchasing Power Parity among Four Industrial Countries: Results for Fixed and Flexible Rates", *Applied Economics*, 22.

Meese, Richard, A. (1986), "Testing for Bubbles in Exchange Markets: A Case of Sparkling Rates?", *Journal of Political Economy*, Vol. 94, no. 2.

Officer, Lawrence, H. (1976), "The Purchasing-Power-Parity Theory of Exchange Rates: A Review Article", *IMF Staff Papers*.

Rush, M. and Husted, S. (1985), "Purchasing Power Parity in the Long Run", *Canadian Journal of Economics*, XVIII.

Summers, R., and Heston, A. (1988), "A New Set of International Comparisons of Real Product and Price Levels: Estimates for 130 Countries, 1950-1985", *Review of Income and Wealth*.

Taylor, Mark P. (1988), "An Empirical Examination of Long-Run Purchasing Power Parity Using Cointegration Techniques", *Applied Economics*, 20.

U.N. and Eurostat (1986), *World Comparisons of Purchasing Power and Real Product for 1980: Part One ; Part Two*, Mimeo: "Detailed Results for 60 Countries", New York and Brussels.

Ward, Michael (1985), *Purchasing Power Parities and Real Expenditures in the OECD*, Paris.

Wood, Adrian (1991), "Global Trends in Real Exchange Rates 1960-1984", *World Development*, 19, no. 4.

World Bank (1983), *World Development Report* 1988, Washington, D.C.: Oxford U.P., June 1988, and previous issues since 1983.

World Bank (1983), *Methodological Problems and Proposals Relating to the Estimation of Internationally Comparable Per Capita GNP Figures*, World Bank Document, Economic Analysis and Projections Department.

World Bank (1993), The World Bank Atlas 1994, Washington, D.C.

STATISTICAL APPENDIX

APPENDIX TABLE 1
"Best-Adjusted" Exchange Rates to the Dollar
20 Countries over 1973-1993.

Country	1973	1974	1975	1976	1977	1978	1979
Bolivia	0.148	0.215	0.209	0.213	0.221	0.228	0.252
Brazil	*3189	*3699	*4742	*5585	*7743	§1077	§1388
Chile	0.155	1.066	4.239	13.99	26.99	39.43	52.98
Colombia	24.05	27.70	31.01	36.67	44.35	48.14	55.05
Costa Rica	7.649	8.659	9.828	10.80	11.83	11.84	11.92
Germany	2.730	2.684	2.592	2.531	2.460	2.379	2.281
Guatemala	0.962	1.022	1.054	1.107	1.208	1.182	1.183
India	10.15	10.99	9.713	9.762	9.470	8.961	9.549
Japan	227.0	250.2	245.0	248.9	248.0	241.4	228.7
Kenya	8.327	8.910	9.043	10.13	11.10	10.62	10.35
Korea	283.9	337.7	390.3	444.8	482.8	544.1	601.7
Malawi	0.927	1.008	0.993	1.031	1.094	1.015	0.967
Mexico	13.91	15.58	16.40	18.50	22.52	24.38	26.87
Pakistan	9.481	10.72	11.95	12.63	13.09	13.22	12.85
Philippines	6.672	8.155	8.120	8.295	8.396	8.536	9.122
Sri Lanka	10.98	12.55	12.01	12.42	13.35	13.76	14.64
Switzerland	2.521	2.481	2.408	2.316	2.176	2.087	1.963
Thailand	21.88	24.14	23.11	22.47	22.36	22.42	23.30
Uruguay	1.118	1.331	2.289	3.112	4.553	6.348	10.31
Venezuela	3.571	4.921	4.586	4.590	4.662	4.584	5.152

* = These figures are intended as preceded by seven decimal places.
§ = These figures are intended as preceded by six decimal places.

APPENDIX TABLE 1 - Continued
"Best-Adjusted" Exchange Rates to the Dollar
20 Countries over 1973-1993.

Country	1980	1981	1982	1983	1984	1985	1986
Bolivia	0.317	0.348	0.915	3.139	43.72	4776	15897
Brazil	§2303	§3928	§7362	ε1403	ε3391	?1004	?3154
Chile	62.22	63.92	65.41	82.39	88.69	108.5	125.9
Colombia	64.10	71.54	84.12	97.71	114.1	137.1	172.2
Costa Rica	12.92	16.58	28.77	34.95	39.94	46.31	53.19
Germany	2.182	2.064	2.029	2.022	1.972	1.931	1.937
Guatemala	1.189	1.173	1.180	1.192	1.187	1.356	1.866
India	10.33	10.35	10.44	10.80	11.14	11.70	12.24
Japan	218.2	205.8	197.1	192.8	188.7	184.3	182.4
Kenya	10.37	10.42	10.92	12.35	13.02	13.55	14.35
Korea	687.3	721.7	744.7	753.6	749.7	750.4	750.4
Malawi	1.020	1.080	1.117	1.192	1.283	1.343	1.485
Mexico	31.06	35.59	53.93	99.12	150.7	226.9	383.8
Pakistan	12.96	13.06	13.52	13.73	14.40	14.47	14.54
Philippines	8.875	9.018	9.237	10.19	14.94	16.89	16.93
Sri Lanka	16.04	17.65	18.05	20.35	23.48	22.69	23.41
Switzerland	1.844	1.794	1.809	1.798	1.766	1.752	1.767
Thailand	25.01	24.55	23.93	23.17	22.11	21.43	21.42
Uruguay	14.60	16.83	18.72	27.62	41.53	69.42	115.8
Venezuela	6.024	6.165	6.058	6.060	8.266	8.480	8.488

§ = these figures are intended as preceded by six decimal places,
ε = by five decimal places,
? = by four decimal places.

APPENDIX TABLE 1 - Continued
"Best-Adjusted" Exchange Rates to the Dollar
20 Countries over 1973-1993.

Country	1987	1988	1989	1990	1991	1992	1993
Bolivia	17808	19400	21037	23228	26847	28956	30591
Brazil	?7589	!2236	0.003	0.079	0.377	4.184	114.4
Chile	160.1	187.4	206.2	236.3	276.0	308.3	347.4
Colombia	205.7	253.2	301.7	371.8	454.0	541.1	644.6
Costa Rica	56.72	64.93	71.49	81.45	100.9	117.2	127.2
Germany	1.915	1.876	1.838	1.834	1.844	1.888	1.898
Guatemala	1.951	2.099	2.225	3.006	3.821	4.120	4.551
India	12.67	13.39	13.90	14.79	16.29	17.47	17.85
Japan	176.8	171.0	166.5	163.6	160.3	159.4	155.7
Kenya	14.65	15.32	15.87	16.68	17.84	20.33	26.39
Korea	752.8	767.8	770.7	817.2	867.7	899.5	916.4
Malawi	1.682	2.060	2.402	2.556	2.789	3.221	3.794
Mexico	890.6	1712	2055	2557	2989	3396	3601
Pakistan	14.71	15.54	16.12	16.49	17.94	19.16	18.66
Philippines	17.54	18.52	19.29	20.94	23.45	24.83	25.75
Sri Lanka	24.55	25.99	27.61	31.90	33.96	36.28	38.86
Switzerland	1.756	1.733	1.724	1.752	1.775	1.784	1.781
Thailand	21.65	22.90	23.15	23.40	23.85	24.28	24.38
Uruguay	193.7	306.2	512.4	987.2	1866	2966	4465
Venezuela	10.95	12.86	22.88	31.57	36.62	45.66	58.42

?= these figures are intended as preceded by four decimal places.
!= these figures are intended as preceded by three decimal places.

APPENDIX TABLE 2
"Best-Adjusted" GDPs: 20 Countries and United States 1973-1993
($ billion)

COUNTRIES	1973	1974	1975	1976	1977	1978	1979
1. USA	1349	1458	1585	1767	1974	2233	2489
2. Japan	495.7	535.5	604.7	668.7	748.0	847.0	970.0
3. Germany(West)	336.6	367.2	397.2	445.0	487.6	543.0	612.2
4. Brazil	81.44	97.33	112.8	131.3	144.2	163.2	189.0
5. India	58.07	63.36	76.27	82.15	94.88	109.1	112.6
6. Mexico	53.65	62.00	71.90	79.51	87.58	102.2	121.1
7. Korea(South)	19.08	22.42	26.20	31.47	37.25	44.55	51.90
8. Switzerland	51.61	56.88	58.23	61.31	67.01	72.70	80.74
9. Thailand	9.899	11.24	12.93	15.03	17.56	20.97	23.88
10. Venezuela	20.51	22.81	25.75	29.44	33.40	36.88	40.32
11. Pakistan	7.053	8.103	9.301	10.32	11.44	13.34	15.17
12. Colombia	10.11	11.64	13.07	14.52	16.15	18.89	21.60
13. Philippines	10.84	12.20	14.13	16.31	18.37	20.82	23.84
14. Chile	7.736	8.634	8.376	9.200	10.66	12.36	14.58
15. Guatemala	2.670	3.093	3.459	3.943	4.537	5.137	5.833
16. Kenya	2.110	2.381	2.646	2.870	3.352	3.860	4.501
17. Sri Lanka	1.676	1.894	2.214	2.432	2.728	3.101	3.578
18. Uruguay	2.683	3.006	3.497	3.856	4.173	4.726	5.433
19. Costa Rica	1.329	1.526	1.710	1.915	2.225	2.551	2.902
20. Bolivia	1.763	2.017	2.360	2.657	2.955	3.295	3.574
21. Malawi	0.393	0.458	0.534	0.594	0.665	0.789	0.894

Note : Countries are ranked according to their "adjusted" GDP figures for 1993.

APPENDIX TABLE 2 - Continued
"Best-Adjusted" GDPs: 20 Countries and United States, 1973-1993
($ billion)

COUNTRIES	1980	1981	1982	1983	1984	1985	1986
1. USA	2708	3031	3150	3405	3777	4039	4269
2. Japan	1100	1251	1373	1463	1595	1745	1841
3. Germany(West)	680.8	748.7	787.1	831.2	897.5	951.5	999.4
4. Brazil	226.3	238.0	254.1	254.1	279.0	314.2	347.3
5. India	131.4	154.1	170.1	191.5	207.0	224.1	239.3
6. Mexico	143.9	172.2	181.7	180.4	195.6	208.9	206.4
7. Korea(South)	55.16	65.15	73.11	84.70	96.90	107.7	124.5
8. Switzerland	92.36	103.0	108.4	113.4	120.7	130.2	137.7
9. Thailand	27.39	32.02	35.35	39.28	44.02	47.33	51.15
10. Venezuela	42.20	46.27	48.08	47.94	50.82	52.95	57.98
11. Pakistan	18.07	21.25	23.97	26.54	29.16	32.63	35.39
12. Colombia	24.64	27.72	29.69	31.26	33.80	36.23	39.41
13. Philippines	27.46	31.23	34.34	36.23	35.11	33.85	35.98
14. Chile	17.28	19.92	18.95	18.91	21.35	23.75	25.79
15. Guatemala	6.629	7.341	7.520	7.591	7.976	8.245	8.489
16. Kenya	5.198	5.951	6.437	6.449	6.857	7.437	8.189
17. Sri Lanka	4.148	4.817	5.498	5.976	6.549	7.157	7.667
18. Uruguay	6.316	7.071	6.786	6.336	6.526	6.894	7.691
19. Costa Rica	3.206	3.445	3.390	3.615	4.082	4.274	4.636
20. Bolivia	3.881	4.307	4.371	4.326	4.568	4.717	4.694
21. Malawi	0.985	1.026	1.115	1.206	1.331	1.448	1.480

Note: Countries are ranked according to their GDP figures for 1993.

APPENDIX TABLE 2 - Continued
"Best-Adjusted" GDPs: 20 Countries and United States, 1973-1993
($ billion)

COUNTRIES	1987	1988	1989	1990	1991	1992	1993
1. USA	4540	4900	5251	5522	5723	6039	6374
2. Japan	1983	2185	2397	2613	2836	2937	3020
3. Germany(West)	1046	1124	1224	1335	1439	1482	1486
4. Brazil	371.5	385.6	416.8	414.5	436.0	441.4	476.0
5. India	259.0	296.2	326.7	358.9	378.0	403.9	434.3
6. Mexico	217.1	228.1	247.0	268.4	289.4	304.2	313.7
7. Korea(South)	144.0	166.7	185.6	211.4	240.0	257.6	279.1
8. Switzerland	145.1	154.9	168.4	179.2	186.5	190.3	194.3
9. Thailand	57.88	68.12	80.19	93.27	105.1	115.4	127.9
10. Venezuela	62.02	68.11	64.93	72.20	82.94	90.49	92.01
11. Pakistan	38.92	43.46	47.75	52.30	57.00	62.76	66.38
12. Colombia	42.89	46.34	50.14	54.40	57.80	61.11	66.02
13. Philippines	38.94	43.16	47.97	51.24	53.06	54.20	56.61
14. Chile	28.36	31.58	36.39	38.95	43.00	48.46	53.25
15. Guatemala	9.076	9.786	10.64	11.42	12.31	13.18	14.08
16. Kenya	8.955	9.870	10.81	11.72	12.38	12.70	13.69
17. Sri Lanka	8.012	8.540	9.124	10.09	10.97	11.67	12.81
18. Uruguay	8.576	8.901	9.445	9.911	10.61	11.64	12.19
19. Costa Rica	5.017	5.386	5.957	6.420	6.835	7.492	8.194
20. Bolivia	4.973	5.358	5.769	6.145	6.695	7.099	7.583
21. Malawi	1.554	1.660	1.827	1.988	2.203	2.070	2.350

Note : Countries are ranked according to their GDP figures for 1993.

APPENDIX TABLE 3
"Best-Adjusted" Per Capita Dollar GDPs
20 Countries and United States,
1973-1993.

COUNTRIES	1993	1990	1980	1973
	$	$	$	$
1. Switzerland	28,250	26,710	14,620	8,030
2. United States	24,750	22,100	11,890	6,370
3. Japan	24,170	21,150	9,420	4,560
4. Germany(West)	23,180	21,110	11,060	5,430
5. Korea(South)	6,270	4,930	1,450	560
6. Venezuela	4,470	3,740	2,810	1,820
7. Uruguay	3,870	3,200	2,170	970
8. Chile	3,850	2,960	1,550	790
9. Mexico	3,440	3,120	2,070	960
10. Brazil	3,040	2,760	1,870	820
11. Costa Rica	2,510	2,150	1,430	710
12. Thailand	2,250	1,660	590	250
13. Colombia	1,940	1,650	950	450
14. Guatemala	1,400	1,240	960	470
15. Bolivia	980	830	690	380
16. Philippines	850	830	570	270
17. Sri Lanka	720	590	280	130
18. Kenya	530	490	310	170
19. Pakistan	520	470	220	110
20. India	480	430	200	100
21. Malawi	220	210	160	80

International Comparisons of Prices, Output and Productivity
Edited by D.S. Prasada Rao and J. Salazar-Carrillo

PRODUCTIVITY,FACTOR ENDOWMENTS, MILITARY EXPENDITURES, AND NATIONAL PRICE LEVELS

Jeffrey H. Bergstrand[1]
Department of Finance and Business Economics
and
Joan B. Kroc Institute for International Peace Studies
University of Notre Dame
Notre Dame, U.S.A

1. Introduction

Economists have found systematic evidence that the general level of prices across countries at a point in time varies dramatically. Irving B. Kravis, Alan W. Heston, and Robert Summers (1982), for example, report that some countries' national price levels are no more than one-third the U.S. price level. Pioneering work by Kravis and Robert E. Lipsey (1983, 1987, 1988) has demonstrated that a positive correlation between the price level and (real) per capita gross domestic product is robust across numerous cross-sectional specifications.

Recently, several studies using the United Nations International Comparisons Program (ICP) data have attempted to disentangle theoretically and empirically the relative effects of productivity differentials, relative factor endowment differences, and the nonhomotheticity of tastes upon national price levels to better understand the "structural" channels through which per capita income differences between countries influence their relative price structures, especially the variation across countries in the relative prices of nontradables (services) to tradables (commodities).

Empirical work in Christopher Clague (1986) and Kravis and Lipsey (1987) assumed that per capita income differences between countries reflected relative productivity differences or relative factor endowment differences. These studies concentrated upon other presumably exogenous variables that might help per capita income explain cross-country variation in general price levels. These variables

[1]The author is very grateful to the Howarth J. Korth Fund for International Programs at the University of Notre Dame for financial support.

included, for instance, the trade balance, tourism receipts' share of GDP, minerals' share of GDP, and the share of nontradables in GDP.

Studies by Clague (1985), Jeffrey H. Bergstrand (1991) and Rodney E. Falvey and Norman Gemmell (1991, 1992) have focused upon understanding the channels through which per capita income differences themselves influence national price level differences. All these studies have in common the role of relative productivity differences, relative factor endowment differences, and the share of expenditures on services as important determinants of relative national price levels. Clague (1985) focused theoretically only on how factor endowment differentials, productivity differentials, and the share of spending on services affected national price levels. Bergstrand (1991) showed theoretically and empirically that per capita income differences influenced relative national price levels as much through relative demand differences as through relative supply (i.e., relative factor endowment and relative productivity) differences. Falvey and Gemmell (1991, 1992) support theoretically and empirically the conclusions of Bergstrand (1991) in the context of exogenous populations and multiple factors, but endogenous per capita incomes.

None of these studies, however, has contemplated the role of exogenous *fiscal spending*, and its influence on endogenous per capita disposable income and national price level differences. This study primarily investigates theoretically and empirically the role of fiscal policy in particular, defence spending – on relative national price levels, in the spirit of Bergstrand (1991, 1992). A secondary goal is of topical interest: How will the imminent reductions of defence spending in numerous industrialized nations affect relative national price levels?

The organization of the remainder of the paper is as follows. Section 2 discusses how the supply of civilian nontradables relative to civilian tradables might be influenced by factor endowments, sectoral productivity levels, military absorption of factors, and relative prices, to derive an estimable relative supply function. Section 3 discusses how the demand for civilian nontradables relative to civilian tradables might be influenced by per capita income, per capita military expenditures, and relative prices, to derive an estimable relative demand function, and discusses the reduced-form relative price level function. Section 4 provides empirical estimates of coefficients of the reduced-form relative price function and of the structural relative demand and supply functions. Section 5 provides conclusions.

2. Supply

I assume a standard simple general equilibrium framework similar to that in Ronald W. Jones (1965) for the production of two goods, tradables (T) and nontradables (N). Tradables and nontradables are consumed by both civilian (X_T^C, X_N^C) and military (X_T^M, X_N^M) sectors. Military absorption is exogenous similar to government absorption in the Frenkel and Razin (1987) framework. Tradables and nontradables are produced using two factors: capital (K) and consumer-workers (L), the endowment of which is fixed intratemporally. Factors are mobile between industries, but not internationally. Perfectly competitive firms are assumed to minimize costs given the constant-returns-to-scale technology, yielding the optimum input requirements per unit of output β_{ij} ($i = K, L$; $j = N, T$). Each β_{ij} is a function of the relative factor price (i.e., the wage rate, W, relative to the rental rate on capital, R) and the state of productivity of factor i in industry $j(\tau_{ij})$. An assumption of full employment of both factors yields:

$$\beta_{LT}X_T^C + \beta_{LT}X_T^M + \beta_{LN}X_N^C + \beta_{LN}X_N^M = L \tag{1}$$

$$\beta_{KT}X_T^C + \beta_{KT}X_T^M + \beta_{KN}X_N^C + \beta_{KN}X_N^M = K \tag{2}$$

In a competitive equilibrium with tradables and nontradables produced, unit costs must reflect market prices of the goods:

$$\beta_{LT}W + \beta_{KT}\,R = P_T \tag{3}$$

$$\beta_{LN}W + \beta_{KN}\,R = P_N \tag{4}$$

where all factor prices (W,R) and goods prices (P_N, P_T) are expressed in terms of a monetary unit.

The four equations (1) - (4) can be differentiated and mathematically manipulated to derive the percentage differences between two countries in key variables; let $\hat{x}$ denote dx/x. Consider first the relationships between goods prices and factor prices. The first-order conditions from profit-maximization are given by equations (3) and (4). Differentiating (4) and dividing both sides by P_N yields:

$$\theta_{LN}\hat{W} + \theta_{KN}\hat{R} + \theta_{LN}\hat{\beta}_{LN} + \theta_{KN}\hat{\beta}_{KN} = \hat{P}_N \tag{5}$$

where $\theta_{LN} = \beta_{LN}W/P_N$ and $\theta_{KN} = \beta_{KN}R/P_N$ are the (average) shares of labor and capital, respectively, in nontradables. Differentiating (3) and dividing both sides by P_T yields:

$$\theta_{LT}\hat{W} + \theta_{KT}\hat{R} + \theta_{LT}\hat{\beta}_{LT} + \theta_{KT}\hat{\beta}_{KT} \;=\; \hat{P}_T \tag{6}$$

where $\theta_{LT} = \beta_{LT}W/P_T$ and $\theta_{KT} = \beta_{KT}R/P_T$. The $\hat{\beta}_{ij}$'s each represent the percentage difference between two countries in the factor i requirement to produce a unit of output j. The factor requirement will differ if relative factor prices (W/R) differ or if the factor's productivity differs between the two countries; expressed as in Jones (1965), section 9:

$$\beta_{ij} \;=\; \beta_{ij}(W/R, t) \qquad i = L, K; j = N, T$$

where t represents the state of productivity or technology. In terms of percentage differences, $\hat{\beta}_{ij}$ can be expressed as:

$$\hat{\beta}_{ij} \;=\; \hat{\gamma}_{ij} - \hat{\tau}_{ij} \tag{7}$$

where $\hat{\gamma}_{ij}$ represents the percentage difference between two countries of the input requirement per unit of output owing specifically to differences in relative factor prices for a given level of productivity and $\hat{\tau}_{ij}$ represents the percentage difference between two countries of productivity of factor i in industry j. Higher levels of τ_{ij} are associated with lower levels of β_{ij} for any given level of relative factor prices; formally, $\hat{\tau}_{ij} = \beta_{ij}^{-1}(d\beta_{ij}/dt)dt > 0$. Substituting (7) into (5) and (6) and some mathematical manipulation yields:

$$\theta_{LN}\hat{W} + \theta_{KN}\hat{R} + (\theta_{LN}\hat{\gamma}_{LN} + \theta_{KN}\hat{\gamma}_{KN}) \;=\; \hat{P}_N + (\theta_{LN}\hat{\tau}_{LN} + \theta_{KN}\hat{\tau}_{KN}) \tag{8}$$

$$\theta_{LT}\hat{W} + \theta_{KT}\hat{R} + (\theta_{LT}\hat{\gamma}_{LT} + \theta_{KT}\hat{\gamma}_{KT}) \;=\; \hat{P}_T + (\theta_{LT}\hat{\tau}_{LT} + \theta_{KT}\hat{\tau}_{KT}) \tag{9}$$

A key assumption in these types of models is that the competitive firm is assumed to maximize profits for given factor prices, goods prices and technology. Hence, as in Jones (1965), any differences in the γ_{ij}'s must satisfy:

$$(\theta_{LN}\hat{\gamma}_{LN} + \theta_{KN}\hat{\gamma}_{KN}) \;=\; 0 \quad or \quad -(W/R) \;=\; d\gamma_{KN}/d\gamma_{LN} \tag{10}$$

$$(\theta_{LT}\hat{\gamma}_{LT} + \theta_{KT}\hat{\gamma}_{KT}) \;=\; 0 \quad or \quad -(W/R) \;=\; d\gamma_{KT}/d\gamma_{LT} \tag{11}$$

Equations (10) and (11) are equivalent to saying that the slope of the isoquant in each industry must equal (in absolute terms) the prevailing wage-rental ratio in equilibrium. Let

$$\hat{\Pi}_N = \theta_{LN}\hat{\tau}_{LN} + \theta_{KN}\hat{\tau}_{KN} \tag{12}$$

$$\hat{\Pi}_T = \theta_{LT}\hat{\tau}_{LT} + \theta_{KT}\hat{\tau}_{KT} \tag{13}$$

represent the percentage difference between two countries in their levels of productivity in the nontradable and tradable industries, respectively. Substituting (10) and (12) into (8), and (11) and (13) into (9), yields:

$$\theta_{LN}\hat{W} + \theta_{KN}\hat{R} = \hat{P}_N + \hat{\Pi}_N \tag{14}$$

$$\theta_{LT}\hat{W} + \theta_{KT}\hat{R} = \hat{P}_T + \hat{\Pi}_T \tag{15}$$

Subtracting (15) from (14) yields:

$$(\theta_{LN} - \theta_{LT})\hat{W} - (\theta_{KT} - \theta_{KN})\hat{R} = (\hat{P}_N - \hat{P}_T) + (\hat{\Pi}_N - \hat{\Pi}_T) \tag{16}$$

Defining

$$\Theta = \begin{bmatrix} \theta_{LN} & \theta_{LT} \\ \theta_{KN} & \theta_{KT} \end{bmatrix}$$

and recalling $\theta_{Lj} + \theta_{Kj} = 1$ for j = N,T, the determinant of Θ is:

$$|\Theta| = \theta_{LN} - \theta_{LT} = \theta_{KT} - \theta_{KN}$$

Substituting $|\Theta|$ into (16) and dividing by $|\Theta|$ yields:

$$(\hat{W} - \hat{R}) = (1/|\Theta|\,[(\hat{P}_N - \hat{P}_T) + (\hat{\Pi}_N - \hat{\Pi}_T)]) \tag{17}$$

Since in a competitive equilibrium (with internal tangencies) the slope of the isoquant in each industry equals (in absolute terms) the ratio of factor prices, the elasticities of substitution can be defined as:

$$\sigma_N = (\hat{\gamma}_{KN} - \hat{\gamma}_{LN})/(\hat{W} - \hat{R}) > 0 \tag{18}$$

$$\sigma_T = (\hat{\gamma}_{KT} - \hat{\gamma}_{LT})/(\hat{W} - \hat{R}) > 0 \tag{19}$$

Each $\hat{\gamma}_{ij}$ can now be solved for in terms of an σ_j, θ_{ij} and the percentage difference in relative factor prices. Solving (10) and (18) simultaneously yields:

$$\hat{\gamma}_{LN} = -\Theta_{KN}\sigma_N(\hat{W} - \hat{R}) \tag{20}$$

$$\hat{\gamma}_{KN} = \Theta_{LN}\sigma_N(\hat{W} - \hat{R}) \tag{21}$$

Solving (11) and (19) simultaneously yields:

$$\hat{\gamma}_{LT} = -\Theta_{KT}\sigma_T(\hat{W} - \hat{R}) \tag{22}$$

$$\hat{\gamma}_{KT} = \Theta_{LT}\sigma_T(\hat{W} - \hat{R}) \tag{23}$$

Consider now the factor endowment constraints (1) and (2). Differentiating (1) and dividing both sides of the resulting equation by L yields:

$$\lambda^C_{LT}\hat{\beta}_{LT} + \lambda^C_{LT}\hat{X}^C_T + \lambda^M_{LT}\hat{\beta}_{LT} + \lambda^C_{LN}\hat{\beta}_{LN} + \lambda^C_{LN}\hat{X}^C_N + \lambda^M_{LN}\hat{\beta}_{LN}$$
$$= \hat{L} - [(\beta_{LT}/L)dX^M_T + (\beta_{LN}/L)dX^M_N] \tag{24}$$

where $\lambda^K_{Lj} = \beta_{Lj}X^K_j/L$ $(j = N,T;\ k = C,M)$ and, by equation (1), $\lambda^C_{LT} + \lambda^M_{LT} + \lambda^C_{LN} + \lambda^M_{LN} = \lambda_{LT} + \lambda_{LN} = 1$. Similarly, differentiate (2) and divide both sides by K:

$$\lambda^C_{KT}\hat{\beta}_{KT} + \lambda^C_{KT}\hat{X}^C_T + \lambda^M_{KT}\hat{\beta}_{KT} + \lambda^C_{KN}\hat{\beta}_{KN} + \lambda^C_{KN}\hat{X}^C_N + \lambda^M_{KN}\hat{\beta}_{KN}$$
$$= \hat{K} - [(\beta_{KT}/K)dX^M_T + (\beta_{KN}/K)dX^M_N] \tag{25}$$

where $\lambda^K_{Kj} = \beta_{Kj}X^K_j/K$ $(j = N,T;\ k = C,M)$ and, by equation (2), $\lambda^C_{KT} + \lambda^M_{KT} + \lambda^C_{KN} + \lambda^M_{KN} = \lambda_{KT} + \lambda_{KN} = 1$.

The two bracketed terms in equations (24) and (25) can be simplified by considering first $dX^M_T > 0$ when $d\beta_{LT} = dX^C_T = d\beta_{LN} = dX^C_N = dX^M_N = dL = d\beta_{KT} = d\beta_{KN} = dK = 0$:

$$-(\beta_{LT}/L)dX^M_T = -(\beta_{KT}/K)dX^M_T \quad or \quad \beta_{LT} = (L/K)\beta_{KT}$$

Second, consider $dX_N^M > 0$ when $d\beta_{LT} = dX_T^C = d\beta_{LN} = dX_N^C = dX_T^M = dL = d\beta_{KT} = d\beta_{KN} = dK = 0$:

$$-(\beta_{LN}/L)dX_N^M = -(\beta_{KN}/K)dX_N^M \quad or \quad \beta_{LN} = (L/K)\beta_{KN}$$

Using the above, we can define:

$$\hat{X}_T^M = \beta_{LT}dX_T^M = \beta_{LT}d(X_T^M/L) = (\beta_{LT}/L)dX_T^M = (\beta_{KT}/K)dX_T^M$$

$$\hat{X}_N^M = \beta_{LN}dX_N^M = \beta_{LN}d(X_N^M/L) = (\beta_{LN}/L)dX_N^M = (\beta_{KT}/K)dX_N^M$$

The above two expressions can be substituted into (24) and (25) to yield:

$$\lambda_{LT}^C\hat{\beta}_{LT} + \lambda_{LT}^C\hat{X}_T^C + \lambda_{LT}^M\hat{\beta}_{LT} + \lambda_{LN}^C\hat{\beta}_{LN} + \lambda_{LN}^C\hat{X}_N^C + \lambda_{LN}^M\hat{\beta}_{LN} = \hat{L} - (\hat{X}_T^M + \hat{X}_N^M) \qquad (26)$$

$$\lambda_{KT}^C\hat{\beta}_{KT} + \lambda_{KT}^C\hat{X}_T^C + \lambda_{KT}^M\hat{\beta}_{KT} + \lambda_{KN}^C\hat{\beta}_{KN} + \lambda_{KN}^C\hat{X}_N^C + \lambda_{KN}^M\hat{\beta}_{KN} = \hat{K} - (\hat{X}_T^M + \hat{X}_N^M) \qquad (27)$$

Substitution of equation (7) into (26) and (27) and some mathematical manipulation yields:

$$\lambda_{LT}^C\hat{X}_T^C + \lambda_{LN}^C\hat{X}_N^C = \hat{L} + [(\lambda_{LT}^C + \lambda_{LT}^M)\hat{\tau}_{LT} + (\lambda_{LN}^C + \lambda_{LN}^M)\hat{\tau}_{LN}] - [(\lambda_{LT}^C + \lambda_{LT}^M)\hat{\gamma}_{LT} + (\lambda_{LN}^C + \gamma_{LN}^M)\hat{\gamma}_{LN}] - (\hat{X}_T^M + \hat{X}_N^M) \qquad (28)$$

$$\lambda_{KT}^C\hat{X}_T^C + \lambda_{KN}^C\hat{X}_N^C = \hat{K} + [(\lambda_{KT}^C + \lambda_{KT}^M)\hat{\tau}_{KT} + (\lambda_{KN}^C + \lambda_{KN}^M)\hat{\tau}_{KN}] - [(\lambda_{KT}^C + \lambda_{KT}^M)\hat{\gamma}_{KT} + (\lambda_{KN}^C + \gamma_{KN}^M)\hat{\gamma}_{KN}] - (\hat{X}_T^M + \hat{X}_N^M) \qquad (29)$$

Let

$$\hat{\Pi}_L = (\lambda_{LT}^C + \lambda_{LT}^M)\hat{\tau}_{LT} + (\lambda_{LN}^C + \lambda_{LN}^M)\hat{\tau}_{LN}$$

be the "labor saving" in factor-productivity differences between countries and

$$\hat{\Pi}_K = (\lambda_{KT}^C + \lambda_{KT}^M)\hat{\tau}_{KT} + (\lambda_{KN}^C + \lambda_{KN}^M)\hat{\tau}_{KN}$$

be the "capital saving" in factor-productivity differences between countries. Substituting these two terms, respectively, into equations (28) and (29) yields:

$$\lambda_{LT}^C \hat{X}_T^C + \lambda_{LN}^C \hat{X}_N^C = \hat{L} + \hat{\Pi}_L - (\hat{X}_T^M + \hat{X}_N^M) - [(\lambda_{LT}^C + \lambda_{LT}^M)\hat{\gamma}_{LT} + (\lambda_{LN}^C + \lambda_{LN}^M)\hat{\gamma}_{LN}] \quad (30)$$

$$\lambda_{KT}^C \hat{X}_T^C + \lambda_{KN}^C \hat{X}_N^C = \hat{K} + \hat{\Pi}_K - (\hat{X}_T^M + \hat{X}_N^M) - [(\lambda_{KT}^C + \lambda_{KT}^M)\hat{\gamma}_{KT} + (\lambda_{KN}^C + \lambda_{KN}^M)\hat{\gamma}_{KN}] \quad (31)$$

In matrix form, (30) and (31) are:

$$\begin{bmatrix} \lambda_{LT}^C & \lambda_{LN}^C \\ \lambda_{KT}^C & \lambda_{KN}^C \end{bmatrix} \begin{bmatrix} \hat{X}_T^C \\ \hat{X}_N^C \end{bmatrix} \quad (32)$$

$$= \begin{bmatrix} \hat{L} + \hat{\Pi}_L - (\hat{X}_T^M + \hat{X}_N^M) - [(\lambda_{LT}^C + \lambda_{LT}^M)\hat{\gamma}_{LT} + (\lambda_{LN}^C + \lambda_{LN}^M)\hat{\gamma}_{LN}] \\ \hat{K} + \hat{\Pi}_K - (\hat{X}_T^M + \hat{X}_N^M) - [(\lambda_{KT}^C + \lambda_{KT}^M)\hat{\gamma}_{KT} + (\lambda_{KN}^C + \lambda_{KN}^M)\hat{\gamma}_{KN}] \end{bmatrix}$$

Premultiplying both sides of (32) by the inverse of

$$\begin{bmatrix} \lambda_{LT}^C & \lambda_{LN}^C \\ \lambda_{KT}^C & \lambda_{KN}^C \end{bmatrix}$$

which is:

$$\begin{bmatrix} \lambda_{LT}^C & \lambda_{LN}^C \\ \lambda_{KT}^C & \lambda_{KN}^C \end{bmatrix}^{-1} = (\lambda_{LT}^C \lambda_{KN}^C - \lambda_{LN}^C \lambda_{KT}^C)^{-1} \begin{bmatrix} \lambda_{KN}^C & -\lambda_{LN}^C \\ -\lambda_{KT}^C & \lambda_{LT}^C \end{bmatrix}$$

yields:

$$\begin{bmatrix} \hat{X}_T^C \\ \hat{X}_N^C \end{bmatrix} = (\lambda_{LT}^C \lambda_{KN}^C - \lambda_{LN}^C \lambda_{KT}^C)^{-1} \begin{bmatrix} \lambda_{KN}^C & -\lambda_{LN}^C \\ -\lambda_{KT}^C & \lambda_{LT}^C \end{bmatrix}$$

$$\begin{bmatrix} \hat{L} + \hat{\Pi}_L - (\hat{X}_T^M + \hat{X}_N^M) - [(\lambda_{LT}^C + \lambda_{LT}^M)\hat{\gamma}_{LT} + (\lambda_{LN}^C + \lambda_{LN}^M)\hat{\gamma}_{LN}] \\ \hat{K} + \hat{\Pi}_K - (\hat{X}_T^M + \hat{X}_N^M) - [(\lambda_{KT}^C + \lambda_{KT}^M)\hat{\gamma}_{KT} + (\lambda_{KN}^C + \lambda_{KN}^M)\hat{\gamma}_{KN}] \end{bmatrix}$$

Simplifying the above yields:

$$\begin{aligned} \hat{X}_N^C = {} & (\lambda_{LT}^C \lambda_{KN}^C - \lambda_{LN}^C \lambda_{KT}^C)^{-1}(-\lambda_{KT}^C) \Big[\hat{L} + \hat{\Pi}_L - (\hat{X}_T^M + \hat{X}_N^M) \\ & -[(\lambda_{LT}^C + \lambda_{LT}^M)\hat{\gamma}_{LT} + (\lambda_{LN}^C + \lambda_{LN}^M)\hat{\gamma}_{LN}]\Big] \\ & +(\lambda_{LT}^C \lambda_{KN}^C - \lambda_{LN}^C \lambda_{KT}^C)^{-1}\lambda_{LT}^C \Big[\hat{K} + \hat{\Pi}_K - (\hat{X}_T^M + \hat{X}_N^M) \\ & - [(\lambda_{KT}^C + \lambda_{KT}^M)\hat{\gamma}_{KT} + (\lambda_{KN}^C + \lambda_{KN}^M)\hat{\gamma}_{KN}]\Big] \end{aligned} \tag{33}$$

$$\begin{aligned} \hat{X}_T^C = {} & (\lambda_{LT}^C \lambda_{KN}^C - \lambda_{LN}^C \lambda_{KT}^C)^{-1}\lambda_{KN}^C) \Big[\hat{L} + \hat{\Pi}_L - (\hat{X}_T^M + \hat{X}_N^M) \\ & -[(\lambda_{LT}^C + \lambda_{LT}^M)\hat{\gamma}_{LT} + (\lambda_{LN}^C + \lambda_{LN}^M)\hat{\gamma}_{LN}]\Big] \\ & -(\lambda_{LT}^C \lambda_{KN}^C - \lambda_{LN}^C \lambda_{KT}^C)^{-1}\lambda_{LN}^C) \Big[\hat{K} + \hat{\Pi}_K - (\hat{X}_T^M + \hat{X}_N^M) \\ & -[(\lambda_{KT}^C + \lambda_{KT}^M)\hat{\gamma}_{KT} + (\lambda_{KN}^C + \lambda_{KN}^M)\hat{\gamma}_{KN}]\Big] \end{aligned} \tag{34}$$

Substitution of equations (20)-(23) for $\hat{\gamma}_{LN}$, $\hat{\gamma}_{KN}$, $\hat{\gamma}_{LT}$, and $\hat{\gamma}_{KT}$, respectively, and $-(\lambda_{KT}^C \lambda_{LN}^C - \lambda_{LT}^C \lambda_{KN}^C)^{-1}$ for $(\lambda_{LT}^C \lambda_{KN}^C - \lambda_{LN}^C \lambda_{KT}^C)^{-1}$, into above two equations yields:

$$\begin{aligned} \hat{X}_N^C = {} & (\lambda_{KT}^C \lambda_{LN}^C - \lambda_{LT}^C \lambda_{KN}^C)^{-1}\lambda_{KT}^C \Big[\hat{L} + \hat{\Pi}_L - (\hat{X}_T^M + \hat{X}_N^M) \\ & +(\lambda_{LT}^C + \lambda_{LT}^M)\theta_{KT}\sigma_T(\hat{W} - \hat{R}) + (\lambda_{LN}^C + \lambda_{LN}^M)\theta_{KN}\sigma_N(\hat{W} - \hat{R})\Big] \\ & -(\lambda_{kT}^C \lambda_{LN}^C - \lambda_{LT}^C \lambda_{KN}^C)^{-1}\lambda_{LT}^C \Big[\hat{K} + \hat{\Pi}_K - (\hat{X}_T^M + \hat{X}_N^M) \\ & - (\lambda_{KT}^C + \lambda_{KT}^M)\theta_{LT}\sigma_T(\hat{W} - \hat{R}) - (\lambda_{KN}^C + \lambda_{KN}^M)\theta_{LN}\sigma_N(\hat{W} - \hat{R})\Big] \end{aligned} \tag{35}$$

$$\hat{X}_T^C = -(\lambda_{KT}^C \lambda_{LN}^C - \lambda_{LT}^C \lambda_{KN}^C)^{-1}\lambda_{KN}^C \Big[\hat{L} + \hat{\Pi}_L - (\hat{X}_T^M + \hat{X}_N^M)$$

$$+ (\lambda_{LT}^{C} + \lambda_{LT}^{M})\theta_{KT}\sigma_{T}(\hat{W} - \hat{R}) + (\lambda_{LN}^{C} + \lambda_{LN}^{M})\theta_{KN}\sigma_{N}(\hat{W} - \hat{R})\Big]$$

$$+ (\lambda_{kT}^{C}\lambda_{LN}^{C} - \lambda_{LT}^{C}\lambda_{KN}^{C})^{-1}\lambda_{LN}^{C}\Big[\hat{K} + \hat{\Pi}_{K} - (\hat{X}_{T}^{M} + \hat{X}_{N}^{M})$$
$$- (\lambda_{KT}^{C} + \lambda_{KT}^{M})\theta_{LT}\sigma_{T}(\hat{W} - \hat{R}) - (\lambda_{KN}^{C} + \lambda_{KN}^{M})\theta_{LN}\sigma_{N}(\hat{W} - \hat{R})\Big] \quad (36)$$

Letting $\lambda^{C} = \lambda_{KT}^{C}\lambda_{LN}^{C} - \lambda_{LT}^{C}\lambda_{KN}^{C}$, $\lambda_{ij} = \lambda_{ij}^{C} + \lambda_{ij}^{M}$ (for all i = K, L and j = N,T), and subtracting equation (36) from (35) yields:

$$\hat{X}^{C} = \hat{X}_{N}^{C} - \hat{X}_{T}^{C} = (\lambda^{C})^{-1}\{(\lambda_{KT}^{C} + \lambda_{KN}^{C})\hat{L} + (\lambda_{KT}^{C} + \lambda_{KN}^{C})\hat{\Pi}_{L} \quad (37)$$
$$+(\lambda_{KT}^{C} + \lambda_{KN}^{C})(\lambda_{LT}\theta_{KT}\sigma_{T} + \lambda_{LN}\theta_{KN}\sigma_{N})(\hat{W} - \hat{R})$$
$$-[(\lambda_{KT}^{C} + \lambda_{KN}^{C}) - (\lambda_{LT}^{C} + \lambda_{LN}^{C})](\hat{X}_{T}^{M} + \hat{X}_{N}^{M}) - (\lambda_{LT}^{C} + \lambda_{LN}^{C})\hat{K}$$
$$-(\lambda_{LT}^{C} + \lambda_{LN}^{C})\hat{\Pi}_{K} + (\lambda_{LT}^{C} + \lambda_{LN}^{C})(\lambda_{KT}\theta_{LT}\sigma_{T} + \lambda_{KN}\theta_{LN}\sigma_{N})(\hat{W} - \hat{R})\}$$

Consolidating and reordering terms, and letting $\lambda_{i}^{C} = \lambda_{iT}^{C} + \lambda_{iN}^{C}$ (for i = K,L), yields:

$$\hat{X}^{C} = (\lambda^{C})^{-1}\{[\lambda_{K}^{C}(\lambda_{LT}\theta_{KT}\sigma_{T} + \lambda_{LN}\theta_{KN}\sigma_{N}) + \lambda_{L}^{C}(\lambda_{KT}\theta_{LT}\sigma_{T}$$
$$+ \lambda_{KN}\theta_{LN}\sigma_{N})](\hat{W} - \hat{R}) - \lambda_{L}^{C}\hat{K} + \lambda_{K}^{C}\hat{L} + \lambda_{K}^{C}\hat{\Pi}_{L} - \lambda_{L}^{C}\hat{\Pi}_{K}$$
$$- (\lambda_{K}^{C} - \lambda_{L}^{C})(\hat{X}_{T}^{M} + \hat{X}_{N}^{M})\} \quad (38)$$

Substituting equation (17) into (38) yields:

$$\hat{X}^{C} = (\lambda^{C})^{-1}\{(\theta_{LN} - \theta_{LT})^{-1}[\lambda_{K}^{C}(\lambda_{LT}\theta_{KT}\sigma_{T} + \lambda_{LN}\theta_{KN}\sigma_{N}) +$$
$$\lambda_{L}^{C}(\lambda_{KT}\theta_{LT}\sigma_{T} + \lambda_{KN}\theta_{LN}\sigma_{N})](\hat{P} + \hat{\Pi}_{N} - \hat{\Pi}_{T}) - \lambda_{L}^{C}\hat{K} + \lambda_{K}^{C}\hat{L}$$
$$-(\lambda_{K}^{C} - \lambda_{L}^{C})(\hat{X}_{T}^{M} + \hat{X}_{N}^{M}) + \lambda_{K}^{c}\hat{\Pi}_{L} - \lambda_{L}^{C}\hat{\Pi}_{K}\} \quad (39)$$

Under the assumption that productivity differentials are "Hicks neutral," we can show that $\lambda_{K}^{C}\hat{\Pi}_{L} - \lambda_{L}^{C}\hat{\Pi}_{K} = (\lambda_{LN} - \lambda_{KN})(\lambda_{K}^{C}\hat{\Pi}_{N} - \lambda_{L}^{C}\hat{\Pi}_{T})$. From the definitions of $\hat{\Pi}_{L}$ and $\hat{\Pi}_{K}$ earlier, we know:

$$\lambda_{K}^{C}\hat{\Pi}_{L} - \lambda_{L}^{C}\hat{\Pi}_{K} = \lambda_{K}^{C}\lambda_{LT}\hat{\tau}_{LT} + \lambda_{K}^{C}\lambda_{LN}\hat{\tau}_{LN} - \lambda_{L}^{C}\lambda_{KT}\hat{\tau}_{KT} - \lambda_{L}^{C}\lambda_{KN}\hat{\tau}_{KN} \quad (40)$$

Since zero-profits requires $\theta_{Li} + \theta_{Ki} = 1$ for i = N,T:

$$\lambda_K^C \hat{\Pi}_L - \lambda_L^C \hat{\Pi}_k$$
$$= \lambda_K^C(\theta_{LT}\lambda_{LT} + \theta_{KT}\lambda_{LT})\hat{\tau}_{LT} + \lambda_K^C \lambda_{LN}\hat{\tau}_{LN} -$$
$$\lambda_L^C(\theta_{LT}\lambda_{KT} + \theta_{KT}\lambda_{KT})\hat{\tau}_{KT} - \lambda_L^C \lambda_{KN}\hat{\tau}_{KN}$$

$$= \lambda_K^C[\theta_{LT}(1-\lambda_{LN}) + \theta_{KT}\lambda_{LT}]\hat{\tau}_{LT} + \lambda_K^C\lambda_{LN}\hat{\tau}_{LN} -$$
$$(\lambda_L^C[\theta_{LT}\lambda_{KT} + \theta_{KT}(1-\lambda_{KN})]\hat{\tau}_{KT} - \lambda_L^C\lambda_{KN}\hat{\tau}_{KN}$$

$$= \lambda_K^C\hat{\tau}_{LT}(\theta_{LT} - \theta_{LT}\lambda_{LN} + \theta_{KT}\lambda_{LT}) + \lambda_K^C\lambda_{LN}\hat{\tau}_{LN} -$$
$$\lambda_L^C\hat{\tau}_{KT}(\theta_{LT}\lambda_{KT} + \theta_{KT} - \theta_{KT}\lambda_{KN}) - \lambda_L^C\lambda_{KN}\hat{\tau}_{KN}$$

$$= \lambda_K^C\hat{\tau}_{LT}[\theta_{LT}(1-\lambda_{KN}) + \theta_{KT}\lambda_{LT} - \theta_{LT}\lambda_{LN} + \theta_{LT}\lambda_{KN}] + \lambda_K^C\lambda_{LN}\hat{\tau}_{LN}$$
$$-\lambda_L^C\hat{\tau}_{KT}[\theta_{LT}\lambda_{KT} + \theta_{KT}(1-\lambda_{LN}) + \theta_{KT}\lambda_{LN} - \theta_{KT}\lambda_{KN}] - \lambda_L^C\lambda_{KN}\hat{\tau}_{KN}$$

$$= \lambda_K^C\hat{\tau}_{LT}(\theta_{LT}\lambda_{KT} + \theta_{KT}\lambda_{LT} - \theta_{LT}\lambda_{LN} + \theta_{LT}\lambda_{KN}) + \lambda_K^C\hat{\tau}_{LN}$$
$$(\theta_{KN}\lambda_{LN} + \theta_{LN}\lambda_{LN}) - \lambda_L^C\hat{\tau}_{KT}(\theta_{LT}\lambda_{KT} + \theta_{KT}\lambda_{LT} + \theta_{KT}\lambda_{LN} - \theta_{KT}\lambda_{KN})$$
$$-\lambda_L^C\hat{\tau}_{KN}(\theta_{LN}\lambda_{KN} + \theta_{KN}\lambda_{KN})$$

$$= \theta_{LN}\lambda_{KN}\lambda_K^C\hat{\tau}_{LN} + \theta_{KN}\lambda_{LN}\lambda_K^C\hat{\tau}_{LN} - \theta_{LN}\lambda_{KN}\lambda_L^C\hat{\tau}_{KN} - \theta_{KN}\lambda_{LN}\lambda_L^C\hat{\tau}_{KN}$$
$$+\theta_{LT}\lambda_{KT}\lambda_K^C\hat{\tau}_{LT} + \theta_{KT}\lambda_{LT}\lambda_K^C\hat{\tau}_{LT} - \theta_{LT}\lambda_{KT}\lambda_L^C\hat{\tau}_{KT} - \theta_{KT}\lambda_{LT}\lambda_L^C\hat{\tau}_{KT}$$
$$+\theta_{LN}\lambda_{LN}\lambda_K^C\hat{\tau}_{LN} + \theta_{KN}\lambda_{LN}\lambda_L^C\hat{\tau}_{KN} - \theta_{LT}\lambda_{LN}\lambda_K^C\hat{\tau}_{LT} - \theta_{KT}\lambda_{LN}\lambda_L^C\hat{\tau}_{KT}$$
$$-\theta_{LN}\lambda_{KN}\lambda_K^C\hat{\tau}_{LN} - \theta_{KN}\lambda_{KN}\lambda_L^C\hat{\tau}_{KN} + \theta_{LT}\lambda_{KN}\lambda_K^C\hat{\tau}_{LT} + \theta_{KT}\lambda_{KN}\lambda_L^C\hat{\tau}_{KT}$$

$$= (\theta_{LN}\lambda_{KN} + \theta_{KN}\lambda_{LN})(\lambda_K^C\hat{\tau}_{LN} - \lambda_L^C\hat{\tau}_{KN})$$
$$+(\theta_{LT}\lambda_{KT} + \theta_{KT}\lambda_{LT})(\lambda_K^C\hat{\tau}_{LT} - \lambda_L^C\hat{\tau}_{KT})$$
$$+(\lambda_{LN} - \lambda_{KN})(\lambda_K^C\theta_{LN}\hat{\tau}_{LN}+\lambda_L^C\theta_{KN}\hat{\tau}_{KN} - \lambda_K^C\theta_{LT}\hat{\tau}_{LT} - \lambda_L^C\theta_{KT}\hat{\tau}_{KT})$$

In matrix form,

$$[\lambda_K^C\ \lambda_L^C]\begin{bmatrix}\hat{\Pi}_L \\ -\hat{\Pi}_K\end{bmatrix} = (\theta_{LN}\lambda_{KN} + \theta_{KN}\lambda_{LN})[\lambda_K^C\ \lambda_L^C]\begin{bmatrix}\hat{\tau}_{LN} \\ -\hat{\tau}_{KN}\end{bmatrix}$$

$$+ (\theta_{LT}\lambda_{KT} + \theta_{KT}\lambda_{LT})[\lambda_K^C\ \lambda_L^C]\begin{bmatrix}\hat{\tau}_{LT} \\ -\hat{\tau}_{KT}\end{bmatrix} + (\lambda_{LN} - \lambda_{KN})[\lambda_K^C\ \lambda_L^C]$$

$$\begin{bmatrix}\theta_{LN}\hat{\tau}_{LN} - \theta_{LT}\hat{\tau}_{LT} \\ \theta_{KN}\hat{\tau}_{KN} - \theta_{KT}\hat{\tau}_{KT}\end{bmatrix} \tag{41}$$

Letting $[\lambda_K^C\ \lambda_L^C]^+$ denote the generalized inverse of $[\lambda_K^C\ \lambda_L^C]$, cf., Henri Theil, Principles of Econometrics, 1971, pp. 269-273, premultiplying both sides of (41) by [1 1] $[\lambda_K^C\ \lambda_L^C]^+$ yields:

$$\hat{\Pi}_L - \hat{\Pi}_K = (\theta_{LN}\lambda_{KN} + \theta_{KN}\lambda_{LN})(\hat{\tau}_{LN} - \hat{\tau}_{KN})$$
$$+(\theta_{LT}\lambda_{KT} + \theta_{KT}\lambda_{LT})(\hat{\tau}_{LT} - \hat{\tau}_{KT})$$
$$+ (\lambda_{LN} - \lambda_{KN})\left[(\theta_{LN}\hat{\tau}_{LN} + \theta_{KN}\hat{\tau}_{KN}) - (\theta_{LT}\hat{\tau}_{LT} + \theta_{KT}\hat{\tau}_{KT})\right]$$

Assuming productivity differentials are Hicks neutral, $\hat{\tau}_{LN} - \hat{\tau}_{KN} = \hat{\tau}_{LT} - \hat{\tau}_{KT} = 0$, and recalling the definitions of Π_N and Π_T in equations (12) and (13):

$$\hat{\Pi}_L - \hat{\Pi}_K = (\lambda_{LN} - \lambda_{KN})(\hat{\Pi}_N - \hat{\Pi}_T)$$

or

$$[1\ \ 1]\begin{bmatrix}\hat{\Pi}_L \\ -\hat{\Pi}_K\end{bmatrix} = (\lambda_{LN} - \lambda_{KN})[1\ \ 1]\begin{bmatrix}\hat{\Pi}_N \\ -\hat{\Pi}_T\end{bmatrix}$$

Premultiplying both sides by $[\lambda_K^C \; \lambda_L^C]\,[1\;1]^+$ yields:

$$\lambda_K^C \hat{\Pi}_L - \lambda_L^C \hat{\Pi}_K = (\lambda_{LN} - \lambda_{KN})\lambda_K^C \hat{\Pi}_N - (\lambda_{LN} - \lambda_{KN})\lambda_L^C \hat{\Pi}_T \quad (42)$$

Substituting (42) into (39) yields:

$$\hat{X}^C = \alpha_1 \hat{P} - \alpha_2 \hat{K} + \alpha_3 \hat{L} + \alpha_4 \hat{\Pi}_N - \alpha_5 \hat{\Pi}_T - \alpha_6 \left[\hat{X}_T^M + \hat{X}_N^M \right] \quad (43)$$

where $\alpha_1 = \lambda_K^C(\lambda_{LT}\theta_{KT}\sigma_T + \lambda_{LN}\theta_{KN}\sigma_N) + \lambda_L^C(\lambda_{KT}\theta_{LT}\sigma_T + \lambda_{KN}\theta_{LN}\sigma_N)]/\lambda^C(\theta_{LN} - \theta_{LT}) > 0$,

$\alpha_2 = \lambda_L^C/\lambda^C > (<)0$ if nontradables are labor (capital) intensive,

$\alpha_3 = \lambda_K^C/\lambda^C > (<)0$ if nontradables are labor (capital) intensive,

$\alpha_4 = \alpha_1 + [\lambda_K^C(\lambda_{LN} - \lambda_{KN})/\lambda^C] > 0$,

$\alpha_5 = \alpha_1 + [\lambda_L^C(\lambda_{LN} - \lambda_{KN})/\lambda^C] > 0$,

$\alpha_6 = (\lambda_L^M - \lambda_K^M)/\lambda^C \gtrless 0$.

Finally, indefinite integration of equation (43), treating α_1 through α_6 as constant parameters, yields:

$$(1nX^C)^S = \alpha_0 + \alpha_1 1n\, p - \alpha_2 1nK + \alpha_3 1nL + \alpha_4\, 1n\, \Pi_N - \alpha_5\, 1n\, \Pi_T - \alpha_6 \left[1nX_T^M + 1nX_N^M \right].$$

from which estimable equation (44) is readily derived:

$$1np = \alpha_0 + (1/\alpha_1)(1nX^C)^S + (\alpha_2/\alpha_1)1nK - (\alpha_3/\alpha_1)1nL - (\alpha_4/\alpha_1)1n\Pi_N + (\alpha_5/\alpha_1)1n\Pi_T + (\alpha_6/\alpha_1)(1nX_T^M + 1nX_N^M) \quad (44)$$

3. Demand

I assume a representative consumer maximizes the nonhomothetic Stone-Geary utility function for civilian goods:

$$u = \left[x_T^C - \tilde{x}_T^C \right]^\delta \left[x_N^C - \tilde{x}_N^C \right]^{1-\delta} \qquad 0 < \delta < 1 \qquad (45)$$

where x_T^C (x_N^C) is the per capita amount consumed of tradables (non-tradables) in the civilian sector and $\tilde{x}_T^C$ ($\tilde{x}_N^C$) is an exogenous minimum-consumption requirement for the civilian sector for the tradable (non-tradable), common to the Stone-Geary utility function. As in Frenkel and Razin (1987), the consumer derives no utility from the government purchases. Assume the budget constraint

$$y = x_T^C + px_N^C + taxes \tag{46}$$

where y is per capita income and taxes $= x_T^M + px_N^M$, both expressed in terms of the tradable (the numeraire). Per capita military expenditures are $x_T^M + px_N^M$.

Maximization of utility function (44) subject to income constraint (46) yields:

$$\frac{\partial u}{\partial x_T^C} = (x_N^C - \tilde{x}_N^C)^{1-\delta}\, \delta(x_T^C - \tilde{x}_T^C)^{\delta-1} - \lambda = 0 \tag{47}$$

$$\frac{\partial u}{\partial x_N^C} = (x_T^C - \tilde{x}_T^C)^{\delta}\, (1-\delta)(x_M^C - \tilde{x}_N^C)^{-\delta} - \lambda = 0 \tag{48}$$

$$\frac{\partial u}{\partial \lambda} = y - x_T^C - px_N^C - x_T^M - px_N^M = 0 \tag{49}$$

Equating (47) and (48) yields:

$$\delta(x_N^C - \tilde{x}_N^C)^{1-\delta}(x_T^C - \tilde{x}_T^C)^{\delta-1} = p^{-1}\,(x_T^C - \tilde{x}_T^C)^{\delta}(1-\delta)(x_N^C - \tilde{x}_N^C)^{-\delta} \tag{50}$$

Solving (50) for x_N^C yields:

$$x_N^C = [(1-\delta)/\delta]\, p^{-1}\,(x_T^C - \tilde{x}_T^C) + \tilde{x}_N^C \tag{51}$$

Substituting (51) into the budget constraint and solving for x_T^C yields:

$$x_T^C = \delta y + (1-\delta)\tilde{x}_T^C - \delta p\tilde{x}_N^C - \delta(x_T^M + px_N^M) \tag{52}$$

Substituting (52) into the budget constraint and solving for x_N^C yields:

$$x_N^C = (1-\delta)p^{-1}y - (1-\delta)p^{-1}\tilde{x}_T^C + \delta\tilde{x}_N^C - (1-\delta)\,(p^{-1}x_T^M + x_N^M) \tag{53}$$

Differentiating equation (52), dividing the resulting equation by x_T^C, and some mathematical manipulation yields:

$$\hat{x}_T^C = -\left[\frac{\delta(\tilde{x}_N^C + x_N^M)\,p}{x_T^C} \right]\hat{p} + \left[1 - \frac{(1-\delta)\tilde{x}_T^C - \delta p\tilde{x}_N^C - \delta(x_T^M + px_N^M)}{x_T^C} \right]\hat{y} -$$

$$\left[\frac{\delta(x_T^M + px_N^M)}{x_T^C} \right](x_T^M + px_N^M) \qquad (54)$$

where

$$(x_T^M + px_N^M) = (dx_T^M + pdx_N^M)/(x_T^M + px_N^M).$$

Differentiating equation (53), dividing the resulting equation by x_N^C, and some mathematical manipulation yields:

$$\hat{x}_N^C = -\left[1 + \frac{(1-\delta)p^{-1}\,(x_T^M + px_N^M) - \delta\tilde{x}_N^C}{x_N^C} \right]\hat{p}$$

$$+\left[1 + \frac{(1-\delta)p^{-1}\tilde{x}_T^C + (1-\delta)p^{-1}\,(x_T^M + px_N^M) - \delta\tilde{x}_N^C}{x_N^C} \right]\hat{y} -$$

$$\left[\frac{(1-\delta)p^{-1}(x_T^M + px_N^M)}{x_N^C} \right](x_T^M + px_N^M). \qquad (55)$$

Subtracting equation (54) from (55) yields:

$$\hat{x}^c = \hat{x}_N^C - \hat{x}_T^C = \hat{x}_N^C - \hat{x}_T^C = -\phi_1\hat{p} + \phi_2\hat{y} - \phi_3(x_T^M + px_N^M) \quad (56)$$

where

$$\phi_1 = 1 + \{[(1-\delta)p^{-1}(x_T^M + px_N^M) - \delta\tilde{x}_N^C]/x_N^C - [\delta(\tilde{x}_N^C + x_N^M)/x_T^C]\}$$
$$\phi_3 = (x_T^M + px_N^M)\,[(1-\delta)x_T^C - \delta px_N^C]/px_N^C x_T^C$$
$$\phi_2 = \phi_3 + (x_T^C + px_N^C)\,[(1-\delta)\tilde{x}_T^C - \delta p\tilde{x}_N^C]/px_N^C x_T^C$$

Finally, indefinite integration of equation (56), treating ϕ_1 , ϕ_2 and ϕ_3 as constant parameters, yields:

$$(1nX^C)^D = \phi_0 - \phi_1 1np + \phi_2 1ny - \phi_3 1n(x_T^M + px_N^M)$$

from which estimable equation (57) is readily derived:

$$1np = \phi_0 - (1/\phi_1)(1nX^C)^D + (\phi_2/\phi_1)1ny - (\phi_3/\phi_1)1n(x_T^M + px_N^M) \tag{57}$$

Finally, the relative price of nontradables in terms of tradables, or real exchange rate, can be solved for as a reduced-form function of the intratemporal supply and demand factors:

$$\begin{aligned} 1np = (\alpha_1 + \phi_1)^{-1} [(\phi_0\phi_1 - \alpha_0\alpha_1) + \alpha_5 1n\Pi_T - \alpha_4 1n\Pi_N + \alpha_2 1nK \\ - \alpha_3 1nL + \phi_2 1ny + (\alpha_6 - \phi_3)1n(x_T^M + px_N^M)] \end{aligned} \tag{58}$$

The reduced form is obtained by equating (44) and (57) and solving for lnp, allowing $1n(x_T^M + px_N^M)$ to represent the unmeasurable variable $(lnx_T^M + lnx_N^M)$. [2] First, higher productivity in tradables (nontradables) will be associated with a higher (lower) real exchange rate, consistent with the Balassa (1964) productivity differential model. Second, a higher capital (labor) stock will be associated with a higher (lower) real exchange rate, if nontradables are labor intensive, consistent with the Bhagwati (1984) relative-factor-endowments theory. Third, a higher per capita income will be associated with a higher real exchange rate, if tastes are nonhomothetic and nontradables (tradables) are luxuries (necessities). Fourth, higher per capita military expenditures will alter the real exchange rate, depending upon the relative factor intensities of civilian and military goods and of civilian tradables and nontradables, and whether civilian nontradables (tradables) are luxuries or necessities in consumption.

[2] The theoretical analysis resulted in slightly different military-expenditure variables for the relative demand and supply functions: $ln(X_T^M + PX_N^M)$ and $lnX_T^M + lnX_N^M$, respectively. As the former was measurable and the latter was not, all equations are estimated using $ln(X_T^M + PX_N^M)$.

4. Empirical Evidence

Reduced-form equation (58) and structural equations (44) and (57) are in forms estimable by ordinary least squares and two-stage least squares, respectively. Data for only 21 countries could be obtained for all of the variables.[3] Data for each country for the price of nontradables relative to that of tradables (relative to that of the United States, US=100), the output of nontradables relative to that of tradables, and per capita GDP in 1975 are from Table 6-12 in Kravis et al. (1982). Capital and labor (LABOR1) for 1975 are from Leamer (1984 appendix table B.1). The level of productivity in nontradables (services) is approximated by the ratio of national output in services in 1975 from Kravis et al. (1982) to the level of employment in services industries in 1975 from the International Labour Organization's Year Book of Labour Statistics (1979) (relative to that of the United States). Per capita military expenditures were obtained by taking the share of military expenditures in gross national product of each country times its per capita gross national product; the military shares were obtained from the SIPRI Yearbook.

Estimation of reduced-form equation (58) yielded:

$$\begin{aligned} ln\, p = & \underset{(3.10)}{-1.10} \underset{(2.05)}{+0.12\, ln\Pi_T} \underset{(3.19)}{-0.28 ln\Pi_N} \underset{(1.11)}{+.09\, lnK} \underset{(1.24)}{-0.11\, lnL} \underset{(2.00)}{+0.28\, lny} \\ & \underset{(0.74)}{+0.04\; ln(x_T^M + px_N^M)}; \qquad (59) \\ see = & \ 0.10; \quad R^2 = 0.95; \quad Adjusted\ R^2 = 0.93 \end{aligned}$$

where numbers in parentheses are absolute values of t-statistics and SEE is the standard error of the regression. A one percent reduction in per capita military spending tends to reduce the price of nontradables relative to that of tradables by only 0.04 percent. Note that all other coefficient estimates' signs conform to the productivity-differential, relative-factor-endowments, and nonhomothetic- tastes theories for departures from absolute PPP, and estimates for Π_T, Π_N

[3] The 21 countries are India, Sri Lanka, Thailand, the Philippines, Korea, Colombia, Jamaica, Brazil, Yugoslavia, Ireland. Italy, Spain, the United Kingdom, Japan, Austria, the Netherlands, Belgium, France, Denmark, Germany, and the United States.

and y are statistically significant at 10 percent (two-tail t-tests).

Although the reduced-form estimates suggest that the impact of military spending reductions on the relative national price level would be economically insignificant, this result does not imply that the intratemporal supply and demand channels are unimportant. In fact, the structural equations' estimates suggest that endogenous supply decisions and nonhomothetic tastes are economically significant channels, but their effects on relative prices are offsetting. Two-stage least squares estimation of equations (43) and (56) yields:

$$\begin{aligned} ln\, p = & \underset{(1.71)}{-0.97} + \underset{(1.31)}{0.46}\,(ln\, X^C)^S + \underset{(3.96)}{0.22}\, lnK - \underset{(4.26)}{0.23}\, lnL - \underset{(2.16)}{0.31}\, ln\Pi_N \\ & + \underset{(1.59)}{0.14}\, ln\Pi_T + \underset{(2.60)}{0.04}\, ln(x_T^M + px_N^M) \\ see = & \ 0.15;\ R^2 = 0.89;\ Adjusted\ R^2 = 0.84 \end{aligned} \tag{60}$$

$$\begin{aligned} ln\, p = & \underset{(15.79)}{-2.22} - \underset{(2.90)}{0.75}\,(ln\, X^C)^D + \underset{(7.46)}{0.58}\, lny - \underset{(1.84)}{0.11}\, ln(x_T^M + px_N^M) \\ see = & \ 0.12;\ R^2 = 0.92;\ Adjusted\ R^2 = 0.90 \end{aligned} \tag{61}$$

Regarding relative supply function (60), coefficient estimates all have signs consistent with the model, and all are statistically significant at 10 percent except for coefficients on $(X^C)^S$ and Π_T. Coefficient estimates for capital and labor suggest that civilian nontradables (tradables) are labor (capital) intensive. If civilian nontradables are labor intensive, then the coefficient estimate for per capita military spending suggests that military production is labor intensive relative to civilian production.

Regarding relative demand function (61), the coefficient estimates all have signs consistent with the model, and all are statistically significant at 10 percent. The results suggest that, due to nonhomothetic preferences, a rise in per capita income raises the relative demand for nontradables, but a rise in per capita military expenditures lowers their relative demand (by lowering per capita disposable income). Hence, via demand military spending reductions will tend to raise the relative price of nontradables in terms of tradables and thus the national price level. However, since the intratemporal supply effect of a one percent decline in military spending on raising production and lowering the price of nontradables relative to tradables (0.14) exceeds the intratemporal nonhomothetic-tastes effect of raising demand and the price of nontradables relative to tradables (0.11), the net effect of smaller military expenditures is to lower the nation's general price level relative to the world average, although the impact turns out to be economically insignificant.

5. Conclusions

Recently, several studies have focused upon better understanding the robust cross-country relationship between per capita incomes and national price levels, or per capita incomes and the price of nontradables relative to tradables. Efforts have been made to disentangle the relative supply versus the relative demand influences of per capita income on relative price levels, in some cases treating per capita incomes as endogenous.

This study has attempted to extend this literature, examining theoretically and empirically the potential channels through which fiscal spending – in particular, exogenous military expenditures – affect per capita disposable income, the absorption of labor and capital endowments, and ultimately the national price level. Theoretically, the effect of military spending reductions on these variables is ambiguous; the effects depend upon the relative factor intensity in production of civilian versus military goods and of civilian tradable versus nontradable goods, and upon the relative importance in utility of civilian tradable versus nontradable goods. Empirically, the model suggests that the effects of reduced military spending on the relative demand for and relative supply of nontradables to tradables are economically and statistically significant. However, because military spending reductions will tend to increase the relative supply only slightly more than the relative demand, the price of nontradables relative to tradables is predicted to decline by only a small amount. Consequently, lower military expenditures are predicted to result in a small real depreciation of a country's currency, and thus only a minor fall in the national price level relative to the world average.

References

Balassa, Bela, (1964), "The Purchasing-Power-Parity Doctrine: A Reappraisal," *Journal of Political Economy*, 72, 584-596.

Bergstrand, Jeffrey H., (1991), "Structural Determinants of Real Exchange Rates and National Price Levels: Some Empirical Evidence," *American Economic Review*, 81, 325-334.

Bergstrand, Jeffrey H., (1992), "Real Exchange Rates, National Price Levels, and the Peace Dividend," *American Economic Review*, 82, 55-61.

Bhagwati, Jagdish N., (1984), "Why are Services Cheaper in the Poor Countries?" *Economic Journal*, 94, 279-286.

Clague, Christopher, (1985), "A Model of Real National Price Levels," *Southern Economic Journal*, 67, 998-1017.

Clague, Christopher, (1986), "Determinants of the National Price Level: Some Empirical Results," *Review of Economics and Statistics*, 68, 320-323.

Falvey, Rodney E. and Gemmell, Norman , (1991), "Explaining Service-Price Differences in International Comparisons," *American Economic Review*, 81, 1295-1309.

Falvey, Rodney E. and Gemmell, Norman , (1992), "Factor Endowments, Factor Productivity, and Service Prices," unpublished manuscript.

Frenkel, Jacob and Razin, Assaf, (1987), *Fiscal Policies and the World Economy*, Cambridge, MA: MIT Press.

Jones, Ronald W. (1965), "The Structure of Simple General Equilibrium Models," *Journal of Political Economy*, 73, 557-572.

Kravis, Irving B., Heston, Alan W., and Summers, Robert, (1982), *World Product and Income*, Baltimore: Johns Hopkins University Press.

Kravis, Irving B. and Lipsey, Robert E., (1983), "Toward an Explanation of National Price Levels," *Princeton Studies in International Finance*, No. 52.

Kravis, Irving B. and Lipsey, Robert E., (1987), "The Assessment of National Price Levels," in Sven W. Arndt and J. David Richardson, eds., *Real-Financial Linkages Among Open Economies*, Cambridge, Massachusetts: MIT Press, 97-134.

Kravis, Irving B. and Lipsey, Robert E., (1988), "National Price Levels and the Prices of Tradables and Nontradables," *American Economic Review*, 78, 474-478.

International Labour Organisation, (1979), *Year Book of Labour Statistics*, Geneva: International Labour Office.

Leamer, Edward E., (1984) , *Sources of International Comparative Advantage*, Cambridge, MA: MIT Press, 69, 488-495.

Index